Elite Mobilities

Small in number but great in influence, mobile elites have shaped the contours of global capitalism. Today these elites continue to flourish globally but in a changing landscape. The current economic crisis – and rising concerns about the moral legitimacy of extreme wealth – coincides with stern warnings over the risks posed by climate change and the unsustainable use of resources. Often an out-of-bounds topic in critical social science, elites are thought of as too inaccessible a group to interview and too variable a minority to measure.

This groundbreaking collection sets out to challenge this perception. Through the careful examination of the movements of the 1 per cent through the everyday spaces of the 99 per cent, *Elite Mobilities* investigates the shared zones elites inhabit alongside the commons: the executive lounge in the airport, the penthouse in the hotel, or the gated community next to the slum. Bringing together the pioneer scholars in critical sociology today, this collection explores how social scientists can research, map, and "track" the flows and residues of objects, wealth, and power surrounding the hypermobile.

Elite Mobilities sets a new benchmark in social science efforts to research the powerful and the privileged. It will appeal to students and scholars interested in mobilities, transport, tourism, social stratification, class, inequality, consumption, and global environmental change.

Thomas Birtchnell is Lecturer in Geography and Sustainable Communities at the University of Wollongong, Australia.

Javier Caletrío is Research Fellow at the Centre for Mobilities Research at Lancaster University, UK.

Changing mobilities
Series Editors: Monika Büscher, Peter Adey

This series explores the transformations of society, politics, and everyday experiences wrought by changing mobilities, and the power of mobilities research to inform constructive responses to these transformations. As a new mobile century is taking shape, international scholars explore motivations, experiences, insecurities, implications, and limitations of mobile living, and opportunities and challenges for design in the broadest sense, from policy to urban planning, new media, and technology design. With world citizens expected to travel 105 billion kilometres per year in 2050, it is critical to make mobilities research and design inform each other.

Elite Mobilities
Edited by Thomas Birtchnell and Javier Caletrío

Forthcoming:

Changing Mobilities
Monika Büscher

Cargomobilities
Moving materials in a global age
Edited by Thomas Birtchnell, Satya Savitzky and John Urry

Elite Mobilities

Edited by Thomas Birtchnell
and Javier Caletrío

LONDON AND NEW YORK

First published 2014 by Routledge

2 Park Square, Milton Park, Abingdon, Oxon OX14 4RN
711 Third Avenue, New York, NY 10017, USA

Routledge is an imprint of the Taylor & Francis Group, an informa business

First issued in paperback 2017

Copyright © 2014 selection and editorial material, Thomas Birtchnell and Javier Caletrío; individual chapters, the contributors

The right of Thomas Birtchnell and Javier Caletrío to be identified as the authors of the editorial material, and of the authors for their individual chapters, has been asserted in accordance with sections 77 and 78 of the Copyright, Designs and Patents Act 1988.

All rights reserved. No part of this book may be reprinted or reproduced or utilised in any form or by any electronic, mechanical, or other means, now known or hereafter invented, including photocopying and recording, or in any information storage or retrieval system, without permission in writing from the publishers.

Notice:
Product or corporate names may be trademarks or registered trademarks, and are used only for identification and explanation without intent to infringe.

British Library Cataloguing in Publication Data
A catalogue record for this book is available from the British Library

Library of Congress Cataloging in Publication Data
Elite mobilities / edited by Thomas Birtchnell and Javier Caletrío.
  pages cm. – (Changing mobilities)
  Includes bibliographical references and index.
  1. Elite (Social sciences) 2. Emigration and immigration.
  3. Globalization. I. Birtchnell, Thomas. II. Caletrío, Javier.
  HT609.E45 2013
  305.52–dc23
                                                    2013012025

ISBN: 978-0-415-65580-4 (hbk)
ISBN: 978-1-138-09377-5 (pbk)

Typeset in Baskerville
by Wearset Ltd, Boldon, Tyne and Wear

Contents

List of figures vii
List of tables viii
Notes on contributors ix
Acknowledgements xii

1 **Introduction: the movement of the few** 1
  THOMAS BIRTCHNELL AND JAVIER CALETRÍO

2 **Elsewhere: tracking the mobile lives of globals** 21
  ANTHONY ELLIOTT

3 **Wealth segmentation and the mobilities of the super-rich: a conceptual framework** 40
  JONATHAN V. BEAVERSTOCK AND
  JAMES R. FAULCONBRIDGE

4 **Elite formation in the third industrial revolution** 62
  THOMAS BIRTCHNELL, GIL VIRY AND JOHN URRY

5 **Aeromobile elites: private business aviation and the global economy** 78
  LUCY BUDD

6 **Super-rich lifestyles** 99
  MIKE FEATHERSTONE

7 **The ease of mobility** 136
  SHAMUS RAHMAN KHAN

8	The uneven pragmatics of "affordable" luxury tourism in inland Yucatán (Mexico)	149
	MATILDE CÓRDOBA AZCÁRATE, ANA GARCÍA DE FUENTES AND JUAN CÓRDOBA ORDÓÑEZ	
9	Visible–invisible: the social semiotics of labour in luxury tourism	176
	CRISPIN THURLOW AND ADAM JAWORSKI	
10	'This is not me': conspicuous consumption and the travel aspirations of the European middle classes	194
	JAVIER CALETRÍO	
11	Tracing the super-rich and their mobilities in a Scandinavian welfare state	209
	MALENE FREUDENDAL-PEDERSEN	
12	The super-rich and offshore worlds	226
	JOHN URRY	
13	Epilogue: the bodies, spaces and tempo of elite formations	241
	MIMI SHELLER	
14	Postscript: elite mobilities and critique	251
	ANDREW SAYER	
	Index	263

Figures

3.1	The geographical distribution of prestige car dealerships in the UK, 2012	51
4.1	Hull co-authorship network of patents for 3D printing	70
4.2	Crump co-authorship network of patents for 3D printing	71
5.1	Growth of the world's business aircraft fleet, 2001–2011	83
5.2	Distribution of business aircraft by world region, 2011	84
8.1	Location map of the Yucatán Peninsula and The Haciendas	152
8.2	Photographs at Hacienda Temozón Sur representing the wedding of a *hacendado* (left) and *peones* (right)	155
8.3	Abandoned Hacienda ex-henequenera Uayalcén, just a few kilometers away from Temozón Sur	157
8.4	Surroundings of the restored Hacienda Temozón Sur	159
8.5	Gated entrance to Hacienda Temozón Sur	162
8.6	Panoramic view of the *casa principal* from inside Hacienda Temozón Sur	164
8.7	Gardeners working at Hacienda Temozón Sur	166
8.8	Waiters catering for tourists at Hacienda Temozón Sur	169
9.1	Beach changing room, Burj al Arab Hotel, Dubai	180
9.2	The lobby, Bellagio Hotel, Las Vegas, USA	181
9.3	A corridor, Bellagio Hotel, Las Vegas, USA	181
9.4	First-floor atrium, Burj al Arab Hotel, Dubai	182
9.5	The Orient Express, Innsbruck station	183
9.6	Kitchen car, the Orient Express	184
9.7	Twentieth floor, Burj al Arab hotel, Dubai	185
9.8	Morning ride, Phinda Private Game Lodge, South Africa	185
9.9	Lunch, Burj al Arab Hotel, Dubai	186
9.10	Breakfast, Phinda Private Game Reserve, South Africa	187
9.11	The Burj al Arab, Dubai	188
9.12	The beach, Burj al Arab, Dubai	189
9.13		191

Tables

3.1	The worldwide population of High Net Worth Individuals and the value of their global wealth, 1996–2011	43
3.2	The composition of the global High Net Worth Individual (HNWI) population, 2002–2011	44
3.3	The global distribution of the High Net Worth Individual (HNWI) population and value of private wealth, 2000–2011	45
3.4	Super-rich mobilities and wealth segmentation	46
3.5	The ten most expensive luxury yachts in the world, 2012	47
3.6	Super-rich charter and sales companies: by sea and air	48
3.7	Super-rich automobilities	49
3.8	The socio-technical basis of super-rich mobilities, differentiated by wealth segmentation	54
4.1	Network indices for the Hull and Crump co-authorship networks	72
5.1	Top 10 business aircraft fleets by country, 2011 (2008 figures in brackets)	84

Contributors

Jonathan V. Beaverstock is Professor of Economic Geography at the University of Nottingham. For over a decade his research has investigated the globalizing strategies of professionals and professional service firms in world cities' knowledge-intensive economies. Recent publications include *Global Cities* (Routledge 2013, co-edited with James R. Faulconbridge and others).

Thomas Birtchnell is Lecturer in Geography and Sustainable Communities at the University of Wollongong. He has published on mobilities, India, elites, 3D printing/additive manufacturing, innovation, and futures. His books include the forthcoming *Cargomobilities: Moving Materials in a Global Age* (Routledge 2014, with Satya Savitzsky and John Urry) and *Indovation: Innovation and a Global Knowledge Economy in India* (Palgrave Macmillan 2013).

Lucy Budd is Senior Lecturer in Air Transport in the School of Civil and Building Engineering at Loughborough University. She has published extensively on the geographies of airspace, air travel, and globalization, aviation and the environment, and the historical development of air transport. She is co-editor of *Technologies of Mobility in the Americas* (Peter Lang 2012).

Javier Caletrío is Research Fellow in the Centre for Mobilities Research at Lancaster University, UK and Scientific Advisor to the Mobile Lives Forum, SNCF, France. His research looks at mobilities, future imaginaries, technological change, and global warming from a cross-cultural perspective. He has co-edited *Mobilities and Forced Migration* (Routledge 2013).

Matilde Córdoba Azcárate was a Postdoctoral Fullbright Fellow at the City University of New York from 2010 to 2012 and is currently a Lecturer at the Department of Social Anthropology at the University of California, San Diego. She has published on tourism mobilities, environmental change, and inequalities in the Yucatán Peninsula (Mexico) and Spain.

Juan Córdoba Ordóñez is Professor of Regional Geography and an expert in cartographic analysis at the Universidad Complutense de Madrid and director of the Research Group on Territory, Development and Culture: Theory and Practice in North–South Dialectics. He has published extensively on globalization, development, inequality, and tourism in Spain and Latin America.

Anthony Elliott is Professor of Sociology at Hawke Research Institute, University of South Australia and Visiting Research Chair at the Open University, UK. A social theorist specializing in the intricate connections between identity and globalization, his publications include *Concepts of the Self* (Polity 2008), *The New Individualism* (Routledge 2006), *Mobile Lives* (Routledge 2010, with John Urry), and *On Society* (Polity 2012, with Bryan Turner).

Mike Featherstone is Professor of Sociology at Goldsmiths, University of London. He is founding editor of the journal *Theory, Culture & Society* and the Theory, Culture & Society Book Series. He is also the editor-in-chief of the journal *Body & Society*. His publications include *Consumer Culture and Postmodernism* (Sage 1991, second edition 2007) and *Undoing Culture: Globalization, Postmodernism and Identity* (Sage 1995).

James R. Faulconbridge is Reader in the Department of Organisation, Work and Technology at Lancaster University Management School. Research interests include the globalization of professional service firms and the role of mobility in the reproduction of global business spaces. He has co-edited *International Business Travel in the Global Economy* (Ashgate 2010).

Malene Freudendal-Pedersen is Lecturer in the Department of Environmental, Social and Spatial Change at Roskilde University, Denmark. Her research focuses on planning, transport, and mobilities in late modern everyday life. Publications include *Mobility in Daily Life* (Ashgate 2009).

Ana García de Fuentes is a Consolidated Researcher in the area of Geography in the Department of Human Ecology at the Centro de Investigación y Estudios Avanzados del IPN Mérida (CINVESTAV) in Mexico. Her research interests are transport infrastructures, space, and development in Mexico, with a special focus on tourism, environmental change, and inequalities in the Yucatán Peninsula.

Adam Jaworski is Professor of Linguistics at the University of Hong Kong. His research interests include discursive and multimodal approaches to tourism, mobility, and globalization; display of languages in space; and text-based art. His publications include *Tourism Discourse: The Language of Global Mobility* (Palgrave Macmillan 2010, with Crispin Thurlow) and *Semiotic Landscapes* (Continuum 2010, co-edited with Crispin Thurlow).

Shamus Rahman Khan is Assistant Professor in the Department of Sociology at Columbia University. He was the inaugural scholar in residence at the Institute for Social and Economic Research and Policy (ISERP) and directs the elite research network. Khan's first book, *Privilege* (Princeton University Press 2011), explored the life of an elite boarding school and he is currently researching the history of elites in New York City.

Andrew Sayer is Professor of Sociology at Lancaster University. He is author of *The Moral Significance of Class* (Cambridge University Press 2005) and is currently writing *Moral Economy: Why We Can't Afford the Rich*, which develops a critique of legitimations and consequences of contemporary forms of economic organization, and discusses popular beliefs about economic justice, particularly the view that differences in income, wealth, and quality of work are deserved.

Mimi Sheller is Professor of Sociology and founding Director of the Center for Mobilities Research and Policy at Drexel University, Philadelphia. She is founding co-editor of the journal *Mobilities*, Associate Editor of the journal *Transfers: Interdisciplinary Journal of Mobility Studies*, and serves on the Scientific Board of the Mobile Lives Forum, SNCF, France.

Crispin Thurlow is Associate Professor of Language and Communication at the University of Washington (Bothell). A strand of his research looks at how identities of privilege and ideologies of inequality are discursively organized and sustained. He has co-authored *Tourism Discourse* (Palgrave Macmillan 2010) and *Semiotic Landscapes* (Continuum 2010), both with Adam Jaworski.

John Urry is Distinguished Professor, co-founder, and Director of the Centre for Mobilities Research at Lancaster University. He is also founding co-editor of the journal *Mobilities* and author of numerous books on globalization, capitalism, tourism, and mobilities. His most recent books include *Climate Change and Society* (Polity 2010) and *Societies Beyond Oil: Oil Dregs and Social Futures* (Zed Books 2013).

Gil Viry is Research Fellow in the School of Social and Political Science at the University of Edinburgh. His research looks at the links between spatial mobility, family life, and networks of intimate relationships using mainly quantitative research methods and social network analysis.

Acknowledgements

This book has benefited from workshops funded by the British Academy (award number LA 100131) and organized by the Centre for Mobilities Research at Lancaster and the Fundaçao Getulio Vargas in Rio de Janeiro and an ESRC-funded research project and workshop on Technologies and Travel, grant number ES/J007455/1.

In the last few years we have learnt a great deal about global elites through conversations with colleagues around the world. In particular, Javier Caletrío would like to thank Joan Carles Cirer in Ibiza and Phil Macnaghten, Ramon Ribera-Fumaz, and Juan Antonio Tomás Carpi for enlightening conversations about elites. Also thanks to Monica Iorio, Carlo Perelli, Giovanni Sistu, Giuliana Mandich, and Valentina Cuzzocrea for their wonderful hospitality during a research visit and mobilities conference in Sardinia in 2012 and Jessica Aquino, Claudia Pitrez, Bianca Freire-Medeiros, Leticia Veloso, Vivian Fonseca, Manolita Correia, and Viviane Riegel for their help and collegiality in Brazil. Thanks as well to the Mobiles Lives Forum and Vincent Kaufmann for many opportunities to meet with like-minded people.

The Centre for Mobilities Research has provided a unique environment to think about our changing world and lives. We are most grateful to Monika Büscher, Bülent Diken, Satya Savitzky, David Tyfield, Saulo Cwerner, John Urry, and many others at Lancaster University.

Our gratitude is also due to all the participants in the workshops that took place in Lancaster and Rio de Janeiro.

Chapter 1

Introduction
The movement of the few

Thomas Birtchnell and Javier Caletrío

> *Nobiliorem, mobiliorem* ... the *nobility* were the *mobility*.
> (Cicero 1755: 233 citing Cato)

In places of mass transit and intense movement – railway stations, airports, harbours, city streets, casinos, skyscrapers, beaches, malls – elite mobilities take place and go ethically and morally unquestioned: they are an accepted facet of everyday life. Within mobility-as-usual there are cordons in place which insulate the few from the travails of travel; these privilege speed, comfort, ease, productivity, elevation and other contemporary virtues for those who can afford them. Such demarcations are ideologically unquestionable (although far from unquestioned) by the majority of the peripatetic or the still. Elite mobilities reinforce the popular images – super-yachts, limousines and biz-jets – of wealthy, powerful and high-status individuals who are super-included in societies and move between them through nested corridors (networks within networks) to distinct nodes or hubs with equally stratified features. Such destinations culminate more often than not in enclaves, compounds, gated communities, gentrified quarters or centres of exclusivity: degrees of stratification simultaneously, and disconcertingly, utterly restricted and yet highly accessible in terms of public visibility and awareness. The characteristics of premium networked spaces and fast-lane corridors for the few and their movement[1] trickle down to the rest of society and perceptually enthral despite flagrant conflict with concerns about the global commons and the wellbeing and equality of the many. All sorts of secrecies ensure that elite mobilities are made unfathomable and beyond audit. Elite mobilities inform cultures of luxury, success and 'the good life' and enforce a self-stylization of global elitism founded on hypermobility, meritocracy and entrepreneurial heroism. In the present liquid era nothing in this styling can stay still for long, neither money nor a regionally fixed identity; therefore, what is needed is a critical mobility-sensitive approach to the residues of evidence emitted, discarded, or put on show in stratified circulations.

This book holds the elite mobilities of the few up to scrutiny by collecting together scholars at the forefront of mobilities research invigorated by this aim.

Within the mobilities turn there has been a rich, yet narrow, seam of engagement with elite mobilities. Founding scholar John Urry was concerned with high-status reference groups across societies in his early work prior to establishing the mobilities paradigm (1973). He was one of the first to note that 'being able to travel, particularly for non-work reasons, was only available to a narrow elite and was itself a mark of status' (1990: 24). Because the few play a formative role in how and why mobilities happen their own forms of movement become foundational, referential, or simply 'normal' ingredients within the flow-architectures of society, empowering some to be more mobile at the expense of others (Massey 1993; Cresswell 2001; Sheller 2008: 29).

While most books begin by claiming an absence of research, the authors in this volume flag recent work by colleagues at the Centre for Research on Socio-Cultural Change (CRESC), which has already started the ball rolling in revamping research on elites. They highlight that elites have been widely researched in the past, but the lapse in quality and memorability of research over the last three decades stems from a lack of clarity about the subject in question – a failure of theory and also a failure of method (Savage and Williams 2008). Seeking to move forward the sociologist John Scott's (2008) solution is to be strict in how the term 'elite' is to be defined by limiting its use to those who exercise or hold power to avoid further dilution. And in uneasy concord, critics of the descendants of classic elite theory's purported folly in ignoring the global are being bidden to take heed that despite a recent glut of activity this body of work is well up to the task of supporting critical analysis on globalization for, as Jan Pakulski puts it, 'elite theory was born "global"' (2011: 3).

Without crusading too much, we recognize the value of classic elite theory and also concur that research on elites demands a different, subtler tack; we identify mobilities as a useful optic for this task in its utter centrality (a veritably global consensus) to how power is exercised and expressed in the world. Various collective nouns have been deployed by the authors in this volume and elsewhere for what we, following Eric Carlton's (1996) typology, call here the 'few' – the aristocracy, the nobility, the principals, the global superclass, the privileged, the top of the pyramid, the wealthy, the High Net Worth (HNW), flexians, the [super, uber, mega, ultra, greedy, filthy] rich, the 1 per cent(ers), globals and so on. At times there appear to be as many collective nouns as there are elite theorists; however, as with fauna, this should be understood to be due to a wealth, rather than a dearth, of curiosity. Despite this partisanship one thread that ties all of these classifications together is mobilities. There are a number of ways the authors in this volume deploy their curiosity.

First there is mobility-as-usual, and what is deemed normal owes its form to pioneering elites and their power agendas of force, speed, ease and other discourses. Mobility-as-usual is stratified not out of poor planning, unforeseen externalities, or as yet unfulfilled technological and financial expectations as commonly claimed by planners, politicians and policy-makers in countless apologetic reports for urban 'splintering' (Graham and Marvin 2001). Infrastructures are designed first with the agendas of the few in view before the social considerations of the rest are addressed. The few set a certain tempo to the movement of the many through space and to their bodily conduct; elite mobilities are instrumental in the setting of speed limits, the location of airports, the provision of urban toll-roads, the comportment and apparel of travel and so on. To challenge mobility-as-usual – whether in relation to concerns about climate change, urban safety or simply in bids for a humbler pace of life – is to question the affordances of the few whose capacity to lobby and influence policy are relentless and pervasive and whose elite mobilities set a now world-recognized standard founded on the growth of economic globalization.

Second, the openness of the world for the few is dependent on the 'staging' of mobility systems and the stratification of mobility, class and territory (as alpha, beta, gamma), which prejudices certain framings of everyday life over others, then reinforced by shared 'structural stories' that make sense of this staging (Freudendal-Pedersen 2009: 1; Jensen 2013). This staging, and its supporting structural stories, privilege elite mobilities and consequently the nitty-gritty of systems is geared towards being easeful for the few at the expense of the mobilities of the many. This prejudice is felt through atmospheres, habitus and temporalities.

Third, the few are interspersed, enmeshed and super-included in the commons, moving rapidly in and out of public spaces, privatizing and making use of them, rather than being exterior to them. The 'enclosure of the commons' in Europe – and elsewhere through the colonial encounter – which Karl Marx historicized was primarily an elite project engaged to mobilize a landed population in order to make it move to factories, cities and industrial farms (1887: 506). This social movement of the few went on alongside other forms of elite mobilities that made movement easeful, but also made others move, marking them as super-unincluded through exile and immurement elsewhere. This unsettling of a stationary majority reliant on the commons through elite mobilities continues apace as anthropologist Laura Nader summarizes in her now famous entreaty to 'study up': 'Never before have so few, by their actions and inactions, had the power of life and death over so many of the species...' (1972: 284). Her entreaty to ethnographers to study the 'colonizers' who continue to lay claim to the global commons (as much as the colonized dispossessed of it) still remains only partially heard and resonates with this volume.

Fourth, power discriminates through mobility. Or to put it another way: it is no coincidence that mobility in popular culture in much of the world is represented according to differing degrees of power: acceleration, might-is-right and velocity. In order to maximize power, elite mobilities are encrypted and enshrouded by secrecies through intermediaries who assure discretion in their labyrinthine services. From Swiss bank accounts to tax haven 'treasure islands' this is a supremely well-orchestrated version of disorganized capitalism.

Fifth, elite mobilities are not just present for the few, but have a residual quality perceivable in luxury products, travel modes, mannerisms, dress, customs, holiday destinations and even the language of those who otherwise cannot be considered elite in any true sense of the word. Elite mobilities are hegemonic in their impacts on other forms of movement and in the size of their ecological footprints. Because of this glut of mobility, residues from the circulations of the few are treasure-troves of research when approached in a critical way.

Critical thought is a powerful ally in mobilizing academic interest on elites. Today elites continue to flourish globally but in a changing landscape. The current economic crisis and rising concerns about the moral legitimacy of extreme wealth coincides with stern warnings over the civilizational risks posed by global warming and the imminent depletion of energy supplies in light of growing levels of demand acknowledged by the Intergovernmental Panel on Climate Change (IPCC) and the International Energy Agency (IEA) respectively. Against a turbulent horizon of climate-related catastrophes, expectations of global equality raise seemingly irresolvable dilemmas that question further the moral legitimacy of mobile elites. In this overarching context the authors raise a number of questions to frame the book.

What conceptual frameworks are best suited to survey and theorize mobile elites? With what tools and instruments can social scientists research, map and 'track' the flows of wealth, influence and objects mustered by the few? How might traces of mobile elites be collected, understood and interpreted in relation to symbolic power and ideas of luxury, prestige and privilege?

Mobility-as-usual

Despite a scientific consensus about the urgency to act on climate change or road fatalities no significant action is taken because of conflict with a commitment from above to 'business-as-usual' or more succinctly mobility-as-usual (Adams 1999; Urry 2004, 2008). This 'practice-consensus' (made up of many practices in concert that just seem to happen without preconceived planning, policy-making or debate) to the tune of elite mobilities is stratified, intensively global, high carbon and expansionist. As a consequence there are ever more flights, trips and commutes, demanding more runways, roads and suburbs, all necessary evils and the symptoms of progress. Elite mobilities are written into this version of everyday life by what appears to be no less than a 'gaming' of what is understood as appropriately civilized everyday movement through the world in order to accommodate the fringe interests of the few and the mainstream aspirations of the rest.

So, for instance, aeromobility, and what Peter Adey (2010) terms 'air-mindedness', began as an elite pastime (Cwerner 2009). An example of this nascent role of the few in air travel is the bizarre appearance of a primitive helicopter over the Scottish moors midway through Alfred Hitchcock's 1935 film *The 39 Steps*, which arose from him learning that a successful industrialist was financing an 'autogyro' for the masses and even commuting to work in this fashion (Bond 2010). Tellingly, in Sao Paulo, Brazilian businesspeople have taken to helicopter commuting to bypass congested and dangerous city streets (Cwerner 2006). Hitchcock's air-mindedness is poignant in light of the global growth of biz-jet culture (Budd this volume).

Railways too, despite representing the democratization of travel, were designed originally for 'goods and elite passengers' (Schivelbusch 1979; Urry 2007: 104; Aguiar 2011). Even after the introduction of mass rail travel the USSR's People's Commissar, Leon Trotsky, had his own 'Trotsky Train' with personnel, restaurant car and line priority for unhindered touring (Service 2010). Indeed, rail travel in most countries continues to cater to an elite market through class divisions demanding different experiences and 'atmospheres' (Urry 1987; Watts and Urry 2008; Bissell 2010). The provision of velocity by the train (and later the automobile) was inextricably linked to their popularity as elite mobilities, lending notions of potency and the feeling and experience of power to those who could afford them (Larsen 2001).

Thorstein Veblen's historical horse-riding elite in *The Theory of the Leisure Class* are driven to exhibitions of force, consequently setting a standard of usual mobility in society through a wider mimicry of their movement styled on 'an uncomfortable posture at a distressing gait', which was originally functionally adopted for fast riding on poor roads (1919: 145). Thus the *nouveau riche* in the nineteenth century overtly came to display material wealth through forceful, 'hyper' mobilities as a 'means of broadcasting social status' (Centeno and Cohen 2010: 113). Like air-mindedness in the late 1890s and early 1900s, motoring began with an evolving 'car-mindedness' involving speed, power, wealth and aesthetic shock. This need for speed emerged among a pioneering group of men and women in elite circles who were investigating the transformative potential of new technology in order to embellish their status (Clarsen 2008: 35; Merriman 2012: 95). Motoring was initially concentrated in the elite due to both their (or their employees') privileged knowledge and their wealth before 'car driving became something for many and not just a few' at the expense of slower forms of travel such as cycling (Shove et al. 2012: 153). Because of these early adopters automobility systems are consequently riven by inequalities harking back to early elite trials with the motorcar and relationships with other more still citizens (Hugill 1985; Gartman 2004; Urry 2004). To this day the ignominy of non-motorized travel is observably constructed as a dialogue with motorized travel, for example in the commodification and cluttering of pedestrian space with street furniture and advertising signage in contrast to the sanctity of the road space for the unopposed carriage of emergency vehicles, motorcades, commuters and high-speed status symbols (Cronin 2010).

Beyond these transport and travel concerns one of the key arguments of this volume is that elite mobilities have not only been a crucial aspect in thinking on the different technical forms of movement (planes, trains and automobiles) and the systems and practices that occur around them. Mobility is inextricably tied up with power, inequality, stratification, governance and decision-making – it is about the 'capacity to move' being engendered by a top-down social movement encouraging an ongoing transition to heightened movement whatever the social cost, including displacement, itinerancy and dispossession (Ohnmacht et al. 2009). So a movement of the few with elite mobilities at its core then permeates complex social systems from property ownership and politics to infrastructure design and investment. Trickle-down and after effects are perceivable here in this wider domain of elite mobilities, for example in the spread of second 'recreational' or 'vacation' homes in order to provide facilities around picturesque landscapes and rural idylls and easy access to them (Halseth 2004). Moreover, some enclosures, such as the Scottish Highlands, owe their very 'nature' to elite practices, such as recreational grouse and deer hunting, and in turn influence the development and ownership of other neoliberal environments (Robbins and Luginbuhl 2007). So then it is a truism to note that the modern world is typified by the idea that while some move others must wait; and this goes as much for queuing in traffic as it does for meritocratic progress or in realizing the dream of a manor with a view.

How does this mobility-as-usual stay normal despite consensual criticism from those concerned about social justice, wellbeing or the climate? A subtle, barely perceptible 'precursory creep' (borrowing the evocative language of seismology) occurs before novel means of movement explode into the mainstream, powered by elite test subjects in the commercialization of innovation (see Geels 2012). These creeping innovations become flows and then solidify into popularized practices originally exercised only by the few. As this precursory creep gathers momentum its gravity suborns the political and industrial elite who then lock it in. These entrenched interests invoke ideologies of neoliberal economic growth to support and perpetuate this mobility-as-usual. The capacity of those few entrusted with systemic responsibility – infrastructure or policy – to distance themselves from their vested interests in easeful or elevated travel allows them to structurally induce a systemic normality which retains its embryonic stratification (Soron 2011). Once vested in mobility-as-usual in this way the few are able to rebut factions of others who champion alternatives (Henderson 2004). Notions of comfort and convenience crafted by elite mobilities, within this mobility-as-usual, trump alternatives not party to these engrained cultural logics originally fastened into place by vested interests.

Mobility-as-usual is calibrated by what Jonathan Beaverstock and James Faulconbridge call socio-technical 'constituents' (Chapter 3 in this volume), which can be usefully unpicked by applying theory to 'blocks' of social practices modelled on elite mobilities (Birtchnell 2012; Shove *et al.* 2012). According to Beaverstock and Faulconbridge the block practices of the few are tied to symbolic meanings in the construction of what is 'normal'. These are social symbolisms that are 'locked in' and the 'ecology' of elite-ness involves all sorts of mediators, support structures, technologies, terms of reference and organizational dimensions that have seen a veritable industry emerge around achieving segmentation and providing semblances of elite mobilities to the rest (Thurlow and Jaworski this volume). Mobility-as-usual acts as a counterweight against efforts to explore alternatives to economic globalization, such as localism or community enterprises, which transgress the practice-consensus for comfort, convenience, speed, productivity, status and flexibility (Budd this volume). Social practices involving the regular and long-distance movement of people have become predictable and even for some a 'staple' of modern life to be defended and lobbied for alongside the right to food or shelter.

Stratification

A densely stratified panoply of the few have made the entire world their oyster and these actors have come to expect the oyster shell to be opened and closed on demand. And with this 'oysterization' has followed the stratification of mobilities, in particular in space. Elite mobilities are concerned not only with flat territories and their enclosures, but also with the stratification of volume: boundaries expressed upwards into space and downwards into the earth. This awareness of territory in '3D' has been considerably neglected in geography (Bridge 2013; Elden 2013). The most obvious form of elevation here is achieved through biz-jets and other forms of elite aeromobility (Budd this volume). So too is elevation at the heart of what Maria Kaika calls 'iconification', as monumental corporate buildings are championed and built by corporate elites who then refuse to occupy them, instead opting for footloose mobile lives (2011). For Kaika these buildings are not dwelling places or zones of productivity, but instead ritual offerings to elite identities, of totemic significance in power plays. Unlike the pyramids of the pharaohs, however, these monumental icons quickly fade into obscurity in an urban canvas too busy for eyes to tarry for long – this obsession with the skyline takes blandness to new heights (Kaika 2010).

What is often unclear in the mobilities turn where the few are concerned is whether space or status or a combination of both is being referred to by this term. The distinctions between social mobility and spatial mobility have most usefully been tackled by Sociologist Vincent Kaufmann by introducing the term 'motility' (see Kaufmann 2011). Discriminations and gradients are present in the most everyday of spatial and social scales: these are realized through capillaries of power in behaviour and politics; by the shaping of infrastructures and land-use; through the dictating of where people dwell and how they move about; and in the rendering of neighbourhoods, cities and countryside more efficient to move through or alternatively utterly pointless for the journeying of the many. The stratification of territory has gained exceptional detail and sensitivity. The elite mobilities of the 'kinetic' few proximate and are exposed to others who are near-dwellers regardless of how insulated or shielded they are: think of slums positioned next to luxury apartments or speedboats on public lakes (Adey 2003; Bissell 2012). Hence many structural decisions about the public space or the commons make little sense to the many as the territorialities of a few leach into governance and policy-making.

As David Harvey illustrates in *Rebel Cities* (2012) the planning of a few, such as Napoleon Bonaparte, modified streets, byways and parks to allow an ideal of intensely stratified travel and urban land-use to become mobility-as-usual while at the same time solving surplus capital and unemployment through planned gentrification. Yet the elite mobilities that put this into place are rarely touched upon. Elite mobilities sculpt and in the process compromise collective 'sustainable' projects in the urban space in favour of discriminatory territorialities privileging efficient travel for individuals between their key nodes: the office, house and leisure facility (Graham and Marvin 2001; Essebo and Baeten 2012).

Mobility systems produce social inequalities through co-ordinated stratification. All sorts of discriminations bolster immobility and stillness for many just as much as they enhance mobility and acceleration for an encapsulated few in the 'fast lane' (Hannam *et al.* 2006; Cresswell 2012). Such discriminations are made based on wealth, prestige, influence and status or combinations of some or all of these rubrics of power. Those stratified areas deemed to be 'alpha' are reserved for those with power to move who can rely on elite mobilities to travel in an unhindered, resource-intensive, exclusive and exceptional way, often detrimental to the commons and public space. And those in power are unlikely to champion transitions such as low-carbon cities, which obstruct the demand for cosmopolitan infrastructure modelled on ideologies of elite standards of economic growth and high-carbon urban functionality (Beck *et al.* 2013). These ideologies of cosmopolitanism are above regional concerns (Elliott this volume) and just a few 'globals', increasingly from regions including India, China and Brazil, pivot off international dimensions of austerity that reinforce regional stratifications for profit and prestige (see Birtchnell 2013). Indeed, understandings of socio-technical transitions must include the few, and the neglect of these powerful actors is a weak point in transitions social theory where grassroots 'bottom-up' change is assumed to be the preferable course of action (Birtchnell 2012).

The concern of this volume is not the discrimination of people per se (who is elite and who is not) but the discrimination of different kinds of mobilities between different geographies. A central thesis of this volume is that, regardless of how exceptional a person is and how privileged the worlds they inhabit are, they still must move to and fro between their places of abode, foci of activity and the rest of the world. While certainly some inhabit entire islands they do not spend all of their time there. Those whose mobilities are nugatory in comparison to more elevated forms of travel still remain partial witnesses to them: the business-jet on the landing strip, the motorcade through the city street, the spacious first-class train carriage, the helicopter landing on the skyscraper helipad, or the super-yacht moored in the public harbour. All of these elite mobilities are disruptive and excessive and exhibit much larger footprints than the rest of the world. Their singular mobility events take precedence over other routine ones around them. Such contrastive castes of mobility are set in stark relief by inequality; they can thus be tracked in real time or traced through various trails left behind of data on wealth, consumption, frequency of travel and investments.

So, unlike offshore financial accounts, island resorts, lodge meetings, or ministerial summits, elite mobilities are neither secretive nor hidden, but are there for all to see (albeit with faces pressed to the windowpane) and perhaps to marvel at in their excesses (see Córdoba Azcárate *et al.* and Caletrío this volume). And the more the eye is cast the more the exercise of power in order to discriminate between forms of movement is revealed as a prerequisite for social systems to run smoothly. To be sure, discriminations in movement are quick to be enforced through more tacit means sensitive to discrete socio-cultural framings. Formal dress codes, limited edition credit cards, private school mannerisms, personal invitations and other trappings of power are advertised as 'essential' in order to be mobile in this fashion. Yet elite mobilities are not just a feature of meritocratic hyper-capitalism and the global inequalities it surely has sown. Elite mobilities are then not only peripheral or accessorial to disorganized capitalism but functional components of the exercise and reward of much wider forms of power. Studying mobilities in this fashion allows a mirror to be held up to the core of what being elite means in relation to the poor, the pedestrian, the second class, the package tourist, the refugee, the sub-prime investor and other subalterns.

Elite mobilities, then, are a useful prism of analysis for an otherwise secretive and inaccessible minority. What the mobilities turn unveils is that the few are by their nature mobile and because of this are interstitial with the rest of a society, regularly crossing over different geographies as part and parcel of their own due processes. And as the world has become more full of people moving, so have the few had to rely on the stratification of movement in order to make sure their mobility options and assets remain a cut above the rest.

Super-inclusion

Journalist Roy Perrott questioned a British aristocrat in the 1960s whose family had been elite since late medieval times – the peer rejected the idea that he stood apart from society, rather: 'We have long since become merged with the general community' (1968: 3). The idea that there is a powerful minority segregated from the rest of society is attractive, yet misguided. As already discussed the few maintain highly discriminatory mobilities, moving through society in distinct ways across, and interspersed with, different geographies, including most dramatically the commons. The mobilities paradigm provides a method to research this complexity – this collection shows that, like an autostereogram or 'Magic Eye' image, elite mobilities can be brought forth from the flux of social life by the right optic to understand what is super-imposed and what is not.

The few, then, are 'super-included' not just in financialization, but within the 'fabric' of modern societies (Leyshon and Thrift 1996). Many of the systems of mobility underpinning contemporary life were put there by, and for, the few so they could travel and communicate according to a social movement affording rapid engagement and disengagement with the commons. This social movement of the few demands that the upper limits of systems are set so that the few can enact their mobilities without compromising their ease regardless of the flavour of social system or government (Freudendal-Pedersen this volume). The ease of the few is more than just a sense of indolence through privilege; it is an entire ideology in the social movement of the few around 'omnivorous' consumption (Khan this volume).

In this volume we evoke mobilities to engage with the few critically, and this includes through asking awkward questions of interviewees and societies more generally, even those that claim to be more equal than others (Freudendal-Pedersen this volume). Strangely, past examinations of elite subjects have been relatively static and fixed, focusing on singular geographies: the boardroom, the mansion, the racecourse, the hotel or the gated community. This is deceptive as most elite activity goes on out of sight and out of mind (Urry this volume). All of the places the few pass through are destinations or starting points for much wider activities and influences. Even so social status enduringly requires the few to press the flesh and enact intensive 'meetingness', much more than those without power, in order to secure their continuing distinction from others, ensuring elites dip into and out of the public domain (Urry 2012).

The 'super-inclusion' of the few in the foundational aspects of societies is by no means a new phenomenon. However, care must be exercised, for as C. Wright Mills noted in 1956 in *The Power Elite*: 'we learn from history that we cannot learn from it' (2000: 23). This rings true in that in an episteme that takes its starting point in the prehistoric emergence of textual, agricultural and architectural forms of evidence, which indicate to observers power and stratification, what has dominated the public and scholarly imagination – as noted by historian Catherine Fletcher blogging in response to the successful DNA identification of Richard III in 2013 (and echoing historian Gustaaf Johannes Renier) – has been 'kings and queens history' (Renier 1950; Fletcher 2013; Kennedy 2013). Indeed, the excitement around the discovery in England of the skeleton of the last Plantagenet king – a long defunct line – ignobly interred after his death in 1485 in what became a car park, merited live feeds from Leicester and front-page press coverage by major global news providers. This curiosity about a long-dead elite met with the ire of other historians as well as Fletcher. Neville Morley, professor of ancient history at the University of Bristol, also blogged, 'why is it that a skeleton is interesting only if it's that of a famous person?' (Kennedy 2013; Morley 2013). And as Fletcher archly hypothesized: 'Imagine that the Leicester archaeologists had uncovered not a royal grave, but a grave of some peasant farmers, results from which completely changed the picture of what we know about human nutrition in the 15th century'; even this 'wouldn't have the media pull of "England's lost king"' (Fletcher 2013; Kennedy 2013).

To remedy 'kings and queens' history Mills suggests that the few must be analysed for every epoch and social structure with due diligence paid to power. This would be an ambitious task and in lieu it is observable that elite mobilities have been a facet of power in many periods and societies. A simultaneous connection and disconnection with the commons through intensive movement has generally been a *sine qua non* of the few, as Cato illustrated in the epigraph in the beginning of this chapter: nobility is mobility. Thinking about the super-inclusion of the few in society means that kings-and-queens history focusing on key heroic individuals, while attractive, can be downplayed in favour of a history of the normalizing of elite practices and their socializing impacts on the subaltern. As well, elite formations composed of tacit networks can be visualized and the heroic sagas of capitalism deconstructed (Birtchnell, Viry and Urry this volume).

So against a kings-and-queens history, two dramatic globalizing systems of elite mobilities in the eighteenth and nineteenth centuries demand brief acknowledgement here. The first was the Grand Tour, where the wealthy and 'high' born would make use of established trade routes, efficient maritime technologies and roads and carriages to tour the European continent and distance themselves from the madding crowd. The second was what was known at the time as the System, which allowed the few in British society to mete out 'transportation' onto the poor, sending them to the ends of the earth. This process of making many people 'super-unincluded' was only moderately successful. As vast numbers of the poor and desperate were transported to penal colonies, often for such trivial offences as swearing or stealing a handkerchief, these vast upheavals implemented in a bid to enforce enclosure of the commons were brought into popular debate. This forced mobility at the whim of the elite was worse than being moved off-world at the time as those transported ruefully reflected – 'at least one could see the moon from England' (Hughes 2010: 77). Where the Grand Tour and the System allowed the few to offshore themselves or the socially unwanted, the redesign and reclassification of extra-legal and territorial 'worlds' emerged as a powerful force for elite mobilities to offshore finances and resources rather than just bodies. These are part of a system of secrecies which elite mobilities underscore.

Secrecies

The premier conspiracy theory is that the world's elites hold a secret meeting every year in order to reach a transnational consensus to secure their own amelioration. In recent years attention has fixed on the Bilderberg Group as the manifestation of this secret society. In an impressive study of 'Bilderberg People', drawing on interviews with participants, Ian Richardson and his colleagues illustrate the underlying dynamics at play in this network. While there is no evidence of a global conspiracy, what is fascinating is that a particular 'brand' of consensus emerges as an unconscious manifestation of the alignment and preference of these actors for distinct relationships that privilege those who are mobile and global – this consensus is 'in service of the forces of economic globalization' (Richardson *et al.* 2011: 217).

In contemporary thought, unlike kings-and-queens history, the few profit from an unspoken social contract: they are overlooked, unmentioned, redacted, and become 'shadows' (Wedel 2008). This is one reason for the indecision about what to term 'the few' despite the wealth of collective nouns on offer. These secrecies and absences are not only a methods problem, but one of theory and episteme as well. Moreover, it serves more than protest to bring to print the observation that only a few shape the contours of global capitalism and also command the payrolls most academics (and publishers) depend upon (Freudendal-Pedersen this volume). Yet lines of command and overarching influences are *de rigueur* kept indistinct and evincing of conspiracy theories.

To lay our cards on the table we contribute that it is not an absence of research or intent that is at fault in not fully critiquing these secrecies, but rather more covert and pervasive elements in the very nature of how 'the few' move through the world and perform their power. Perhaps the first to question the secrecies of the few in recent times were Jonathon Beaverstock and his colleagues who in 2004 sought to expose how the super-rich were 'getting away with it' through examining their geographies of activity (Beaverstock *et al.* 2004). In an unprecedented counter-movement the secrecies of the few were brought to light by the global financial crisis. Savage and Williams offered the well-timed question at this time: 'Where ... are the social theorists who focus on these processes as central to understanding the contemporary dynamics of social change?' (2008: 1). And fortifying this question was a now infamous article in the *Guardian* newspaper by Aditya Chakrabortty asking 'Where are the sociologists?' Chakrabortty named and shamed social scientists for focusing not on the global economic meltdown or the inegalitarianism of subprime markets, but instead on niche topics (perhaps unfairly) such as bodybuilding in later life (2012). In a public debate at Lancaster University in October 2012 with Professors John Urry, Sylvia Walby, Andrew Sayer and Bob Jessop, Chakrabortty sympathized with arguments that many sociologists feel as if they are on the outside looking in when it comes to topics of power, wealth and status; however, he stressed that they should persevere in developing critical instruments rather than solely engage with subaltern or apolitical topics alone.

The authors in this volume are keen to bring into the open the secrecies of the few and illuminate the shadowy mobilities of finances, resources and people through what is emerging to be, like dark matter, impossibly vast but unobservable through current instruments (Urry this volume; Featherstone this volume; Beaverstock and Faulconbridge this volume). It is perhaps a sign of things to come that scrutiny of these secrecies is being dealt out by social scientists.

Residues

The notion that the few are under-researched in comparison to subalterns in the social sciences is a perennial issue. Sociologists Savage and Williams maintain that elite studies needs to be 'kick-started' and elites 'remembered' (2008). But not only do elites need remembering; as well the insufficiency of the tools of social research to engage with the few as a subject of inquiry demands redress. As Savage has noted elsewhere (Savage and Burrows 2007) the 'confessional' modes of research (interviews, questionnaires, sample surveys) are confounded by inaccessible, powerful and valorized actors, although tactical approaches do exist (see Caletrío 2012). Those who attempt to tackle the few according to reigning conventions do so with extensive caveats: ethics approval could not be obtained; invitation letters were ignored or returned unread; emails bounced or went unnoticed; questions were analysed, edited and redacted; surveys, tests and questionnaires were too time-consuming to complete; access to the building could not be granted; diary dates were not available; data were censored afterwards; the sample was too small for generalization; anonymity could not be assured; the travel costs of close observation were too high.

In 1974 Sociologist Anthony Giddens adamantly asserted that first and foremost empirical research is required to remedy the lack of exploration of elites (Stanworth and Giddens 1974). But traditional methodologies are undermined by the very nature of elite mobilities. For instance, conventional ethnographic research based on a year's fieldwork on the few is logistically and politically dubious and would require almost superhuman resources and skills. Take the film *Goldfinger* (1964), which crosses through an overwhelming number of elite mobilities. The MI6 spy James Bond discovers the eponymous magnate is smuggling gold in the bodywork of his car across international borders through an assignment that involves a game of cards in a Miami Beach five-star hotel, a game of golf in Buckinghamshire, a car chase in Switzerland, a race course in Kentucky and a trip in the villain's personal jet. The film finishes with Goldfinger being sucked out of an aeroplane and plunging to his death while Bond parachutes to safety. We would all like to conduct our research like this, but ethics committees, deans, academic supervisors and risk managers would hardly approve. Of course there are some valuable exceptions where the few have been shadowed through their mobilities (Elliott this volume). Other social scientists, however, can get busy in different ways by tracing personalized biz-jet number-plates (Budd this volume), sorting technology founders' citation histories in patent data (Birtchnell, Viry and Urry this volume), frequenting privileged private schools (Khan this volume), being flies on the wall in top resorts (Córdoba Azcárate *et al.* this volume), chatting and photographing servants and maids (Thurlow and Jaworski this volume), bothering beachgoers about luxury lifestyles (Caletrío this volume), subjecting the wealthy to a clinical classification system (Beaverstock and Faulconbridge this volume) or simply talking to bodyguards about their clients (Freudendal-Pedersen this volume). In all these cases residues of elite mobilities are made a topic of interest just as journalists might sort through the garbage of celebrities in order to uncover their dirty secrets.

Interestingly the sociologist Vilfredo Pareto laid the groundwork for this approach early in the twentieth century in his key formulation that elites 'circulate' and leave 'residues' (1963). For Pareto and his disciples circulations and their symbolic 'residues' were strictly in terms of power and woven accordingly into a totemistic social theory. But elites also circulate spatially as well and this occurs in an interplay with social mobility so that many interesting residues are laid about the public domain waiting for those willing to get their analytical hands dirty. This wealth of possible research is hardly surprising as the extent of elites' circulations are truly staggering. Summing up her four-year career as the US Secretary of State Hillary Clinton referenced the impressive network capital she had accumulated on her circulations of the globe – covering 956,733 miles to 112 countries (with a photo from each one), her travelling time adds up to 86.8 days (Ghattas 2013). Elites circulate not only in terms of station, one elite replacing another, but also literally, in terms of mobility. Such intensive circulations leave many residues, which critical mobile methods are sensitive to through the methodology's openness to academic innovation (Büscher, Urry and Witchger 2010).

Predefined global circuits have become synonymous with transnational professionals and are an obvious place to inquire into elite mobilities (Sassen 2008). Elites 'live large' and they oscillate, touring with ease extra-territorially. Whether it is a club, a board meeting, a conference or a summit, regardless of the purpose of their movement all of these elites are used to a lifestyle where they, at times, see a new city every night, but travel in relative comfort and ease. Mobilities in this fashion represent a perk and symbol of achievement (Elliott this volume). Intensive mobilities have become a meritocratic ideal that is both a curse and a reward for high achievement. So, then, the few have a heightened sense of mobility, both literally, as ensconced in the top floors of skyscrapers and in business jets, and experientially, as in a greater need and opportunity for and performance of movement. The movement of the few is rapid, technologically empowered and global, and social scientists must be sensitive to this in the way they engage with these subjects. This volume hopes to contribute to such an enterprise.

Conclusion

'Never was so much owed by so few to so many' (Cherny 2001: 199). The few who make up the subject of this book are not just out there waiting patiently for social scientists to remember to include them in a sample survey, test their IQ, or ask them to fill out a questionnaire. These powerful actors are small in number but great in influence, and their power extends to control over the research methods used on them. In this volume we contend that social scientists must pay attention to tracing their residues; shadowing their flows; scrutinizing their secrecies or absences; and questioning their claim-making, stratification projects and enclosures of the commons. The mobilities turn and mobile methods offer a springboard to accomplish these investigations without direct confrontations that jeopardize critical thought, on the one hand, or social and economic survival, on the other. The authors in this volume show too that geographies are a complementary optic to mobilities: occupying the top tier of the so-called 'human pyramid' elites' activities are scrutinized, emulated and benchmarked in the production of urban and leisure landscapes. These associations of movement and landscape form a brand vocabulary that the global elite aspire to and promote through an embarrassment of riches that manifest in venues like Dubai, perhaps the wildest materialization of an age of excess. A few highly mobile, high net-worth individuals are instrumental in the socialization of desire for unattainable and unsustainable standards of consumption styled as luxury, privilege, prestige and 'class'. The extravagant lifestyles of the rich, super-rich and, increasingly, mega-rich, modulate between these nodes of power and elite identity and free-floating, unhindered mobility.

That mobile elites, who have unlimited access to the world's resources, are also part of the ordinary, everyday world constitutes the main thesis of this book. In this regard, a number of tasks are extant here. First, to clarify whether the new economic and moral order is a passing trend or whether it signifies the beginning of a vigorous contestation of the lifestyles of the few; second, to understand the implications for global mobilities in terms of potentially diminishing resources, on the one hand, and ongoing hypermobility on the other; third, to unpack the impacts of a growing class of mobile elite on social practices; fourth, to renew social science techniques only currently applied in other domains; and finally, to discover which conceptual and theoretical tools might be most appropriate to identify path dependencies, lock-ins, tipping points and critical transitions in high-carbon mobility regimes.

Elite mobilities are at the same time both obvious and discreet. How to resolve this conundrum critically? In this book the power, spaces, luxuries, and movements of the few are theorized, tracked and traced to draw out this contradiction through the latest mobile methods and the mobilities turn. While there is a rash of public content on leadership, top management, celebrities, the rich and the successful there is paltry critical analysis of elites and their mobilities. However, new instruments and techniques in geography and sociology offer an optic on the implicit flow-architectures and explicit power dynamics of this group. By addressing this lacuna *Elite Mobilities* engages with and further develops standard academic perspectives on elites in current public and media debates and provides insights into the future trajectories, meritocratic or not, of imbalanced and inegalitarian societies.

Note

1 The word movement is used here in a dual sense to indicate a 'social movement' as well as social/spatial mobility. Many of the authors in this volume describe elite mobilities in terms of a set of organizing principles resembling a social movement (or a 'revolution of the rich') for economic globalization, wealth accumulation, enclosure of the commons, tax evasion and other concerns.

References

Adams, J. (1999). *The Social Implications of Hypermobility*. Report for OECD Project on Environmentally Sustainable Transport. Paris, OECD.
Adey, P. (2003). 'Secured and Sorted Mobilities: Examples from the Airport'. *Surveillance & Society* 1 (4): 500–551.
Adey, P. (2010). *Aerial Life: Spaces, Mobilities, Affects*. Chichester, Wiley-Blackwell.
Aguiar, M. (2011). *Tracking Modernity: India's Railway and the Culture of Mobility*. Minneapolis, University of Minnesota Press.
Beaverstock, J. V., P. Hubbard and J. Rennie Short (2004). 'Getting Away with It? Exposing the Geographies of the Super-Rich'. *Geoforum* 35 (4): 401–407.
Beck, U., A. Blok, D. Tyfield and J. Y. Zhang (2013). 'Cosmopolitan Communities of Climate Risk: Conceptual and Empirical Suggestions for a New Research Agenda'. *Global Networks* 13 (1): 1–21.
Birtchnell, T. (2012). 'Elites, Elements and Events: Practice Theory and Scale'. *Journal of Transport Geography* 24: 497–502.
Birtchnell, T. (2013). *Indovation: Innovation and a Global Knowledge Economy in India*. Basingstoke, Palgrave Macmillan.
Bissell, D. (2010). 'Passenger Mobilities: Affective Atmospheres and the Sociality of Public Transport'. *Environment and Planning D: Society and Space* 28 (2): 270–289.
Bissell, D. (2012). 'Pointless Mobilities: Rethinking Proximity through the Loops of Neighbourhood'. *Mobilities*. DOI: 10.1080/17450101.2012.696343.
Bond, A. (2010). 'Travelling at the Edge of Space.' Accessed 18 March 2010 at http://ewds.strath.ac.uk/space/OnDemandSeminar/tabid/4560/articleType/ArticleView/articleId/288/Travelling-at-the-edge-of-space–10-March-2010.aspx.
Bridge, G. (2013). 'Territory, Now in 3D!' *Political Geography*. Accessed 26 April 2013 at http://dx.doi.org/10.1016/j.polgeo.2013.01.005.
Büscher, M., J. Urry and K. Witchger (2010). *Mobile Methods*. Abingdon, Routledge.
Caletrío, J. (2012). 'Global Elites, Privilege and Mobilities in Post-Organized Capitalism'. *Theory, Culture & Society* 29 (2): 135–149.
Carlton, E. (1996). *The Few and the Many*. Farnham, Ashgate.
Centeno, M. A. and J. N. Cohen (2010). *Global Capitalism: A Sociological Perspective*. Cambridge, Polity.
Chakrabortty, A. (2012). 'Economics Has Failed Us: But Where Are the Fresh Voices?' *Guardian*, 16 April.
Cherny, A. (2001). *The Next Deal: The Future of Public Life in the Information Age*. New York, Basic Books.
Cicero, M. T. (1755). *M. T. Cicero De Oratore: Or, His Three Dialogues Upon the Character and Qualifications of an Orator; Translated into English, with Notes Historical and Explanatory, and an Introductory Preface*. London, Printed for T. Waller.

Clarsen, G. (2008). *Eat My Dust: Early Women Motorists*. Baltimore, Johns Hopkins University Press.

Cresswell, T. (2001). 'The Production of Mobilities'. *New Formations* **43**: 11–25.

Cresswell, T. (2012). 'Mobilities II Still'. *Progress in Human Geography* **36** (5): 645–653.

Cronin, A. (2010). *Advertising, Commercial Spaces and the Urban*. Basingstoke, Palgrave Macmillan.

Cwerner, S. B. (2006). 'Vertical Flight and Urban Mobilities: The Promise and Reality of Helicopter Travel'. *Mobilities* **1** (2): 10.1080/17450100600726589: 191–215.

Cwerner, S. B. (2009). 'Introducing Aeromobilities'. In S. B. Cwerner, S. Kesselring and J. Urry (eds) *Introducing Aeromobilities*. Abingdon: Routledge, pp. 1–22.

Elden, S. (2013). 'Secure the Volume: Vertical Geopolitics and the Depth of Power'. *Political Geography*. Accessed 26 April 2013 at http://dx.doi.org/10.1016/j.polgeo.2012.12.009.

Essebo, M. and G. Baeten (2012). 'Contradictions of "Sustainable Mobility" – the Illogic of Growth and the Logic of Myth'. *Tijdschrift voor economische en sociale geografie* **103** (5): 555–565.

Fletcher, C. (2013). '(Dead) Kings and Queens History: Richard III and the Car Park Saga'. *History Matters*. Accessed 4 February 2013 at www.historymatters.group.shef.ac.uk/richard-iiidead-kings-queens-history/.

Freudendal-Pedersen, M. (2009). *Mobility in Daily Life: Between Freedom and Unfreedom*. London, Ashgate.

Gartman, D. (2004). 'Three Ages of the Automobile: The Cultural Logics of the Car'. *Theory, Culture & Society* **21** (4–5): 10.1177/0263276404046066: 169–195.

Geels, F. W. (2012). 'A Socio-Technical Analysis of Low-Carbon Transitions: Introducing the Multi-Level Perspective into Transport Studies'. *Journal of Transport Geography* **24**: 471–482.

Ghattas, K. (2013). 'Hillary Clinton: A Long Journey.' *BBC News*. Accessed 2 February 2013 at www.bbc.co.uk/news/magazine-20311170.

Graham, S. and S. Marvin (2001). *Splintering Urbanism: Networked Infrastructures, Technological Mobilities and the Urban Condition*. London, Routledge.

Halseth, G. (2004). 'The "Cottage" Privilege: Increasingly Elite Landscapes of Second Homes in Canada'. In C. M. Hall and D. K. Müller (eds) *Tourism, Mobility, and Second Homes: Between Elite Landscape and Common Ground*. Clevedon, Channel View Books, pp. 35–54.

Hannam, K., M. Sheller and J. Urry (2006). 'Editorial: Mobilities, Immobilities and Moorings'. *Mobilities* **1** (1): 1–22.

Harvey, D. (2012). *Rebel Cities: From the Right to the City to the Urban Revolution*. London, Verso.

Henderson, J. (2004). 'The Politics of Mobility and Business Elites in Atlanta, Georgia'. *Urban Geography* **25** (3): 193–216.

Hughes, R. (2010). *The Fatal Shore*. London, Vintage Books.

Hugill, P. J. (1985). 'The Rediscovery of America: Elite Automobile Touring'. *Annals of Tourism Research* **12** (3): http://dx.doi.org/10.1016/0160-7383(85)90008-8: 435–447.

Jensen, O. B. (2013). *Staging Mobilities*. Abingdon, Routledge.

Kaika, M. (2010). 'Architecture and Crisis: Re-Inventing the Icon, Re-Imag(in)ing

London and Re-Branding the City'. *Transactions of the Institute of British Geographers* **35** (4): 10.1111/j.1475-5661.2010.00398.x: 453–474.

Kaika, M. (2011). 'Autistic Architecture: The Fall of the Icon and the Rise of the Serial Object of Architecture'. *Environment and Planning D: Society and Space* **29** (6): 968–992.

Kaufmann, V. (2011). *Rethinking the City: Urban Dynamics and Motility*. Abingdon, Routledge.

Kennedy, M. (2013). 'Richard III's Scarred Skeleton Becomes a Battlefield for Academics'. *Guardian*, 4 February. Accessed 4 February 2013 at www.guardian.co.uk/uk/2013/feb/04/richard-third-skeleton-confirmed-leicester.

Larsen, J. (2001). 'Tourism Mobilities and the Travel Glance: Experiences of Being on the Move'. *Scandinavian Journal of Hospitality and Tourism* **1** (2): 10.1080/150222501317244010: 80–98.

Leyshon, A. and N. Thrift (1996). 'Financial Exclusion and the Shifting Boundaries of the Financial System'. *Environment and Planning A* **28** (7): 1150–1156.

Marx, K. (1887). *Capital: A Critical Analysis of Capitalist Production*. London, Sonnenschein.

Massey, D. (1993). 'Power-Geometry and a Progressive Sense of Place'. In J. Bird, B. Curtis, T. Putnam, G. Robertson and L. Tickner (eds) *Mapping the Futures: Local Cultures, Global Change*. New York, Routledge, pp. 60–70.

Merriman, P. (2012). *Mobility, Space and Culture*. Abingdon, Routledge.

Mills, C. W. (2000). *The Power Elite*. New York, Oxford University Press.

Morley, N. (2013). 'Bah. And Furthermore, Humbug.' *Sphinx: The Bristol Classics Blog*, 4 February. Accessed 4 February 2014 at http://bristolclassics.wordpress.com/2013/02/04/bah-and-furthermore-humbug/.

Nader, L. (1972). 'Up the Anthropologist: Perspectives Gained from Studying Up'. In D. H. Hymes (ed.) *Reinventing Anthropology*. Ann Arbor, University of Michigan Press, pp. 284–311.

Ohnmacht, T., H. Maksim and M. M. Bergman (2009). 'Mobilities and Inequality – Making Connections'. In T. Ohnmacht, H. Maksim and M. M. Bergman (eds) *Mobility and Inequality*. Abingdon, Ashgate, pp. 7–26.

Pakulski, J. (2011). 'Global Elite: A Myth or Reality?' *ECPR General Conference*, ed. J. Higley and U. Hoffmann-Lange. Reykjavik.

Pareto, V. (1963). *The Mind and Society: A Treatise on General Sociology*. New York, Dover Publications.

Perrott, R. (1968). *The Aristocrats*. London, Weidenfeld & Nicolson.

Renier, G. J. (1950). *History, Its Purpose and Method*. London, Allen & Unwin.

Richardson, I. N., A. P. Kakabadse and N. K. Kakabadse (2011). *Bilderberg People: Elite Power and Consensus in World Affairs*. Abingdon, Routledge.

Robbins, P. and A. Luginbuhl (2007). 'The Last Enclosure: Resisting Privatization of Wildlife in the Western United States'. In N. Heynen, J. McCarthy, S. Prudham and P. Robbins (eds) *Neoliberal Environments: False Promises and Unnatural Consequences*. Abingdon, Routledge, pp. 25–37.

Sassen, S. (2008). 'Two Stops in Today's New Global Geographies: Shaping Novel Labor Supplies and Employment Regimes'. *American Behavioral Scientist* **52** (3): 457–496.

Savage, M. and R. Burrows (2007). 'The Coming Crisis of Empirical Sociology'. *Sociology* **41** (5): 10.1177/0038038507080443: 885–899.

Savage, M. and K. Williams (2008). 'Elites: Remembered in Capitalism and Forgotten by Social Sciences'. In *Remembering Elites*. Oxford, Blackwell Publishing, pp. 1–24.

Schivelbusch, W. (1979). *The Railway Journey: Trains and Travel in the Nineteenth Century*. New York, Urizen Books.

Scott, J. (2008). 'Modes of Power and the Re-Conceptualisation of Elites'. In M. Savage and K. Williams (eds) *Remembering Elites*. Oxford, Blackwell Publishing, pp. 25–43.

Service, R. (2010). *Trotsky: A Biography*. London, Pan.

Sheller, M. (2008). 'The Ethics of Mobilities'. In S. Bergmann and T. Sager (eds) *The Ethics of Mobilities: Rethinking Place, Exclusion, Freedom and Environment*. Aldershot, Ashgate, pp. 25–38.

Shove, E., M. Pantzar and M. Watson (2012). *The Dynamics of Social Practice: Everyday Life and How It Changes*. London, Sage.

Soron, D. (2011). 'Road Kill: Commodity Fetishism and Structural Violence'. In J. Sanbonmatsu (ed.) *Critical Theory and Animal Liberation*. Plymouth, Rowman & Littlefield.

Stanworth, P. and A. Giddens (1974). *Elites and Power in British Society*. Cambridge, Cambridge University Press.

Urry, J. (1973). *Reference Groups and the Theory of Revolution*. London, Routledge & Kegan Paul.

Urry, J. (1987). 'Some Social and Spatial Aspects of Services'. *Environment and Planning D: Society and Space* **5** (1): 5–26.

Urry, J. (1990). 'The 'Consumption' of Tourism.' *Sociology* **24** (1): 10.1177/0038038590024001004: 23–35.

Urry, J. (2004). 'The "System" of Automobility.' *Theory, Culture & Society* **21** (4–5): 25–39.

Urry, J. (2007). *Mobilities*. London, Polity.

Urry, J. (2008). 'Climate Change, Travel and Complex Futures'. *The British Journal of Sociology* **59** (2): 261–279.

Urry, J. (2012). 'Social Networks, Mobile Lives and Social Inequalities'. *Journal of Transport Geography* **21**: 24–30.

Veblen, T. (1919). *The Theory of the Leisure Class: An Economic Study in the Evolution of Institutions*. New York, B. W. Huebsch.

Watts, L. and J. Urry (2008). 'Moving Methods, Travelling Times'. *Environment and Planning D: Society and Space* **26** (5): 860–874.

Wedel, J. (2008). *The Shadow Elite: The New Agents of Power and Influence Who Are Undermining Government, Free Enterprise, and Democracy*. New York, Perseus Books Group.

Chapter 2

Elsewhere
Tracking the mobile lives of globals

Anthony Elliott

In the twenty-first century, it is arguably the case that no signifier exerts as much socio-economic force as money. Not surprisingly when it comes to mega-wealth, the impact of such signification is raised to the second power. Today's cultural fascination with mega-wealth is increasingly evident in various displays of lavish, conspicuous consumption – from US$100+ million homes and personal tropical islands to 500-foot super-yachts and personal jets.

Culture in the expensive, polished cites of the West is a form of life which, seemingly automatically, bends the knee at all signs of extreme wealth. If this is true of the global field of fame and celebrity, it is equally true of a new corporate elite and the super-rich. The emergence of a new transnational corporate elite – whom I shall call, following Zygmunt Bauman, 'the globals' – is intricately interwoven with the formation of integrated global financial markets and interlocking information networks. The globals are those contemporary women and men roaming the planet through multiple mobilities and mutliplex careers – overseeing vast capital investments, transnational operations, endless organizational downsizings and corporate remodellings. As a first approximation, let me propose the following formula for the analysis of today's stateless, hyper-mobile global elite: the more money a person has at their disposal, the more mobile they are because everything (or just about everything) becomes possible. This formulation should of course only serve as an initial orientation to thinking about global elites: there are many other central social forces at work in the production and performance of the lives of globals. The intricate connections between money and mobilities is key in this connection. Why, for example, do globals travel as much as they do? What is it about the mobilities of new global elites that captivates and disturbs? These are some of the central issues I wish to explore in this chapter. But this is rushing ahead. To grasp the increasingly rootless, nomadic, season-driven lifestyles of global elites, it is necessary to situate such hyper-mobile lives in the context of the financial deregulation of markets and the comprehensive privatization of 'social things' (Lemert 2008). Seeking to capture the socio-economic contours of the new economy, analysts have spoken of an age of 'turbo-capitalism', 'late capitalism', 'neo-liberalism', 'disorganized capitalism' and 'liquid modernity' (e.g. Luttwak 1998; Jameson 1999; Lash and Urry 1987; Bauman 2000). There have been many economic and financial developments that have shaped the emergence of our new mobile age of light, disorganized capitalism. These developments are complex, and some of the most significant of these economic transformations include: the collapse of Bretton Woods; President Nixon's repudiation of gold in the 1970s; the oil shocks of 1973; the Wall Street crash of 1987; the dot-com bubble and subsequent wreck; the September 11 terror attacks; and the global financial meltdown of the late 2000s and early 2010s.

Against this socio-economic backcloth, several factors are worth noting at the outset as regards today's globals – particularly if we are to adequately distinguish them from the global elite of yesteryear. First, today's globals – operating in an institutional context of fast-paced networking and mobile life – are, for the most part, relatively unconstrained by nations, national societies or communities. I will return to this point in more detail later in the chapter, but for now note that the international mobile realm of the twenty-first century is the first to generate a socio-economic elite that is genuinely global. Second, not only are the assets and financial holdings of globals truly staggering (as will be shortly reviewed), but the speed and dynamism with which globals generate, increase and multiply their total annual incomes has intensified on a dramatic scale (Haseler 2000: 4–7). From foreign-exchange dealing on Wall Street to software innovation in Silicon Valley, globals command vast personal agglomerations of wealth, travelling in transatlantic private jets to designer mansions dotted around the world. And, crucially, the private jets are an indication not only of super-wealth but of the highly mobile nature of globals themselves and of their money – shifting as they do between various countries and regions, tax regimes and legal systems, whilst living extraordinary sumptuous lifestyles well over and above even the highest standards of 'locals' living in territorially fixed societies.

Exploring, and developing upon, previous work I have undertaken on the relationship between money, mobilities and identities (Elliott and Urry 2010; Elliott 2012), I want here to explore a range of practices and experiences associated with the rise of new global elites.[1] I am especially interested in exploring the escapist dimensions of the lives of globals – that is to say, what it is that globals (as opposed to ordinary identities) manage to escape from, and also what they escape to, in the living of elite lifestyles. I want to bear in mind that contemporary culture appears increasingly spellbound by ideas of the escapism of globals, and yet largely lacking in knowledge as to the demands and disturbances of such lifestyles. In a sense, then, I am interested in the question of our 'pictures' of the lifestyles of new global elites – and of whether these pictures adequately capture the thrills and spills of lives lived by globals. The chapter examines in detail the mobile lives of globals, situated in terms of recent sweeping changes to national economies, identities and cultures. The chapter begins by considering various connections between new global elites and the world of hyper-mobilities. What is absent from many recent discussions of global elites is any sustained consideration of the 'experiential texture' of the lives of globals, as well as the rich networked individualism such lives entail, and the remainder of the chapter seeks to develop an alternative approach sufficiently alert to the tracking of the mobile lives of globals. I review the methodological precepts that have underpinned recent studies of the 'moving targets' of mobile global elites I have undertaken, and I then go on to outline a case-study of one such global high in network capital. In the final section of the chapter, some more general lines of analysis from the case-study are considered, highlighting the central social forms in and through which the identities of globals are constituted, reproduced and transformed.

The globals and hyper-mobilities

Notwithstanding the global financial crisis of the late 2000s and early 2010s, the stunningly opulent lifestyles of global elites have continued to blossom, transcending geographical boundaries and nation-state regulations as a result of the privileges of multiple mobilities. Contemporary sociologies of wealth, financial power and studies of the super-rich suggest various indicators of widening social inequality (Walby 2009). Selected somewhat at random from a range of recent studies, consider the following indicators of wealth expansion, mobility acceleration and excessive lifestyle choices of globals:

- A 2011 report estimates the overall number of global ultra wealthy worth at least US$500 million at about 4,650. These globals together hold an estimated US$6.25 trillion in assets (Pizzigati 2012).
- Elites increasingly enjoy tax-free global citizenship (on tax and offshoring see Urry in this volume). 'Homeless' German billionaire Nicolas Berggruen is one such global who has been criticized for such tax evasion, largely for deploying his US$2.3 billion fortune 'hopping the world from one five-star hotel to another' (Pizzigati 2012).
- Hyper-mobile global lifestyles have led to the stateless super-rich buying the large bulk of the world's most expensive homes. The superprime property markets are increasingly dominated by global elites: for example, 100 per cent of Monaco's super-prime properties are sold to international buyers; it is estimated that globals also purchase as many as 95 per cent of the most expensive homes in Paris, and 85 per cent in London (Powley and Warwick-Ching 2012).

- One report estimates that the average global spends US$157,000 a year on hotels and resorts, and US$224,000 a year on events at hotels and resorts; US$107,000 a year at spas around the world; US$226,000 per year on cars, and US$404,000 a year on yacht rentals; US$542,000 a year on home improvements; and, US$1.75 million a year on art (Kostigen 2012.)
- In 2012, the US bank Wells Fargo announced the appointment of a 'wealth psychologist', offering counsel to those with upwards of US$50 million (Eichelberger 2012).

What helps to constitute global elites, then, also figures as a central element of the performativity of transnational lifestyles. For globals the power of money concerns, among other things, the liberating force of mobilities. According to Knight Frank's 2012 Wealth Report, today's 63,000-strong global elite – with assets of $US100 million or more – live lives of unparalleled cultural, climatic and geographic diversity, as indicated by high-frequency worldwide travel and the frenetic buying of multiple homes across the globe. To live life as a global, to be sure, requires the demonstration of a surplus of economic and cultural capital. And yet economic and cultural capital is not all in grasping the lives of globals. In our book *Mobile Lives* (2010), John Urry and I developed the argument that there is another type of power – what we term 'network power' – that is fundamental to the lives of globals. Bluntly put, network power is essential to successful 'networking' in the global financial markets of the rich North, and is intricately interwoven with new forms of travel, movement and mobility. Life today, Urry and I argue, is fundamentally experienced as 'life on the move', and nowhere is this is more obviously so than when we look at the lives of new corporate elites. In clearing an analytical space for network power in studying global elites, it is crucial also, as we shall see throughout this chapter, to reflect on the idea of mobilities and the continued movement of globals.

Access to complex, contradictory and digitized mobility systems – from mobile phones and computer databases to yachts and private jets – is central to contemporary global experiences of great wealth, power and prestige. Yet the rapid increase in the wealth of globals during recent years has occurred at the cost of unprecedented levels of poverty. As Edward Luttwak notes, 'all countries that have undergone turbo-capitalist change, from the United Kingdom to Argentina, from Finland to New Zealand, now have their new billionaires or at least centi-millionaires, as they all have their new poor' (1998: 5). To which it might be added that one central defining feature of the new poverty to which Luttwak draws attention concerns its embedding in complex systems of immobility – for example, the contracted cleaning staff that service the business and first-class airport lounges that globals routinely pass through.

In sociological terms, the emergence of a new global elite should be cast against the backdrop of the institutional shift from organized, solid modernity to disorganized, liquid modernity (Bauman 2000; Lash and Urry 1987). The idea here is that the 'shake-out' of nationally organized economies and societies by the dislocating processes of globalization has penetrated all the way down to the restructuring of work, the professions, social divisions and status processes. John Scott expresses this as follows: 'national capitalist classes themselves are being increasingly fragmented along the lines of the globalized circuits of capital and investment that they are involved in' (1997: 312). Scott's assessment of the logic of wealth transformation occurs from the standpoint of methodological nationalism, with the 'global' represented as an external force rewriting the 'local'. But if we switch optics and consider the question from a more global perspective, we begin to see that these changes are even more far-reaching. Specifically global finance, new technologies and multinational firms are creating highly mobile, detached forms of professional and executive experience that are transformational to the new economy.

Toward a sociology of global mobile elites: research methodology

The research I report in this chapter is drawn from a five-year theoretical and empirical study of contemporary global elites, which I term 'the globals'. The aim was to develop an investigation of mobile elite life-strategies and their cultural complexities as wrought by the advent of advanced globalization: this involves exploring, among other things, individuals' understanding of themselves, others and their geographical, social and virtual locations in the world. The research was specifically focused on mobile identities, with particular reference to the theoretical paradigm of 'mobilities' (Urry 2007; Elliott and Urry 2010). The research avoids simply rehearsing or repeating what has already been investigated on the relations between identity, work and globalization (e.g. Sennett 2000). Rather, the research developed new methodological approaches for mapping the impacts of transnationalism, globalization and cosmopolitanism upon elite mobile identities in the field of work. The values of the new economy are especially evident here in a number of cutting-edge fields, such as financial services, high-tech industries and the media, and it is for this reason that this research was primarily concerned with global mobile identities.

The project involves multiple research strategies, and will extend the new methodological approach of 'mobile methods' (Büscher *et al.* 2010). Mobile methods – such as 'mobile shadowing' and 'mobile free-association interviewing' – are especially well suited to investigating global elites and the mobile lives conducted and performed in transnational business mobilities. Specifically, this methodology builds upon recent innovative work in psychodynamic, narrative and 'mobile free-association' analysis (Hollway and Jefferson 2000; Frosh *et al.* 2002; Elliott and Urry 2010). In-depth interviewing 'on the move' unsettles the impression management techniques of interviewees, and is likely to bring to the fore emotional contradictions, tensions and difficulties (Elliott 2008). There is now a substantial body of research in psychodynamic, narrative and discourse traditions of interview procedures, and the proposed synthesis of these traditions is appropriate to this research programme because: (a) psychoanalytic approaches engage with the complex ways individuals emotionally invest positions of discourse and subjectivity (Henriques *et al* 1984); and, (b) materials produced are of sufficient detail to facilitate investigation of complex research ideas.

The research involved recruitment of 75 'globals' for in-depth individual interviews. Interviews were conducted with global mobile elites working in Australia, Singapore, Japan, the UK and Europe. The aim was to interview subjects in individual interviews, with each seen twice. The relatively small numbers of interviews are not viewed as problematic, since the research methodology is based in the psychodynamic and social-theoretical traditions and does not seek to make statistically informed generalizations.

The approach is narrative-centred, exploratory and psychodynamic in design: in-depth qualitative interviews were conducted with global mobile elites through which the research team listened to people, alone and in groups, explain themselves, their fears and hopes of globalism. Drawing from and reflexively engaging with the social theory of global identities detailed above, the aim was, among other things, to distil difficulties, contradictions and ambiguities which appear in these personal accounts of identity, work and globalization.

The methodological approach builds upon recent innovative work in psychodynamic, narrative and discourse analysis (Hollway and Jefferson 2000; Frosh *et al.* 2002), and in particular seeks to extend and refine the 'clinical interviewing' technique described by Hollway and Jefferson (1998, 2000). A major concern of the interviews was to allow for reflection upon and reappraisal of interviews' narratives, and hence subjects were interviewed twice. The research team paid particular attention to the gaps in the discourse of interviewees, particularly the contradictions, silences and other absences in their narrative accounts of identity.

In addition to interviews, in-depth observational studies were also undertaken of organizations that deploy extensive international fast travel of global elites. This research involved the sustained shadowing of key individuals as 'moving targets' within particularly emblematic mobile organizations. This included observing the daily organizational practices that promote and accelerate international travel and fast mobilities, with specific attention to investigating how key individuals contingently maintain business and social connections across varied and multiple distances (Thrift 2004; Urry 2007); sitting in on meetings between local and visiting overseas staff; and observing the encounters, events and understandings of such actors in order to explore the mobile practices of organizational life, rather than focus only on the exciting or idealized narrative accounts that sometimes characterize semi-structured interviews (Holton 2008). Given the lack of research on the changing character of organizational practices in relation to global business mobilities, the focus of this ethnographic research is less concerned with the 'take-up' rates of international fast travel and more concerned with the complex internal refinement of embryonic extant organizational practices. When researching these kinds of emergent organizational practices of global elites, the project adopted the ethnographic methods of organizational observation, especially the ideas of relayed creativity and distributed innovation (Born 2005).

Case-study: Mr X

This third section of the chapter presents a case-study of a member of the global elite whom I have called 'Mr X'.[2] 'Mr X' is, in fact, a composite description amalgamated together from two of the interviews that were conducted. The descriptions from these two interviews were used to form 'Mr X' because, taken together, the two interviews highlighted, and were representative of, certain key themes that were consistently repeated throughout the 75 interviews that were conducted among members of the global elite discussed in this chapter.

Mr X is a London-based investment banker. At our first interview, Mr X talks to me against the backdrop of a bank of screens displaying movements across world markets. As it happens, the screens are not a distraction to the interviewee: Mr X answers all questions thoughtfully and carefully, whilst all the time keeping an eye on the ratings of the large banks, investment houses and insurance companies.

The interviews with Mr X had been scheduled several months in advance of the researcher's trip to the UK. As a result of the 2008 global economic meltdown, however, the first scheduled interview was cancelled at short notice due to his need to travel to the United States. An impromptu interview was subsequently arranged (again, at very short notice), as the day following the interview Mr X was leaving the UK for ten days' further travel in Asia, the Middle East and Australia. Such scheduling and re-scheduling, most often at the last minute, was an integral aspect of Mr X's daily working life.

Mr X got rich investing other people's money in short-term money markets, futures and hedge funds. He then got even richer through investments made in the rapid industrialization of China and India, as well as the buying up of cheap stocks in the leading Asian economies. Armed with an economics degree from the University of Chicago, he was one of the few who smelled trouble with the American sub-prime housing crisis of late 2007, and made the calculated move to sell up his own investments across world stock markets. He subsequently began putting his money to work elsewhere, and decided that the time was right for a change of job along the way. As a reward for timing the market to near perfection, he took three months off work. During that time, he and his wife – a successful businesswoman in her own right – holidayed at various exclusive resorts. The remainder of the time they divided their time between their four homes; they also commenced renovating a mansion recently purchased in Brittany.

At the time of interview, Mr X had been heading up a private investment bank in London for three months. He explained that the global crisis of 2008 represented an enormous professional challenge, though he also noted that his working schedule hadn't really changed from what he was doing previously.

> Usually I am up at around five in the morning and at the office by six thirty. I meet with clients throughout the day, which more often than not involves email and phone calls – unless I am meeting with a client for lunch. I go home at about seven, have dinner, and try to find some time to talk on the phone with my teenage daughter – who is at a private boarding school. Then it's back to the paperwork and late-night conference calls.

The late-night calls, it transpires, are routine: Mr X is part of his bank's Global Leadership Program, which involves dealing with the New York office several times a week. All this is presented as 'routine', although tellingly Mr X casually mentions that he is often abroad for work. As it happens, he was working away from home on a staggering 268 nights in 2007 – a figure calculated by his secretary at the conclusion of our first interview.

Life in the fast lane of investment banking has changed enormously in recent years, mostly as a result of communications and travel revolutions. Investment bankers cultivate the look less of the dashing businessman than of the prosperous tourist: expensive suits, open-neck designer shirts and lots of business/first-class travel. Mr X is able to travel the globe so regularly partly because the individuals and firms which employ him demand this and partly because new information technologies make it so easy to track and trace the movements of his staff back in London.

The elite network of globals in which Mr X operates is one of short-term projects, business-on-the-move and continual mobility. What supports the flowing work worlds of such globals, however, is the largely immobile staff based at head offices. Implicated in all global mobile lives are various immobility regimes (Urry 2007).

That mobility is always intricately intertwined with immobility is a point that clearly applies to Mr X's professional and personal situation – for example, he and his wife employ a live-in housekeeper as well as a personal assistant. The personal assistant is charged with 'organizing' their professional and social lives, right down to 'scheduling' weekend get-togethers with their daughter, often in far-away cities where one of the parents is located for work. As regards work itself, Mr X's extensive mobilities depend primarily on the management strategies he deploys for running the office at a distance. 'One thing I've learned over time in the management of staff', he comments, 'is that you get the best out of people by leaving them to get on and produce, but also keeping tabs on their productivity and performance just so that people know that they must deliver.' From such a calculated and detached perspective, Mr X is able to retain management control without being overly burdened by the daily detail of the office. As a result, he estimates that only around 15 per cent of his time is ever spent on management or administrative duties.

Attachment is the prevailing vice of those who have not managed to adapt to the new ethos of 'flexibility' promoted by the global electronic economy. Without explicitly saying so, Mr X makes it evident that there is little room in his professional life for attachment to colleagues or places. The new regime of short-term projects, episodic contacts and fast-assembled/disassembled teams means that the course of his daily life has little sense of continuity or routine. Mr X captures this nicely in his self-description of professional roles and responsibilities: whether performing as investment banker, or a manager, an expert on hedge funds, a networker or real estate guru, it is part of Mr X's talent to make any contradictions between these roles appear untroubling. Indeed one of the most noticeable aspects of his working life, as he recounts it, is the requirement to continually shift between different sectors of the broader economy; almost all aspects of the global marketplace and its dazzling new technologies are used by Mr X to fashion and restructure his working life involving continual mobility, detached cooperativeness, short-term connections and networked associations.

Overall there is much that is supremely attractive, indeed seductive, about Mr X's professional life of intensive mobilities and fast happenings. A vast income, luxury residences, global travel, high social connections and a 'designer' lifestyle: Mr X confides that he and his wife are the envy of their friends and acquaintances. Intriguingly, the relentless demands of travel and networking arising from his job aren't experienced as constraining. Far from the stereotypical 'time poor' senior executive, he describes how he finds himself 'plunging' into ever-new projects, work tasks or networked possibilities. In fact, the global lifestyle which allows Mr X to 'get away from it all' (the office, colleagues, family) recasts him as someone always getting ahead of himself. He is, on his own reckoning, always planning and re-planning the future. His professional networks appear to feed ongoing financial and work possibilities which drift in his self-imposed manoeuvrings and compulsive reinventions of self. If Mr X's world of corporate entries and exits engenders increased personal freedom, this is partly because he is a self-described 'global', and certainly a man hugely rich in network capital. As he navigates the complex systems of the global economy (electronic money flows, financial databases and the spreadsheet culture of investment banking) with ease, Mr X's language is resolutely that of the corporate 'insider'.

But there are significant limits here as well. First, there is a familiar conflict between the global and the local which raises seemingly insurmountable dilemmas as regards Mr X's experience of the world. He describes, for example, a sense of feeling overwhelmed – 'sometimes I become quite flat' – upon returning home from corporate travel. He talks about his family's demands on his time; his daughter has suffered from various illnesses (including eating disorders) in recent years, and he finds himself carrying out 'make-up' or 'repair' time in their relationship when making time to see her after periods away. Then there is his marriage: 'it's odd going from weeks of phone calls and texting to sitting opposite each other in the kitchen.' And, finally, the demands of his staff. He finds it irritating that his staff so often present issues as urgent the moment he arrives home – just when he is trying to 'catch up' with domestic demands. Second, switching between the time of work-related travel and the time of routine practices is unnerving to him. There is undoubtedly a somewhat cold, detached pleasure which he derives from the 'empty time' of global roaming – airport check-ins, first-class lounges, limousine transfers, hotel business suites. There are sites where obligations to others are minimal, and Mr X can engage his passion for de-contextualized living to the hilt. The more fixed social relations he experiences in London, by comparison, are drab.

Elsewhere: on the arts of elite escape

The new institutional mobile realm, with its ever-changing, frenetic networking, promotes a novel relationship to the self, to other people as well as to shared cultural life among present and aspiring members of the global elite. As we can glean from Mr X's experiences, the new institutional regime puts a special emphasis on swiftness, speed, weightlessness, dexterity and flexibility (Sennett 2000; Bauman 2000; Elliott and Urry 2010). These are ideological values coveted by advanced capitalism; but the point to note is that they press in deeply upon the self. Subjected to these institutional changes, the globals have been the fastest to embrace this ideology. There are six important forms in and through which the making and remaking of the lifestyles and life-strategies of global elites now occurs. These social forms comprise detached engagement; floating; speed; networked possibilities; distance from locality; and mapping of escape routes.

First, life in the fast lane with other globals requires a sense of detached engagement. Such engagement through disengagement ranges from 'dropping in' to organizational discussions through email whilst working abroad to the monitoring of professional contacts in thick networks. It is also evident that the prospects for the detached engagement of individualized actors increase the higher one is within an organization or firm. At the top, crisis is normalized and change ever-present, and so shifting from one network to another network with speed and agility becomes central to professional and personal success. Knowing how to move in the networked world, perhaps even more so than the acquisition of specific technical skills themselves, is fundamental to what Luc Boltanski and Eve Chiapello call 'the new spirit of capitalism'. As Boltanski and Chiapello summarize this ethos, the global business elite are 'putting an accent on polyvalence, on flexibility of employment, on the ability to learn and to adapt to new functions rather than on the possession of skills and acquired qualification, on the capacity to gain trust, to communicate, to "relate"' (2007: 187). We should perhaps note that the inverted commas here around 'relate' do not, in our view, indicate a lack of expenditure of emotional energy invested in work and professional networking. On the contrary, and as Mr X's narrative indicates, many globals feel themselves to be taxed to their limit in terms of their daily communications and relationships with colleagues. But the point is that less and less often in today's fast-paced mobile world does the growing speed of networked communications lead many globals to 'open themselves up' to others. From one angle, this is hardly surprising. Living in networked time means being continually on the move, both physically and emotionally.

Second, abetted by various economic forces including financial deregulation, globals turn towards floating both their organizational responsibilities and their control over subordinates within firms. By floating, I mean to stress the collapse of managerially structured executive routines, as well as of the mentality of long-term 'careers' (Sennett 2000). To say that mobile-driven organizations promote this floating orientation is to say that, like all obsolescent paradigms, the 'scientific' approach to management which dominated the advanced societies during the late twentieth century – involving the continuous presence of executives and ongoing surveillance of employees – has become a formidable barrier to progress in the early twenty-first century. By contrast, and strikingly, the new approach to management involves a kind of non-management. The French economist Daniel Cohen (1998) says of today's global business elite: 'there are no more white collars who give orders to blue collars – there are only collars of mixed colours who confront the task they have to resolve.' And the task to be resolved, we might add, is more often than not an episodic project – each of which creates further opportunities for networking as well as the likely improvement in opportunities for employment elsewhere or further promotion. This is why floating is both network-driven and self-interested. Mr X could afford to start job discussions with other companies so soon after commencing his new executive position because much of his working time is spent on short-term, fast-changing projects. Not only is there the opportunity to engage in these networking discussions with other senior professionals, but the networked identities promoted by mobile organizations seem to demand this of these individuals.

Third, globals define their identities increasingly through the intensity and extensity of their mobilities – especially their speed. For example, Mr X is arguably a new kind of global to the extent that he is a technician of speed – always on the move, ready to travel at a moment's notice, adept at navigating the corporate sensation of speed and global shift of movement. Multi-tasking across space and time is part of this; but another part is thinking and acting in instant-response mode – as the next corporate directive arrives by email, text or fax. It is as if, shifting through the fast lanes of the global electronic economy, part of Mr X's talent is to 'swoop down' on particular corporate institutions, possible mergers or financial deals and show companies how they have become trapped in set ways of doing things. Note again, though, that it is the speed of Mr X's command over mobility systems that makes a difference to the financial world in which he moves. He is at the centre of global finance working in London; he is ever-ready for 'virtual consultation' via his mobile or video-conferencing; he arrives to 'lock in' the deal (in Singapore, Hong Kong or Dubai) and then, just as swiftly, has exited. 'Speed of movement', writes Zygmunt Bauman, 'has become today a major, perhaps the paramount factor in social stratification and the hierarchy of domination' (2002: 27). Mr X's speed of movement is necessary to 'keep up' with the networking, deal-making and swirl of contemporary market forces.

Fourth, globals organize much of their professional and personal lives in and through networked possibilities – the basis upon which those high in network capital achieve ever higher forms of connectivity with other globals via networks, connectors and hubs. Here the 'networked' dimensions of the self, in contrast to the self as a generic phenomenon, presume a reflexive architecture of informational connections. How far certain individuals are able to exploit networked possibilities depends to a large extent on how rich they are in terms of informational connectivity.

Fifth, if globals are intricately interwoven with the culture of global capitalism, this is partly because they have learnt the language of cosmopolitanism. As a political doctrine, cosmopolitanism is concerned with – among other things – what we owe each other as persons as the result of a shared humanity (e.g. Appiah 2007). As an element of the lived experience of the elite we are considering here, however, the cosmopolitanism of globals retains the more attractive qualities of the high culture propagated by political theorists and philosophers, but combines this with an understanding of 'humanity' fashioned in the image of the consumerist space of designer brands and opulent living. That is to say, this is a version of cosmopolitanism which fits hand in glove with the values of transnational corporations, or as some have dubbed it a kind of depoliticized postmodern culture (Eagleton 2000). Elsewhere this has been termed 'banal globalization' (Szerszynski and Urry 2006). What can be said is that this is a worldview pitched towards the postnational or transnational, certainly as far as business, economics, media, information and technology are concerned. As such, distance from locality – expressed as distaste for traditional identities and communities – is a key social form influencing the making of identities of globals under conditions of mobile life.

Finally, the mobile life of globals is almost exclusively about elsewhere. Much of Mr X's professional and personal life, for example, can be seen as a detailed mapping of possible escape routes. We are, essentially, talking about life experienced as a series of exits. From this angle, each exit is in turn followed by new entrances. And these entrances then entail further exits. This notion of escapism raises, of course, the thorny question of what it is, exactly, that globals are escaping from? For those preoccupied with escapism, the lure of what one is escaping to is often imagined as altogether different from what one is escaping from. But this is rarely the case. Psychotherapist Adam Phillips, in a recent study of escapism, writes:

> If we privilege what we are escaping from as more real – or in one way or another, more valuable – than what we are escaping to, we are preferring what we fear to what we seem to desire. Fear of something (or someone), and the wish to escape from it, confer a spectacular reality on it.
>
> (2001: 26–7)

Phillips raises here a fascinating question about the emotional geography of our lives: both what we wish to escape from and what we wish to escape to. Fear, in this psychoanalytic context, is the prospect of being overwhelmed by anxieties that concern entrapment, fixity, enclosure. The impulse to get away, to escape, is enacted and re-enacted across cultures and societies; but in our own time of intensive globalization and multiple mobilities such an emotional impulse emerges in a new light. Extending the insights of Phillips, we might say that the globalized world of multiple mobilities encourages new forms of escapism and especially encourages us to be impressed (possibly seduced?) by elite enactments of fast escape. Conversely, dread of immobility penetrates to the very roots of the contemporary psyche, partly because to be immobile in a society of intensively mobile processes is a kind of 'symbolic death'. By contrast, to be 'on the move' provides a mode of orientation which, on the level of daily life, provides for a sense of independence as well as feelings of emotional security. The ultra-mobilities of globals might thus be seen as an attempt to 'master' an otherwise unsettling and dangerous world: the capacity to always be elsewhere is the capacity to thwart whatever debilitating circumstances arise within local contexts (Iyer 2001).

Here is Phillips again, this time in a more speculative framing: 'Perhaps one can define the times, and the individual people who live through them, by their exits; by what they think of themselves as having to escape from, and to confront, in order to have the lives they want' (2001: 149–150). As regards globals, places of escape – indeed the whole notion of escape – are valuable to the extent that the debilitating fear of immobility is cancelled out (or, more accurately, is imagined cancelled) through modes of action invoking instantaneity. It is the speed of escape today that is paramount. Indeed, it is arguable that globals have made escapism an end in itself – the ultimate symbolic prestige is a kind of escape (whether on a private jet, into virtual realities or to a communicative 'elsewhere') which sets the scene for further acts of escape, and on and on in an infinite regress. The production and performance of life lived as 'elsewhere' is the essential symbol of success in the world of globals.

The self-stylization of globals

The life of the global can be thought of as a kind of aesthetic performance. That is to say, the power and prestige of global elites is less a pre-existing social or structural category than it is a type of identity that has to be enacted, performed and represented to others.[3] Just as Mr X performs a global elitism for others through his relentless business travel, incessant virtual communications and lavish lifestyle, so other globals around the world undertake the ongoing daily work of an unconscious enactment and subjective representation of this new elitism.

Throughout the last ten to 15 years, sociologists have sought to understand better the social practices which affirm a sense of exclusivity, superiority, status and wealth. These social practices of 'distinction', to invoke Pierre Bourdieu's term, turn increasingly on the symbolism of luxury, exclusiveness and expense in legitimating the growing separation between global elites and the less well off. Many sociologists have emphasized in this connection the key significance of society's shift from industrial to post-industrial economies, bound up as this has been with a thoroughgoing transformation away from production and towards consumption. In looking for clues as to what such large-scale shifts in the economy entail for today's inequalities of wealth and status, social theorists have concentrated in particular on the social value derived from consumerism and consumer capitalism. One influential argument is that disorganized capitalism differs from organized capitalism through, among other things, its increasing semioticization of economic life (Lash and Urry 1994). A focus on the growing semiotic dimensions of the new economy – finance, information technology and the service sectors – has also been pivotal to much recent social science research (du Gay and Pryke 2002).

Movement – relentless, tireless, burdensome – has become the degree zero of contemporary societies, at once an index of social status (ranging from enforced migration to luxuriant global tourism) and the medium through which social relations are organized. It is not only that many people are travelling faster and further than in any previous historical era, although that is surely the case. It is rather that more and more people voluntarily travel without end – without ever arriving at a final destination – and that such travel in itself confers prestige, power and symbolic status. The mobile world, for its part, opens up to a new reckoning of economy and the political, and in the process confers an endlessly expanding multitude of new possibilities, pleasures and perils. The desirable life is not only about money and possessions; it is about mobilities, the capacity to escape – to be elsewhere. Mobility status today stands for an addiction to power and pleasure.

Today the styling and stylization of 'the global' has become an increasingly well-identified social figure. As the spending and investment strategies of the wealthy reaches such unprecedented levels as to generate an increasingly separate economy of the super-elite, globals undertake a series of stylizations aimed at the pursuit of luxury, good taste, exclusivity, authenticity, glamour and knowledge. From Bulgari luxury fashion goods to Bentley convertibles, from Louis Vuitton luggage to Prada designer clothes: the gap between wealth and extreme wealth is more and more defined through the acquisition, consumption and display of expensive goods, products and services.

Whilst others can no doubt be found, globals have had one key lifestyle thread in common: relentless travel. Whether illustrious investment bankers, new economy entrepreneurs or globe-trotting architects, their lifestyles were linked through chauffeured limousines, airport business-class lounges and five-star hotels. Life 'on the move' was at once personally exhilarating and professionally taxing, but all agreed that they felt at the edge of a massive cultural shift. For few of the old social coordinates (career, family, social routine) held much weight any longer; life at the top had moved on at least for these interviewees, and this seemed to produce lifestyles that were mobile, weightless, plural and freeing. It was as if, for these globals, someone had said 'you don't have to live the way your parents did'. Quite a number of these interviewees were people born into considerable wealth, and so their childhoods had been filled with travel, journeys and adventures. But these were still mobilities with a fixed reference point of 'home' at the back of their minds. By contrast, the world of mobilities lived by many globals today is more rootless. With homes dotted throughout the world, endless business travel and family life restructured around episodic get-togethers, the old social coordinates divided between firmly around work and home have somewhat evaporated.

Communication analysts Crispin Thurlow and Adam Jaworski (2006) have sought to probe the semiotic conditions and consequences of what they call 'superelitism', specifically with reference to the stylization of elites in frequent-flyer programmes. Frequent-flyer programmes, they argue, at once generate social anxieties about status and confer symbolic prestige and power upon their members. According to this view, the normative production of luxury is intricately interwoven with a personalized framework by which 'rewards', 'awards', 'privileges' and 'entitlements' accrue to identities marked as 'elite'. This framework extends from material benefits such as wider cabin legroom or priority airport check-in to more semiotic indulgences such as luxury brand champagne or the refined elegance of business and first-class lounges. As Thurlow and Jaworski note,

> frequent flyer programmes go to great lengths to promote design over substance, seducing passengers with the expressive utility of things and appealing to the indefinable nature of 'good taste'. Given the relative immateriality but semiotic potency of all these resources, frequent-flyer programmes are thereby able to fabricate an aspirational lifestyle by which to stylize their passengers as distinctive and superior.
>
> (2006: 131)

To adequately generate all these new desires, affects, aspirations and addictions, as well as inscribe them with broader symbolic markers of distinction, the intensive mobile fields of globalization must do more than rely on attitudes of distinctiveness and superiority. In the society of multiple and intensive mobilities, the gap between those keeping on the move and those less on the move – to say nothing of those not moving at all – is of fundamental significance to contemporary boundaries between self and others. 'To travel', as Robert Louis Stevenson famously put it, 'is a better thing than to arrive' – which in our own time of interdependent digitized systems of mobility has been raised to the second power. We are dealing, then, with a symbolic register in which anxiety becomes expressed in and around the differentiated field of mobilities. 'Keeping on the move' appeals increasingly as a glamorously stylish life-strategy, linking as mobility does with new possibilities of desire, difference, otherness, exotica and plenitude. Concomitantly, and from the other angle, fears of 'getting stuck' become debilitating.

Globals, mobilities, space

Since globals are largely de-anchored from traditional social coordinates of routine work, family commitments and community responsibilities, the experimental nature of their lives – the thrills and spills of globality, as it were – is particularly pronounced. To navigate these professional and personal complexities, globals employ a number of mobile life-strategies to create novel connections with their own identities, the lives of others and the wider network society. This chapter has identified various identity forms used by globals – consisting of detached engagement, speed, networked possibilities, distance from locality and the mapping of escape routes.

The social practices of globals suggest the new formulation of mobilities and mobile lifestyles. It must be acknowledged, of course, that the ultra-mobile ways of living charted by globals remain a form of life conducted by only a small elite. Nevertheless, it is the mobile lifestyles of globals that are routinely held up as a normative ideal by many sections of society – especially in popular culture and the media – and in turn mimicked by many other people across lower social strata. The cultural influence of globals, in other words, should not be underestimated.

Notes

1 Some of the material in this chapter was reported in a slightly different form in my book with John Urry, *Mobile Lives*, London and New York: Routledge, 2010, chapter 4. I have revised and adapted this material for the argument I develop in this chapter. But the influence of John Urry has made all the difference for thinking about the mobilities of globals, and I am much indebted to him for his advice.
2 The case-study of Mr X derives from research funded by the Australian Research Council, 2008–2011, and was originally reported in Chapter 4 of Elliott and Urry

(2010). Mr X is a composite figure of two of the people interviewed for this project, and this fictionalized character has been deployed in order to disguise individual identities.
3 Social science research concerned with wealth and power has, for the most part, been preoccupied with the descriptive or objective description of elitism. See, for example, E. Carlton, *The Few and the Many: A Typology of Elites*, Aldershot: Scolar Press, 1996 and M. Dogan, *Elite Configurations at the Apex of Power*, Leiden: Brill, 2003.

References

Appiah, K. A. (2007) *Cosmopolitanism: Ethics in a World of Strangers*, New York: Norton.
Bauman, Z. (2000) *Liquid Modernity*, Cambridge: Polity.
Bauman, Z. (2002) *The Individualized Society*, Cambridge: Polity.
Born, G. (2005) 'On musical mediation: ontology, technology and creativity', *Twentieth-Century Music* 2(1): 7–36.
Boltanski, L. and Chiapello, E. (2007) *The New Spirit of Capitalism*, London: Verso.
Büscher, M., Urry, J. and Witcgher, K. (2010) *Mobile Methods*, London: Routledge.
Cohen, D. (1998) *Richesse du monde: parvretes des nations*, Paris: Flammarion.
du Gay, P. and Pryke, M. (eds) (2002) *Cultural Economy*, London: Sage.
Eagleton, T. (2000) *The Idea of Culture*, Oxford: Blackwell.
Eichelberger, E. (2012) 'Sad About Being in the 1 Percent? There's a Therapist for That', viewed 26 April 2013, at www.motherjones.com/politics/2012/04/bank-therapy-super-rich-occupy-wall-street.
Elliott, A. (1996) *Subject to Ourselves: Social Theory, Psychoanalysis and Postmodernity*, Cambridge: Polity.
Elliott, A. (2008) *Making the Cut: How Cosmetic Surgery is Transforming our Lives*, London: Reaktion.
Elliott, A. (2012) 'New Global Elites' in P. Beilharz and T. Hogan (eds), *Sociology: Antipodean Perspectives*, Oxford: Oxford University Press.
Elliott, A. and Urry, J. (2010) *Mobile Lives*, London: Routledge.
Frosh, S. (2002) *After Words*, London: Palgrave.
Haseler, S. (2000) *The Super-Rich: The Unjust New World of Global Capitalism*, London: Macmillan.
Henriques, J., Hollway, W., Urwin, C., Venn, C. and Walkerdine, V. (1984) *Changing the Subject: Psychology, Social Regulation and Subjectivity*, London: Methuen.
Hollway, W. and Jefferson, T. (1998) '"A Kiss is Just a Kiss": Date Rape, Gender and Subjectivity', *Sexualities* 1: 405–423.
Hollway, W. and Jefferson, T. (2000) *Doing Qualitative Research Differently: Free Association, Narrative and the Interview Method*, London: Sage.
Holton, R. J. (2008) *Global Networks*, Basingstoke: Palgrave Macmillan.
Iyer, P. (2001) *The Global Soul: Jet Lag, Shopping Malls, and the Search for Home*, New York: Vintage.
Jameson, F. (1999) *Postmodernism, or the Cultural Logic of Late Capitalism*, Durham: Duke University Press.
Kostigen, T. (2012), 'The Jet Set's Shopping List Unmasked', viewed 10 May 2013 at http://biz.yahoo.com/special/luxury083106_article1.html.

Lash, S. and Urry, J. (1987) *The End of Organized Capitalism*, Cambridge: Polity Press.
Lash, S. and Urry, J. (1994) *Economies of Signs and Spaces*, London: Sage.
Lemert, C. (2008) *Social Things*, Lanham: Rowman and Littlefield.
Luttwak, E. (1998) *Turbo-Capitalism: Winners and Losers in The Global Economy*, London: HarperCollins.
Phillips, A. (2001) *Houdini's Box: On The Arts of Escape*, London: Faber and Faber.
Pizzigati, S. (2012) 'Wealthy People of the World, Unite – and Party!', *inequality.org*, viewed 26 April 2013 at http://inequality.org/wealthy-world-unite-party/.
Powley, T. and Warwick-Ching, L. (2012) 'Stateless and Super-Rich', *Financial Times*, 28 April, viewed 26 April 2013 at www.ft.com/cms/s/2/740fff32-8d34-11e1-8b49-00144feab49a.html.
Sennett, R. (2000) *The Corrosion of Character*, New York: Norton.
Szerszynski, B. and Urry, J. (2006) 'Visuality, mobility and the cosmopolitan: inhabiting the world from afar', *British Journal of Sociology* 57(1): 113–131.
Thrift, N. (2004) 'Remembering the technological unconscious by foregrounding knowledges of position', *Environment and Planning D: Society and Space* 22: 175–190.
Thurlow, C. and Jaworski, A. (2006) 'The alchemy of the upwardly mobile: symbolic capital and the stylization of elites in frequent-flyer programmes', *Discourse and Society* 17(1): 99–135.
Urry, J. (2007) *Mobilities*, Cambridge: Polity.
Walby, S. (2009) *Globalization and Inequalities*, London: Sage.

Chapter 3

Wealth segmentation and the mobilities of the super-rich
A conceptual framework

Jonathan V. Beaverstock and James R. Faulconbridge

Introduction

Running parallel to everyday mobilities in society there exists a privileged circuit of capital accumulation which is bespoke to the *normal* lives of the so-called 'super-rich' or 'plutocrats': the multi-millionaires and billionaires of the world (Beaverstock *et al.* 2004; Beaverstock 2012; Elliott and Urry 2010; Freeland 2012). From private jets, first class and luxurious limousine travel, to super-yachts, collections of prestige cars and concierge services, the mobilities of the super-rich, whose number reached over ten million worldwide from 2009 (Capgemini Merrill Lynch Global Wealth Management [CMLGWM] 2010; 2011), occupy an intriguing juxtaposition in the mobilities discourse. On the one hand, super-rich mobilities are often invisible, as for example in the fleets of private jets or helicopters that ferry the Forbes rich-list individuals, company CEOs and celebrities on business trips. But, on the other hand, the super-rich display in very overt and opulent ways their luxurious mobilities (Kaplan 2007), such as Roman Abramovich's world's biggest (and most expensive at £740 million) super-yacht, *Eclipse* (*The Sunday Times* 2010), which has become 'fair game' for the global press and paparazzi (McNamara 2009). The purpose of this chapter is to provide the first conceptual framework which unpicks the wealth segments of the super-rich, starting at liquid assets of US$1 million (high net worth individuals) and up to the 'top-tier' billionaires like Carlos Slim Helu – Telecoms (US$69 billion), Bill Gates III – Microsoft (US$61.0 billion) and Warren Buffett – Berkshire Hathaway (US$44 billion) (Forbes World Billionaires List 2011). The framework benchmarks such wealth segmentation with the different ownership, modes and carriage of mobilities and asks questions about the way we understand the embeddedness of different forms of mobility in the lives of the super-rich.

In order to develop the posited conceptual framework for super-rich mobilities, the chapter will specify what we refer to as the 'socio-technical systems of super-rich' mobilities, this being an approach which illustrates the different traits of mobilities in diverse wealth segments and the underlying foundations that embed these forms of mobility in the lives of the super-rich. The chapter is organised into five major parts. In the first part, the super-rich and their wealth segments are defined, followed in part two by an outline of our conceptual framework for understanding such segmentation and super-rich mobilities. In part three, we discuss the social technical systems of super-rich mobilities, before in part four drawing on empirical examples from corporate life and the social worlds of the super-rich to illustrate the usefulness of this framework. Finally, we report several conclusions and offer a research agenda for future research on super-rich mobilities.

Our subject of study: the super-rich

In times of economic decline and widening disparities between personal income, the popular media, public intellectuals and political commentators have all turned their attention to exposing the luxurious and exclusive lifestyles of the so-called super-rich (Freeland 2012; Simmons and Morrow 2011). With the advent of publically available digests identifying the super-rich, like *Forbes' List of World Billionaires* and *The Sunday Times Rich List*, and popular magazines reporting the lifestyles of the 'celeb' super-rich (such as Simon Cowell, Sir Elton John and David and Victoria Beckham), the privileged lives of this minuscule, yet disproportionately asset-rich, segment of the world population has never been so ingrained in the public consciousness. But there is more to the make-up of the super-rich than meets the superficial eyes of the popular press, commentators and ephemeral social groups decrying their self-perpetuating global wealth and exclusivity in civil society. Three pertinent points can be made about our subjects of study.

First, the label, 'super-rich', is both a relative and a sweeping category to pigeon-hole the wealthy into one amorphous social stratum. Ironically, there are significant wealth inequalities amongst the super-rich. For example, Haseler (1999: 2–3) identified three wealth categories for the super-rich: (a) millionaires, who were 'by no means lavishly well off'; (b) multi-millionaires, who were, 'at the very lowest reaches ... of the super-rich'; and, (c) the mega-rich (>US$50 million) and billionaires (US$1,000 million+). More recently, Frank's (2007) depiction of the virtual global society of the super-rich, named Richi$tan, distinguished between four socio-spatial groups: Lower Richi$tan (net worth US$1 million to US$10 million); Middle Richi$tan (net worth US$10 million to US$100 million); Upper Richi$tan (net worth US$100 million to US$1 billion); and Billionaireville (net worth over US$1 billion).

Importantly, since the early 1990s, the super-rich have been categorised as a retail private wealth management financial market in their own right with the advent of their classification as High Net Worth Individuals

(HNWIs), defined as 'those with US$1 million or more at their disposal for investing' (Capgemini and RBC Wealth Management 2012: 3; see also Beaverstock, Hall and Wainwright 2013; Hay and Muller 2012). Capgemini, one of the world's leading specialist consultancies focusing on analysing the global population of HNWIs and the stock of world private wealth (and who worked previously with Merrill Lynch) distinguishes this market for HNWIs into three identifiable wealth bands:

> those with US$1 million to US$5 million in investable assets (so-called 'millionaires next door'); those with US$5 million to US$30 million (so-called 'mid-tier millionaires') and those with US$30 million or more ('ultra-HNWIs').

Since the development of this financial technology by Capgemini (and others; see for example Boston Consulting Group 2011; Pricewaterhouse-Coopers 2009), which clearly defines and classifies the super-rich as HNWIs by wealth bands, empirical intelligence has been available to estimate the worldwide population of HNWIs by wealth band and global world region.

Second, with few exceptions, there has been a continuous increase in the worldwide population of the super-rich (HNWIs) and the value of their private wealth since the end of the 1980s (Boston Consulting Group 2011; Irvin 2008; Lundberg 1988; Smith 2001). In 2011, the world population of HNWIs stood at 11 million (Capgemini and RBC Wealth Management 2012), which is almost a threefold increase (+144 per cent) in absolute terms since data was first collected in 1996, identifying 4.5 million HNWIs worldwide (Table 3.1). Significantly, much of the absolute growth in the HNWI market during this period has been in the 'millionaire next door' and 'mid-tier millionaires' associated with the advent of 'new money' wealth originating from exorbitant executive remuneration, financial returns on investments (e.g. hedge funds) and real estate, and the stock market flotation of private companies (Frank 2007; Irvin 2008) (Table 3.2). But it is pertinent to note that the 100,000 or so Ultra-High Net Worth Individuals, who are regularly listed in the Forbes List of Billionaires, and the almost 1 million number of 'mid-tier millionaires' accounted for over half of all global investible wealth (US$42 trillion) in 2011 (Capgemini and RBC Wealth Management 2012).

Third, and highly important, the highest net relative growth in the global population of HNWIs is now to be found in the emerging markets of the Asia-Pacific (including China and India) and Latin America (Table 3.3). In 2010, the Asia-Pacific region surpassed Europe in terms of the stock of HNWIs and in 2011 was comparable to North America for the first time with 3.4 million HNWIs (Capgemini and RBC Wealth Management 2012). Between 2010 and 2011, Brazil and China experienced the

Table 3.1 The worldwide population of High Net Worth Individuals and the value of their global wealth, 1996–2011

	Number (millions)	Change (%)	Wealth (US$ trillions)	Change (%)
1996	4.5	–	16.6	–
1997	5.2	+15.6	19.1	+15.1
1998	5.9	+13.5	21.6	+13.1
1999	7.0	+18.6	25.5	+18.1
2000	7.2	+2.9	27.0	+5.9
2001	7.1	−1.4	26.2	−3.7
2002	7.3	+2.8	26.7	+2.7
2003	7.7	+5.5	28.5	+6.7
2004	8.2	+6.5	30.7	+7.7
2005	8.8	+7.3	33.4	+8.8
2006	9.5	+8.0	37.2	+11.4
2007	10.1	+6.3	40.7	+9.4
2008	8.6	−14.9	32.8	−19.4
2009	10.0	+17.1	39.0	+18.9
2010	10.9	+8.3	42.7	+9.7
2011	11.0	+0.8	42.0	−1.7

Sources: Capgemini Merrill Lynch Global Wealth Management (2008; 2009, 2010, 2011); Capgemini Merrill Lynch (2002, 2007); Capgemini and RBC Wealth Management (2012).

highest relative growth rates in the population of HNWIs of +6.2 per cent (from 155,000 to 156,000) and +5.2 per cent (from 535,000 to 562,000), respectively (Capgemini and RBC Wealth Management, 2012). Turning to the geographical location of the world HNWI population, the top five locations remain: the USA (3.1 million), Japan (1.8 million), Germany (0.951 million), China (0.562 million) and the UK (0.441 million).

In order to understand the 'extraordinary sumptuous lifestyles ... [and] ... literal mobility' (Haseler 1999: 3) of the global super-rich, we suggest that it is vitally important to begin by looking beyond the popular image of super-yachts and privately owned jets, so as to conceptualise the modes, ownership and consumption of such mobilities as they apply to the wealth bands of the global HNWI population.

Wealth segmentation and super-rich mobilities

As we have already demonstrated, the wealth bands of high net worth individuals can vary enormously, from the 'mere' millionaire to the ultra-high net worth individual (up to US$30 million) and up to the truly global super-rich who regularly rank in the Forbes List of Billionaires (with investible assets over US$1 billion). Thus, we would expect the mobilities of the wide spectrum of the super-rich to vary considerably depending on the level of their personal wealth and power. As Haseler (1999: 3) observes, 'Amongst multi-millionaires there is a sharp distinction to be

Table 3.2 The composition of the global High Net Worth Individual (HNWI) population, 2002–2011

Category	Percentage of the total population of HNWIs									
	2002	2003	2004	2005	2006	2007	2008	2009	2010	2011
Ultra-high NWI	0.8	0.9	0.9	1.0	1.0	1.0	0.9	0.9	0.9	0.9
Mid-tier millionaire & 'millionaire next door'	99.2	99.1	99.1	99.0	99.0	99.0	99.1	99.1	99.1	99.1
Total number of HNWI (millions)	7.3	7.7	8.2	8.8	9.5	10.1	8.6	10.0	10.9	11.0

Sources: Capgemini Merrill Lynch (2002, 2007); Capgemini Merrill Lynch Global Wealth Management (2008–2010 inclusive); Capgemini and RBC Wealth Management (2012).

Table 3.3 The global distribution of the High Net Worth Individual (HNWI) population and value of private wealth, 2000–2011

	HNWIs (millions)		Growth (%)	Value of private wealth (US$ trillion)		
	2000	2011		2000	2011	% growth
North America	2.2	3.4	+55	7.5	11.4	+52
Asia-Pacific	1.6	3.4	+113	4.8	10.7	+123
Europe	2.5	3.2	+28	8.4	10.1	+20
Latin America	0.3	0.5	+67	3.2	7.1	+122
Middle East	0.3	0.5	+67	1.0	1.7	+70
Africa	0.1.	0.1	0	0.6	1.1	+83
Totals	6.9	11.0	+59	25.5	42.0	+67.7

Sources: Capgemini Merrill Lynch (2002); Capgemini Merrill Lynch Global Wealth Management (2009, 2010); Capgemini and RBC Wealth Management (2012).

made between those at the lower end ... and those at the higher end – say the $500 million plus households. The distinction is one of power, not lifestyle.' Britain's top rich list entry, Lakshmi Mittal and his family (net worth £12,700 million according to *The Sunday Times Rich List* 2012) and those individuals with net worth in the hundreds of millions theoretically (and practically) should display a portfolio of mobilities for business and leisure which are completely separated from the meagre millionaire, whose net worth may lie in the millions or tens of millions of US dollars, euros or GB pounds. In the following we posit a conceptual typology of mobilities for the super-rich which are segmented by wealth bands in order to tease out the different modes, ownership patterns, consumption and carriage for the wide spectrum that are the super-rich, from millionaire to billionaire.

Our conceptual typology of mobilities for the super-rich is divided into the three Capgemini and RBC Wealth Management wealth bands: ultra-high net worth (over US$30 million); 'mid-tier millionaires' (which we term 'very high net worth'); and 'millionaires next door' (or just 'high net worth'). For each of these wealth bands we set out the main attributes of their mobilities lifestyles, noting particularly the very wide gulf in wealth and mobilities between the rest and the ultra-high net worth category which effectively goes upward from US$30 million to the Forbes billionaires.

The typology of super-rich mobilities is set out in Table 3.4. Before we explain the typology for each wealth band it is important to note two caveats. First, the typology is conceptual in nature in that it is constructed from our observations of the practices of the super-rich, which are themselves informed by the academy, popular press and media. Second, we must remember that the super-rich present in the very high and ultra-wealth bands often lead very highly mobile but secretive and anonymous lifestyles, flowing between multiple luxurious residences scattered around

Table 3.4 Super-rich mobilities and wealth segmentation[1]

Wealth segmentation	Mode of mobility	Ownership	Consumption	Carriage
Ultra-high net worth over US$30 million	Private fleet (e.g. jet helicopter, car) Sea (e.g. luxurious yacht) Prestige (e.g. car)	Propensity for 100% ownership Selected leasing Liquid assets (e.g. classic cars)	Family office Concierge services Management companies Personal	'Super-rich' class First class
Very-high net worth ('mid-tier millionaires') US$5 million–US$30 million	As above, with exceptions (e.g. 'normal' yacht) Private, chartered and scheduled	Mixture of ownership, and leasing Liquid assets (e.g. car)	As above, except limited family office	Predominately first class
High net worth ('millionaires next door') US$1 million–US$5 million	Predominately scheduled airline, road, rail Prestige car	Mixture of leased and ownership Executive travel Limited liquid assets (e.g. classic car)	Chauffeur service Personal	Predominately business class

Note
1 Wealth segmentation benchmarks are Capgemini and RBC Wealth Management (2012) wealth bands.

the world. The ultra-super-rich (billionaires and multi-billionaires) or, as Beaverstock (2012: 389) has referred to them, the global super-class, inhabit 'their own global society within global society' which inevitably reproduces a portfolio of mobilities which are out of reach, but also out of view of the rest of society. This poses a range of methodological challenges which we return to later in the chapter. Nonetheless, each of the three different wealth band super-rich mobilities will be unpacked in turn below.

Ultra-high net worth mobilities

As we have already pointed out, the ultra-high wealth band begins at US$30 million and extends to the richest of the rich; the multi-billionaires like Warren Buffett, Bill Gates and George Soros (www.forbes.com). The first and foremost characteristic of the mobilities of these individuals is that their mode of mobility is one of exclusivity, luxury and, importantly, privacy. At the upper spectrum of the wealth band, it would be expected that these individuals would have at their disposal a private fleet of yachts, jet planes, helicopters and prestige, high-performance and/or classic car collections, which may be distributed between their multiple residences in different countries. The popular press and media often make reference to the billionaire super-yachts (Table 3.5), but less is known about other modes of transport beyond reference made to individual billionaire or multi-millionaire cars and helicopters. As for ownership, there is a high propensity for the ultra-high net worth super-rich to own these assets which are managed by the 'family estate' (management company) of the individual. We would argue that the further down the pyramid an

Table 3.5 The ten most expensive luxury yachts in the world, 2012

Yacht	Length (m)	Price (US$m)	Owner	Wealth (Forbes 2012 rank)
Eclipse	163	485	Roman Abramovich	US$12.1 billion (#68th)
'A'	119	323	Andrey Melnichenko	US$10.8 billion (#81st)
Dubai	162	300+	Sheikh Mohammed bin-Rashid Al Makhtoum	N.A.
Pelorus	115	300	David Geffen	US$5.5 billion (#128th)
Dilbar	110	256	Alisher Usmanov	US$18.1 billion (#28th)
Rising Sun	138	200+	David Geffen	US$5.5 billion (#128th)
Al Salamah	139	200	Sultan bin Abdul Aziz	N.A.
Lady Moura	105	200	Nasser Al Rasheed	N.A.
Octopus	126	200	Paul G. Allen	US$14.2 billion (#48th)
Tatoosch	92	162	Paul G. Allen	US$14.2 billion (#48th)

Sources: www.bornrich.com/entry/top-12-high-tech-luxury-yachts; www.boatinternational.com/yachts/the-register/top-100-largest-yachts; www.forbes.com/billionaires (all accessed 15 August 2012).

individual sits in this wealth band, the higher the probably that mobilities assets (especially high-value items like yachts and jets) would be leased or chartered to the individual's estate. For example, Edminston and PremAir charter lease yachts and private jets respectively to the super-rich (Table 3.6). Bespoke concierge services would be employed by the 'family office' (Effinger and Ody 2011) to support, maintain and service these mobilities assets, for example Blue Ocean Yacht Management (www.blueoceanyachting.com). Moreover, it would be expected that where these individuals did engage with the normality of everyday mobilities, expected further down this wealth pyramid band, it would be in first class carriage, especially on long-haul schedule airlines for business or leisure. A final point to make about the mobilities of the ultra-super-rich is that high-performance and prestige cars (perhaps used for everyday travel, and including for example Bugatti, Rolls-Royce, Maserati and McLaren; see Table 3.7) and classic car collections are also significant liquid assets for the family estate, replicated between different country residences.

Very high net worth mobilities

The super-rich mobilities of the very high net worth individuals, at the top spectrum of this wealth band, would mirror those of the lower echelons of the ultra-high net worth pyramid, as discussed earlier. Three distinctive characteristics of this mobilities wealth band would be: (i) a high propensity of leasing for high-value assets, like yachts, boats and private jets (Table 3.6) for those with tens of millions of investible assets; (ii) the use of chartered companies and a high frequency of first class travel on scheduled transport for those with investible assets at the lower end of this wealth band; and (iii) the ownership of high-performance and prestige cars as liquid assets, drawn from a very wide range of makes and models

Table 3.6 Super-rich charter and sales companies: by sea and air.

Yacht charter and sales	
Edmiston	www.edmiston.com
Burgess	www.burgessyachts.com
Camper & Nicholsons	www.camperandnicholsons.com
Princes Motor Yacht sales	www.princess.com
Liveras Yachts	www.liverasyachts.com
Fraser Yachts	www.fraseryachts.com
Private jet charter	
PremAir	www.premieraviation.com
Air Partner	www.airpartner.com
Netjets	www.netjetseurope.com
Vista jet	www.vistajet.com
Luna jets	www.lunajets.com

Source: websites listed above, accessed 17 August 2012.

Table 3.7 Super-rich automobilities

Make	Model	Typical price OTR[1]
Alpina (BMW)	B7 saloon	£95,850–£98,850
Aston Martin	DBS Volante (5.9 V12)	£185,152
Audi	R8 Spyder	£96,625–£117,740
Bentley	Mulsanne Saloon (6.75 V8)	£224,700
Bugatti	Veyron 8.0 W16 Grand Sport	£1,130,000*
BMW	M5 Saloon (4.4)	£73,000
Ferrari	F12 Coupe (6.3 V12)	£250,000
Jaguar	XK Convertible	£71,430–£103,430
Lamborghini	Aventador Coupe (6.5 LP700-4)	£242,280
Land Rover	Range Rover 4 × 4	£70,020–£86,925
Lotus	Evora Coupe (3.5 V6 +2 IPS)	£65,745
Maserati	Grancabrio Open	£98,200–£102,615
McLaren	MP4–12C Coupe (3.8 V8)	£168,500
Mercedes-Benz	S-Class Saloon AMG (S65L)	£176,925
Noble	M600 Coupe	£200,000
Porsche	911 Coupe	£67,270–£128,466
Rolls-Royce	Ghost Saloon	£200,500–£230,000
	Phantom Saloon	£285,200–£336,700

Source: *What Car?* August 2012; *TopGear Magazine*, August 2012.

Note
1 On the road price, excluding additional specifications.

(Table 3.7). As with the ultra-high net worth individuals, the use of private jets becomes a normalised mode of mobilities for both social and business use (Budd and Hubbard 2010). Throughout this wealth band, there would be less of an involvement of family offices, in favour of more specialist and mainstream private wealth management providers who advise on the ownership, security and protection of liquid assets (Beaverstock *et al.* 2013). Those individuals with investible assets on the boundary with the high net worth wealth band, around US$5 million, would benchmark their mobilities lifestyles much closer to this segment of the wealth pyramid.

High net worth

This is the 'millionaires next door' wealth band where the main modes of mobilities lifestyles would be predominately scheduled and in the public domain, like business class air and first class train travel. There would be very little evidence of yacht or private jet ownership or leasing, but they may be chartered for occasional leisure and business activities (Table 3.6; Budd and Hubbard 2010). A significant characteristic of the mobilites assets of these individuals would be the ownership of high-performance and prestige cars, such as Aston Martin, BMW Alpina, Range Rover, Porsche and Mercedes, whose main distributors are located in the major cities or close to prestige motor car racing circuits (e.g. Silverstone, Northamptonshire; see Figure 3.1 in the UK context). Private chauffeur services would be close to the norm for those at the top end of this wealth band. A range of private wealth management companies would service those with multi-millions, but those on or close to US$1 million in investible assets would probably use high street bank 'premier' wealth management services (Beaverstock *et al.* 2013). Many of the new breed of financial elites (Economist 2011; Folkman *et al.* 2007; Hall 2009), employed in banking and professional services, would populate this wealth band, and encroach into the very high net worth category, where business class carriage would dominate these super-rich mobilities, especially for working practices.

A socio-technical perspective on super-rich mobilities

From one perspective, the various modes of mobility discussed above, from the prestige car to the super-yacht, could be seen as a form of lavish excess, the super-rich spending money because they have it, or as investments in mobility as a way of transforming surplus capital into assets. Both interpretations would undoubtedly stand up to scrutiny. Here, however, we suggest there is another interpretation that also deserves consideration; that mobility acts as a form of conspicuous consumption that is embedded in the lifestyles of the super-rich. From this perspective, the prestige car, super-yacht or any other form of mobility asset becomes part of the performance of a particular way of life, this way of life being symbolically meaningful as well as functional. We label this a socio-technical perspective on the mobilities of the super-rich and in the rest of this section of the chapter build the perspective using ideas from work on theories of practice.

A theories-of-practice-informed analysis of the socio-technical constituents of mobility has been gradually gaining traction over recent years (Birtchnell 2012; Shove *et al.* 2012; Watson 2012), something which builds on and subtly reconfigures earlier work on mobility systems (Cohen 2010; Urry 2004). Underlying a practice perspective is an insistence that the development of technological systems of mobility, such as those detailed in Table 3.4, is interpreted through a lens that connects their use to wider forms of meaning and competency. Specifically, a practice is defined as a 'block' (Reckwitz 2002) of materials, meanings and competencies that together form a taken-for-granted way of being and doing, in the case in question here this being a taken-for-granted way of achieving mobility for the super-rich. Consequently, the use of a yacht, private jet or any other material technology by the super-rich gets interpreted as a taken-for-granted way of travelling not only because of the affordances that such mobility modes offer. It is also taken for granted because of the symbolic

Figure 3.1 The geographical distribution of prestige car dealerships in the UK, 2012.

meanings attached to the use of the mode of mobility and the competency as a member of the super-rich demonstrated by use of the mode.

The significance of a practice interpretation of super-rich mobility is threefold. First, in a practice perspective the variations in mode, ownership, consumption and carriage of the super-rich according to their net worth (Table 3.4) are interpreted as being closely tied to their symbolic meaning and construction as normal and needed. The ownership or not of a yacht, the use of a private jet versus scheduled airlines etc. is associated not only with what is 'affordable', but also with what is taken for granted in the particular financially constructed social class to which an individual belongs. Failure to perform mobility in the way expected would be viewed as lack of competence and illegitimacy as a member of any particular class. Second, a practice perspective suggests that the forms of super-rich mobility noted above are *locked in* by the social symbolism and meaning of consumption associated with the mobility form. This is significant because of the resource-intensive nature of super-rich mobilities – private jets and yachts and the oil they consume being an extreme example of the aspiration-driven unsustainability that Cohen (2010) discusses. Any attempt to derail super-rich, high carbon mobilities needs, therefore, to consider not only substitutes for the affordances of the modes of mobility used, but also new forms of meaning and competency that are tied to the super-rich classes outlined above. Finally, third, a practice perspective draws our attention to the importance of the ecology of corporate actors who reproduce super-rich mobilities. The private wealth management companies, yacht and private jet operating/chartering groups and other providers of services to the super-rich all play a crucial role in defining and reproducing the meanings and competencies that render certain forms of mobility as taken for granted, normal and needed. Not only do the companies devise and maintain the material technologies needed to uphold the mobile lives of the super-rich, but they also imbue the products with meaning and set the terms of reference for their competent use.

In the next section of the chapter, we therefore examine the sociotechnical assemblages associated with different forms of mobility for the classes of super-rich outlined above. In doing this we reveal the absolute centrality of certain forms of mobility in the public–private lives of the super-rich, something indicative of the wider relevance of mobility practices to class status in society generally.

The constituents of super-rich mobility practices

Table 3.8 outlines how the modes of mobility associated with different categories of high net worths are intimately related to different meanings and competences. These meanings and competencies are important because they are a core part of the practice 'block' that give the use of different forms of mobility taken-for-granted and normal status and that help distinguish one class of high net worth from another. The modes of mobility and the meanings and competencies associated with them are, then, to use Bourdieu's (1985; 1990) terminology, the forms of cultural capital that an individual is expected to display in order to fit into a particular social grouping. This does not mean the connections to economic capital of the practice blocks outlined in Table 3.8 are insignificant. The mode of mobility and the meaning and competencies attached to it are all intimately related to the economic capital available for investment in mobility technologies. But the way wealth creates cultural expectations and social pressures that have to be attended to is as important as the economic capital available in influencing mobility investments, especially for those in the ultra-high and very high net worth classes.

The connections between mobility practice and class expectations can be better understood by pulling apart the meanings detailed in Table 3.8. For the ultra-high network worths, the private fleets of exclusive mobility modes represent both their class status at the pinnacle of the super-rich cohort, and understandings of what the ultra-high net worth needs in order to go about everyday life. This understanding of need is worth analysing a little further. It relates, first, to understandings of the role of mobility in the life of the ultra-high net worth. Mobility for these individuals is a constituent part of how they do business, consume and network, and hence having a globally distributed fleet of mobility assets, available on demand, is crucial for the fulfilling of these components of everyday life. In addition, second, the private fleet has meaning because of the privacy and security it offers. With ultra-high net worth goes a degree of vulnerability – to kidnap, corporate espionage and/or press intrusion – private fleets being presented as one solution to such inconveniences. Together, these two components of the meaning of mobility systems embed private fleets into the everyday life of the ultra-high net worths.

A similar role is played by the meanings detailed for the very high and high net worths, but with varying logics existing that support the distinctive mobility systems employed by the different classes. For the very high net worths the meanings are closely related to those of the ultra-highs, albeit with the limitations imposed by economic capital resulting in the translation of meaning into subtly different modes of mobility. For the high net worths the meanings are, however, different. Mobility modes are primarily associated with comfort and convenience, with class of travel distinguishing this group from the non-high net worth traveller. Scheduled first class services provide privacy and flexibility unavailable to the masses in standard class, but in a way that cannot parallel what private jets and yachts offer. Hence for the high net worths economic capital (or relative lack of kit) is significant because of how it produces different meanings

Table 3.8 The socio-technical basis of super-rich mobilities, differentiated by wealth segmentation[1]

Wealth segmentation	Material technologies and systems of mobility provision	Meanings	Competencies
Ultra-high net worth Over US$30 million	Private fleet (e.g. jet helicopter, car) Sea (e.g. luxurious yacht) Prestige chauffeured car	Exclusivity, privacy, security, complete personal freedom, membership of the 'elite of the elite' class	Occasional use (demonstrating wealth that allows a fleet big enough to facilitate constant movement between assets which appear to non-ultra-high net worths to be underused and a frivolous waste of investment funds); loaning to only most exclusive of guests; understated use with few overt and deliberate attention-grabbing public displays of mobility assets
Very-high net worth ('mid-tier millionaires') US$5 million–US$30 million	'Normal' yacht Chartered fleet and first class scheduled travel Prestige chauffeured car	Privacy, bespoke travel; differentiation from the high net worth masses	Overt performances (that draw attention, often via the media, to the use of forms of mobility not available to the masses); strategic use of charters to display mobility capital in the right place at the right time (e.g. the Cannes Film Festival); use of exclusive providers of mobility services to ensure concierge style services available
High net worth ('millionaires next door') US$1 million–US$5 million	Predominantly scheduled business or first class Rail and prestige car Prestige (probably self-driven) car	Comfort, luxury and convenience; identity formation and differentiation by indulgence in exclusive versions of everyday products; the ability to rise above the masses of the non-high net worths	Use of elite booking/management agents to distinguish from the mass market; effective use of affordances/services offered to demonstrate 'fit' in elites classes of everyday mobility services (e.g. first class air); downplaying of mobility mode itself (not distinctive enough to warrant overt attention) and emphasis on being seen in the right places thanks to what mobility allows

Note
1 Wealth segmentation benchmarks are Capgemini and RBC Wealth Management (2012) wealth bands.

for mobility. This point becomes clearer when the role of competencies in constituting super-rich mobility practices is considered.

The competencies outlined in Table 3.8 are significant in two ways. First, they reinforce the meanings already discussed, in particular by tying the use of particular modes of mobility and the meaning of this to certain kinds of public–private performance. As such, competencies define not which mode of mobility 'should' be used – this is the role of meanings – but *how* a mode of mobility should be used. Using the mode appropriately is a key part of reproducing the class identity associated with a particular high net worth tier. The main distinction portrayed in Table 3.8 concerns the overtness of mobility performance between the classes. For the ultra-high net worths, mobility is something that should occur covertly and, as much as possible, below the radar of the paparazzi and press. Whilst hiding one of the exclusive private yachts detailed in Table 3.5 in a harbour is not a realistic prospect, the whole point of the private fleet is to allow privacy and, as such, drawing unnecessary attention to oneself is deemed inappropriate. This contrasts with the very high net worths, where the overt performance of mobility is an important part of identity construction. Displaying mobility capital, both by being in the right place at the right time and being seen using the appropriate mode of mobility, for example being photographed on a chartered yacht, is central to identity making. As such, for the very high net worths the privacy of charter yachts and flights is juxtaposed with the public performance of the use of such modes of mobility. Different again are the high net worths. For this class, mode of mobility lacks the glamour and prestige needed to be a part of identity formation. Instead, effective use of scheduled first class travel to be seen in the right places, looking unfazed by hyper-mobility and jetlag like the average traveller might, is the legitimate way to be mobile. The photograph of a high net worth individual walking through the airport is perhaps the best exemplar of a legitimate performance for this class.

The mobility practices of the super-rich are, then, multi-dimensional assemblages that are tied to the economic capital of different classes of super-rich, but also the meanings of mobility that go with certain modes of mobility and definitions of competent mobility performance. In many ways, these all-important meanings and competencies that underlie super-rich mobility travel practice blocks are, however, deliberate constructions by a variety of interested parties. Companies manufacturing various modes of mobility – yachts, private jets etc. – alongside companies providing operational or chartering services for these technologies all work to construct meanings and definitions of competency that create demand for their products. Take, for instance, Bombardier, who manufacture the Learjet brand as well as a much wider range of long- and short-haul private jets. Through their promotional material they are clear about why the super-rich 'need' to invest in one of their products. As they suggest:

> Every aircraft is an outstanding example of aviation engineering, designed to meet and exceed the expectations of the world's most discerning travellers. From performance superiority, to reliability and cost efficiency, to unequalled comfort and uncompromising luxury.... The Global 8000 business jet's unprecedented 7,900 nautical mile (14,631 km) range capability with 8 passengers empowers leaders, with key route possibilities more in tune with both current and emerging world economic models. Enjoying unparalleled productivity and an unmatched comfort experience over these extended distances, global leaders are more able to maintain the unrestrictive agenda and flexibility that their positions of power command.
>
> (Bombardier 2012)

Such discourse is an integral part of the production of the meanings detailed in Table 3.8. It helps to shape the understanding of the ultra-high and high net worths in terms of how they should travel, whether they own or hire mobility technologies. Thanks to this kind of promotional material, travelling by private jet becomes meaningful because, to replicate the language in the Bombardier discourse, it is the reliable, cost-efficient, comfortable, luxurious and flexible thing to do. It is also what a competent member of the (business in particular) super-rich should do, empowering them to engage in the kinds of hyper-mobility associated with a high and ultra-high net worth lifestyle and putting them in tune with the changing geography of the world (cultural as well as business) economy. Indeed, the tagline for Bombardier's Global 8000 aircraft is 'I am global', whilst for the Global 5000 it is 'time and space redefined'.

Service providers such as those who will operate or hire you a private jet also help produce the meanings and competencies detailed in Table 3.8. The Private Jet Company (2012) notes, for instance, that:

> No longer an optional luxury ... a private aircraft is an operational essential in a world of unforgiving expectations. But, it's only part of the global executive transport challenge ... we take a holistic, solution-oriented approach to help you get there safely, efficiently and comfortably with none of the hassles.

Of course, underlying such discourses is an economic motive – to sell more jets, jet management contracts, etc. As Cohen (2010) therefore notes, the corporate ecology behind mobility systems such as the private jet plays a fundamental role in generating and sustaining the logics that lead to demand. In the case of the super-rich, this means that various services associated with the consumption of mobility detailed in Table 3.4 play a fundamental role alongside the producers of mobility technologies themselves in generating a socio-technical system that normalises lavish modes of travel. The meanings and competencies alongside the affordances of technology embed and lock in certain mobility practices in ways that make them taken-for-granted parts of the everyday life of the super-rich. And what is taken for granted is intimately related to the apparent ability of the super-rich to evade questions about the impacts of their mobile lifestyles. In particular, private yachts and jets, high-powered prestige cars, and even first class travel are all examples of a super-high-carbon lifestyle associated with the super-rich. This means the super-rich have a disproportionate carbon impact because of their hyper-mobility, but also because of their use of modes of mobility that generate several times more carbon per mile travelled than that generated by non-super-rich mobility. For instance, Pearce (2009) reports on a survey that suggests private jets generate ten times more carbon dioxide per hour's flying time than a standard scheduled flight. Whilst many private jet charter companies now offer or compel carbon offsetting, it is clear from such statistics that the super-rich are super-guilty when it comes to carbon emissions associated with mobility.

Challenging super-rich mobility practices that have such a high carbon impact is likely, though, to be difficult because of the meaning and competencies that form practice 'blocks'. Just like the everyday citizen who, because of the role of the car in everyday practice, is unwilling to switch to cycling (Watson 2012), the super-rich are unlikely to give up their high-carbon mobility modes because of their centrality to their identity and way of life. Unless, that is, a new brand of super-rich identity was to emerge, the green high net worth for instance, who uses her/his status to champion a lower carbon lifestyle. If Birtchnell (2012) is right and elites can act as role models in ways that change practices, then perhaps a green high net worth figure could have a significant impact, on the carbon impacts of the super-rich and on the carbon impact of mass mobility more generally. But who will be willing to challenge the existing super-rich mobility system and its meanings and competencies?

Conclusions

In this chapter we have provided one of the first analyses of the segmentation of super-rich mobilities. In doing this we have highlighted the various modes of mobility, supporting infrastructures and forms of consumption associated with different high net worth classes and discussed their socio-spatial characteristics. We have also developed a socio-technical conceptualisation of the mobility practices of different segments of the super-rich which draws attention to the way that the use of modes of mobility relates not only to economic capital, but also to the meanings and competencies tied to forms of cultural capital associated with a class. This cultural capital is, we have suggested, one of the forces embedding certain forms of mobility in the lives of the super-rich, something that is significant in the context of the increasingly obvious super-carbon impact of the modes of mobility discussed in this chapter.

The analysis provided here is significant in several ways. First, the analysis helps differentiate between the mobilities of different classes of super-rich, in the process acting as a reminder of the importance of mobility as a form of capital (Kaufmann *et al.* 2004), social distinguisher (Nowicka 2006) and meaningful practice (Cresswell 2010). In this sense, the chapter offers a novel insight into the way that systems of mobility are embedded within the often secretive, obscure and hard-to-access world of the super-rich. At one level this suggests that, just like for the masses, mobility is now a fundamental component of the everyday life of the super-rich. But, as the discussion of modes of mobility reveals, at another level the chapter also makes clear that super-rich mobility takes a form and function that is unrecognisable to the majority of the population, this unrecognisability being central to the differentiation of the super-rich class from the 'rest'. Second, the chapter is important because of the way it begins to break the silence surrounding the impacts of super-rich mobility. Whilst not the heart of the analysis here, the conceptual framing developed in the chapter provides a way to think through both the embeddedness of super-high carbon mobility in the lives of the super-rich, and the difficulties that might be faced by those wishing to challenge excesses such as private jets and yachts. As such, the strength of the analysis here is the way connections are drawn between the first half of the chapter, where the characteristics of super-rich mobility are described, and the second half of the chapter, where a conceptual framing is provided of the social significance of these mobilities, their impacts and embeddedness. Together, the two halves thus provide a powerful way of taking forward research on super-rich mobilities. We suggest two key directions for such research.

First, more attention should be paid both to the particularities of the kinds of services provided by the various companies servicing the mobility needs of the super-rich and to the way these companies construct meanings and competencies of mobility. The discussion in this chapter has begun both tasks, but there is much to do in order to add empirical depth to our knowledge of the work of the corporate ecology surrounding super-rich mobilities. Of course, there are major methodological challenges associated with such work. By definition the companies in question are secretive about their work in order to protect the privacy, security and mystique of their clients. Negotiating access, or the need to use innovative data sources such as ex-employees of companies, is thus likely to be a major hurdle to such research, but one that needs to be overcome if knowledge is to be deepened of this economically, culturally and environmentally significant dimension of mobility. Second, the relationships between the mobility practices of the super-rich and those of the masses might be examined more carefully. As the conceptual framing presented here suggests, in many ways the practices of the super-rich are designed to distinguish them from each other as well as from the masses. It therefore seems feasible that the way the super-rich travel, where they travel to, and the way this is reported in the media has a significant influence on the practices of the masses as they aspire to mimic, as far as financial resource allows, the super-rich. Such an interpretation fits with the suggestion that elites are powerful figures for generating new practices (Birtchnell 2012) and, if this is the case, studies of the super-rich may yield important insights into the influences that sustain hyper-mobile lives and high-carbon mobility practices.

This chapter acts as the foundation for a much deeper and conceptually sophisticated analysis of super-rich mobilities, something that has relevance not only to those interested in the super-rich themselves, but also to those interested in the role of mobility in everyday life more generally.

References

Beaverstock, J. V. (2012) 'The privileged world city: Private banking, wealth management and the bespoke servicing of the global super-rich', in P. J. Taylor, M. Hoyler, B. Derudder and F. Witlox (eds), *International Handbook of Globalization and World Cities*, Cheltenham: Edward Elgar.

Beaverstock, J. V., Hall, S. and Wainwright, T. (2013) 'Servicing the super-rich: new financial elites and the rise of the private wealth management retail ecology', *Regional Studies* (in press).

Beaverstock, J. V., Hubbard, P. J. and Short, J. R. (2004) 'Getting away with it? Exposing the geographies of the super-rich', *Geoforum* 35: 401–407.

Birtchnell, T. (2012) 'Elites, elements and events: Practice theory and scale', *Journal of Transport Geography*, 24: 497–502.

Bombardier (2012) *Ebrochures*. Available at: http://businessaircraft.bombardier.com/ebrochures, accessed 22 August 2012.

Boston Consulting Group (2011) *Global Wealth 2011: Shaping a New World*. Available at: www.bcg.com, accessed 13 March 2012.

Bourdieu, P. (1985) 'The social space and the genesis of groups', *Theory and Society*, 14 (6): 723–744.

Bourdieu, P. (1990). *The Logic of Practice*, Stanford: Stanford University Press.

Budd, L and Hubbard, P. (2010) 'The "Bizjet" set: Business aviation and the social geographies of private flight', in J. V. Beaverstock, B. Derudder, J. R. Faulconbridge and F. Witlox (eds) (2010) *International Business Travel in the Global Economy*, London: Ashgate.

Capgemini and RBC Wealth Management (2012) *World Wealth Report 2012*. Available at: www.capgemini.com/insights-and-resources/by-publication/world-wealth-report-2012-spotlight, accessed 21 June 2012.

Capgemini Merrill Lynch [CML] (2002) *World Wealth Report 2001*. Available at: www.ml.com, accessed 6 January 2010.

CML (2007) *World Wealth Report 10th Anniversary 1997–2006*. Available at: www.ml.com, accessed 6 January 2010.
Capgemini Merrill Lynch Global Wealth Management (CMLGWM) (2008) *World Wealth Report 2007*. Available at: www.ml.com, accessed 6 January 2010.
CMLGWM (2009) *World Wealth Report 2008*. Available at: www.ml.com, accessed 6 January 2010.
CMLGWM (2010) *World Wealth Report 2009*. Available at: www.ml.com, accessed 6 January 2010.
CMLGWM (2011) *World Wealth Report 2010*. Available at: www.ml.com, accessed 13 March 2012.
Cohen, M. J. (2010) 'Destination unknown: pursuing sustainable mobility in the face of rival societal aspirations, *Research Policy*, 39: 459–470.
Cresswell, T. (2010) 'Towards a politics of mobility', *Environment and Planning D: Society and Space*, 28: 17–31.
Economist, The (2011) 'Wall Street bonuses.' Available at: www.economist.com/node/18231330, accessed 11 May 2011.
Effinger, A. and Ody, E. (2011) 'HSBC tops family office list as money firms manage rises 17%'. Available at: www.bloomberg.com/news/2011-08-08/hsbc-tops-family-office-list-as-money-firms-manage-rises-17-.html, accessed 18 October 2011.
Elliott, A. and Urry, J. (2010) *Mobile Lives*, Oxford: Routledge.
Folkman, P., Froud, J., Johal, S. and Williams, K. (2007) 'Working for themselves? Capital market intermediaries and present day capitalism', *Business History*, 49 (4): 552–572.
Forbes (2011) *The World's Billionnaires 2011*. Available at: www.forbes.com, accessed 12 March 2012.
Frank, R. (2007) *Richi$tan. A Journey through the 21st Century Wealth Boom and the Lives of the New Rich*, New York: Piatkus.
Freeland, C. (2012) *Plutocrats: The Rise of the New Global Super Rich*, New York: Penguin.
Hall, S. (2009) 'Financialised elites and the changing nature of finance capitalism: Investment bankers in London's financial district', *Competition and Change*, 13 (2): 173–189.
Haseler, S. (1999) *The Super-Rich. The Unjust New World of Global Capitalism*, London: St. Martin's Press.
Hay, I. and S. Muller (2012) ' "That tiny, stratospheric apex that owns most of the world": Exploring geographies of the super-rich', *Geographical Research*, 50 (1): 75–88.
Irvin, G. (2008) *Super Rich. The Rise of Inequality in Britain and the United States*, London: Polity.
Kaufmann, V., Bergman, M. M., and Joye, D. (2004) 'Motility: mobility as capital', *International Journal of Urban and Regional Research*, 28 (4): 745–756.
Kaplan, D. A. (2007) *Mine's Bigger: Tom Perkins and the Making of the Greatest Sailing Machine Ever Built*. New York: HarperCollins.
Lundberg, F. (1988) *The Rich and the Super-Rich*, New York: Citadel Press.
McNamara, K. (2009) 'Publicizing private lives: celebrities, image control and the re-configuration of public space', *Social and Cultural Geography*, 10 (1): 9–23.
Nowicka, M. (2006). *Transnational Professionals and their Cosmopolitan Universes*, Frankfurt and New York: Camous Verlag.

Pearce, F. (2009) 'Green private jets? Don't make me laugh', *Guardian*, 29 October. Available at: www.guardian.co.uk/environment/2009/oct/29/private-jets-green, accessed 2 August 2012.

PricewaterhouseCoopers (2009) *Global Private Banking/Wealth Management Survey*. Available at: www.pwc.com, accessed 30 April 2013.

Private Jet Company (2012) *The Private Jet Company*. Available at www.privatejetco.im, accessed 22 August 2012.

Reckwitz, A. (2002) 'Toward a theory of social practices: a development in culturalist theorizing', *European Journal of Social Theory*, 5 (2): 243–263.

Shove, E., Pantzar, M. and Watson, M. (2012). *The Dynamics of Social Practice: Everyday life and how it changes*. London: Sage.

Simmons, R. and Morrow, C. (2011) *Super-Rich. A Guide to Having it All*. New York: Penguin.

Smith, R. C. (2001) *The Wealth Creators*, New York: Truman Books.

Sunday Times (2010) *Sunday Times Rich List 2010*, 26 April.

Sunday Times (2012) *Sunday Times Rich List 2012*, 29 April.

Top Gear Magazine (2012), August. London: Immediate Media Co.

Urry, J. (2004). 'The "system" of automobility', *Theory, Culture and Society*, 21 (4–5): 25–39.

Watson, M. (2012) 'How theories of practice can inform transition to a decarbonised transport system', *Journal of Transport Geography*, 24: 488–496.

What Car? (2012) August. London: Haymarket Media Group.

Chapter 4

Elite formation in the third industrial revolution

Thomas Birtchnell, Gil Viry and John Urry

The heroes

This chapter brings together two topics normally understood separately: the study of elites and the processes by which new 'technologies' develop. We discuss these in the context of the new technology known as additive manufacturing or 3D printing. We examine how it was that elites came to be formed in this new and as yet still-to-be-fully-formed area of development. We show that behind every elite are formations of complex mobilities. We extract and visualize public patent data from the early history of this technology and consider the mobilities of innovation across organizations, relationships and affiliations. Social network analysis (SNA) is used here to examine critically the popular notion that elites are uniquely and individually responsible for what may be significant game-changing innovations.

Of course, behind every general is an army and behind every prime minister is a party; however, scholarly studies of 'leaders' or 'managers' within specific organizations generally fail to capture the thick intensities over time of social interactions. By providing interpretable examples of such relationships, SNA challenges the legitimation of those who are located within elite positions.

Indeed, in thinking elites it is necessary to move beyond the hagiography often found in the media. Innovators are treated as gurus, role models and spokespeople for entire technologies. Self-made myths about apical technology elites, such as Facebook's Mark Zuckerberg, the world's twenty-third richest person in 2011, feature strongly in the ways that founders of information technology (IT) companies are treated as singularly innovative (Miller *et al.* 2012). This understanding of elite individuals spans back to the early innovative entrepreneurs in the computer revolution and before that to those developing various corporate empires in oil, cars, film, fast food and so on. What are disregarded in these myths of self-made singular elites are the roles and relationships between key actors and companies. The use of SNA offers a method to explore this structure of ties linking actors and their position within this structure that appear to be singular (Froud *et al.* 2006).

We begin by briefly considering two such 3D innovators, Chuck Hull and Scott Crump, and some of the stories told about them. Together these two company founders represent the key 'heroic' founding innovators of 3D printing and we subsequently examine their 'social networks' as revealed by patent data from the 1980s onwards.

In 2012 researchers working at the MIT Media Lab launched a campaign to raise funds for an affordable desktop printer that 'prints' exceptionally detailed objects in three dimensions. The company, Form Labs, used the online initiative Kickstarter, which raises support by deploying crowdsourcing techniques. Their innovation uses a patent resin material hardened in the printing process by exposure to a computer-guided laser. This avoids the ribbed, rough surface texture of many conventional 3D printed objects, a byproduct of the layer-by-layer extrusion melting process. The Form Labs 3D printer is marketed to customers requiring near-perfect scale prototypes to be used in architecture, engineering and design (Falconer 2012). But there is a catch. The current market leader in 3D printing, 3D Systems, has sued Form Labs and, controversially, Kickstarter for patent infringement ('Kickstarter Sued over 3D Systems' Printer Patent' 2012). It is alleged by 3D Systems that Form Labs violated patents dating back to the 1980s regarding a process they termed stereolithography, most clearly in the 1997 patent 'Simultaneous Multiple Layer Curing in Stereolithography' (Smalley *et al.* 1997).

The co-founder of the company 3D Systems, Charlie 'Chuck' Hull, is considered by many to be the 'inventor' of 3D printing. He patented some of the first innovations as a chemical engineer and then founded 3D Systems following his invention of the Stereolithography Rapid Printing System.

Hull coined the term 'stereolithography' in his 1983 patent 'Apparatus for Production of Three-Dimensional Objects by Stereolithography'. In 1987 the *Sunday Times* reported that Hull, then a Vice-President of UVP in San Gabriel – experts in ultra violet (UV) light technology – had invented a process of 'three-dimensional printing' through computer-controlled layer-formation and UV curable polymers (Matthews 1987). Much of his tinkering had been done after hours and, facing a company lay-off, Hull and some of his colleagues decided to leave and start 3D Systems: 'There I was a 40-something-year-old doing a startup', he later reminisced (Vance 2012: 2).

Hull found his way into public imagination decades before Form Labs in a science segment on the TV show *Good Morning America* broadcast on 30 January 1989. The feature described how 'the auto industry spends twice as much money designing car parts as making them' and how it used to make models out of clay – 'both expensive and time consuming' (Good

Morning America 1989). Hull summarizes in an interview from this feature what he plans to undertake:

> I think a good way to describe it is a three-dimensional printer ... in the broader sense you might say it does for engineering and manufacturing what the Xerox machine or word processor or both of those do for the office environment.
>
> (Good Morning America 1989)

Raymond Freed, the CEO of 3D Systems at the time, elaborated further:

> I think the technology is capable of what I call just-in-time manufacturing, which is what the world is trying to really do, which means that you would produce the part just as you need it ... I think we would revolutionize the way industry works.
>
> (Good Morning America 1989)

Two decades or so later, in 2011, Chuck Hull, along with 3D Systems CEO Abe Reichentel, received the Ernst and Young Carolinas Entrepreneur of the Year award ('3D Systems' CEO and Co-Founder Receive Prestigious E&Y Entrepreneur of the Year Award' 2011). Hull continues to play a key role in the organization, appearing at a recent investors' meeting in the same year.

Alongside Hull, the other elite hero of 3D printing is the co-founder (with his wife Lisa) of the company Stratasys, Scott Crump. Crump was an engineer manufacturing load cells for commercial aviation, where he came into contact with traditional methods of prototyping before tooling up items in factories. This process was time-consuming and expensive using wood, clay or foam. The company Stratasys started life in the 1980s when Crump is credited with having invented the Fused Deposition Modeling (FDM) process. This is now widely used in many low-end 3D printers, from the open-source RepRap to the kit, or pre-built, company Makerbot's range. Thermoplastic wire is liquefied and then deposited by an extrusion head following a path set by a digital CAD file from a computer. This technique proved to be much more affordable than other forms of 3D printing, such as stereolithography or laser sintering, albeit with some material limitations. For example, FDM is not suitable for metals or most resins, which must be in a powder form in order to be printed.

The widely narrated story goes that Crump got the idea for FDM from experimenting with a hot glue gun at home in order to make a toy frog for his daughter. 'I decided to create a toy froggy ... once I saw my daughter using the part ... and having gone through a number of years trying to get to market with a product, that's when the "aha" moment occurred' (Insley 2011). Crump continued to experiment in his kitchen and garage until he produced one of the first office prototyping machines available on the market, allowing plastic models to be made quickly and cheaply. From his solitary beginning as 'A Man and His Glue Gun' experimenting with candlewax and plastics and 'ruining every frying pan in the house', Crump went on to become the 'Father of FDM' and winner of the Ernst and Young Entrepreneur of the Year Award in 2005 (Mantey 2012).

In this chapter we focus on the innovation lineages of these key ideas in the socio-technical transition that may develop around 3D printing and what some call the third industrial revolution. The later sections examine data showing 'families' of innovators and the 'ancestral' roles of founding elites. From these relationships lineages of networks in patent citations (which are formalized and legalized 'ideas') stemming from 'common ancestors' can be visualized. These are articulable as self-organizing and informal distributions of power alongside corporate takeovers, technological innovations and the sponsorship and acquisition of intellectual property (IP) and relative patents. The emphasis on social networks of innovators allows a comparison and critique of heroic inventors at the apex of elite formation (Scott 2008). These are new methods to probe the chronological career progressions of elites and the strategies, key moments and fortuitous alliances behind innovation stories. As well, a critical examination of the managerial myths around lone heroic 'garage' technology inventors is made more plausible (Godelier 2007).

In this chapter we thus analyse some of the first patents for the most widely identified elites that involve 3D printing/additive manufacturing. A current intensification of activity in 3D printing is the context here. The recent acquisition of the company Z Corporation – primary innovator in itself – by competitor 3D Systems is a key moment. At the same time Stratasys has acquired the company Objet. The emergence of two major corporate institutions echoes the maturation of the computer sector. But so far 3D printing has yet to see the emergence of one common consumer product such as the Personal Computer (PC). There is currently a range of 3D printers designed for specific uses. For instance, Direct Laser Melting (DLM) and laser sintering has uses in jewellery making and in the production of complexly innovative automobile and aeroplane parts. These technologies in their current form are unlikely to become widely available for general home use although 3D System's creative director Janne Kyttanen suggests 3D printing at home is now 'cheaper than shopping' (Fairs 2012). However, printers could emerge in local bureaus or community centres, or in the office.

Mobilities and elites

It is not only people that move, but also many objects are moved about, or afford movement. And these objects must first be made by hand, or by machine, or both. There are what Latour terms non-human actors (1997). Objects, unlike but derived from raw resources, possess many physical, symbolic and cognitive aspects.

Made objects are distinct from raw resources in that their making requires a further sort of movement to precede them, the *mobilities of ideas* (Cresswell 2005). Ideas are not always 'open source' but are marked by ownership in the same fashion as objects or property. And those who have, or claim to own, ideas (brands, patents, copyrights, designs) profit from them and may become part of elite formations. Such elite formations are the fabric of corporations, governments and more informal institutions that own knowledge and exercise power (Scott 2012).

Stratification in social networks is a crucial issue for understanding power, inequality and elites, but there has not been adequate attention to SNA in relation to the mobilities of ideas or to the objects that get made. We synthesize the SNA approach with data from qualitative interviews and future scenario building exercises. Through a combination of discourse analysis, media mining and SNA on patent data we focus on elites within highly stratified organizations. We understand their role in major socio-technical transitions as founders, innovators, inventors and 'movers' of people, objects and ideas.

The use of SNA offers the chance of capturing relations between elites. In synthesizing these methods we follow Savage and his colleagues, who suggest that the 'glaring invisibility of elites' can be uncovered by looking not for direct contact with them as subjects for interviews or surveys, but instead for residual evidence around their relationships, activities, formations and movements (Savage and Williams 2008: 2).

We use the term 'elite formation' to indicate that those at the apex of power are never solely responsible for their achievements or status, but are rather surrounded by social structures making them participants within a process of what may turn out to be an innovation. Apical elites act as proxies for the ideas produced from social networks. Traditionally SNA research on elites has been most successfully applied to global corporate directorates (Carroll 2012). In combination with the mobilities paradigm, SNA promises to capture elite formations in more diverse settings, in this case in what can be understood as innovation networks (Caletrío 2012). Studies of stratification in anthropology, archaeology and history make use of the term 'apical elites' to identity those at the top of the social pyramid (Mandondo 1997; Anderson 1998; Schwake and Iannone 2010). This is useful in understanding how transitions 'dribble down' from the apex to the wider society. According to Bre Pettis, CEO of 3D printing startup Makerbot, 'the biggest most exciting thing that just happened is this technology that was really only available for the elite is now in the hands of anyone' (Simmons 2012).

Social networks in the third industrial revolution

With 3D printing there is the promise of transforming digital bits into physical atoms, blurring the line between ideas and objects. Virtual bits of data can be fabricated (or fabbed) into atoms at any place with many ramifications for many mobilities (Gershenfeld 2007). Commentators in the *Economist* describe this as a possible third industrial revolution. Jeremy Rifkin views 3D printing as one part of a range of disruptive innovations (2011: 220). This speculation goes alongside discussions of a 'manufacturing renaissance' for the United States as bureaucratic 'fab-less' organizations move towards innovative 'fabbing' organizations (Khanna 2012; Pisano and Shih 2012: 67). A significant caveat here is that without advances in localized recycling technologies with 3D printers the process crucially still requires resources for feedstock production and transport; however, recycling innovations are also taking place alongside production ones.

According to commentators the first industrial revolution began with the gradual shift from cottage industries and distributed skilled labourers crafting by hand to factories with concentrated and mechanized unskilled workers (Markillie 2012). The second industrial revolution occurred in the twentieth century with mechanized assembly lines and mass production, coinciding with the discovery of vast oil reserves and culminating in complex global production networks spanning the world. At the end of the second industrial revolution came complex data and network technologies allowing remote labour to be regulated and organizational tasks to be outsourced. The heroic exploits of the elites of the second industrial revolution, such as Microsoft's Bill Gates, Apple Computer's Steve Jobs or Virgin's Richard Branson, and the social networks that afforded them their success and consequent status, are well documented.

And from these innovations emerged what some commentators perceive is a third industrial revolution through a convergence of smart materials, 3D printers and network technologies. In this revolution services and manufacturing could be more localized and the lines between them blurred. Digital files will be shared and sold online and be printable at the touch of a button. Mass customization and the demand for unique, bespoke objects could overtake the desire of consumers for disposable and cheap mass-manufactured items.

Key to this third industrial revolution is 3D printing, where objects are not produced through a global network but rather are printed near to or by the user from standardized material resources, much like a photocopier or paper printer combines feeds of ink and paper to produce many different images and texts (Birtchnell and Urry 2012). And just as the key indicators of the second industrial revolution – the computer, the microprocessor, the microchip, the Internet and the digital network – involved social networks of garage innovators, entrepreneurs, venture capitalists, techno tinkerers, scientists and policymakers, so too does 3D printing.

Elite formations and the social networks they encompass are so far obscure in the third industrial revolution. This chapter seeks to rectify this absence through SNA techniques within the framework of the mobilities turn. Global production networks (GPNs) and the 'outsourcing' of manufacturing from the Global North to the Global South enables profit to be made from much lower wages and much less strict labour regulations. These GPNs also allow political pressure to be redirected on climate change mitigation towards those with the least historical responsibility for emissions from energy use, such as China, India and Brazil. So too is avoidance made possible of third party auditing of taxation and financial gains as well as responsibility for regulatory and legal claims against product quality, safety and longevity, assignable in GPNs to remote sub-contractors.

But following oil price spikes, rising wages in Asia, falling wages in the United States and potential efficiencies from the proximity of workers to designers and managers is a move towards insourcing – the return of manufacturing to the Global North by companies such as General Electric (Fishman 2012). Alongside this the question is now increasingly being asked: 'Can 3D printing change the [manufacturing] world' (Campbell *et al.* 2011)? Some commentators speculate that 3D printing is a sign of the collapse of the multi-national corporation as every town could be equipped with 'a high-end DIY facility capable of producing products from scratch based on digital designs' and local 'solutions for producing, distributing, and sharing can provide functional alternatives to corporations for both production and employment' (Davis 2012: 2–3). The use of 3D printing offers a new 'elegance' through the disruption of global supply chains, logistics and factory-based production (Mirchandani 2012: 97).

In order to understand something of the formation of an emerging elite we begin with a Google Ngram search of keyword references to the term '3D Printing' on the Internet. This analysis reveals the dramatic development of accounts of this new technology from 1990 onwards. There is a really rapid climb to the present very wide exposure in the media and public awareness. This suggests that there is here a 'revolution' in thought at least.

Similarly, a Google Trend analysis shows there has been a growth and consolidation of semantic interest and 'hype' in the media, especially in the last two or three years. Steady interest during the 2000s has now turned into a torrent of interest, with discussion and debate especially in the business press deciding whether 3D printing is the 'new big thing'.

We turn now to an SNA analysis of *relations* between key innovators of 3D printing, of those that turned out to be elites in this emerging field. We focus here on the co-authorship ties between innovators establishing patents related to 3D printing. Information about patent co-authorship was collected via the Google Patent search website. Two co-authorship networks of innovators were analysed. The first network was based on 428 patents published by May 2012, each having cited the seminal 1986 patent of Charles W. Hull (# U4575330). The second network was similarly built around the 237 patents citing the 1992 patent of Steven Scott Crump (# U5121329). This definition of ties means that only innovators that were collectively publishing patents were deemed to be part of the network. In our analysis, we did not account for the various degrees of importance and influence of single patents.

The initial Hull co-authorship network consisted of 475 innovators, fragmented into 79 components of size two and more (a component is a subset of a network where the largest number of innovators are connected). The largest component was composed of 84 inventors (most working for 3D Systems), the second largest of 46 (MIT and Z Corporation) and the next six components ranged from 10 to 20. For the purpose of analysis here only the largest component was examined – this consisting of 84 innovators.

The initial Crump co-authorship network consisted of 293 innovators, fragmented into 36 components of size two and more. Sizes of the largest components were, in descending order: 67 (Stratasys), 34 (MIT and Z Corporation), 33 (3D Systems), 17 and 12. As for the Hull network, only the largest component was used for the present analysis in order to focus on the core network around the two elite innovators.

Figures 4.1 and 4.2 show the two co-authorship networks. The names of Charles W. Hull and Steven Scott Crump are illustrated in larger print than the other innovators. Both numbers and shades of grey indicate which companies the innovators were working for at the time of the patent application. Innovators holding patents on behalf of different companies were illustrated in black (marked with a figure five). They acted as bridges between companies. Visual inspection of both graphs shows the pre-eminence of 3D Systems and Stratasys, respectively. Charles W. Hull and Steven Scott Crump and their co-authors hardly published for other companies while citing their original patents. This one-company pre-eminence is even stronger in the case of 3D Systems. This finding supports evidence that the two elites attract and cluster innovators within their own companies rather than work across different organizations. However, because patents are usually published within single companies, patent co-authorship networks are not suitable for revealing the ties of influence and collaboration across companies that may exist in other ways and forms other than collective patenting.

Various SNA measures may be used to characterize relational structures (Wasserman and Faust 1994; Scott 2000; Burt 2002). Some of these focus on the cohesion of network members, while others aim to assess the degree of inequality in power or resources between network members.

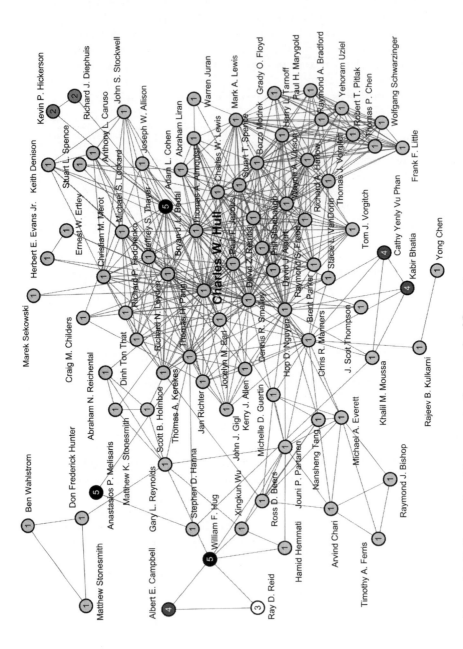

Figure 4.1 Hull co-authorship network of patents for 3D printing.

Notes
1 3D Systems, Inc. 2 Desktop Factory, Inc. 3 Omnichrome Corporation. 4 N/A. 5 Plural affiliation.

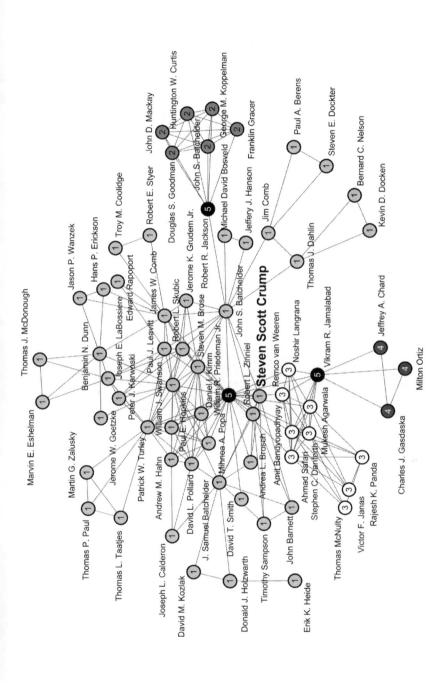

Figure 4.2 Crump co-authorship network of patents for 3D printing

Notes

1 Stratasys, Inc. 2 International Business Machines Corporation (IBM). 3 Rutgers, The State University of New Jersey. 4 Honeywell International, Inc. 5 Plural affiliation.

In the present study, we use the network density as a measure of overall cohesion. Network density is equal to the number of existing ties divided by the total number of possible co-authorship ties.

In order to estimate the inequality of prominence of innovators in the network, two measures of network centralization were computed: the degree and betweenness centralization. These two indices capture different conceptual dimensions of the centrality of actors within the network. The degree centrality of a given actor is simply the number of direct ties this actor has, calculated as a proportion of the total possible number of ties. At the level of the network, degree centralization expresses the variability (or inequality) among innovators with respect to degree centrality. The network is said to be centralized (in terms of degree) if a small number of innovators have many direct ties and a large number of innovators have few ties. This centrality measure provides information on the local dimension of centralization, as an innovator may have collaborated within a rather isolated subgroup of innovators.

Quite distinctly, betweenness centrality measures the extent to which an actor is located on the path between any pairs of actors. Betweenness centralization measures the variability of betweenness centrality among innovators. A network where a small number of innovators lie between all other innovators' chains of relationships has a strong betweenness centralization measure. Degree and betweenness centralization are expressed as a percentage, where 100 per cent is the centralization of a 'star network'. The theoretical star network where there is one person connected to every other person in the network and no other ties is the most centralized network. The degree and the betweenness centrality of Charles W. Hull, Steven Scott Crump and some other key innovators were also computed.

Table 4.1 shows that in the case of Hull and 3D Systems there is a relatively densely connected and highly unequal network in terms of number of co-authorship ties (using the software UCINET; see Borgatti et al. 2002). Hull plays a very central role. By contrast Crump's network is more sparsely knit, less asymmetrical in terms of number of co-authorship ties and highly centralized in terms of betweenness. Contrary to Hull, Crump does not hold a central position, neither in terms of number of co-authors, nor in terms of strategic position between disconnected parts of the network. John S. Batchelder and, more importantly, William R. Priedeman from Stratasys conversely occupy this central position.

Table 4.1 Network indices for the Hull and Crump co-authorship networks

	Hull network	Crump network
Density (%)	13.9	9.2
Degree centralization (%)	42.5	28.0
Betweenness centralization (%)	25.9	40.6

Hull possessed 46 co-authorship ties among the 83 innovators, which corresponds to 190 co-authors if multiple collaborations with the same innovator are accounted for. In other words, he co-wrote patents with around 55 per cent of the whole network. He is the most central innovator of the network, although differences with the following most central innovators are not particularly marked (47 per cent for Smalley, 40 per cent for Almquist or Nguyen). A handful of his colleagues from 3D Systems have also published with a large proportion of other innovators of the company. However, the network degree centralization reaches a high value of 43 per cent (almost half that of the most unequal star network), as half of the innovators published patents with fewer than 10 other colleagues. In average, innovators published patents with 12 other large innovators.

The high connectivity of the core of the network prevents some actors playing the role of compulsory intermediaries between other actors. Consequently, betweenness centralization is relatively low (26 per cent). Hull is by far the most central actor, with a betweenness centrality of 27 per cent by comparison with 14 per cent for the second most central actor (Nguyen).

By contrast with Hull's network, innovators in Crump's network's core are much less connected, so that degree centralization barely reaches 30 per cent. William R. Priedeman is the most connected innovator in the network, having co-authorship ties with 36 per cent of the network. The second most connected innovator is William J. Swanson (27 per cent). Steven Scott Crump was co-author with only seven other colleagues (11 per cent of the network and 12 co-authors if multiple collaborations are accounted for), which is just over the average of six direct ties. This sparse network fosters structural holes (Burt 2002), enabling some key actors to benefit from their position as compulsory intermediaries between disconnected clusters of innovators. Accordingly, the betweenness centralization of the network is much higher than the one in Hull's network (41 per cent versus 26 per cent). Crump (centrality of 3 per cent) is not one of those few innovators who bridge disconnected parts of the network. William R. Priedeman (43 per cent) and John S. Batchelder (40 per cent) play this role, sometimes across companies (see Figure 4.2).

This analysis shows that apical elites are embedded in a densely connected set of interdependent collaborators, challenging the image of innovation arising from lone entrepreneurs and personal 'genius'. These findings suggest that in order to be successful their inventions have to be further developed and applied by a collective enterprise within and in some cases across companies and research institutions. The company provides the apical elites with the financial, technical, commercial, managerial and relational resources that they need on the path to entrepreneurial and economic success. As well it provides a network consistency arising from a common symbolic goal. This being said, we observed that the apical elites do not necessarily hold the most central position within the patent co-authorship network. While Hull is central in 3D Systems, Crump holds a relatively peripheral position (at least in relation to this original patent), leaving other innovators in Stratasys to expand his initial work through new innovations and patents.

Conclusion

We thus identified from desk research, qualitative interviews and a workshop with experts the elite formations in 3D printing, as McNulty summarizes: these 'patent-holding, individuals-turned-entrepreneurs successfully commercialized 3D printing technology, with Scott Crump of Stratasys, Inc., and Chuck Hull of 3D Systems as prime examples' (McNulty et al. 2012: 11). We surveyed the most significant patent histories to the present filed by these two innovators and visualized varied 'elite formations'. We analysed patent data from the US Patent and Trademark Office (USPTO), using self-assigned patent citations as a control (Griffiths et al. 2008). We focused on Scott Crump and Chuck Hull and their respective companies, Stratasys and 3D Systems. These are, following various key takeovers/mergers of competitors (Objet and Z Corporation), the market leaders in the possible third industrial revolution of 3D printing and related system developments.

The research dynamically examined snapshots over a single patent's citation history from the original date of issue to the latest cited patent at the time of research in the Google Patent search engine. The original patent was elected because it was attributed to the founder of a company now part of an elite formation. Two founders' patents were selected for analysis as hubs in a citation network. These two represent the most significant corporate players in 3D printing. We analysed the histories of two patents; and there may be a bias in selecting these and not others. However, the scale of activity through a number of decades is evidence of the importance of these patents to the careers of these 3D elites.

As only patents are given a unique identifying code and inventors are not, we drew on single elites as a retrospective 'common ancestor', which gave us a starting point for a network analysis of these elite formations. In the process we sought to establish the patterns involved in how some founding inventors become treated as heroic elite members in key innovative corporations through processes of collaboration, acquisition and new technology funding and creation. Without the huge number of collaborators these heroes of 3D would not have emerged and come to occupy elite positions within the possibly emerging third industrial revolution.

Note

The research reported here was conducted in an Economic and Social Research Council (ESRC) funded project at the Centre for Mobilities Research (CeMoRe) at Lancaster University (ESRC ES/J007455/1).

References

'3D Systems' CEO and Co-Founder Receive Prestigious E&Y Entrepreneur of the Year Award'. (2011). Accessed 13 June 2011 at www.3dsystems.com/press-releases/3d-systems-ceo-and-co-founder-receive-prestigious-ey-entrepreneur-yearr-award.

Anderson, D. G. (1998). 'Swift Creek in a Regional Perspective'. In M. Williams and D. T. Elliott (eds) *A World Engraved: Archaeology of the Swift Creek Culture.* Tuscaloosa: University of Alabama Press, pp. 274–300.

Birtchnell, T. and J. Urry (2012). 'Fabricating Futures and the Movement of Objects'. *Mobilities*: published online: 26 November. DOI: 10.1080/17450101. 2012.745697.

Borgatti, S., M. Everett and L. Freeman (2002). 'UCINET for Windows: Software for Social Network Analysis.' Harvard: Analytic Technologies.

Burt, R. S. (2002). 'The Social Capital of Structural Holes'. In M. F. Guillén, R. Collins, P. England and M. Meyers (eds) *The New Economic Sociology: Developments in an Emerging Field.* New York: Russell Sage Foundation, pp. 148–190.

Caletrío, J. (2012). 'Global Elites, Privilege and Mobilities in Post-Organized Capitalism'. *Theory, Culture and Society* **29** (2): 135–149.

Campbell, T., C. Williams, O. Ivanova and B. Garrett (2011). 'Could 3D Printing Change the World?'. Washington: Atlantic Council.

Carroll, W. K. (2012). 'Capital Relations and Directorate Interlocking: The Global Network in 2007'. In G. Murray and J. Scott (eds) *Financial Elites and Transnational Business: Who Rules the World?* Cheltenham: Edward Elgar, pp. 54–75.

Cresswell, T. (2005). 'Mobilising the Movement: The Role of Mobility in the Suffrage Politics of Florence Luscomb and Margaret Foley, 1911–1915'. *Gender, Place and Culture* **12** (4): 447–461.

Davis, G. F. (2012). *Re-Imagining the Corporation.* Ann Arbor: The University of Michigan.

Fairs, M. (2012) 'Printing Products at Home Is "Cheaper Than Shopping"'. *Dezeen Magazine,* 21 October. London: Dezeen Limited.

Falconer, J. (2012). 'Formlabs Creates Blu-Ray Based Prosumer 3D Printer.' *Gizmag,* 26 September. Accessed 1 May 2013 at www.gizmag.com/formlabs-blu-ray-prosumer-3d-printer/24300.

Fishman, C. (2012). 'The Insourcing Boom'. *The Atlantic,* 28 November. Accessed 1 May 2013 at www.theatlantic.com/magazine/archive/2012/12/the-insourcing-boom/309166.

Froud, J., M. Savage, G. Tampubolon and K. Williams (2006). 'Rethinking Elite Research'. *Journal of Management and Social Sciences* **2** (1): 25–41.

Gershenfeld, N. (2007). *Fab: The Coming Revolution on Your Desktop – from Personal Computers to Personal Fabrication.* New York: Basic Books.

Godelier, E. (2007). "Do You Have a Garage?' Discussion of Some Myths About Entrepreneurship'. *Business and Economic History Online* **5**: 1–20.

Good Morning America. (1989). 'Science Segment with 3D Systems'. January. Accessed 5 September 2012 at www.youtube.com/watch?v=NpRDuJ5YgoQ.

Griffiths, D., A. Miles and M. Savage (2008). 'The End of the English Cultural Elite?' In M. Savage and K Williams (eds) *Remembering Elites*. Oxford: Blackwell Publishing, pp. 189–210.

Insley, K. (2011). 'Stratasys Takes 3D Printing Mainstream.' *Kare*, 19 January. Accessed 23 January 2011 at www.kare11.com/news/career/article/901211/376/Stratasys-takes-3D-printing-mainstream.

Khanna, R. (2012). *Entrepreneurial Nation: Why Manufacturing Is Still Key to America's Future*. New York: McGraw-Hill.

'Kickstarter Sued over 3D Systems' Printer Patent.' (2012). *BBC News*, 21 November. Accessed 22 November 2012 at www.bbc.co.uk/news/technology-20434031.

Latour, B. (1997). 'Where Are the Missing Masses? The Sociology of a Few Mundane Artifacts.' In W. E. Bijker and J. Law (eds) *Shaping Technology/Building Society: Studies in Socio-Technical Change*. Oxford: Oxford University Press, pp. 225–258.

Mandondo, A. (1997). 'Trees and Spaces as Emotion and Norm Laden Components of Local Ecosystems in Nyamaropa Communal Land, Nyanga District, Zimbabwe'. *Agriculture and Human Values* **14** (4): 353–372.

Mantey, D. (2012) 'A Man & His Glue Gun.' *PD&D Magazine*, 6 November. Madison: Product Design and Development. Accessed 8 November 2012 at www.pddnet.com/articles/2012/06/man-his-glue-gun.

Markillie, P. (2012). 'A Third Industrial Revolution.' *The Economist*, 21 April. Accessed 1 May 2013 at date www.economist.com/node/21552901.

Matthews, R. (1987). 'Innovation: Prototype Professionals – 3-D Prints Give Ideas Shape.' *Sunday Times*, 25 January.

McNulty, C. M., N. Arnas and T. A. Campbell (2012). 'Toward the Printed World: Additive Manufacturing and Implications for National Security'. *Defense Horizons* **73**: 1–16.

Miller, B., M. Lapham, B. Gates and C. Collins (2012). *The Self-Made Myth: And the Truth About How Government Helps Individuals and Businesses Succeed*, San Francisco: Berrett-Koehler Publishers.

Mirchandani, V. (2012). *The New Technology Elite: How Great Companies Optimize Both Technology Consumption and Production*, Hoboken: John Wiley & Sons.

Pisano, G. P. and W. C. Shih (2012). *Producing Prosperity: Why America Needs a Manufacturing Renaissance*. Boston: Harvard Business Review Press.

Rifkin, J. (2011). *The Third Industrial Revolution: How Lateral Power is Transforming Energy, the Economy, and the World*. Basingstoke: Palgrave Macmillan.

Savage, M. and K. Williams (2008). 'Elites: Remembered in Capitalism and Forgotten by Social Sciences'. In M. Savage and K. Williams (eds) *Remembering Elites*. Oxford: Blackwell Publishing, pp. 1–24.

Schwake, S. A. and G. Iannone (2010). 'Ritual Remains and Collective Memory: Maya Examples from West Central Belize'. *Ancient Mesoamerica* **21** (02): 331–339.

Scott, J. (2000). *Social Network Analysis: A Handbook*. London: Sage.

Scott, J. (2008). 'Modes of Power and the Re-Conceptualization of Elites. In M.

Savage and K. Williams (eds) *Remembering Elites*. Oxford: Blackwell Publishing, pp. 27–44.

Scott, J. (2012). 'Capital Mobilization, Transnational Structures, and Capitalist Classes'. In G. Murray and J. Scott (eds) *Financial Elites and Transnational Business: Who Rules the World?* Cheltenham: Edward Elgar, pp. 1–25.

Simmons, D. (2012). 'From Toys to Cars – What Will You Make on a 3D Printer?' *Click* (BBC), 19 November. Accessed 20 November 2012 at http://news.bbc.co.uk/2/hi/programmes/click_online/9770565.stm.

Smalley, D. R., T. J. Vorgitch, C. R. Manners, C. W. Hull and S. L. VanDorin (1997). 'Simultaneous Multiple Layer Curing in Stereolithography'. United States Patent No. 5,597,520.

Vance, A. (2012). '3D Printers: Make Whatever You Want'. *Business Week*, 26 April. Accessed 5 December 2012 at www.businessweek.com/articles/2012-04-26/3d-printers-make-whatever-you-want, p. 2.

Wasserman, S. and K. Faust (1994). *Social Network Analysis: Methods and Applications*. Cambridge: Cambridge University Press.

Chapter 5

Aeromobile elites
Private business aviation and the global economy

Lucy Budd

> There is no debate about whether flying privately is more productive. You control when, where and with whom you fly. You skip the check-ins, connections, baggage handling and delays that can make flying such a headache. And you replace those problems with more meetings, more time with clients and more sales.
>
> (NetJets 2010)

Introduction

The opening vignette, taken from the website of one of the world's largest operators of business aircraft, NetJets, is unequivocal: business aviation saves time and enhances productivity by enabling users to avoid the stresses, delays, and congestion associated with conventional passenger air travel. For the sector's critics, however, particularly during times of economic downturn, it represents a profligate, highly inequitable, and environmentally unsustainable manifestation of capitalist production which enables a small number of cash-rich but time-poor politicians, corporate executives, royalty, and celebrities to bypass the spatial and temporal constraints imposed by conventional airline schedules and fly around the world in comfort, at a time and in the company of their choosing, to destinations they desire to visit in an aeromobile vehicle that effectively insulates and isolates them from less affluent others.

Although business aviation only accounts for a small (albeit very high yield) segment of the global air transport market, its socio-cultural impacts are profound and the 'bizjet', in particular, has become a powerful cultural symbol of wealth, social-political status, and prestige. Indeed, in an era of unprecedented global aeromobility in which over two billion people board a commercial flight every year, *how* one flies has become an increasingly important social differentiator and indicator of relative power and status. While full-service airlines have conventionally offered multiple classes of travel to separate higher-yielding First and Business Class passengers from customers flying in Economy, these crude forms of aerial segregation still oblige passengers to travel in the company of strangers and depart from particular airports at times that suit the airline, not the individual. As a consequence of the strict social and spatial regimes imposed by commercial airlines, a distinct subcategory of commercial aviation practice emerged in the United States in the mid 1920s and rapidly spread around the world to serve the particular and often demanding mobility needs of society's most affluent members.

For a wealthy few, business aviation, along with other forms of elite surface and maritime mobility (on which see Atkinson and Flint 2004; Atkinson 2006; and Atkinson and Blandy 2009), enable users to bypass conventional forms of transport and timetabled spaces of flow and create personalised and bespoke geographies of movement. By facilitating the selective reconfiguration of global time-space and effectively cleaving the trajectories of the super-rich away from those of the less affluent, business aviation creates and reproduces highly exclusionary spaces of corporeal mobility which present an exciting prospect for mobilities research. Yet while a number of studies have begun to investigate the oft-hidden mobilities and interior spaces of luxury trains, yachts, and cruise ships, comparatively little work has explored the unique spatialities and choreographies of private business or corporate aviation.

Taking its cue from the developing literature on the multiple socialities of passenger aviation (on which see Adey 2010; Adey *et al.* 2007; Budd 2011; Budd and Hubbard 2010), this chapter examines the bespoke aerial mobilities that are performed by the space-rich yet time-poor users of private business aircraft. More specifically, it analyses the motivations for, and users of, business aircraft and examines the role and the implications that the creation and maintenance of new 'affluent infrastructures' of aeromobility, including private jets and dedicated business aircraft registers, have had for the organisation and reproduction of global society.

Structure of the chapter

The chapter is divided into eight subsections. The first defines and then charts the development of private business aviation from the early 1920s to the present day. This is followed by an examination of the scale and scope of contemporary business aviation activities around the world. Sections three and four respectively provide an insight into who uses business aviation and how business aircraft are used while section five offers a critical consideration of the extent to which six key discourses – of comfort, convenience, speed, productivity, status, and flexibility – collectively create a need for, and access to, exclusionary spaces of mobility that reinforce the social stratification of the super-rich and create new geographies of connectivity and socio-economic interaction. The dedicated corporate aircraft register on the Isle of Man is offered, in section six, as an exemplar of how the global business aviation sector is becoming increasingly fragmented as the wealthiest business aviation users seek new ways to subtly differentiate themselves from other groups. The seventh section identifies some of the contemporary challenges associated with conducting research into elite aeromobilities. The penultimate section discusses possible future trajectories of future of business aviation and the chapter concludes by discussing the extent to which contemporary forms of elite aeromobility may require current understandings of aerial travel to be reframed.

Taking flight – the elite practices of business aviation

The term 'business aviation' invariably conjures up images of sleek, streamlined jets, and connotations of wealth, opulence, and prestige. As a mobility genre, business aviation is habitually constructed as something that is desirable and which is routinely compared favourably with the perceived stresses, indignities, and delays associated with flying on scheduled commercial aircraft. The sector is also depicted as catering for the mobility needs of a small group of socially privileged individuals, including film, television, music, and sport celebrities, CEOs, and royalty. According to the International Business Aviation Council (IBAC 2008) business aviation differs from commercial aviation because the former involves the operation or use of aircraft that are generally *not* available for public hire by companies or individuals 'for the carriage of passengers or goods as an aid to the conduct of their business'. As a consequence, Cwerner suggests that business aviation 'provides strategic network capabilities to an increasing number of corporations and industries' and plays a 'growing role in shaping ... the social relations that underpin the global economy' (2009: 226).

While the use of specialist aircraft for business purposes can be traced back to the early 1920s when major US corporations began using private aircraft to shuttle executives between company headquarters and manufacturing sites that were not linked by regular commercial services (Sheehan 2003), business aviation really emerged as a distinct subset of civil aviation practice from the late 1950s and early 1960s onwards when a new range of dedicated aircraft, including jets, began to be produced for the executive market (Bilstein 1984). Today, business aviation activities encompass a wide range of business models and operating characteristics, ranging from fixed-wing corporate flights in twin-seater turboprop aircraft, to 'VVIP' business jets and owner-operated helicopters. However, despite the apparent diversity, all these activities can be classified as belonging to one of three types, namely commercial, corporate, or owner-operated business aviation, according to the type of business model adopted.

The first, commercial business aviation, describes a situation in which a third-party operator flies a business aircraft on behalf of a private client.

These third-party operators may offer ad hoc (on demand) aircraft charter and/or air taxi services or operate fractional ownership schemes that allow corporations or individuals to purchase defined units of flight time on a particular aircraft in their fleet. Under these arrangements, the third-party operators supply everything that is needed for a flight, including aircraft, flight and cabin crew, fuel, insurance, maintenance, catering, and flight plans. These 'timeshares in the sky' allow companies or individuals to buy access to a private aircraft for a set number of hours per year at a fraction of the cost of purchasing the aircraft outright. The price of the service depends on the size of the aircraft and the number of flight hours that are required. Typically, customers buy a share in an aircraft in blocks of 25 hours (or multiples thereof) and pay a monthly maintenance fee in addition to 'pay as you fly' fuel, catering, landing fees, and navigation charges. The high level of integration that these commercial operators achieve facilitates the rapid 'go now' creation of bespoke travel arrangements, and aircraft can be in the air at as little as ten hours' notice, 24 hours a day, 365 days a year, to satisfy the mobility needs of the most demanding and discerning of clients. Such modes of operation are reportedly popular among small and medium-sized enterprises as well as individuals who want access to a private aircraft but do not want to pay the purchase price and ongoing maintenance and crew costs associated with owing an aircraft outright.

The second principal type of operation, corporate business aviation, refers to a situation in which a company or an individual owns an aircraft outright and directly employs the personnel required to operate it. This regime enables the majority of flight operations to be performed 'in house' without the need for external providers (as described above). However, the high start-up and ongoing management costs of this type of operation render it beyond the financial means of all but the largest and wealthiest of corporations or individuals. As its name implies, the final category, owner-operated business aviation, describes flights where an aircraft's owner also acts as its pilot.

In order to fulfil the operational needs of a diverse group of users and flight missions, a wide range of fixed- and rotor-wing aircraft have been developed for the business aviation market. These aircraft range in size and performance from single-seat propeller-powered aircraft, which can operate from very short runways, to executive helicopters, long-range business jets, and 'VVIP' aircraft such as the Airbus 319 Corporate Jet, the Boeing Business Jet (which is based on a 737 aircraft) and executive Boeing 747s and Airbus A340s. However, the aircraft type that is arguably most synonymous with business aviation is the mid-range six-to-ten seat 'bizjet'.

These sleek and aerodynamic aircraft were first developed in the late 1950s when jet engines were becoming the propulsion mode of choice for civilian aircraft. In 1957, the world's first executive jet took off on its maiden flight. Lockheed hoped that its new JetStar, which could cruise at

550 miles per hour at an altitude of 33,000 ft, would generate considerable numbers of commercial sales but the purchase price of US$1.5 million discouraged many potential buyers (Bilstein 1984). However, despite the JetStar's disappointing sales figures, American entrepreneur William Lear believed an untapped market for executive jets existed and he sought to develop his own aircraft. The performance of the resulting Learjet far exceeded that of the JetStar and an aggressive sales strategy combined with detailed attention to costs stimulated unprecedented demand for the new product. By the autumn of 1964, barely a year after the first flight, over 100 Learjets had been sold, and other US and foreign aircraft manufacturers began to design their own business jets to take advantage of the emerging market (Bushell 2000).

Today, there are well over a dozen major aerospace companies who manufacture business aircraft. Some, such as Cessna, Piper, and Beech, have been involved in executive aircraft manufacture since before the Second World War whereas others, including Embraer, Gulfstream, Grob, Boeing, and Bombardier entered the market more recently. Between them, they produce over 50 different types of business aircraft, from single-engine light aircraft to long-range business jets that cost tens of millions of US dollars when new. Buyers are encouraged to configure their aircraft's exterior paintwork and interior fittings to their own exacting personal requirements to create a luxurious aerial 'home from home' or an office in the sky. However, the high acquisition and ongoing operating costs (which include, but are not limited to, crew salaries, fuel, maintenance, insurance, airport fees, and navigation charges) mean that bizjets, in particular, are a luxury obtainable only by a wealthy few. As a result, business jets have become the mobility tool of choice for the global super-rich, political elites, and celebrities and their cultural cachet has endured. Indeed, access to a bizjet has become a major barometer of social status and thus personal and professional success.

The scale and scope of global business aviation

There are currently in excess of 31,000 dedicated business aircraft in operation around the world. This compares with around 17,500 commercial aircraft. Like its commercial counterpart, business aviation occurs on all seven continents but its geographic distribution is highly uneven. Unlike commercial aviation, however, business aviation was relatively unaffected by the global slump in passenger demand for air travel that followed the 9/11 terrorist attacks, record oil prices, and the recent economic downturn. Between 2001 and 2011, the world's business aviation fleet increased by almost 50 per cent from 21,459 to 31,166 units and growth was recorded every year except for 2007 (Figure 5.1). This contrasts sharply with the situation in the commercial sector, where many

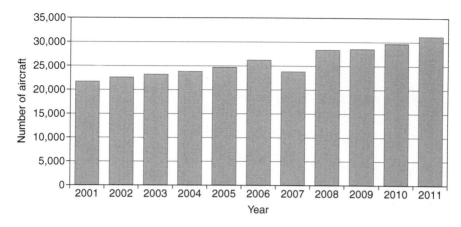

Figure 5.1 Growth of the world's business aircraft fleet, 2001–2011.

airlines were declared bankrupt while others rationalised their route network, cut their workforce, and deferred aircraft deliveries in a desperate bid to remain operational.

Historically, business aircraft have been concentrated in a small number of the most economically developed countries in North America and western Europe but recent economic growth combined with structural and regulatory changes in other aviation markets has led to rapid growth elsewhere. In 2008, 72 per cent of the world's business aircraft were registered in North America, with 10 per cent in Europe and only 6 per cent in South America (Budd and Graham 2009). By 2011, slowdown in US and Canadian markets combined with rapid growth in other world regions meant that North America accounted for only 45 per cent of the world's business aircraft fleet while the proportions in Europe and South America had grown to 21 per cent and 20 per cent respectively (see Figure 5.2). Particularly notable growth occurred in Brazil and Venezuela, but despite economic growth in the Middle East, Pacific Rim, Asia, and Africa relatively few business aircraft are registered in these regions.

Although business aviation is an almost global phenomenon, the spatialities of business aircraft registrations are highly concentrated and uneven. Global aeronautical regulations stipulate that all civilian aircraft, irrespective of size or performance, are registered in a single country and display a unique alpha/numerical registration mark on the fuselage. All aircraft on the UK civil aviation registration list, for example, have a registration mark that follows the format G-xxxx (where the xxxx are capital letters), while those on the Canadian register are similarly marked C-xxxx, and those on the German register D-xxxx. Civil aircraft registers can thus be used to determine where in the world business aircraft are registered.

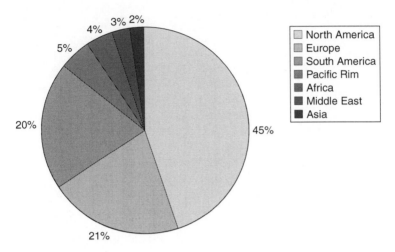

Figure 5.2 Distribution of business aircraft by world region, 2011.

At the time of writing, only seven countries in the world have more than 500 business aircraft on their national aircraft registers and only four have more than 1,000. The country with by far the highest number of business aircraft registrations is the United States. In 2011, almost 18,000 business aircraft were registered in the United States, nearly 15 times as many as second-placed Brazil and 27 times as many as Germany, the country with the higher number of business aircraft in Europe (Table 5.1). Interestingly, the top ten countries for business aircraft registrations in 2008 were the same in 2011 although the position within the rankings had changed. With the exception of the USA, the business aircraft fleet in every country in the list grew between 2008 and 2011 despite the global economic downturn and recession in many key world markets (see Table 5.1). The fact that business aircraft registrations continued to grow during this period indicates that the business aviation sector was shielded from the effects of the downturn.

Table 5.1 Top 10 business aircraft fleets by country, 2011 (2008 figures in brackets)

Country	Number of aircraft	Country	Number of aircraft
United States	17,937 (18,772)	UK	639 (316)
Brazil	1,225 (759)	Venezuela	587 (397)
Canada	1,117 (927)	Australia	480 (317)
Mexico	1,035 (887)	South Africa	464 (330)
Germany	664 (496)	France	424 (398)

Sources: AvData NetJet (2011) and Budd and Graham (2009).

While aircraft registrations provide a useful overview of the spatialities of global business aviation, they cannot offer any insights into where in the world the individual aircraft are used. Indeed, for reasons of business expediency, political neutrality, or taxation, a business aircraft that is registered in Bermuda could be based in Europe while another registered in the USA could predominately be used on inter-island services in Australasia. Thus, in order to uncover where, how, and why business aircraft are used it is necessary to examine the type of people and organisations who are using them.

The global high (net worth) flyers

It is estimated that 60 per cent of the world's business aircraft are owned by major multinational corporations, 20 per cent by national governments, 17 per cent by small and medium-sized enterprises, and the remaining 3 per cent (or around 930 units) by wealthy individuals (Pricewaterhouse-Coopers 2009). According to the US-based business aviation trade organisation the National Business Aviation Association (NBAA), business aircraft are 'productivity multipliers that allow passengers to conduct business en route in complete privacy while reducing the stresses associated with travelling on commercial carriers' (NBAA 2004: 3). In 2001, a study of Fortune 500 companies reported that those that used business aircraft generated 146 per cent more in cumulative returns than non-users and that CEOs believed business aircraft helped their company to identify and execute 'strategic opportunities' for new relationships, increase contact and visibility with clients, and develop new markets. Many of these advantages are the result of the inherent flexibility of business aviation. Having access to a private business aircraft immediately frees companies from the temporal constraints imposed by conventional airline schedules, allowing them to react to emerging market opportunities and reach them before their competitors, and fly at a time that suits them. In addition, business aircraft enable companies to access airports which may be nearer to emerging opportunities but which commercial carriers do not serve.

In addition to enhanced temporal and spatial flexibility, the creation of on-demand and bespoke *private* aerial mobilities removes many of the stresses, congestion, and delays associated with major commercial airports, improves the safety and security of key personnel, and reduces opportunities for industrial espionage (Sheehan 2003; IBAC 2008). It also makes employees feel valued and arguably helps a company or an individual project a positive and successful image. Passenger surveys have reported that employees feel that they are significantly more productive when they are flying on business aircraft than they would have been on conventional airlines (or even in their own office) and three times less likely to be resting or reading non-work-related materials during the flight (NBAA

2004). According to the NBAA (2004: 19), these attributes collectively mean that 'business aircraft are good for the bottom line' as they enable users to 'consistently outperform non-operators in key economic performance measures, [including] annual sales volume, number of employees, value of assets, stockholders' equity and annual income'.

While 77 per cent of the world's business aircraft fleet are owned and operated by multinational corporations and small and medium-sized enterprises, the remainder are owned by a small group of very wealthy individuals. According to the 2010 World Wealth Report, the global population of High Net Worth Individuals (HNWIs), here defined as people with investible assets exceeding US$1 trillion, grew by 17.1 per cent in 2009 to ten million and their collective wealth increased by 18.9 per cent to US$39 trillion (Capgemini and Merrill Lynch 2010). This growth was facilitated, in part, by GDP growth and policies of national fiscal stimulation that helped to reverse the effects of the 2008 global economic downturn, but also by the growing value of private corporations, particularly in Latin America and Asia-Pacific (ibid.). As a consequence of their superior (and growing) purchasing power, HNWIs have historically invested in luxury consumer items including antiques, fine art and wine, racehorses, vintage cars, yachts, and aircraft (Beaverstock *et al.* 2004). While the majority of these so-called 'passion collectables' are material statements of social status and accumulated wealth that enable their owners to engage in particular practices of leisure and consumption, personal aircraft enable the production of a specific jet-setting lifestyle that is underpinned by unfettered access to rapid global mobility.

Business aviation: an entirely different type of flying?

Clearly, the relative wealth of business aviation users vis-à-vis the general flying public means that the embodied practices and experiences of flying on a private aircraft differ quite considerably from those of passengers flying on conventional airlines. Indeed it is the very ability to socially and spatially segregate oneself from the stresses and unpleasantness of normal routines of flying that is one of the primary attractions of business aviation. Yet for all the apparent differences, a number of common refrains remain. Business aviation, like its commercial counterpart, transports people from where they are to where they want to be.

One of the primary uses of business aircraft is the transport of company employees. Typically, this will involve flying staff between offices and production sites, taking them to visit clients or enabling them to participate in trade shows, or ensuring that they arrive ahead of any competitor to secure new business when opportunities emerge. As later sections of this chapter will show, discourses of convenience, flexibility, and comfort have become instrumental in structuring how, when, and why business aircraft are used for this purpose. In addition to transporting company employees and executives, business aircraft may also be used to transport clients to and from meetings and reward high-performing employees. The possibility of flying on a private aircraft not only confers corporate status on the operator but may also act as a powerful incentive for employees to exceed sales targets or profit forecasts.

As well as moving people, business aircraft are also used for the carriage of samples, supplies, and documents. Usually, these constitute very high value, delicate, and often confidential or perishable products that have to be moved in accordance with strict deadlines under defined handling conditions and security protocols. Depending on the nature of the product, it may have to be transported in a protective container, packed into a strong cool box, and/or be accompanied by in-house couriers or security personnel at all times along the journey. By using business aircraft to transport financially or intellectually valuable goods, companies ensure that they are in control of their supply chains and distribution channels at all times, thus reducing the potential for delays, damage, or commercial espionage.

A further way in which business aircraft are used is for humanitarian and/or charity missions. Owing to their smaller size and ability to use less developed airfields, business aircraft can be used to take medical supplies and emergency aid to destinations that large conventional cargo aircraft cannot reach. They can also be mobilised relatively quickly and be the first to arrive at the scene of a natural disaster. Employing aircraft on such relief flights helps business aviation users to demonstrate their corporate social responsibility credentials. However, one of the most distinctive uses for business aircraft concerns direct applications or 'aerial services' such as aerial photography, atmospheric measurement, environmental monitoring, and aerial surveying. Here, the aircraft themselves are used as a platform for monitoring, advertising, crop spraying, or scientific experiments that could not be conducted in any other way. Many energy and infrastructure firms use helicopters and aircraft to survey electricity pylons, gas installations, and oil pipelines while national law enforcers and border control agencies may use them to police the integrity of borders and detect illegal activity. Consequently, as well as providing different ways of flying, business aircraft also arguably offer users a much more pleasant environment in which to fly.

Business aircraft: a better way to fly?

By the late 1920s, business aviation had become an accepted, if not exactly widespread, feature of American commerce. For American aviation historian Roger Bilstein (1984), the growth in business aviation in the United States in the late 1920s and early 1930s can be attributed to increased industrialisation and the fact that many US airports lacked a regular scheduled air service. Consequently, many business executives discovered that private aircraft offered them tangible benefits of enhanced convenience, flexibility, speed, productivity, comfort, and status.

Convenience

For centuries, mobility has been a prized asset. Access to transportation, whether on horseback or, later, ship, road, rail, and air, enables people to travel to places outside their normal sphere of influence and take advantages of any personal, political, or commercial opportunities that may exist there. In the case of civil aviation, aircraft have enabled travellers to complete, in a matter of hours, journeys that would once have taken many days or weeks to accomplish by other modes. However, despite its advantages, conventional commercial air travel is rarely convenient. Passengers have to travel to the airport and fly at a time that suits the airline, not the individual, and in the company of strangers. In contrast, business aviation aims to make flying much more convenient by putting the user in charge of flight schedules and itineraries. 'The company owned plane', opined an editorial in *Factory and Management Magazine* in 1928, 'is almost indispensable' as it shortens travel time and increases 'the range of action of executives' (cited in Bilstein 1984: 64) and this discourse of the convenience of private flying continues today.

In 2008, Grob Aerospace ran a series of printed advertisements for their new business jet which claimed that the new sp^n 'reaches places that others can't'. Interestingly, rather than draw attention to the aircraft's performance characteristics, the advertisement sought to emphasise the global reach of using their aircraft. Thanks to their smaller size, lower weight, and minimal ground handling requirements, business jets such as the sp^n can access airports that commercial aircraft cannot serve. This enables users to access new markets and land at airports that are nearer to their clients, thereby saving time and reducing the need for lengthy ground transport connections to/from commercial airports. Studies of the business aviation sectors in Europe and the United States discovered that the scale, scope, and concentration of business aviation services within these two regions were very different from those of commercial services. Indeed, whereas the scheduled airline market is concentrated on a relatively small number of key routes and key airports, the business aviation market is more diffuse.

In Europe, the business aviation sector connects in excess of 100,000 airport pairs a year compared with the 30,000 airport pairs linked by scheduled airlines, while in the United States, business aviation serves ten times as many airports as all the commercial carriers combined (Marsh 2006; NBAA 2010). Thus, business aviation is not replicating the network of scheduled airlines but actively creating new links and patterns of aerial connectivity. Only 5 per cent of all business aviation flights performed in Europe had a scheduled alternative (defined as having at least one scheduled flight every working day) while 64 per cent of respondents to a 2010 study reported that they used business aircraft to support schedules that are not supported by conventional airlines, such as accessing multiple destinations within one working day (NBAA 2010). As a result, business aircraft are not only creating new aerial connections but also offering users the opportunity to perform new strategies of mobility.

In order to improve productivity and minimise ground time, most business aviation users choose to fly from smaller, less congested airports, that are as close to the intended destination as possible. In the case of London, this means flying into Farnborough, Northolt, or Biggin Hill as opposed to Heathrow or Gatwick and in Paris using Le Bourget in preference to Charles de Gaulle. These alternative airports are favoured by business aviation users and business aircraft operators because they are smaller and less congested, do not suffer from capacity constraints, offer a more attractive environment, and provide services that are specifically tailored to the needs of business aviation users (such as the option of being driven out to the aircraft by your chauffeur and met again at the door of the aircraft on arrival).

Flexibility

In addition to exhibiting distinctive spatial patterns, business aviation also creates distinctive temporal patterns which arise from the inherent flexibility of the product. Access to a business aircraft, whether as a corporate or commercial user or as an owner-operator, enables the rapid creation of 'go now' flights that can be in the air within as little as 60 to 90 minutes of the service being requested. The abilities to reach multiple destinations in the course of a single day and change itineraries in response to evolving situations are important drivers of business aviation growth. A 2001 study reported that access to such flexible regimes of aerial mobility improved organisational agility and enabled business aviation users to take advantage of new strategic opportunities, improved knowledge integration, and faster transaction speeds (Andersen 2001).

Speed

Paralleling the discourses of convenience and flexibility is that of speed. As early as the mid 1920s, the advantages of the speed of business aircraft were being strongly advocated and potential users tempted with the idea that time saved equals money saved (Bilstein 1984). Clearly any advantages that are associated with being able to access a wide range of airports at convenient times would be negated if competitors arrived there first and 'sealed the deal' while you were still travelling. For that reason, business aircraft manufacturers developed a range of jet-powered business aircraft that cruise at speeds that are comparable to (and in some cases exceed) those achieved by commercial aircraft. The Gulfstream G650, for example, can achieve a top speed of Mach .925 and is marketed as being the fastest civil aircraft in the sky (Gulfstream 2012). However, while much has been made of the 'need for speed' it could be argued that it is as much a cultural construct designed to sell aircraft as it is a commercial necessity. Certainly the contemporary marketing rhetoric that is used to sell business aircraft reinforces the idea that speed is good, powerful, and necessary and that the time that is saved by flying in a business aircraft is money well spent. 'Only the Citation X operates in that exclusive neighbourhood of Mach-calibre speed. Only in a X are you the first to every opportunity...' (Cessna 2008). 'If time is money, then the time saved [by travelling in a business jet] is money in the bank' (Gulfstream 2012).

Productivity

Part of the attraction of speed is that it allows people to cover greater distances in ever shorter periods of time. The Supersonic Concorde, which flew at twice the speed of sound and could cross the northern Atlantic Ocean in under three hours, was marketed as a 'time machine' that, thanks to the conventions of world timekeeping, allowed passengers to land in New York apparently before they had left London and therefore achieve more in a day. Business aviation operators similarly claim that the cumulative benefits of convenience, flexibility, and speed mean that people are more productive on business aircraft than they would have been on regular scheduled services or even in their own office.

Some of this improved productivity stems from the shorter turnaround times and reduced ground transport connections associated with business aviation, but the remainder is achieved during flight. An NBAA survey in 2010 reported that business aviation users spend 36 per cent of a flight in productive meetings with company employees compared with just 3 per cent on commercial airlines (NBAA 2010). Employees were also found to be significantly more likely to spend their time on individual work-related tasks or in discussions with potential clients or customers (NBAA 2010). There is also anecdotal evidence that employees feel inspired (or perhaps compelled) to work harder and improve their productivity to justify the expense and privileges that their bosses have afforded to them (Andersen 2001).

Comfort

In addition to providing new opportunities for productive work and enabling the creation of bespoke mobilities, another important factor promoting the desirability of business aviation is the higher level of comfort it affords to its users. While the economic liberalisation of global aviation markets is often considered to be a socio-economic success that has 'democratised' air travel and enabled more people to fly to more places more often, customer dissatisfaction is growing and, as Budd and Hubbard (2010) have shown, long queues, poor customer service, inadequate legroom, contradictory or confusing baggage restrictions, cancellations, delays, and boredom have become part of the lexicon of modern air travel. In comparison, business aviation operators claim that the stresses and unpleasantness that are often associated with commercial flying are almost absent when one flies on a business aircraft.

In recognition of the fact that many business aviation users use their aircraft as an extension of their boardroom, aircraft manufacturers have gone to considerable lengths to create 'offices in the sky' that are comfortable and thus conducive to productive work. The development of pressurised cabins mean that business jets can fly above the most turbulent weather and offer passengers a smoother ride. The cabin interior is often luxuriously appointed with sumptuous fabrics, furnishings, and fittings. Dedicated workspaces with ergonomically designed tables and seats are fitted as standard while other value-added customer preferences and amenities, including mood lighting, in-flight e-conferencing and telecommunications equipment, washrooms, galleys (stocked with luxury food and drink brands), and, in some of the larger aircraft, bedrooms, are provided. In order to lessen some of the undesirable physical sensations and bodily consequences of flight, the cabins of business aircraft are designed to be light and airy and are pressurised at relatively low altitudes to reduce the effects of fatigue and changes in atmospheric pressure.

Status

The sixth and final discourse of business aviation concerns that of status. There can be little argument that business aircraft, and bizjets in particular, are emblematic symbols of elite aeromobility. The aircraft, once purchased, are configured to reflect and expand the lifestyles of their users and are paraded as statements of wealth and social, political, or commercial status. Specialist publications such as *Business Jet Interiors International* magazine publish items on luxury aerial living and advise bizjet owners on the latest range of aircraft cabin fragrances, coffee-table books, tableware, hardwoods, fabrics, leathers, and interior design innovations to have entered the market. Already there is a considerable demand for 'value-added' customer preferences as owners and operators vie for the latest and most opulent interior fixtures and fittings that are designed by some of the world's leading luxury brands including Versace and BMW. In comparison with the opulence of the interior, the paint schemes that are applied to the exterior of the aircraft are often subtle and understated. It is rare for a company or an individual to paint their name or other recognisable symbol on the airframe. Indeed, anonymous cheatlines and restrained design marks appear to be the livery of choice for the majority of owners and operators. However, within the last couple of years a new, albeit rather discreet, way of visually differentiating business aircraft has emerged: the dedicated corporate aircraft register.

'Make mine a Manx' – new infrastructures of elite aeromobility

Many of the infrastructures of elite aeromobility, including dedicated business aircraft and business airports, while not always overt, are at least to be expected. A variety of business aircraft have been developed to serve the mobility needs of a range of private and commercial customers while dedicated business aviation airports have enabled business traffic to avoid the congestion and delays of major commercial airports and passenger terminals. These aircraft and airports are constructed, supported, and maintained by a network of aerospace companies, aircraft brokers, air chartering services, banks, private equity firms, and customer support teams which collectively work to ensure the efficient social and spatial segregation of business aviation. One of the most recent and interesting developments has been the establishment of a new type of infrastructure of elite aeromobility – the dedicated corporate aircraft register – and the extent to which the resulting 'clustering of affluence' is generating new types of segregation within an already elite sector.

On 1 May 2007, Europe's first dedicated corporate aircraft register was established. Based on the Isle of Man, a semi-autonomous island in the Irish Sea, the Manx aircraft register only accepts 'high quality' twin turbine helicopters and fixed-wing aircraft weighing more than 5,700 kg (smaller aircraft are accepted only if they belong to residents or businesses based on the Isle of Man). Crucially, and unlike other national aircraft registers, aircraft on the Manx register are not permitted to operate public transport flights (Isle of Man Government 2012), rendering it an exclusive register for the aeronautical elite.

According to the Isle of Man Government, the Manx register offers a number of key benefits including the island's stable legal and political environment, its high regulatory standards, its lack of insurance premium tax, and its taxation regime which collectively render it a low-risk investment proposition. The neutral registration prefix 'M-' is also considered an advantage as it not only 'depoliticises' the aircraft (although the decision by some Isle of Man residents to re-register their aircraft on it can be interpreted as being a political statement) but also enables aircraft owners to acquire personalised registration markings in the sequence M-xxxx. Current examples of these personalised registrations include 'M-AGIC', 'M-IDAS' 'M-YFLY', 'M-YJET', 'M-GULF' (on a Gulfstream jet) and 'M-LEAR' (on a Learjet).

Although it only became operational in May 2007, the Manx register has expanded quickly. By the spring of 2010, it was ranked 15th in the world in terms of the number of bizjets registered on it and by March 2012 there were 343 active registrations.

The majority of registrations are for business jets, and most are in the five- to twelve-seat range. There are also a number of larger aircraft including VIP versions of Airbus and Boeing aircraft, the largest of these currently being an A340, and helicopters. Some 28 per cent of registrations are for aircraft that belong to companies or individuals based in the Isle of Man. A further 20 per cent belong to companies or individuals resident in the British Virgin Islands, and 15 per cent, 8 per cent and 7 per cent to companies or individuals based in the UK, the Channel Islands and Bermuda respectively. The given address of other Manx-registered aircraft includes Gibraltar, The Commonwealth of Dominica, the Cayman Islands, Luxembourg, the Seychelles, Liechtenstein, Switzerland, and Belize.

With the exception of the Channel Islands, Gibraltar, and Liechtenstein, all the other countries in the list have their own national aircraft register. While there is no empirical evidence that explains why these owners chose to re-register their existing aircraft in the Isle of Man, it is not unreasonable to assume that a combination of factors, including considerations of tax, reputation, and status/prestige, may have played a part. At the time of writing, aircraft have been transferred onto the Manx register from over 30 countries, including the USA, Turkey, France, Bermuda, India, Canada, Austria, Mexico, Norway, and Ukraine, while a small number of aircraft formerly on the Manx register have been de-listed and re-registered abroad. Evidence of such transactions would appear to indicate that there is a global market in business aircraft registrations, and the fact that the Manx register is the fastest-growing corporate aircraft register in the world suggests that the acquisition of a Manx registration is considered an important statement of difference and prestige.

The challenge of researching elite aeromobilities

While the Isle of Man aircraft register provides an insight into the types of aircraft that are being flown and the individuals and companies who own them, the fact remains that it is far harder to obtain accurate and up-to-date empirical information on business aviation than it is about commercial aviation. This is no coincidence. Business aviation users choose to fly on private aircraft precisely because they do not want to share a flight with members of the public and they can afford to purchase the discretion and privacy that business aviation offers. The ad hoc nature of business aviation operations means that flight schedules are not published or publicised in advance (and so details of the origin, departure, and timings of services do not appear on websites or printed timetables) and commercial operators may have signed non-disclosure agreements with their clients which mean they are unable or unwilling to reveal information about their services to third parties. As a consequence, these discourses of secrecy, security and client confidentiality render the acquisition of data inherently challenging.

While it is possible to gain some insight into the spatialities of the global business aviation network by using proxy sources, such as national aircraft registers, directories of business aviation companies, and data from air traffic control organisations (where available), such sources often provide information only about individual aircraft or individual flightplans. Even potential new sources of flight information such as flight tracking websites and flight radar apps for smartphones and tablet computers can only offer information about where individual aircraft are at any given point in time. By their very nature such sources are unable to provide information about where individual aircraft are based, how often they are used, who uses them, the purposes for which they are used, and the views of people who use and service them. While there is an emerging body of non-academic literature that examines selected aspects of business aviation (for example its economic impact, on which see NEXA 2010), such reports are often produced by external consultants in response to a particular brief or by companies pursuing particular business or political agendas. As such, they rarely consider challenging questions surrounding the longer term social, economic and environmental sustainability of the sector. It is to these themes that the penultimate section of this chapter now turns.

Growing pains: the future of elite aeromobilities

If, as it has been argued, the business aviation sector is an important barometer of the health of the global economy then the period from 2007 onwards has been a tale of the 'have gots' versus the 'have lots'. On the one hand, the global financial crisis resulted in a dramatic downturn in demand for *particular types* of business aviation and a rapid contraction of the lower end of the market. Annual deliveries of small and medium-sized business jets fell from a high of 1,200 units in 2008 to 700 the following year and two manufacturers, Eclipse and Epic, who were engaged in designing a new generation of smaller 'very light jets' for owner-operators, ceased trading. As demand for fractional and ad hoc commercial business aviation operations fell, many providers of business aviation services were forced to dramatically downsize their operation, ground or sell their aircraft, and reduce the size of their workforce.

Globally, the biggest reductions in demand were seen in parts of Asia, the Caribbean, and the Middle East as companies were forced to reduce travel expenditure and 'trade down' to commercial airlines. In the United States and parts of Europe too, there was (albeit largely anecdotal) evidence of shareholders criticising the apparent profligacy of corporate flight at a time of falling interest rates and a volatile stock market. However, while certain sections within the business aviation market were affected by falling demand, demand for very high value products and services was seemingly unaffected. Indeed, growth in the 'VVIP' sector remained strong throughout and helped to offset demand reductions elsewhere. As a consequence, it would appear that the business aviation market is becoming increasingly polarised between the low and high ends of the sector. As the Isle of Man corporate aircraft register shows, new business aviation products and services are emerging that are furthering the internal fragmentation of an already elite sector.

While it appears that growth is returning to certain markets, the vexed question remains as to exactly how much further growth can be expected. If one subscribes to the argument that the market for business aviation in North America and parts of western Europe is nearing saturation, business aviation operators must look to new and emerging economies in South America and Asia where the potential for uptake may be significant. Considerable growth in business aviation activities has already been recorded in the 'BRIC' economies of Brazil, Russia, India, and China and, given the size of these countries' populations and economic aspirations, it is not unreasonable to assume that this growth will continue for the foreseeable future.

The current scale and likely future growth of the business aviation sector raises challenging questions about the sector's environmental sustainability. Commercial aviation contributes approximately 2 to 3 per cent of all anthropogenic carbon dioxide emissions but continued expansion combined with emissions reductions elsewhere has meant that aviation is rapidly becoming one of the fastest-growing sources of pollution. Flying on a private aircraft represents a particularly carbon-intensive form of mobility that, thanks to existing legislation, enjoys a largely favourable operating environment. Aircraft fuel is not taxed, and the taxes and charges that are levied on airline passengers are often avoided by private flyers by virtue of the fact that their aircraft are too small to trigger them, and business aircraft flying within Europe will not initially be included in the European Union's Emissions Trading Scheme, a cap and trade system that aims to make the polluter pay for their carbon emissions. This means that it may prove more cost-effective (if environmentally damaging) for a company to charter a private jet than pay for a group of employees to travel first or business class on a conventional airline. While various national governments and legislators have promised to address the environmental externalities of the business aviation sector, they appear wary of imposing additional taxes that may cause wealth-creators, entrepreneurs, and multinational corporations to move overseas to countries where environmental taxes are not imposed. There is a need, therefore, to quantify the environmental impact of business aviation operations at all stages of the service chain, from aircraft manufacture to disposal, and identify how best to improve the sector's environmental performance and help it adjust to an increasingly oil-scarce world.

Conclusion

Business aviation represents a small but high-value segment of the global air transport industry. It is used by wealthy individuals and corporations as an aid to the conduct of their business and, increasingly, as a lifestyle tool that enables users to engage in particular practices of leisure and consumption. The development of business aviation has been described as a reaction against the perceived inadequacies (spatial, temporal, and social) of conventional passenger aviation, but as the sector has evolved, access to private business aircraft has come to embody notions of personal and professional success. As significantly, in the context of this chapter, new discourses of convenience, flexibility, speed, comfort, productivity, and status have collectively (re)invented private flying as a necessity and promoted it as a rational (and often cost-effective) alternative to more conventional forms of aeromobility. This, in turn, has promoted the creation and maintenance of exclusionary spaces of automobile affluence and the existence of a 'hidden' set of supporting infrastructures of operators, airports, maintenance engineers, aerospace companies, specialist finance, and marketing regimes that operate in parallel with, but are distinct from, the more familiar routines of commercial flight.

As the business aviation sector moves into its second century, it is confronted by a range of challenges and opportunities. While many will undoubtedly be overcome through the application of advanced technology, new operating procedures, or updated legislation, all will require a greater understanding of human behaviour and a more nuanced appreciation of the motivations for, and alternatives to, elite aeromobility to be effective. This represents the continued challenged for mobilities research.

References

Adey, P. (2010) *Aerial Life: Spaces, Mobilities, Affects*, RGS/IBG Book Series, Chichester: Wiley-Blackwell.

Adey, P., Budd, L. C. S., and Hubbard, P. J. (2007) Flying lessons: the social and cultural geographies of global air travel, *Progress in Human Geography* 31(6): 773–791.

Andersen Associates (2001) *Business aviation in today's economy. A shareholder value perspective*, White Paper Series Number 4 (Spring), Andersen Associates.

Atkinson, R. (2006) Padding the bunker: Strategies of middle-class disaffiliation and colonisation in the city, *Urban Studies* 43: 819–832.

Atkinson, R. and Flint, J. (2004) Fortress UK? Gated communities, the spatial revolt of the elites and time-space trajectories of segregation, *Housing Studies* 19: 875–892.

Atkinson, R. and Blandy, S. (2009) A picture of the floating world: grounding the secessionary affluence of the residential cruise liner, *Antipode* 41(1): 92–110.

Beaverstock, J. V., Hubbard, P. J., and Short, J. R. (2004) Getting away with it? Exposing the geographies of the global super rich, *Geoforum* 35: 401–407.

Bilstein, R. E. (1984) *Flight in America. From the Wrights to the Astronauts*, Baltimore: Johns Hopkins University Press.

Budd, L. (2011) On being aeromobile: airline passengers and the affective experiences of flight, *Journal of Transport Geography* 19: 1010–1016.

Budd, L. and Graham, B. (2009) Unintended trajectories: liberalization and the geographies of private business flight, *Journal of Transport Geography* 17: 285–292.

Budd, L. and Hubbard, P. J. (2010) The 'bizjet set': business avaition and the social geographies of private flight, in Beaverstock, J. V., Derudder, B., Faulconbridge, J., and Witlox, F. (eds) *International Business Travel in the Global Economy*, Farnham: Ashgate.

Bushell, S. (2000) Business aviation, in Jarrett, J. (ed.) *Modern Air Transport: Worldwide Air Transport from 1945 to the Present*, London: Putnam.

Capgemini and Merrill Lynch. (2010) *World Wealth Report 2010*, Capgemini/Merrill Lynch. Retrieved from www.capgemini.com/resources/world-wealth-report-2010 on 10 May 2013.

Cessna (2008) Printed advertisement for the Cessna Citation X. Sourced from *Flight International*, various dates.

Cwerner, S. (2009) Helipads, heliports and urban space: governing the contested infrastructure of helicopter travel, in Cwerner, S., Kesselring, S., and Urry, J. (eds) *Aeromobilities*, London: Routledge.

Grob Aerospace. (2008) Printed advertisements for the sp^n business jet. Sourced from *Flight International*, various dates.

Gulfstream. (2012) Gulfstream corporate homepage. Retrieved from www.gulfstream.com on 26 March 2012.

IBAC (International Business Aviation Council) (2008). Corporate homepage: About us. Retrieved from www.ibac.com on 11 July 2008.

JetNet AvData Report (2011) Retrieved from www.jetnet.com/avdata.shtml on 26 March 2012.

Isle of Man Government. (2012) Isle of Man Aircraft Registry pages. Retrieved from www.gov.im/ded/aircraft 26 March 2012.

Marsh, D. (2006) *Getting to the point: business aviation in Europe*. Trends in Air Traffic, Volume 1. Brussels: Eurocontrol.

National Business Aviation Association. (2004) *NBAA Business Aviation Fact Book 2004*, Washington DC: NBAA.

National Business Aviation Association. (2010) *NBAA Business Aviation Fact Book 2010*, Washington DC: NBAA.

NetJets. (2010) *Our value proposition*. Retrieved from www.netjetseurope.com/wps/portal/njecust/netjets/wps/wcm/connect/netjetseu_en/netjets/welcome-to-netjets/our-value-proposition on 7 December 2010.

NEXA (2010) *Business Aviation. An Enterprise Value Perspective*, Washington DC: NEXA Advisers.

PricewaterhouseCoopers (2009) *The economic impact of business aviation in Europe*, London: PwC.

Sheehan, J. J. (2003) *Business and Corporate Aviation Management: On-demand Air Travel*, New York: McGraw-Hill Professional.

Chapter 6

Super-rich lifestyles

Mike Featherstone

> For high net worth individuals, luxury is not a lifestyle but a prerequisite.
> (The Luxury Brands Club, 2011)

Over the last twenty to 30 years a group of extremely wealthy people have come to prominence, first in the West and in the last decade globally, who have become widely known as the super-rich. This group has attracted some negative attention since the financial crisis of 2008 and subsequent global recession, as the increased levels of sovereign and individual debt and unemployment have lead some in the media to ask questions about the their wealth at a time of growing social inequalities. There has been some condemnation and questioning of their lack of responsibility ('the greedy rich') evident in their capacity to move their money around the world through a network of tax-favourable offshore companies and trusts, along with their apparent immunity from national taxation in numerous locations. There has been a build-up of media interest in the extent of their fortunes alongside the provision of more regular information and detailed metrics about the extent of their wealth, manifest in the growing number of billionaires' lists and wealth reports which are now widely available. Their lifestyles continue to fascinate and raise questions. 'What do the rich do?' 'Where do they live?' 'How do they spend their money?' Yet despite the raising of some critical voices, the super-rich lifestyles continue to be presented as the acme of success, the ideal ways for people to enjoy happiness and fulfilment. This chapter will examine the recent rise to prominence of this new cohort of the rich and super-rich and attempt to throw some light on their modus operandi, examining their lifestyles, living spaces, consumption activities, charitable pursuits, wealth maintenance and investment patterns.

The enterprising rich

In the West images of the rich and super-rich in the popular media have tended to swing between admiration for their entrepreneurial flair and hard work, and condemning their inactivity and idleness, as in the popular phrase 'the idle rich'. The image of the rich as active and successful entrepreneurs, who should be allowed to enjoy the fruits of their labours, resonates with the neoliberal emphasis on enterprise. Indeed, one feature of the rich and super-rich frequently lauded is that they are self-made and have not inherited family fortunes. The *2012 Fidelity Millionaire Outlook*, for example, suggests that 86 per cent of current US millionaires are self-made.[1] Another report by Forbes and Société Generale Private Banking entitled *Driving Global Wealth* (Forbes Insights 2011) used the Forbes database of billionaires to analyse the fortunes of ultra-high net worth individuals in twelve countries around the world in 2011.[2] It found that in the British sample, 80 per cent were entirely 'self-made', with the equivalent figure of rich in the United States being 68 per cent. In the BRIC countries (Brazil, China, India and Russia) the self-made make up more than 60 per cent of ultra-high net worth individuals (in Forbes's definition those with fortunes of over one billion US dollars – although the figure used for India and China is $500 million).

These figures may seem surprising, for a number of reasons which will be discussed below, but they reinforce the connection between super-rich self-made persons and the neoliberal emphasis upon the enterprising self. This connects to the earlier remark about neoliberalism seeking to foster the type of person who is 'an entrepreneur of himself'. Foucault (2008: 226) goes on to suggest that this means a person being for 'himself his own producer' and the source of his earnings. There are two ramifications here that Foucault considers which are interesting.

The first is to suggest that we should follow Gary Becker in exploring this mode of analysis not just in production but also in consumption and think of consumption as enterprise activity, in which the consumer should be seen as a producer, one whose activity is geared to producing her or his own satisfaction. The notion of enterprising consumption, the consumer as an active lifestyle innovator and investor in her or his self, has a good deal of potential for understanding the consumption of the rich and we will return to this shortly. Foucault's second point draws on the work of Gary Becker, Theodore Schultz and other theorists of human capital, to explore the argument that income is allocated on the basis of human capital, which is comprised of innate (hereditary, embodied) and acquired elements. The latter are formed over the lifespan and involve parental time spent in feeding, training and giving affection to their children as well as educational investments, professional training, health care and investments in mobility (the ability to migrate). Human capital investment, then, is seen as the key to growth, for the individual, but also for nation-states.[3]

Since the 1980s, with the take-up of neoliberal ideas in the West, the programme of investment in enterprise has grown markedly with terms such as 'the enterprise society', 'creatives', 'creative cities', 'cultural entrepreneurs', 'creative industries' and 'the creative class' being taken up by policy makers, politicians and others as part of a series of strategies designed to promote an expansion of the cultural sector, along with arts-led social regeneration and a closer relationship between business and the arts (Raunig *et al.* 2011; Gill and Pratt 2008).[4] The notion of creative innovation, enterprise and initiative has long been seen as central to business. Entrepreneurs such as Bill Gates, Alan Sugar, Steve Jobs, Richard Branson, Oprah Winfrey and Simon Cowell regularly have their careers dissected in attempts to discover the secret of their success. There are a great many popular books, television programmes and internet sites which focus on the qualities needed to succeed in business.[5] Indeed, neoliberal enterprise culture connects with many deep-seated beliefs in the middle and working classes, and the long history of 'how to do it' self-help literature.

According to the *Forbes* World Billionaires List, 65 per cent of the 1,625 global billionaires appear to meet the self-made category, with the other 35 per cent being those who inherited wealth (Sanandaji 2012). Particularly noticeable on the 2012 list are those people working in computing, information technology and the new media sector. Amounting to ten out of the world's top 100 billionaires, many of this set benefitted from the dot.com boom and accumulated massive wealth in a relatively short period of time. In addition a sizeable proportion made large fortunes at a very young age.[6] Another noticeable set on the Forbes list are the twelve people in the top 100 billionaires who have made their fortunes in the financial sector.[7]

These two sectors – new media/information technology and finance – became more interconnected with the digitalization of the global markets in the mid-eighties with a dramatic increase in trading and production of new financial instruments and types of product selling in the more deregulated neoliberal financial atmosphere of the 1990s. New financial intermediaries, especially in global financial centres such as London and New York, were encouraged to develop instruments which minimized risk and encouraged securitization through derivatives, credit default swaps, short selling and sub-prime mortgages, in which many traditional safeguards to banking leverage were sidestepped and the conditions for a new financial bubble effectively created (Mallaby 2010; Venn forthcoming). The downside outcome was the 2007/2008 financial crisis and global recession, which has seen a massive accumulation of banking and financial sector debt, which in many cases has been absorbed into sovereign debt, with resultant economic stagnation and a decline in living standards for the vast majority of the population. At a time of increasing austerity for many, public anger about the salary levels and bonuses of bankers and financial sector workers in particular, and senior executives in general, has mounted.[8]

Although there have been attempts to reregulate the sector, much of the financial apparatus is still intact and while returns from the global stock markets have fallen, there are still many opportunities for profitable investment. In addition the offshore financial apparatus continues to provide a wide range of opportunities for systematic tax avoidance. This has been the case in Britain and the United States: London in particular, now the world's leading financial centre, has a long history of providing a range of offshore financial services to people around the world through trusts, tax havens and other shadowy strategies to reduce tax bills for companies and rich individuals (Shaxson 2011).[9] When coupled with the increased volume and speed of trading through ubiquitous digital network technologies, this maze of trusts, companies and financial instruments makes it easy to draw down profits, shares and collateral in the most favourable tax economical global sites. Hence 'going offshore' doesn't entail physical movement from the office or hotel room around the world; it just means contacting financial advisers who will select and deliver the best investment vehicles and tax efficiency; in addition, the returns offered on investments and tax savings increase exponentially with the volume of money at stake. Hedge funds are a good example here, being a widespread form of investment for the rich and super-rich given their high rate of return. Leading funds have given profits to investors of over 40 per cent, even in the bad year of 2011. They currently exclude most ordinary people through their initial capital requirements, level of risk and stringent vetting process.[10] With reference to the salaries accumulated by managers, in 2011 Raymond Dalio, the founder of Bridgewater Associates, the world's biggest hedge fund, made an estimated $3 billion, as his funds produced net returns in the 20 per cent range.

The salaries of top business executives pale in comparison with the hedge fund managers, but can hardly be described as modest. The top of the Forbes List of America's Highest Paid Executives for 2011 was John Hammergren of McKesson, who earned $131 million in total pay, including stock options, salary and bonus. Second was Ralph Lauren of Ralph Lauren, with $67 million, and third was Michael D. Fascitelli of Vornado Realty with $64 million. In 2011 the chief executives of the 500 biggest companies in the United States gained a pay raise of 16 per cent, which brought the average salary up to $10.5 million (De Carlo 2012).[11] When compared to the 1950s, the financial sector and CEO salaries paid today seem enormous and the amount of tax paid on them miniscule.

The income increases at the upper levels are reflected in the growth of income inequalities since the 1980s; this is especially evident in

English-speaking countries along with India and China, but not in continental European countries or Japan (Atkinson *et al.* 2011; Saez 2012. In the 1970s the wealthiest 1 per cent of Americans took home 9 per cent of the national income; now it is near 24 per cent and is the highest level since 1928. In terms of tax paid in the United States in the 1950s the top rate of income tax was over 90 per cent; now it is 35 per cent. In Britain the rate peaked at 83 per cent in the 1970s and is now 40 per cent. In Britain too, the 550 or so people earning more than £1 million a year pay a lower average rate of tax than those with an annual income of £200,000, and 33 of these paid a tax rate of less than 10 per cent (Alkan 2012).[12] This trend since the 1980s of lower taxes for the rich has been combined with the driving down of middle and lower incomes in the West, as corporations have taken advantage of cheaper labour and friendly taxation regimes abroad through globalization to relocate production anywhere around the world (Reich 1991). This has helped to hold down working-class and lower-end wage levels in the West, a trend which is now eroding the middle classes, while upper-class incomes continue to rise (Freeland 2011b).[13]

The upper classes in English-speaking countries (in particular the United States, United Kingdom, Canada and Australia) have not only gained massively in terms of income levels, at the same time they have possessed the financial and knowledge resources to fully exploit the financial apparatus. Hedge fund managers can obtain their massive salaries because they have clients who are happy to invest and gain annual returns of up to 65 per cent on their capital. They are one element in a financial services apparatus for wealth management, which has been established to cater for the rich and super-rich. Financial services entrepreneurs do not just offer steady returns on investments, but pay large salaries to attract the brightest graduates globally to work in 'tax boutiques' to research and develop new financial instruments and tax solutions. The potential rate of return, then, on investments and tax-economical solutions are stacked in favour of the highest levels within the rich whose fortunes therefore continue to grow rapidly and widen the gap between the extremely wealthy and the rest. The super-rich, then, are leaving the rich behind, with a disproportionate rise in the assets of ultra-high net worth individuals (UHNWIs – those with over $30 million in investible assets), as compared to high net worth individuals (HNWIs – people having investible assets of over US$1 million) (World Wealth Report 2011, 2012; Beaverstock 2010).[14] Yet there is a further massive gap between the UHNWIs and the billionaires who are the genuine super-rich (see also Beaverstock *et al.* 2004). It is the latter two groups – the UHNWIs and the billionaires – who are the most visible: the people who appear in the various rich lists.

A notable recent trend is the expansion of numbers of billionaires outside the West, which has seen the United States joined by Russia and

China, who also now have more than 100 billionaires each (Forbes Insights and Société Générale study referred to in Vellacott 2011). The average age of China's 115 billionaires and Russia's 101 is, respectively, 50 and 49. This makes them over a decade younger than the next youngest cohort, from India, and a quarter-century younger than the oldest cohort, from France. (The average age of US billionaires is 66.) Many of this new group of Chinese and Russian billionaires are self-made.

Despite the global recession, HNWIs are now clearly a global phenomenon, with the 2012 *World Wealth Report* stating that the global population of millionaires is now eleven million, with assets of $42 trillion. The Asia-Pacific region has 3.37 million men and women with more than $1 million in investible assets, overtaking the 3.35 million in North America for the first time in 2011. A study of Chinese high net worth individuals by China Merchants Bank and Bain & Company in 2011 remarks that that the majority were entrepreneurs with at least 100 million Yuan (around $15.3 million) to invest (China Merchants Bank and Bain & Company 2011). At the end of 2010, the near 500,000 high net worth individuals, including more than 20,000 ultra-high net worth individuals, held about 15 trillion Yuan available to invest. The survey also suggests that around 60 per cent of this group have emigrated or are seriously thinking of doing so. The tendency to want to emigrate is highest among China's wealthiest; 27 per cent of those entrepreneurs with a net worth of $15 million or more have already completed the formalities required to emigrate through investment schemes in countries like the United States, or cities such as Hong Kong. Many rich Chinese generally prefer to move to countries such as the United States, Canada and Australia. High taxes were cited as a reason for leaving China (Chen 2011).[15]

There is now an increasing amount of data available for the study of the global rich and super-rich, but analysis is only in its preliminary stage. The current phase of financial deregulation and globalization over the last 30 years has opened up major changes in how and where the rich make and invest their wealth. There are important long-term trends which need to be investigated. The twentieth century saw major changes in the composition of the rich and wealthy, with the decline of the aristocracy and those relying on rent as their main source of income. The effects of two world wars and the economic depression of the 1930s along with progressive income and estate taxation in the United States and other countries provided major impediments for the accumulation and preservation of large fortunes. At the same time, while the rich have recovered a good deal of ground since the 1960s it is notable that the working rich have replaced the rentiers at the top of the income distribution table (Saez and Piketty 2007).[16]

It is also clear that the working rich are now in a better position to make their wealth work for them than ever before, given the mobility of capital and sophistication of wealth management through the network of offshore finance. The fact that the numbers of millionaires in the Asia-Pacific region eclipsed those in North America for the first time in 2011, and China has had a 15 per cent increase in the number of millionaires with more than $1 million in assets at a time when North America has experienced a 1 per cent negative growth in private wealth, points to a larger trend and shift in the global balance of economic power (New 2012).[17] We are witnessing only the latest in a series of shifts and counter-shifts, which has pushed the manufacture of consumer goods to East Asia, consequently increasing the numbers of rich and super-rich. Also to be noted is the predicted rising growth trajectory of not just Asian countries, and Latin American ones such as Brazil and Mexico, but also the rise of African countries, especially Nigeria and Egypt. At the same time the ongoing shift in global economic power still has a considerable way to go with emerging markets still accounting for only 27 per cent of the world's private wealth of $122.8 trillion in 2011, with North America, Western Europe and Japan still controlling nearly three-quarters of the world's wealth according to a recent Boston Consultancy Group study (New 2012).

Lifestyles of the rich and super-rich

There has long been a fascination with the lifestyles of the rich and super-rich. In our consumer culture being rich is invariably presented as a worthy high-status goal for all as it opens up the possibility of purchasing a wide range of goods and exciting, fulfilling experiences which are linked to the positive qualities of youth, beauty, romance, exotica, status, novelty and empowerment. The greater the wealth, the greater the potential for active lifestyle construction, for sampling the full range of luxuries and pleasures offering the transformation of body, self and social relationships in a range of exciting and exotic settings around the world. In the media, internet and mediatized urban landscape, there are constant flows of images of beautiful people enjoying exclusive luxury goods. The media fascination with the lives of the super-rich, then, is hardly surprising. In the United States a television series *Lifestyles of the Rich and Famous* ran from 1984 to 1995.[18] It profiled wealthy people, celebrities, entertainers, businessmen and sports personalities, featuring their opulent residences and glamorous lifestyles. The programme examined the lives of a different 'rich and famous' person each week, giving special attention to the luxuries such as homes and cars (emphasizing the price paid along with special features such as helipads, basement tennis courts, swimming pools, chandeliers and gold-plated bathroom fittings) purchased by those who could afford 'the best of everything'. Viewers were encouraged by the presenters to stimulate their 'champagne wishes and caviar dreams'.

What is interesting about the current phase of the global economy in the wake of the 2008 economic crisis, with hopes of recovery dented by the sovereign debt crisis, is that the consumption of the super-rich and the rich has continued practically unabated. Of course not all wealthy people are actively seeking consumer lifestyles. There are a myriad of opportunities for consumption open to the wealthy given that they are both information and resource rich and able to potentially sample the full range of pleasures, luxuries and experiences available, and seek them out, or have them summoned to them, from whatever distant parts of the world in which they may reside.[19] At the same time they are under no obligation to engage in intensive consumption and some prominent figures have more of a 'workstyle' than a lifestyle, or at best engage in limited or austere consumption.

Yet for the vast majority of people the ready availability of credit, in the recent phase from the 1980s to the sub-prime mortgage crisis of 2007, has stimulated the purchase of houses, cars, vacations and a wide range of consumer goods. Consumer culture has encouraged people to not just aspire and dream about lifestyles and consumption experiences previously limited to the wealthy, but to sample scaled-down versions themselves. Consumer culture not only provides images of the good life, the home with sumptuous fittings inhabited by stylish well-dressed people with well-honed healthy bodies, it provides an endless series of narratives and how-to-do-it advice and commentary (Featherstone 2007, 2010b). Yet for many of the wealthy credit does not enter into the equation, indeed the opposite in some cases can be said to operate: not living beyond their means, but living below their means.[20]

When we think of lifestyles, there can be a tendency to be forced into an active/passive dichotomy with consumer culture lifestyles presented as passive, with consumers manipulated to follow the images of consumption available in the mass media and advertising. In contrast, consumption in artistic, bohemian and counter-cultural groups has often been seen as circumscribed and subordinated to the active construction of lifestyle. This is not just an emphasis on active or productive consumption, on reworking the meaning of consumer goods and objects, but a more general disregard for and even opposition to much of the paraphernalia of consumer culture. Rather, the emphasis should not be just on the 'style' element in life*style*, but more on the energies that go into becoming an artist of life: the artist who is *in* life; the artist who doesn't paint, yet who actively fashions life.[21] The emphasis on experiment and invention is also central to Michel Foucault's (1991) discussion of the cultural dimension of modernism, where he approvingly cites Baudelaire's notion of the modern person as 'the man who invents himself'. The active cultivation of social relations and an ethics of the self is also something which some see as a feature of Foucault's own life orientation and experiences (Rabinow 2009; Revel 2009; Brigstock 2013). A number of points can be made at this juncture.

First, lifestyle can take us beyond consumer culture through the emphasis upon active consumption and stylistic assemblage. Consumer goods may be a part of this, but mass-produced and marketed goods lack the necessary individuality which advertising promises, even though differentiated short-batch production is now more common. This suggests that lifestyle cultivation becomes increasingly important within capitalism which, as Foucault (2008: 115) reminds us, should not be regarded as a 'one-dimensional mass society' with its striving towards standardization and normalization. Rather consumer culture encourages active consumption along with a more general sense of enterprise: the investment in lifestyle infrastructure, the planning, buying and selling and self-formation processes on the part of people who are entrepreneurs of themselves. In this sense what some would depict as the oppositional gap between bohemias, youth cultures and counter culture becomes minimalized, as the good consumer also becomes an active lifestyle constructor with the emphasis on invention and innovation. This is the other side of Schumpeter's (1976) emphasis on innovation in which the artist and businessmen share similar forms and means of orientation as part of their modus operandi, even though they handle very different contents.[22] There are, of course, expanding numbers of cultural, lifestyle and financial intermediaries, who as we will see below are eager to offer advice, training and customised packages for the *nouveau* riche (see Featherstone 2007, forthcoming).

Under neoliberalism competition, the market and enterprise not only become generalized and applicable throughout the work world, where everyone has to think like an entrepreneur, but also penetrate into family life, leisure and consumption where the same active calculus, incentivization and securitization are increasingly deemed appropriate modes of orientation. Everyone's life course should be conceived as a journey in which innovation, invention and the will to succeed should be appropriately rewarded. The corollary is that the wealthy should, therefore, be celebrated as the most successful competitors who are able to enjoy not only work success, but also have the potential for the most productive and fullest lifestyle cultivation, exploration and switching.

Second, for the rich, wealth is manifest in property, evident in the satisfactions and social status that relate to the mastery of things.[23] Consumer culture does not just offer an endless series of images but also things; objects which can be purchased, gazed at, used and accumulated. It is this appetite for the appropriation and possession of things which points to the capacity for exclusive enjoyment (others can be legally excluded from the process by security personnel and surveillance systems). Some things may well be objects already endowed with prestige, as with luxury objects, works of art and architecturally designed locations, which may be sought out because they already have a certain memorableness and are assumed to be useful as resources for the construction of ambient memories. At the same time, things may well be discarded and replaced by new sets whose particular assemblage holds out the promise of new memorable experiences. Or they may be just sold and not replaced, but transformed into money, collateral and other transitory immaterial forms. From this perspective all property becomes a propensity, a potential whose value can be readily calculated and realised through the financial apparatus and services. The increasing double life of things which are in principle calculable and increasingly seen as transitory investments is central to a money economy with a high degree of liquidity as noted and discussed at length by Simmel (2004).

It is therefore hardly surprising to see the expansion of the luxury market over the last twenty years, which has sought to extend the range of luxuries on offer through a 'trickle down' effect to the middle classes as part of a more general 'democratization of luxury' and development of 'mass luxuries' within consumer culture (Featherstone 2010a; forthcoming).[24] At the same time, the opposite tendency needs to be noted: the swing towards greater distinction with new ranges of 'super-luxuries', even more exclusive brands and products aimed not just at the rich, but at the super-rich.[25] It is noticeable that the luxury market in general, and the upper-end luxury market in particular, has been highly resilient since the global recession of 2008, with the overall market for luxury goods expected to have grown by 14.5 per cent in 2012, according to the Boston Consulting Group (Bellaiche *et al.* 2012).[26]

In recent years many people in the luxury business have been casting an eye on China, given that the number of Asia-Pacific millionaires surpassed that of North America for the first time in 2012. China possesses 271 billionaires along with 1.02 million dollar millionaires, and the greater purchasing power of these groups is evident in the way in which *HuRun*'s luxury price index has outpaced the consumer price index by 38 per cent over the past six years (Zeveloff 2012).[27] While it has often been commented on that in the recent phase of luxury purchasing in China, high-status brands have been central, with a typical nouveau riche concern for conspicuous consumption manifest in the display of high-value labels, it is also the case that over time wealthy people move on to different forms of luxury consumption. One prominent recent example of Chinese conspicuous consumption was the publicity stunt of a Nanjing jeweller who had a sports car gold plated and driven around the city (*Daily Mail* 2011).[28]

There are a range of up-market magazines[29] which cater for specialist consumer tastes and lifestyle aspirations of the super-rich. They regular feature top-end luxury items, such as customized mobile office/mobile mansion jumbo jets, super-yachts and high-performance cars.[30] The accumulation of specially designed status symbols which go beyond the world of branded goods has proved to be especially attractive for the nouveau riche and nouveau super-riche. This has been accompanied by an expansion in luxury concierge and high-end travel services which offer exclusive customised 'lifestyle managers,' along with 'once in a lifetime' experiences, be they vacations, getaway breaks or bespoke treats, which according to one survey now account for more than half of the luxury goods and services total spend (Wood 2012).[31] The top-end luxury market continues to be significant in its own right, with a report by Moody's Analytics indicating that the top 5 per cent of the richest households in the United States actually account for 37 per cent of all consumer spending (Sen 2012).[32] But as the title of a recent article indicates, 'The Real Wealth Gap' occurs between the super-rich and the rich, with the wealth differential between the top 0.01 per cent and the top 1 percent rising the most steeply (Frank 2012).

The possession of cars, jets and yachts offers the prospect of ultra-mobility, pleasurable and comfortable means of travel, leisure and escape, as people move between global cities and exclusive resorts. They are means to move between the spaces of face-to-face encounters where deals are done, relationships cemented and networks enlarged, the spaces of spectacular architecture and luxury building developments such as Dubai, Qatar, Singapore, New York, London, Shanghai and Hong Kong, which themselves also throw up new opportunities for investment. The spaces in which the super-rich are always welcome and are greeted as cosmopolitan global citizens.[33]

Properties of wealth: spaces for the super-rich

One area that doesn't feature in most taxonomies, but is central to the notion of luxury lifestyles, is property. There are a plethora of magazines and websites with titles such as *Luxury Property, Christie's International Real Estate* and *PropGOLuxury.com*. The last-named has a regular feature on the 'Top World's Most Expensive Homes,' which it takes from the US magazine *Forbes* with 'The Manor' Beverly Hills currently the number one real estate property for sale at $150 million.[34] Another major source of information on the wealthy property market is *The Wealth Report 2012* from Knight Frank which has a section on Prime Luxury Property. The report states that while the prime residential market covers the top 1 or 2 per cent of the world's homes, within this group is an elite super-prime category of the world's wealthiest individuals. It remarks that if we wish to focus on the so-called 'centa-millionaires' – people with assets of $100 million and above which includes the billionaires[35] – then we need to consider locations which have a regular number of over $20 million transactions a year which will attract foreign buyers.

This 'super-prime' market includes, in Europe, London, Paris, the Côte d'Azur, Monaco, the French and Swiss Alps and Geneva. In the Americas there are New York, Miami and Los Angeles, with São Paulo now on the list (although as yet struggling to attract foreign purchasers). The rest of the world includes Hong Kong, Singapore, Moscow and, in the Caribbean, the Bahamas, Mustique, Barbados and the British Virgin Islands. The report suggests that for the super-rich it is not just a question of first or second homes, but also the investment potential of having an 'opportunity' portfolio which can mean advantages from investment in new markets and currency switching. For those for whom price is no restriction, such as the billionaires, there can always be the search for the perfect home or 'trophy apartment', coupled with the willingness to wait until one becomes available. This opens up a space for top-level real estate intermediaries, who seek to induce owners of exclusive properties that never come on the market in the $30 million plus range, to make a deal (Barrionuevo 2012).

London is top of Knight Frank's *Wealth Report* annual ranking of urban centres, having long attracted capital flight from all around the world as the home of offshore investments with its range of tax and business advantages for the wealthy; a role which continues unabated and is now further boosted through attracting capital from Eurozone sovereign debt crisis countries. London, then, has a long history as a property investment market for the wealthy, but in the last decade or so it has become the home of a new range of luxury developments. Some have involved the refurbishment of traditional upper-class areas such as Mayfair. One recent example here is the Grosvenor Holdings redevelopment of Mount Street. A project which purports to provide a 'glamorous, but villagey atmosphere' which seeks to go beyond 'mainstream luxury' by replacing the former carpet and antique dealers with a series of exclusive upper-end fashion and accessories shops, restaurants and clubs and careful re-design to provide a traditional pedestrianized street feel, in an exclusive but ungated urban area which is highly attractive to the wealthy (Sanai 2010). Another project in the construction of luxury living for the 'über-rich' is One Hyde Park in Knightsbridge, which allows residents access to hotel and concierge facilities at the five-star Mandarin Oriental hotel next door (Neate 2011).[36] London's position as the leading city for the super-rich has been reinforced by the completion of the 310-metre Shard which dominates the skyline of London's South Bank. Its larger apartments on the upper floors sell for around £30 million each, and it marks a trend in the development of new urban towers in which the wealthy can live in a high degree of security.[37]

Investing passion

Art, wine and sport are often referred to as investments of passion in terms of their unusual combination of luxury pleasure coupled with investment potential. In this they open up a dimension beyond disposable consumer goods and can offer the individuality and emotional investment which mass consumption always sought to provide, but rarely realized. The term consumption here, then, suggests *active* consumption in line with our earlier discussion, with the emphasis on broader enterprise and caring for, and in some cases direct involvement in, production. In the case of sport, this may typically entail spectatorship, but the type of spectatorship is far from the alleged passive or distracted television viewer.

Financial investment, then, in the case of art, wine and sport may not be primarily about the bottom line and level of profitability, but brings with it certain responsibilities which relate to owning rare things, things which other people feel they also have an important emotional stake in. In this sense, while it entails the purchase, ownership and the possession of property, the fame the entity has accumulated brings with it expectations of public responsibility in terms of care and preservation. To some extent this involves an inversion of our usual definition of property, given the wider emotional investment of the many people who know about its qualities and who may feel familiarity and quasi-ownership, guardianship and proxy responsibility for its fate, despite being legally defined as non-owners.

There are a wide range of emotional investment possibilities, from the transitory deal to make money from a quick resale, to the life-long pursuit of a particular work of art or ownership of a prestigious vineyard or sports club, to the interest in a more general education of taste, acquisition of cultural capital and understanding of the many dimensions of the field within which the particular object or entity lies. This can involve collecting and learning to be a connoisseur, as is often the case with art and wine. Similarly, becoming an expert and exercising judgement also applies in the purchase of a promising racehorse or footballer, who then needs to be developed, paraded and trained to succeed under one's colours. Yet, there is always the expectation of passion and potential struggles with fate, destiny and eventfulness as is evident in our use of the qualifier 'lover': the art lover, the wine lover, the sports lover.

In the case of sport, a prominent example is the English Premier League which has many football teams owned by overseas billionaires and wealthy people, with one of the most successful being Roman Abramovich, the Russian oligarch owner of London's Chelsea FC. Here involvement is not just running the club as a business, but also entails risking the wrath of fans over investments in new players, or the appointment of a poor manager. It means participation in the team and collective fan ethos, with its intense emotional charge: sharing in the dressing room atmosphere and the euphoria of winning competitions; feeling to be almost one of the players and enjoying the strong social bonding; enduring the despair of failures. This involves participating in the sphere of risk and fate, where people risk their bodies and in some instances their lives, gambling near the limits of their talent and endurance.

Given the globalization of sport, the lucrative television rights and advertising deals for successful teams in prominent leagues also mean potential high returns too – or losses as was the case with the North American investors in Liverpool FC. Sport involves the generation of intensities which can become eventful and memorable. Sport has regularly been noted for its capacity to produce a different sense of time in participants and spectators – the intensely focused time, the absorption of 'flow' or 'edgework', which contrasts with the time of everyday routines with their distractions and interruptions; the sealed-in time of the adventure and the heroic life; a world in which a different register of emotional involvement is anticipated and eagerly expected (Featherstone 1995; Csikszentmihalyi 2008; Csikszentmihalyi and Halton 1980; Lyng 2004).

The pursuit of fine wines and art takes the wealthy into different areas. The football fan can experience the intensity of watching his or her team succeed and also become knowledgeable about the history of the club and develop an interest in classifications, records and statistics on which to hang memories. But the level of direct involvement may differ from a player and owner of the club. With wine and art there can be similar graded distinctions. It is different owning one's own vineyard and producing a *premier cru* Bordeaux, or owning a Picasso and gazing at it every day, than reading about it or seeing magazine reproductions. With wealth comes the potential for direct experience and not only deepening the knowledge of a particular example, but also direct encounters with experts and connoisseurs, who can teach the initiate how to appreciate fine things and develop knowledge of the framework within which the particular item resides. In short, connoisseurship involves not only learning how to taste, educating the palate or nose (cf. Latour 2004, on learning how to smell perfume), but also opens up the joys of classification, of weighing up the value of a particular thing against a range of standards and frames. To live amidst fine things, in the company of people who give fine performances and make fine judgements, involves demanding and potentially exciting development and the education of taste and the senses (Featherstone 2010a). Yet the learning process, the *Bildungsprozess*, can be absorbing not just because of its step-by-step accretion, but also because it opens up the possibility of being captured or captivated by things. People who buy Picassos speak of falling in love with a particular painting and it being a life-changing event. Such are the passions of collecting and connoisseurship; and the wealthy have always been in a position to participate or become a player in this world.

At the same time there is also the additional potential financial benefit of having made a wise choice and seeing value grow and being able to realise one's investment. According to *The Wealth Report 2012*, art, wine and sport, so-called 'investments of passion', are currently enjoying a growing popularity among investors and experienced a sharp rise in demand in 2011 (Shirley 2012). Likewise fine wine investments have performed well since the recession as a hedge against stock market volatility and risk, as well as being bolstered by increasing demand from the Asia-Pacific region. There is even now a passion investing website, www.passion-investments.org, which operates out of Geneva Switzerland. The site tells us that

> Passion Investments guarantees its clients a return on their investment, whether it is a financial return, a return in terms of enhanced reputation, privileges, special access to information, places, exceptional people or a return from participating in the project.... Your seat at the Cannes film festival, your exhibition room in a museum in Rome, your vineyard in Bordeaux, your room in a chateau in the Loire Valley, your research institute in Munich, the artist that you patronize personally in Moscow, your golf course in Tuscany, etc., thanks to your Passion Investments. But pleasure and pride do not mean a lack of financial benefits: most Passion Investments provide for investors to share in the financial success of projects, together with tax breaks for investors.
>
> (cited in Kime 2010)

Another site, www.emotionalassets.com, seeks to further merge the worlds of collecting and investing. Emotional assets are defined as art, photography, contemporary design, antique carpets, vintage watches, vintage jewellery, ceramics, musical instruments, architecture, rare coins, rare stamps, maps and atlases, rare manuscripts and rare antiquities. There is also a Fine Art Fund. One of the conundrums this new sphere of interest opens up is time economy; as Matt Woolsey (2007) remarks in *Forbes*, 'It's not always easy being rich. For the jet set, scheduling, disclosure of finances and setting time tables for buying everything from houses to Gulfstream V's can be difficult' (cf. the discussion of the 'harried leisure class' in Linder 1970; Featherstone 2007).

There has always been a close relationship between the wealthy and art which goes back at least as far as the commissioning of art works in the Renaissance. In the late nineteenth century Henry Tate, who made his fortune through sugar, built museums to house his collection of Victorian art, and John D. Rockefeller's family helped found The Museum of Modern Art (MOMA) in New York in the 1920s. Concomitantly, with the recent shift of the global economy towards Asia and with it the substantial rise in the numbers of billionaires and millionaires, there is a new interest in art museums. China's best-known art collectors, Wang Wei and her husband have spent nearly two billion Yuan ($317 million) on art in the past two years, according to a report in the state-run *China Daily* cited in an article by Kelvin Chan (2012). Wang's 'Long' museum, which opened in Shanghai in December 2012, will cost $1.6 million a year to run. The museum not only gives her the space to show off her collection of Chinese revolutionary and contemporary art, but also enables her to provide nouveau riche compatriots with a cultural education. 'The rich housewives have money but do not know how to spend it without shopping,' Wang remarked, adding 'I want to teach them to be more tasteful' (Chan 2012).[38]

Lifestyle and the centrality of work

While the popular media are replete with images which present the super-rich and celebrities enjoying leisure lifestyles, rarely do we see them at work, unless it is an image which reinforces the charisma of the powerful: marching through the architect-designer spacious lobby of a financial institution or corporate headquarters to attend meetings, or stepping out of a limousine, jet or helicopter. Yet, as mentioned above, the leisure images tend to conflict with the centrality of work and entrepreneurship for of many of the wealthy. In line with the classic description of the entrepreneur in Max Weber's *The Protestant Ethic and the Spirit of Capitalism* (2008), the work habitus can carry over into the rest of life, as the virtues of economising, work discipline and frugality become ingrained dispositions. This notion is reinforced by an article by Angie Mohr on *Investopedia.com* entitled 'The Everyday Life of Frugal Billionaires' in which we are given details of the frugal lifestyles of Warren, Buffet, Mark Zuckerberg, Carlos Slim Helu and John Caudwell (Mohr 2012; see also Hawkins 2007). In addition, it is clear that some of the younger generation of super-rich, do not consider the projection of a powerful image and maintenance of a glamorous lifestyle to be importance.[39]

For many of the super-rich, workstyle and lifestyle can be separated, merged and re-assembled to suit the dictates of the day, or their own particular desires or whims. Today's digital systems mean that communications can be carried out instantly from anywhere in the world and the office brought to you. The latest and most extensive market data as well as information about new business possibilities, along with the speed of jet and helicopter travel, facilitate quickly arranged face-to-face meetings around the world, to offer new major forms of logistic empowerment. In a hyper-mobile world of rapid transportation and speeded-up digital communications, the capacity to purchase the latest technologies offers an important advantage for the new 'globals' who enjoy 'miniaturized mobilities' (smartphones, digital devices) which extend the 'globalization of mobility to the core of the self' (Elliott and Urry 2010; see also Sheller and Urry 2006; Urry 2010b).

This extreme capacity for mobility is linked closely to a massive capacity for choice to the super-rich. Some millionaires, of course, may need to stay close to their original network of business contacts and the culture in which they succeeded. Yet at a certain point on the wealth scale this type of concern may become irrelevant. According to James Meek (2006), 'When you're a billionaire, you don't live anywhere, and neither does your money. Or rather you live everywhere, and so does your money.' The capacity for mobility, then, has led to some interesting migration patterns for the super-rich.[40]

This is the context of the emergence of an elite group of 'stateless super-rich', who can choose to lead more nomadic season-driven or impulse driven lives. Powley and Warwick-Ching (2012), who advance this thesis, cite Jeremy Davidson, a London property consultant who deals in properties that cost £10 million or more in the most sought-after areas of London:

> The more money you have, the more *rootless* you become because everything is possible. I have clients who wake up in the morning and say, 'Let's go to Venice for lunch.' If you've got that sort of money the world becomes a very small place. They tend to have a diminished sense of place, of where their roots are.

This has led to the super-rich not only buying properties in global cities such as London, Paris or New York and an extra holiday home, but additionally investing in portfolios of super-prime properties, to the extent that according to Knight Frank in London 95 per cent of super-prime property now goes to international buyers, whose mobility and high proportion of second, third or fourth homes means that many are left vacant for significant periods of the year. As Powley and Warwick-Ching (2012) put it, 'These individuals will spend a few months in St Moritz, before moving to their trophy mansion in London, and then on to their luxury villa in Sardinia for the summer months.' This annual rhythm suggests that when in residence the super-rich often fail to participate in local life and often live in isolation.[41]

Such a lifestyle, with its high level of mobility and mixture of regular and spontaneous migrations, can take a good deal of planning and organizing. It is for this reason the super-rich employ personal assistants or a personal or family office to handle their itinerary and movements. There are a growing number of concierge and special services companies who can be relied on to provide all the arrangements. London in particular has seen an unprecedented upsurge and clients typically pay a retainer of around £5,000 a month, for which they expect 24-hour service, but need to meet all other costs. Given the influx of international super-rich, there is a growing demand for this type of gatekeepers or cultural intermediaries. Alastair Gill, the manager of Mayfair Concierge, remarks that

> What they share is a desire for certain aspects of British life – private education, hunting and fishing – as well as everything they might expect from a playboy's paradise, such as reservations at restaurants and nightclubs, and sometimes even drugs and prostitutes. But going to the right shoot, ensuring your child jumps the school waiting list or getting a seat at a restaurant that is fully booked for the next year require skills and contacts beyond most of us.
>
> (quoted in Urquhart 2012)

For Gill the typical concierge is someone who has worked in five or six-star hotels and 'loves people and is well-balanced, understands what people want and is unshockable' (Urquhart 2012). Another company recounts how it was requested to organize a two-hour shopping spree with an unlimited budget for a client and her two friends in the style of the film *Pretty Woman* and rapidly managed to obtain the co-operation of managers and assistants at over a dozen stores, including Louis Vuitton, Christian Dior, Hermès, Chanel and Yves St Laurent. The spree resulted in the purchase of £250,000 worth of shoes, clothes and accessories (Urquhart 2012).

In some cases the responsibilities for concierge and specialist services will be subsumed into a personal family office, or Single Family Office (known as an SFO), which can also contain a set of financial specialists to handle investments (Amit *et al.* 2008).[42] The family office, then, can also contain a full-time team of financial experts, accountants and lawyers who have the sole aim of protecting and enhancing the family wealth. The long-term planning evident here and the focus on the family as the key unit is interesting at the current juncture with family trusts representing an attractive option as they curtail potential individual irresponsibility and enable families to plan two or three generations into the future to conserve the wealth for the long-term benefit of the proto-dynasty. For some of the super-rich, then, the prime attachment is to their own family, something which suggests they have moved to becoming a 'citizen of their own family' rather than a citizen of any one country' (Meek 2006).[43]

For the super-rich, then, the separation between work and leisure can be made flexible given their capacity to communicate through personal assistants on any aspect of their business, financial and other activities, when the inclination takes them, either directly or through mobile technologies. The family is bound together financially through family trusts and administered by the family office, but the flexibility built into their work and lifestyle gives them the potential to disengage, take time out, and sample whatever business, financial and personal adventures they see fit. This may lead to a more fragmented life, but it also offers the possibilities of greater control.[44]

As Georg Simmel (2004) reminds us in his *Philosophy of Money* the danger of a life of calculation means that money as the 'absolute means' can become the 'absolute end', relegating all values including 'wisdom and art' and even 'beauty and love' to means (Blumenberg 2012; Darmon and Frade 2012). It also suggests the difficulty of ordering time as well as money. As Simmel suggests, passing time is the predicate for practically everything we enjoy doing, whereas 'saving time' is often the goal of our exertions. This has been put well by Hans Blumenberg (2012):

> In order to pass the time, we save it. The same is true of money: one wants to amass it in order to spend it – provided one is not a miser, that is. Precisely the time we devote to 'pastimes' is not measured time; whoever is passing the time stays away from clocks, since he has the time to banish [*vertreiben*] all thought of time. Similarly, the wish for money is connected with the limit-value of no longer having to spare it a thought.

It is in this sense that Blumenberg (2012) argues that we are forced to accept one of the most odious formulations: having money is the only definite form of happiness we can possibly name: 'The reason for this lies in [that] … only the pure potentiality of money can satisfy the pure subjectivity of the concept of happiness.'

Giving and philanthocapitalism

In contrast to the popular images of the super-rich as enjoying a life of pleasure, high living and luxury, there are a significant number who opt for a life in which their work can be seen as amounting to something akin to a 'calling'.[45] For others the direction to attain happiness and a sense of salvation is related to 'good works'. Charitable giving and philanthropy, then, can be seen to offer solutions to those troubled by intransigent social problems such as the disease, sickness, inequalities, poverty, natural disasters and the accumulated problems which confront humanity and the planet. One contemporary example of charitable initiative is 'The Giving Pledge' from Warren Buffet and Bill and Melinda Gates. In 2010 they decided to try to persuade the wealthiest people in America to commit to giving over 50 per cent of their wealth to a charitable cause or philanthropic organization and as a consequence over fifty of the wealthiest people in the United States took the pledge. It is estimated that Buffet himself committed to give $36 billion and Gates $31 billion to their respective foundations (Bishop and Green 2008). Buffet and Gates also travelled abroad to persuade other wealthy people to participate. When questioned about what percentage of the rich he thought would give back, he responded: 'I think it will be a high percentage. More like 70 per cent than 15 per cent' (Bishop and Green 2008: 5).[46]

The *Forbes Insights* (2011) report on ultra-high net worth individuals suggests that over 40 per cent of the UHNWIs either fund or run their own foundations, or gave other substantial charitable contributions without having their own or a family foundation.[47] There are therefore concerns to present a more acceptable public face for neoliberalism and find ways to counter the accusations of the indifference of the wealthy to human suffering, inequalities and broader social problems; hence philanthropy regularly appears on the agenda at the various gatherings of the super-rich.[48] In effect, there are attempts to make philanthropy more central to the lives of the super-rich and discover a new sense of *noblesse oblige*, which goes beyond the negative depiction of critics such as Christopher Lasch in his *Revolt of the Elites* (1996). The difficult problem here is how to construct a viable ethic of generosity and responsibility that is deemed appropriate for the cosmopolitan global elite.[49]

Some of these concerns have stimulated the discussion of 'Philanthrocapitalism', an attempt to rethink charitable giving in terms of 'venture philanthropy' put forward by a new body of 'philanthroentrepreneurs', who seek to apply the skill set and methods of the entrepreneurial super-rich and 'creative capitalism'. The aim is to find innovative solutions to wider social problems: in effect the mission to create social as opposed to private value (Bishop and Green 2008: 6). It is suggested that charities and foundations should take on some of the qualities of hedge funds: become more adventurous and innovative, and willing to resort to leverage to access additional resources so they can intervene more strongly to back a particular strategic decision (Bishop and Green 2008: 88).[50]

At the same time, one of the major arguments about the super-rich revolves around the negative view of their general contribution to society. While the ambition of new foundations such as the Gates Foundation in trying to find imaginative solutions to endemic diseases such as malaria and other problems in the Global South is generally applauded, the philanthropy of the rich attracts many critics. There are those who consider both the tax avoidance strategies of individuals and families in conserving their fortunes, along with the use of offshore tax havens by the corporations they run, as amounting to an undeniable part of the set of global problems that have been created. In effect the governmental tax capture in many parts of the world is seen as increasingly inadequate for their welfare, infrastructure, research and development programmes. Governments have the experience and institutional structures for better long-term problem solving than individual initiatives, which can be sporadic and idiosyncratic. In the context of this debate it is interesting to note that one of the richest men in England, David Harding, founder of the Winston Capital hedge fund, felt some moral obligation to pay his full tax demand, amounting to £34 million out of his £87 million income in 2011 (*Daily Mail* 2012).

Nevertheless, there is still a good deal of suspicion surrounding the charitable giving of the rich. In some cases it may merely be a tax efficient device, in which the trustees and administrators run up large bills for expenses. Another problem is that the manifest purpose of the foundation, charity or trust is purely at the discretion of the founder and may be idiosyncratic and in some instances furnish funds for areas of low relative need or importance. In other cases the choice may be self-interested, as when gifts are made to leading universities such as Harvard or private schools, which younger family members could well attend. There is also considerable knowledge and expertise accumulated by governments, their advisers, think tanks and public sphere discussants of welfare and charitable priorities along with relevant intervention tactics and strategies, which suggest that the channelling of funds through governments could be more efficient.

The general question of debt transfer also has to be faced, especially with regard to the banking sector and stock market bubbles such as the recent financial crisis. In the final analysis it is governments that end up bailing out the financial sector, and while those at the bottom may have difficulties in repaying loans, it is the wealthy, especially the super-rich with single family offices who are alert to contingent possibilities and constantly monitoring the markets, who can readily move their money into safer havens and continue to obtain high returns on their investments, in periods of crises and downturn. Neoliberalism tends to operate with a neo-Darwinist philosophy of the survival of the fittest, with competition, league tables, performance measurement and metrics which reward the winners and punish the losers the order of the day (Terranova 2009; Venn 2009, forthcoming; Smart 2011). Yet there are still many who remain to be convinced that this is the only viable logic for contemporary societies, as the protests against bankers and financiers in London, New York, Madrid and other cities by the 'Occupy Movement' testifies. The problem of resource transfer, from public to private, has resulted in widespread hardships such as increased unemployment, wage freezes, inflation, reduced public services, negative equity on house purchases and unsustainable levels of debt. Indeed, there are some who point to the long history of the central significance of debt in social life and its key role under the recent phase of neoliberalism (Graeber 2011; Lazzarato 2012). This has led to an emphasis on the need to think about the move beyond neoliberalism, or create more radical solutions to the stability of the money supply and lending.[51]

At the same time an increasingly alert media and internet regularly remind us that the rich, the bankers, financiers and corporate CEOs continue to award themselves massive salaries and manage to pay very little tax. As the above discussion of philanthrocapitalist solutions put forward by members of the super-rich indicates, the problem they face is legitimacy. Many of the super-rich continue to distrust and side-step governments; they do not wish to see their contribution swallowed up in what they see as a black hole of public debt and nation-state deficit financing.

They do not want to consider the persuasive and well-researched argument that the rich can at the same time pay more taxes and still be better off.[52]

Over time it is possible that some members of the super-rich will become more globally oriented and help create new alliances and funding for broader public sphere and political structures beyond the nation-state. Yet in the long term this would also mean granting the new emergent state a monopoly over taxation and the means of violence, something many would be reluctant to consider. But in the longer term, given the stacking up of problems resulting from the increasing integration of the world economy and social life, along with the need to deal with planetary ecological threats, new forms of global governance cannot be ruled out. If the super-rich are to play an active part in this process they must overcome the public image of selfishness and greed and actively embrace greater social responsibilities for the fate of others.[53]

If history is any guide, when massive inequalities build up and the social bond and responsibilities are reneged on, questions of social justice resurface. At the moment it is relatively easy to suppress dissent and protest, as there would seem to be no global alternative to neoliberalism. But the demands to tax the super-rich on a fairer basis through direct taxation, or indirectly through some form of transaction tax, will continue to grow. This suggests that questions will continue to be raised about the lavish consumer culture lifestyles, the excesses and wastefulness, along with the overall sense of responsibility of the rich and super-rich.

Notes

1 https://fidelityinstitutional.fidelity.com/fi/campaigns/mobasi/index.html accessed 3 September 2012.
2 There are conflicting uses of the terms high net worth individuals (HNWIs) and ultra-high net worth individuals (UHNWIs). Usually the latter refers to people with financial resources of more than $30 million – see discussion below and also the use by Beaverstock (2010).
3 Foucault (2008: 232) discusses the neoliberal take-up of the problem of innovation and the view that the growth of Western countries and Japan since the 1930s has depended on the ways in which human capital has been formed, augmented and invested in. Likewise the economic take-off of the West since the sixteenth century and the problems of Third World economies in the late twentieth century are seen in terms of human capital accumulation. The extent to which Foucault's position was close to and sympathetic to the human capital theories of neoliberalism is contentious. François Ewald and Gary Becker in a May 2012 symposium were content to explore communalities (Becker et al. 2012); others might find this highly contentious.
4 As critics point out, in many cases the demands for young people to invest their own human capital and work more flexibly has led to greater insecurity and 'precarity', with the growth of a range of hybrid employer/employee statuses: the expansion of a group of people who are 'neither wage-earners, nor

entrepreneurs nor employees' (Lazzarato 2011: 53). To succeed one needs to invest, but also gamble: to spend time in a project to try to win a major competition, or have a big hit of one's own. This is a 'winner takes all' reality which has been referred to as 'the Hollywood effect' and 'Los Angelisation', which involves a total mobilization of self and unsustainable level of self-belief (McRobbie 2011: 125).

5 *Metro* newspaper launched its 'Creative Pioneers Challenge' under the headline 'Metro is looking for the next Mark Zuckerberg or Lord Alan Sugar in a competition launched by culture minister Ed Vaizey' (12 January 2012). This also relates to the current popular media fascination with talent contests in which ordinary people are propelled to stardom, such as *The X Factor*, *Britain's Got Talent*, and the host of imitators and fellow travellers. Richard Branson has been particularly successful in writing a string of books giving advice on business success. Alan Sugar also has a string of books spinning off from his popular BBC television series *The Apprentice* (2006–); the original US series on NBC (2004–) was hosted by Donald Trump. Spin-offs include *Celebrity Apprentice* and the form has migrated into business education. The audition, talent show, reality TV format has many resonances with *The X Factor*, developed by Simon Cowell in 2004, which involves a prolonged series of local competitive elimination events to produce contestants for the live finals. It has proved immensely popular and there are similar series in many parts of the world.

6 At the top (second on the overall billionaires list) is Bill Gates, co-founder of Microsoft, whose net worth is estimated by *Forbes* at $61 billion, despite the fact that he continues to give a large proportion away. Gates is followed by Larry Ellison, boss of Oracle, with $36 billion, and Michael Bloomberg with $22 billion. Larry Page and Sergey Brin, co-founders of Google, occupy joint 24th place with $18.7 billion each. Jeff Bezos of Amazon is number 26 with $18.4 billion while Mark Zuckerberg of Facebook sits at no. 35 with £17.5 billion. Michael Dell, founder of the computer manufacturer, is at no. 41 with $15.9 billion while Steve Ballmer, Microsoft's CEO, is three places lower on $15.7 billion and Paul Allen, co-founder of Microsoft, is at no. 48; his former partner Steve Jobs, who was worth about $9 billion when he died, is not listed (Naughton 2012). Also to be considered, currently in their late twenties or early thirties, are Dustin Moskovitz with $3.5 billion, Eduardo Saverin with $2 billion and Sean Parker with $2.1 billion, all of whom worked on Facebook.

7 This set of the list which includes bankers, hedge fund and investments people, is headed by Warren Buffet who has a fortune of $44 billion and includes Michael Bloomberg ($22 billion), George Soros ($20 billion) and Al-Waleed bin Talal ($18 billion). Three of the ten (Soros, John Paulson and James Simons) have made their money through hedge funds. In addition to the *Forbes Billionaires Lists* it is also useful to consult the Bloomberg Billionaires Index which started in 2012 and updates people's fortunes and rate of change on a daily basis; see www.bloomberg.com/billionaires (accessed 7 May 2013).

8 A recent case is Bob Diamond, Chief Executive of Barclays Bank, who was eventually forced to resign in July 2012 over a scandal about fixing interest rates and providing misleading information to the Bank of England. His payoff is said to have been between 20 and 30 million pounds.

9 Trusts are secret compacts administered by third parties under oath of non-disclosure and can be traced back to the European Middle Ages. In recent years the maze of electronically networked offshore banks, trusts and financial services has extended beyond ex-British colonies (Cyprus, Malta, Mauritius, Singapore, Hong Kong, the Bahamas, Virgin Islands, etc.) and quasi-independent crown domains such as Jersey, Guernsey and the Isle of Man, to

many other locations around the world, such as Panama, Dubai, Labuan and Vanuatu, all of whom seem eager to attract new money and maintain high levels of confidentiality.

10 The estimated size of the global hedge fund industry in April 2012 was $2.13 trillion (Chung 2012). It is widely acknowledged that 2011 was a particularly bad year with the average hedge fund falling by 5 per cent, yet the leading funds such as Charles Pace Coleman's Tiger Global returned 45 per cent in the first ten months of 2011. Over the three-year period (2008 to 2011) the winner of Barron's annual ranking of the top 100 Hedge funds was Christian Zugel's Zias Opportunity Fund, which returned an average of 78.5 per cent annually (Uhlfelder 2012). The commission taken by fund managers is estimated at between 20 and 48 per cent. Not anyone can join a hedge fund; for most funds you need to be either *an accredited private investor* with a net worth of more than $1 million and annual income of $200,000 or a *qualified purchaser* who must have $5 million in investments. The typical hedge fund minimum investment is between $500,000 and $1 million (Mallaby 2010).

11 There are a number of different rich lists including Forbes, Bloomberg, the *Sunday Times* and BornRich.com and the various methodologies used need to be investigated. See also the GMI (Governance Metrics International) Ratings for CEOs; for the 2012 report see GMI Ratings 2012.

12 It is also easier for the taxation departments such as the Inland Revenue in the UK to accurately tax around 99 per cent of salary income, but only 70 per cent of business and investment income, which is disproportionately high in the upper levels, because of inaccurate reporting (Johnston 2007).

13 The US Congressional Budget Office (CBO) revealed in October 2011 the proportion of income gains since the late 1970s, which had gone to the richest 1 per cent of households. Over the 28 years US incomes had increased overall by 62 per cent, allowing for tax and inflation. The lowest-paid 20 per cent gained a small share with their incomes having grown by 18 per cent. Middle-income households were also well below the average with gains of 37 per cent. While the majority of America's richest households had gains of just above the overall average at 67 per cent, the top 1 per cent of US households' income increased by a massive rise of 275 per cent. In the UK a comparison of income between 1997 and 2007 showed that in 1997 the bottom 90 per cent had average income of £10,500 with the top 1 per cent having income 18 times bigger. By 2007 the average income of the bottom 90 per cent had increased slightly to just under £12,500, whereas the income of the top 0.1 per cent had increased by 95 times, averaging well over £1 million a year (Robinson 2012).

14 Capgemini, the central force behind the *World Wealth Report*, describes itself as one of the world's foremost providers of consulting, technology and outsourcing services and provides 'The industry's leading benchmark for High New Worth market information' (www.capgemini.com/wwr12, accessed 14 May 2013). The reports from 2007 to 2011 were produced by Merrill Lynch and Capegemini. From 2012 onwards they were produced by Capgemini in collaboration with a new partner, the Royal Bank of Canada Wealth Management.

15 India's population of HNWIs grew by 20.8 per cent in 2010, according to the *World Wealth Report*, making India's HNWI population the world's twelfth largest; although it experienced a slump in 2011. Increasingly, Indian ultra-high net worth individuals invest in risky financial vehicles, such as hedge funds, private equity, structured products and derivatives with private equity managers, who have been very active in India in recent years. The growth of the private equity sector and hedge funds has produced greater investment in start-ups and new companies, which has, in turn, helped to

develop a new class of first-time entrepreneurs, who are now also joining the club of the super-rich.
16 From one perspective it should be possible to relate the waves of academic and critical interest in the super-rich to particular phases of the long-wave cycles of economic growth, such as the 50-year Kondratieff cycle. One might expect interest and public condemnation of the excesses of the rich, their alleged public irresponsibility and greed to peak immediately after an economic crisis and depression as the gaps between the rich and poor widen, as in our current time. Unfortunately, this pattern cannot easily be detected. Books such as Lundberg's (1968) study of the rich and super-rich in the United States in the sixties, or C. Wright Mills' *The Power Elite* (1956) were not published in the down cycle. For the argument for a return to the study of elites see Savage and Williams (2008).
17 For a discussion of the current Eastward shift in global GDP see Quah (2011). Such shifts are of course not new. Jack Goody and others have noted that historically there have been a number of swings in economic power between the two sides of Eurasia as opportunity cost and cheap labour moved across the continent between China and Europe (Goody 2009; Frank 1998; Featherstone 2007, 2009).
18 See http://en.wikipedia.org/wiki/Lifestyles_of_the_Rich_and_Famous (accessed 7 May 2013).
19 For a discussion of the concept of multiplicity and topology, both of which are relevant to the ways of theorizing complex relatively open sets see Deleuze (1999).
20 See Mohr (2012) where she discusses the frugal lives of Warren Buffett, Mark Zuckerberg, Calos Slim Helu and John Caudwell.
21 To look stylish, to fashion one's own life in a unique expressive way has been described in relation to youth cultures by Dick Hebdige (1979) and queer cultures by Henning Bech (1998). A notable account of the will to forge a new identity through actively making a lifestyle is Quentin Crisp's (1998) *How to Have a Life-Style.*
22 For a discussion of entrepreneurship in relation to the nineteenth century innovative artist see Wuggenig (2011).
23 The writings of Gabriel Tarde (2012) on property and monadology are relevant here. For Tarde society is to be seen as 'reciprocal possession' composed of monads who are possessive agencies eager to possess others and avoid being appropriated (see also Debaise 2008).
24 The development of mass luxuries is exacerbated, with for example celebrated designer houses creating 'capsule collections' in collaboration with massmarket and fast-fashion retail brands, sparking a proliferation of similar looking but cheaper products to those of the luxury labels. Jimmy Choo and Versace have been on sale at H&M and Karl Lagerfeld has a capsule line for Macy's (Bellaiche *et al.* 2012). At the same time certain brands may feel they have gone too far down into the mass market and if there is the perception, as was the case with Louis Vuitton, that too many women possessed a mass-produced Vuitton handbag, then new ranges with exclusive designer credentials will be developed and marketed. This is currently the case with a major promotion of a new Vuitton collection, the product of a collaboration with the Japanese artists Yayoi Kusama, which has led to a new handbag line promoted in major department stores around the world. In September 2012 at Selfridges, Oxford Street, London, for example all the show windows featured her art with its prominent dot patterns in various displays, along with a specially designed Vuitton–Kusama 'Concept Store' on the ground floor which produced a sort of

designer-wonderland. The department store and art space merge and aestheticization and consumer design go into overload (see http://kusama.selfridges.com, accessed 7 May 2013). Fashion magazines, discount houses and outlet stores also speed up the affordable look-alike process. Exclusivity then is a highly marketable attribute and companies are quick to see and exploit the potential.

25 Apart from the example of Vuitton and Yayoi Kusama mentioned in the previous note, the ultra-luxury market segment has a strong dynamic given that consumers today want something distinctive and exclusive in a world of mass production, and highly value quality craftsmanship, artistic inspiration and connoisseurship, not just status. Indeed the status phase may be found more in the early phases of nouveau riche consumption, with the *arrivistes* seeking comfort and endorsement in brands and the type of luxury goods they were previously denied. Certain eras, the boom times such as the Gilded Age and the current phase from 1980 to 2008, tend to throw up new generations of *arrivistes*. Given that the global economy tends to fire differential growth cycles which favour different parts of the world, the booms can be more marked in certain phases and certain countries – e.g. the USA in the 1920s, China in the 2000s, etc.

26 Another indicator is the 'Cost of Living Extremely Well Index', which was created by Forbes in 1976 based on a selection of 40 goods and services for very rich customers, which continues to increase at double the rate of inflation (De Carlo 2011). A further indicator is the rise in duty-free and travel retail sales of perfumes, cosmetics and luxury goods, with sales increasing by 28 per cent between 2008 and 2011 and expected to rise a further 25 per cent to $44.5 billion over the next two years, according to the Swedish data company Generation Research (Moulds 2012). A good part of this increase has been put down to the rising numbers of wealthy travellers from China, Russia, Brazil and the Middle East who have boosted airport sales.

27 According to Russell Flannery of Forbes, 'The number of billionaires among China's richest 400 people increased to a record 146 from 128 a year earlier, according to the annual survey ... by Forbes Asia' (Flannery 2011).

28 China is currently enjoying what has been referred to as a 'pandemic of luxury-goods stores openings'. There are increasing numbers of high-end ultra-luxury or sports and performance cars to cater for the demands of the wealthy which are making a visible impact in the China market. It is also worth mentioning that, apart from the fact that countries may be at different stages in the cycle of luxury consumption, as a comparison of consumption in China, India and Japan would immediately show, there is also the question of cultural differences which have emerged over time. It is therefore possible to see different definitions of luxury operating in various countries in Europe, Asia and the Americas. Spending on luxury goods in the United States has its own distinctive pattern and cars are central to the definition. When asked to cite the top luxury brands, Americans name car makers such as Lexus, BMW and Cadillac. The US mindset about luxury differs from that in other regions (there is strong attention to price relative to other countries, and hence value must be clearly communicated). The United States accounts for only 19 per cent of the world's spending on personal luxury goods, but has 37 per cent of global high-end-car purchasing (Bellaiche *et al.* 2012).

29 The top-end luxury market has spawned a number of specialist magazines for the super-rich such as the *Robb Report, Luxurious Magazine, Elite Traveller, Wealth Collection Magazine, Prestige Magazine, Lusso Magazine, Jetset Magazine* and *Elephant Lifestyle*. The last-named is 'The Oil & Gas Year's Luxury Edition for Energy Tycoons' with the slogan 'Hit Big, Live Large'. It offers pages of 'luxury living

advice' with galleries full of yachts, jets, helicopters, sports cars and even islands – all priced neatly in barrels of oil; along with reviews of cities, vacations and hotels, features on oil moguls, leisure, style events and of course margins replete with highly crafted sophisticated advertisements for all kinds of luxury goods. There are also numerous websites with names such as *Luxury Lifestyles, Luxury Insider, Elite Choice, Global Luxury Lifestyle Living, Luxury Culture, Luxury Society, Luxury Institute* and *Born Rich: the Home of Luxury*. The *Luxury Brands Club* has a 'Luxury Clinic' offering individually tailored solutions via 'Private Client' adviser teams targeting the high net worth and ultra-high net worth individuals, with this type of specialist tailored lifestyle and travel management services a common feature. A typical taxonomy taken from *Luxurious Magazine* employs the following categories: Art and Collectables; Aviation; Cars and Boats; Classic Art; Design and Construction; Electronics and Gadgets; Fine Dining; General News; Luxurious Sounds; People and Interviews; Retro Luxury; Style and Fashion; Travel; Watches and Jewellery.

30 The customised VIP jumbo jets such as the wide-bodied Boeing 767 'execuliner' can have bedrooms, dining rooms, movie theatres and private baths, along with 'standard butler service and a private chef' and cost around $150 million each. Super-yachts, such as Roman Abramovich's *Eclipse*, costing an estimated one billion dollars, are prominently discussed in the media. The yacht has nine decks and a crew of 70; it also possesses a missile defence system and mobile submarine (for discussion of specialist super-yacht builder Lürssen of Bremen, see Paterson 2011).

31 Red Carpet Enterprises in London, for example, specializes in the 'making dreams come true' business and can arrange for a *Top Gun* experience of flying in a jet fighter, or drinking champagne halfway up a Swiss mountain, or playing a five-a-side football game on the deck of a battleship, or helicopter skiing in Alaska (Macalister and Wood 2012).

32 The annual spend of $1.5 trillion in 2012 becomes a modest figure when set against the $42 trillion total assets which the world's wealthiest have at their disposal.

33 Such new super-rich spaces have attracted a range of critics. They have been dubbed 'Evil Paradises' (Davis and Monk 2007). The excessive carbon consumption lifestyle of the rich at a time of intensified climate change has also drawn criticism (Urry 2010a).

34 The site tells us that the *Wall Street Journal* has recently launched a Global Property section in conjunction with *PropGOLuxury*. It also claims that this confirms its 'status as the market leader in greater China, Asia, and the World' and that it provides 'the most comprehensive luxury property portal reaching the largest audience of affluent property consumers in greater China and globally' (George Varvitsiotis, Managing Director, PropGOLuxury.com: PropGOLuxury.com 2010).

35 *The Wealth Report 2012* remarks that:

> There are now 63,000 people worldwide with $100 million or more in assets, according to Ledbury Research, which specialises in monitoring global wealth trends. The number of these centa-millionaires has increased by 29% since 2006 and is forecast to rise even further.
>
> (Shirley 2012)

36 One Hyde Park (developed by the Candy brothers) has what is described as the world's most expensive apartment following the $160 million sale of one of the penthouses, part of the 86-apartment complex (Barrionnuevo 2012). One Hyde Park is apparently the world's most expensive block of flats and like the

Shard is owned by the Qatar Investment Authority. The QIA also owns sizeable slices of the City of London Financial Centre at Canary Wharf, the London Stock Exchange and other parts of London.

37 This is proving to be a global trend and in China, India, the Gulf States and many other places 'supertall' skyscrapers are being built. If one definition of the skyscraper is 'a machine for making the land pay' then the new boom in high towers or supertall buildings (classified as 300 metres or over) is seen as providing 'mini metropoles' with not only luxury apartments on their highest floors, but high-end hotels and shopping malls, restaurants and entertainment areas in the middle floors, and offices on the lower levels (Heathcote 2012). The best example is the Burj Khalifa in Dubai, at 829 metres by far the tallest building in the world. Despite the global recession, Dubai and other gulf states such as Qatar continue to build dozens of supertall buildings along with a series of mega-projects such as the Palm Jumeirah island complex with its vast range of residences, hotels, leisure facilities and yacht marinas.

38 The Hong Kong Art Fair held its first private museum forum in 2011. Some forty private museum owners and collectors from Australia, Japan, Indonesia and China were expected to attend the 2012 event. One central player is Budiardjo Tek, president of Sierad Produce, a $155 million company listed on the Jakarta stock exchange. Tek says he maintains a modest lifestyle and remarks: 'The action of opening the museum is an extension of love to society.' Tek, Wang and other wealthy collectors have turned Hong Kong into the world's third biggest auction hub as they build up their collections of contemporary Chinese art. That segment boomed in recent years, but has softened lately (Chan 2012).

39 The world's youngest self-made billionaire, Facebook co-founder and former Mark Zuckerberg roommate Dustin Moskovitz, now works with his friend Justin Rosenstein, another former Facebook worker, to head a company called Asana, which recently launched an online project management service. During an interview at their modest offices, Rosenstein remarked: 'When we think of work, we think of work as an act of service, as an act of love for humanity.' In keeping with the recent start-up anti-hierarchical trend, the pair sit among their 24 other employees at Asana. Like Zuckerberg, they dress down, Moskovitz in an untucked shirt, Rosenstein in a sweater (Wohlsen 2012). There is also an additional generational dimension here. The self-made billionaire or millionaire often has very different dispositions and attitudes towards spending money, leisure pursuits and the rich lifestyle from those of her or his children, who have been expensively educated into the world of culture and the art of living by finishing schools, top universities, exclusive clubs and social networks.

40 Apparently, for 'lifestyle nomads', a typical super-rich individual's portfolio will consist of four or five properties, which include established super-prime homes in London, southern Europe, the Alps, the United States and the Caribbean, with their migratory patterns driven by seasonal pursuits and filtered through family background and connections. As Cole (2012) puts it,

> With skiing, or *après-ski*, in mind, the new wealthy Brazilians join Americans on the slopes of Vail and Aspen, while Christmas sees the British and Europeans head for their chalets in the Alps, where old money has long graced the sophistication of Gstaad and Megève.

For Russians, on the other hand, currently some of the most active players in the European super-prime market, the Caribbean becomes the sun-seekers' refuge of choice from November to March, with the Russians congregating on St Barts – recently brought to prominence by the lavish parties of Roman

Abramovich, whose 70-acre estate cost a reported £59 million in 2009. Cole (2012) also mentions that, apart from Mustique and the Bahamas, Barbados boasts the highest proportion of billionaires. London is also seen as attractive for children's education, personal safety, economic and investment security, as well as its cosmopolitan culture, shopping and centrality. The Côte d'Azur continues to attract Russian, American and Arab clients and their yachts, mingling with the old money Europeans in Cap Ferrat, and Cap d'Antibes 'billionaires' bay', whose property prices continues to rise and regularly top €30 million.

41 This has led some critiques to argue that this not only aggravates housing shortages, but as Saskia Sassen indicates, it also means in some cases that poorer local residents start to develop a sense of distance from their city: 'In my research I found that in several cities across the world, locals – often high-income and old rich locals – did not mince their words when saying that all of this was a loss to their neighbourhood and city' (cited in Powley and Warwick-Ching 2012). The current unease in the UK is part of a more general reaction to the absent super-rich, which has led Singapore to introduce a 10 per cent additional buyer's stamp duty on all foreign purchases, the French government to talk of introducing steeper property taxes for foreigners and the Swiss to support a referendum for a 20 per cent limit on second homes.

42 According to Amit *et al.* (2008) SFOs and the families behind them tend to view their SFOs as private investment services, more focused on maintaining and growing wealth than on personal or concierge services – a hedge fund expert shouldn't be distracted by having to deal with domestic staff issues. According to a *Forbes Insights* (2011) report on Global Wealth it is expected that the biggest growth in family offices will occur in Asia. Philanthropy can also be handled via SFOs – see further discussion later.

43 To describe the shift to becoming a citizen of the family could seem too strong as the two forms, 'citizenship' and 'family', would at first seem to work on different dynamics. There has been a clear process of the formalization of rights and obligations and more general codification and rationalization of the family within modern societies (e.g. emergence of women's rights, spelling out husband's and father's obligations, then children's rights, etc.). But the formalization of citizenship within the contemporary upper class would prove to be an interesting variant: this being a family which essentially establishes its own laws and obligations and seeks to avoid the normal nation-state citizenship duties linked to representation and taxation, for more informal modes of operating across societies, in conditions of mobility and multiple affiliations. Likewise the upper-class family is bound together by money, not just blood: the legal rules governing money flows, as well as blood ties, make an interesting mix of obligations and rights. The use of the medieval notion of trusts, now transformed into a financial instrument for secrecy and tax efficiency aimed at securing the long-term transmission of wealth, with safeguards against squandering the fortune by capricious family members, is also interesting. An economic relationship involving money quantification and calculation, and used in the midst of the mobility, speed and flows of the global financial system, can therefore sustain a dynastic form, which many academics assumed following the logic of modernization theory and the drive to individualization (cf. Beck and Beck-Gernsheim 2002), is becoming obsolete, with family structures being sidestepped or breaking up through divorce and separation, in many of the leading countries of the world. Returning to the affective and economic ties of family, as opposed to those of nation, could be seen as a positive step by some; but it also contains the dangers of romanticizing the mafia-type family as the prime defensive unit to face an allegedly hostile world. The emphasis on dynasties in

the upper classes, in the face of opposite trends in the bulk of the population and its relation to finance, would have been a worthy topic for Georg Simmel (2004) in his *Philosophy of Money*, with his wonderfully flexible capacity to see reverse tendencies and the way quantitative phenomena give rise to qualitative changes and vice versa.

44 The importance placed on the handling, planning and protection of wealth, along with the fluidity of forms of sociation made on the move, or in the face of pressing deadlines can, it is suggested, encourage people to develop more flexible dispositions and even amount to a new 'flexian' character (Wedel 2009; Caletrío 2012). Flexians operate in flexible networks between financial, business, political and official elites and can act as specialist policy advisers. In effect, they are a shadow elite with a new transnational mobile habitus that thrives on turbulence and disorder. The 'flexians' and super-rich are the groups with the potential to develop means of handling life on the move, and mobile systems with greater informational connectivity. It is in this flexible work life, with the potential to blur the lines between work, play and family and readily shift contexts, but calculate the costs and benefits for all, amidst the shifting matrix of network alliances and possibilities, that a new sense of the good life becomes nurtured.

45 There is a long history of biographical and fictional accounts of reclusive, miserly and spendthrift wealthy people. One interesting contemporary case is that of Ingvar Kamprad, the billionaire founder of the Swedish furniture and home goods company IKEA. He allegedly takes EasyJet flights, drives himself around in a fifteen-year-old Volvo and has his modest house almost entirely furnished with IKEA items – which he assembled himself. On visits to London he only uses the Tube or buses. Explaining his frugal nature, he remarked:

> I am a bit tight with money, a sort of Swedish Scotsman. But so what? If I start to acquire luxurious things then this will only incite others to follow suit. It's important that leaders set an example. I look at the money I'm about to spend on myself and ask if Ikea's customers could afford it. From time to time I like to buy a nice shirt and cravat – and eat Swedish fish roe.
> (Ballinder 2008)

It is stated that the IKEA Group is owned by a non-profit foundation and pays no tax, although IKEA Systems collects franchise fees and is owned by the Kamprad family and is registered in Luxembourg. More recently it emerged that Kamprad admitted to controlling the company through a secret foundation worth 100 billion kronor ($15.34 billion), according to a Sveriges Television (SVT) report (The Local 2011).

46 Estimates of existing percentages vary, but Bishop and Green (2008: 28) cite the *World Wealth Report* as stating that only 11 per cent of the global rich give to charitable sources, whereas the figure is higher, at 17 per cent for the ultra-rich.

47 Some people tend to think of philanthropy as an American notion, and indeed in the United States 55 per cent of UHNW individuals operate charitable foundations. At the same time in the Middle East some 63 per cent of UHNWIs fund charitable foundations; yet the figure for China is just 7 per cent. Cultural factors, such as Sharia Law in the Middle East, along with the tax advantages of giving (United States) and the perception of the state's role in social welfare (China) could be relevant to explain the differences (*Forbes Insights* 2011).

48 The extent to which philanthropy features in the regular round of communal activities and gatherings of the super-rich and 'plutocrats' is an interesting question. The World Economic Forum's annual meeting in Davos, Switzerland, is well known. The Bilderberg Group, which meets annually in Europe and

North America, is more exclusive and secretive, focusing more on geopolitics and less on global business and philanthropy. The Boao Forum for Asia, held on China's Hainan Island each spring, is also important. Others to be noted are: the TED conferences (the acronym stands for 'Technology, Entertainment, Design'); Herb Allen's Sun Valley gathering, for media moguls; and the Aspen Institute's Ideas Festival. These various gatherings and circuits not only increase information exchange and networking to link together 'people like us', which can be seen as the 'network society' that really matters; they also offer the basis to develop scenario planning for alternative global futures (Freeland 2011a, 2012).

49 It would be interesting to compare the late nineteenth-century Gilded Age businessmen such as Rockefeller and Carnegie with today's generation of philanthropists, such as Gates, Buffet, Soros, Branson *et al.*

50 Peter Drucker, a long-standing advocate of social entrepreneurship, has been referred to as 'the high priest of philanthrocapitalism' (Bishop and Green 2008: 95). Drucker, a regular participant at the World Economic Forum, Davos and in the Clinton Global Initiative, urges that the rich bring down 'the five global goliaths': spiritual emptiness, egocentric leadership, extreme poverty, pandemic diseases, and illiteracy and lack of education.

51 One recent interesting IMF proposal is the idea to replace private bank-created money (approximately 97 per cent of the money supply) with state-created money. This would mean an attack on 'fractional reserve banking', under the assumption that if lenders are obliged to put up 100 per cent reserve backing for deposits, they cannot create new money, which would allow the state to regain sovereign control over the money supply. See the IMF study by Jaromir Benes and Michael Kumhof (2012; also mentioned in Evans-Pritchard 2012).

52 One key proponent, Claude Rosenberg, who died in 2008, argued that America's super-rich could increase their annual contributions to charity tenfold and still end up with higher personal fortunes. Rosenberg started a research group dedicated to spreading the message and wrote a book (Rosenberg 1994) and many articles in periodicals read by rich people with all the figures. In the year 2000, Rosenberg's researchers documented that households with $1 million or more in income could have given $128 billion more to charity than they actually did, without losing any net worth over the course of the year (Inequality.org Staff 2011).

53 Questions continue to be asked about the greed and the dishonesty of the super-rich, bankers and financiers. See for example Robert Peston *Super Rich: The Greed Game* (2006); a version of this programme is available on the internet on *YouTube*. Recent research suggests there may be some foundation in these common perceptions of greed and dishonesty. Psychologists at the University of California in Berkeley covertly observed people's behaviour in the open and in a series of follow-up studies in the laboratory. Social psychologist Paul Piff and his colleagues claim that self-interest may be a 'more fundamental motive among society's elite' and selfishness may be 'a shared cultural norm'. The scientists also found a strong link between social status and greed, a connection they suspect might exacerbate the economic gulf between the rich and poor. The work builds on previous research that suggests the upper classes are less aware of others, worse at reading other people's emotions and less altruistic than individuals in lower social classes (Sample 2012). Additional arguments continue about whether the super-rich actually create new wealth or merely redistribute existing wealth; a question which goes to the heart of the basis for generating financial wealth and its relation to economic and other forms of value (see Lansley 2008, 2012).

References

Alkan, C. (2012) 'Tax the rich: the minefield of high-level taxation', *Economia*, 3 July.
Amit, R., Liechtenstein, H. and Prats, M. J. (2008) 'Single family offices: private wealth management in the family context', Wharton School, University of Pennsylvania.
Atkinson, A. B., Piketty, T. and Saez, E. (2011) 'Top incomes in the long run of history', *Journal of Economic Literature* 49(1): 3–71.
Ballinder, L. (2008) 'He lives in a bungalow, flies EasyJet and "dries out" three times a year ... the man who founded Ikea and is worth £15bn', *Daily Mail*, 14 April.
Barrionuevo, A. (2012) 'Trophy hunting', *New York Times Real Estate*, 7 June.
Beaverstock, J. (2010) 'The privileged world city: private banking, wealth management and the bespoke servicing of the global super-rich', *GaWC [Globalization and World Cities Research Network] Research Bulletin* 338.
Beaverstock, J., Hubbard, P. and Short, J. R. (2004) 'Getting away with it? Exposing the geographies of the super-rich', *Geoforum* 35: 401–407.
Bech, H. (1998) 'Citysex: representing lust in public', Special Issue on Love and Eroticism, *Theory, Culture & Society* 15(3–4).
Beck, U. and Beck-Gernsheim, E. (2002) *Individualization*. London: Sage.
Becker, G., Ewald, F. and Harcourt, B. (2012) 'American neoliberalism: Michel Foucault's birth of biopolitics lectures', open seminar at the University of Chicago, 9 May, http://vimeo.com/43984248 (accessed 7 May 2013).
Bellaiche J.-M., Eirinberg Kluz, M., Mei-Pochtler, A. and Wiederin, E. (2012) 'Luxe redux: Raising the bar for the selling of luxuries', *BCG Perspectives*, Boston Consultancy Group, 5 June, www.luxesf.com/wp-content/uploads/2012/06/BCG-Luxe-Redux.pdf (accessed 7 May 2013).
Benes, J. and Kumhof, M. (2012) 'The Chicago Plan revisited', *IMF Working Papers*, August.
Bishop, M. and Green, M. (2008) *Philanthrocapitalism: How Giving Can Save the World*. London: A & C Black.
Blumenberg, H. (2012) 'Money or life: Metaphors of Georg Simmel's philosophy', *Theory, Culture & Society* 29(7–8).
Brigstock, J. (2013) 'Artistic parrhesia and the genealogy of Ethics in Foucault and Benjamin', *Theory, Culture & Society* 30(1).
Caletrío, J. (2012), 'Global elites, privilege and mobilities in post-organised capitalism', *Theory, Culture & Society* 29(2).
Chen, G. (2011) 'High net worth individuals: China's new export', *Reuters*, 20 April.
Chan, K. (2012) 'China super rich use boom money to open their own art museums', *Huffington Post Business*, 5 September, www.huffingtonpost.com/2012/05/09/china-super-rich_n_1502446.html?ref=business (accessed 7 May 2013).
China Merchants Bank and Bain & Company (2011) *China Private Wealth Report 2011*, www.bain.com/Images/2011_China_wealth_management_report.pdf (accessed 14 May 2013)/
Chung, J. (2012) 'Hedges' assets: $5 trillion', *Wall Street Journal*, 11 June.
Cole, T. L. (2012) 'Lifestyle nomads', *Financial Times*, 6 July.

Crisp, Q. (1998) *How to Have a Life-Style*. New York: Alyson.
Csikszentmihalyi, M. (2008) *Flow: the Psychology of Optimal Experience*. New York: Harper.
Csikszentmihalyi, M. and Halton, E. (1980) *The Meaning of Things: Domestic Symbols and the Self*. Cambridge: Cambridge University Press.
Daily Mail (2011) 'At least he'll be able to pay the fine: Gold-plated car is impounded by police … after owner forgot to tax it', *Daily Mail*, 1 April, www.dailymail.co.uk/news/article-1372409/At-ll-able-pay-fine-Gold-plated-car-impounded-police-owner-forgot-tax-it.html (accessed 7 May 2013).
Daily Mail (2012) 'Britain's highest earner actually pays his fair share of taxes: Hedge fund chief pays £34m out of £87m salary', *Daily Mail*, 30 September, www.dailymail.co.uk/news/article-2210717/Britains-highest-earner-actually-pays-fair-share-taxes-Hedge-fund-chief-pays-34m-87m-salary.html (accessed 7 May 2013).
Darmon, I. and Frade, C. (2012) 'Beneath and beyond the fragments: the charms of Simmel's philosophical path for contemporary subjectivities', *Theory, Culture & Society* 29 (7–8).
Davis, M. and Monk, D. B. (eds) (2007) *Evil Paradises: Dreamworlds of Neoliberalism*. New York: New Press.
Debaise, D. (2008) 'The dynamics of possession. An introduction to the sociology of Gabriel Tarde', in D. Skribna (ed.) *Mind that Abides: Panpsychism in the New Millennium*. Amsterdam: John Benjamins.
De Carlo, S. (2011) 'Cost of Living Extremely Well Index: the price of living large is up', *Forbes*, 26 September.
De Carlo, S. (2012) 'America's highest paid CEOs', *Forbes*, 4 April.
Elliott, A. and Urry, J. (2010) *Mobile Lives*. New York: Routledge.
Evans-Pritchard, A. (2012) 'IMF's epic plan to conjure away debt and dethrone bankers', *Daily Telegraph*, 21 October.
Featherstone, M. (1995) *Undoing Culture: Globalization, Postmodernism and Identity*. London: Sage.
Featherstone, M. (2007) *Consumer Culture and Postmodernism* (2nd edition). London: Sage.
Featherstone, M. (2009) 'Introduction to Jack Goody: occidentalism and comparative history', *Theory, Culture & Society* 26(7–8).
Featherstone, M. (2010a) 'The sense of luxury: consumer culture and sumptuary dynamics', *Les Cahiers Européens de l'Imaginaire*, CNRS Editions, March.
Featherstone, M. (2010b) 'Body, image and affect in consumer culture', *Body & Society* 17(1).
Featherstone, M. (forthcoming) 'The rich and the super-rich: mobility, consumption and luxury lifestyles' in N. Mathur (ed.) *Consumer Culture, Modernity and Identity*. New Delhi: Sage.
Flannery, R. (2011) 'A new no. 1 on the Forbes Rich List', *Forbes*, 7 September, www.forbes.com/sites/russellflannery/2011/09/07/a-new-no-1-on-the-forbes-china-rich-list (accessed 7 May 2013).
Forbes Insights (2011) *Driving Global Wealth: Mapping ultra high net worth individuals around the globe*. New York: Forbes Insights, in association with Societe Generale Private Banking, http://images.forbes.com/forbesinsights/StudyPDFs/Driving_Global_Wealth_May2011.pdf (accessed 7 May 2013).

Foucault, M. (1991) 'What is enlightenment?' in P. Rabinow (ed.) *The Foucault Reader*. Harmondsworth: Penguin.
Foucault, M. (2008) *The Birth of Biopolitics: Lectures at the College de France 1978–79*. Houndsmills: Palgrave Macmillan.
Frank, A. G. (1998) *ReORIENT: Global Economy in the Asian Age*. Berkeley: University of California Press.
Frank, R. (2012) 'The real wealth gap: between the rich and the super-rich', *WSJ Blogs*, 30 April, http://blogs.wsj.com/wealth/ (accessed 7 May 2013).
Freeland, C. (2011a) 'The rise of the new global elite', *The Atlantic*, January/February.
Freeland, C. (2011b) 'Capitalism is failing the middle class', *Reuters*, 15 April.
Freeland, C. (2012) *The Plutocrats: The Rise of the New Global Super-Rich*. London: Penguin.
Gill, A. and Pratt, A. (2008) 'Introduction to precarity and cultural work', *Theory, Culture & Society* 25(7–8).
GMI Ratings (2012) 'GMI Ratings' latest report details a second straight year of double digit pay increases in the Russell 3000', 3 May, www3.gmiratings.com/home/2012/05/gmi-ratings%E2%80%99-latest-report-details-a-second-straight-year-of-double-digit-pay-increases-in-the-russell-3000 (accessed 14 May 2013).
Goody, J. (2009) *The Eurasian Miracle*. Cambridge: Cambridge University Press.
Graeber, D. (2011) *Debt: The First 5000 Years*. London: Melville House.
Hawkins, A. (2007) 'The frugal billionaires', *Forbes.com*, 14 November, www.forbes.com/2007/11/14/billionaires-walton-buffett-biz-cz_ah_1114frugalbillies.html (accessed 7 May 2013).
Heathcote, E. (2012) 'High society', *Financial Times*, 9 June.
Hebdige D. (1979) *Subculture: The Meaning of Style*. London: Routledge.
Inequality.org Staff (2011) 'The global super-rich stash: now 25 trillion,' *inequality.org*, 12 November, http://inequality.org/global-super-rich-stash-25-trillion (accessed 14 May 2013).
Johnston, D. C. (2007) 'Income gap is widening, data shows', *New York Times*, 29 March.
Kime, S. (2010) 'A thing of beauty is a joy forever … and a good investment? The return of passion investing', *Luxist*, 30 September, www.luxist.com/2010/09/30/a-thing-of-beauty-is-a-joy-forever-and-a-good-investment-th (accessed 7 May 2013).
Lansley, S. (2008) 'Do the Super-Rich Matter?' London: Touchstone/TUC, www.tuc.org.uk/extras/touchstonesuperrich.pdf (accessed 14 May 2013).
Lansley, S. (2012) *The Cost of Inequality*. London: Gibson Square Books.
Lasch, C. (1996) *Revolt of the Elites*. New York: Norton.
Latour, B. (2004) 'How to talk about the body? The Normative dimension of science studies', *Body & Society* 10(2–3).
Lazzarato, M. (2011) 'The misfortunes of the artistic critique and cultural employment', in G. Raunig, G. Ray and U. Wuggenig (eds) *Critique of Creativity: Precarity, Subjectivity and Resistance in the 'Creative Industries'*. London: May Fly Books.
Lazzarato, M. (2012) *The Making of the Indebted Man: Essay on the Neoliberal Condition*. Cambridge MA: MIT Press.
Linder, S. B. (1970) *The Harried Leisure Class*. New York: Columbia University Press.
Local, The (2011) 'Ikea founder admits to secret foundation', *The Local: Swedish News in English*, 26 January, www.thelocal.se/31650/20110126/ (accessed 7 May 2013).

Lundberg, F. (1968) *The Rich and the Super-Rich: A Study in the Power of Money Today*. New York: Lyle Stuart.
Lyng, S. (ed.) (2004) *Edgework: the Sociology of Risk-Taking*. London: Routledge.
Macalister, T. and Wood, Z. (2012) 'Luxury retail defies the slump by selling the things only money can buy', *Observer*, 24 June.
Mallaby, S. (2010) *More Money than God: Hedge Funds and the Making of a New Elite*. London: Bloomsbury.
McRobbie, A. (2011) 'The Los Angelisation of London', in G. Raunig, G. Ray and U. Wuggenig (eds) *Critique of Creativity: Precarity, Subjectivity and Resistance in the 'Creative Industries'*. London: May Fly Books.
Meek, J. (2006) 'Super rich', *Guardian*, 17 April.
Mills, C. W. (1956) *The Power Elite*. New York: Oxford University Press.
Mohr, A. (2012) 'The everyday life of frugal billionaires', *Investopedia*, Yahoo Finance, 26 April, http://finance.yahoo.com/news/everyday-lives-frugal-billionaires-150330781.html (accessed 7 May 2013).
Moulds, C. (2012) 'Wealthy travellers boost airport sales of luxury brands', *The Guardian*, 4 July.
Naughton, J. (2012) 'New tech moguls: the modern robber barons?' *The Observer Magazine*, 1 July.
Neate, R. (2011) 'Lower taxes lure foreign buyers to spend £4bn on London properties', *Guardian*, 23 December.
New, C. (2012) 'United States losing millionaires As China, India gain them, study says', *The Huffington Post*, 31 May.
Paterson, T. (2011) 'Yachts with champagne showers tempt the world's super-rich to Germany', *Independent*, 2 February.
Peston, R. (2008) *Super Rich: The Greed Game*. BBC Documentary.
Powley, T. and Warwick-Ching, L. (2012) 'Stateless and super-rich', *Financial Times*, 28 April.
PropGOLuxury.com (2010) 'PropGOLuxury and the Wall Street Journal join forces!' 17 April, www.propgoluxury.com/EN/PropertyNews/Hong-Kong/840-Wall-Street-Journal-partnership.html (accessed 7 May 2013).
Quah, D. (2011) 'The global economy's shifting centre of gravity', *Global Policy*, January.
Rabinow, P. (2009) 'Foucault's untimely struggle: towards a form of spirituality', Special Issue on Michel Foucault, *Theory, Culture & Society* 26(6).
Raunig, G., Ray, G. and Wuggenig, U. (eds) (2011) *Critique of Creativity: Precarity, Subjectivity and Resistance in the 'Creative Industries'*. London: May Fly Books.
Reich, R. (1991) *The Work of Nations*. New York: Knopf.
Revel, J. (2009) 'Identity, nature, life: three biopolitical deconstructions', Special Issue on Michel Foucault, *Theory, Culture & Society* 26(6).
Robinson, M. (2012) 'The wealth gap – inequality in numbers', BBC World Service radio broadcast 17 January.
Rosenberg, C. (1994) *Wealthy and Wise: How You and America Can Get the Most Out of Your Giving*. Boston: Little, Brown.
Saez, E. (2012) 'Striking it richer: the evolution of top incomes in the United States', http://elsa.berkeley.edu/~saez/saez-UStopincomes-2011.pdf (accessed 7 May 2013).

Saez, E. and T. Piketty (2007) 'Income inequality in the United States, 1913–1998', *Quarterly Journal of Economics* 118(1) [2003]: 1–39.
Sample, I. (2012) 'Upper-class people are more likely to behave selfishly, study suggests', *Guardian*, 27 February.
Sanai, D. (2010) 'Beyond luxury', *Lux; Luxury Lifestyles Magazine*, 32, Winter.
Sanandaji, T. (2012) 'The international mobility of the super-rich.' IFN Working Paper no. 904, Research Institute of Industrial Economics, Stockholm, www.ifn.se/wfiles/wp/wp904.pdf (accessed 7 May 2013).
Savage, M. and Williams, K. (eds) (2008) *Remembering Elites*. Oxford: Blackwell.
Schumpeter, J. A. (1976) *Capitalism, Socialism and Democracy*. London: Allen & Unwin.
Sen, W. (2012) 'How the super-rich are spending their money', *Born Rich: Home of Luxury*, 13 March, www.bornrich.com/how-super-rich-spending-money.html (accessed 7 May 2013).
Shaxson, N. (2011) *Treasure Islands: Tax Havens and the Men who Stole the World*. London: Bodley Head.
Sheller, M. and Urry, J. (2006) 'The new mobilities paradigm', *Environment and Planning A* 38: 207–226.
Shirley, A. (2012) 'Passion play', *The Wealth Report* 2012, Knight Frank.
Simmel, G. (2004) *The Philosophy of Money*, 3rd edition, translated by D. Frisby. London: Routledge.
Smart, B. (2011) 'Another "great transformation" or common ruin: prospects and possibilities', *Theory, Culture & Society* 28(2).
Tarde, G. (2012) *Monadologie and Sociology*. Melbourne: re. press.
Terranova, T. (2009) 'Another life: political economy in Foucault's Genealogy of Biopolitics', Special Issue on Michel Foucault, *Theory, Culture & Society* 26(6).
Uhlfelder, E. (2012) 'Best 100 Hedge Funds', *Barron's Penta*, 19 May, http://online.barrons.com/article/SB50001424053111904571704577404264215025458.html (accessed 14 May 2013).
Urquhart, C. (2012) 'No problem, sir: concierge firms boom as the rich flee to London', *Observer*, 10 June.
Urry, J. (2010a) 'Consuming the planet to excess', Special Issue on Changing Climates, *Theory, Culture & Society* 27(2–3).
Urry, J. (2010b) 'Mobile Sociology', *British Journal of Sociology*.
Vellacott, C. (2011) 'Britain has higher rate of self-made rich than U.S.', *Reuters*, 26 May, www.reuters.com/article/2011/05/26/us-wealth-selfmade-rich-idUSTRE74P2XX20110526 (accessed 14 May 2013).
Venn, C. (2009) 'Biopolitics, Political Economy and Power: A Transcolonial Genealogy of Inequality', Special Issue on Michel Foucault', *Theory, Culture & Society* 26(6).
Venn, C. (forthcoming) ' Bankrupt capitalism: debt, the crash, and neoliberal accumulation', in *Protocols for a Postcapitalist World*. Unpublished manuscript.
Weber, M. (2008) *The Protestant Ethic and the Spirit of Capitalism*. 4th Edition. Translated and introduced by Stephen Kalberg. Oxford: Oxford University Press.
Wedel, J. R. (2009) *Shadow Elites: How the World's new Power Brokers Undermine Democracy, Government, and the Free Market*. New York: Basic Books.
Wohlsen, M. (2012) 'Why the world's youngest self-made billionaire shuns life of luxury', Associated Press, 30 April, http://jobs.aol.com/articles/2012/04/30/

why-worlds-youngest-self-made-billionaire-shuns-life-of-luxury (accessed 7 May 2013).
Wuggenig, U. (2011) 'Creativity and innovation in the Nineteenth Century: Harrison C. White and the Impressionist Revolution reconsidered', in G. Raunig, G. Ray and U. Wuggenig (eds) *Critique of Creativity: Precarity, Subjectivity and Resistance in the 'Creative Industries'*. London: May Fly Books.
Wood, A. (2012) 'World's super-wealthy spend their riches on luxury travel adventures', *The Guardiani*, 5 June.
Woolsey, M. (2007) 'Living super large: How wall street titans spend their cash', *Forbes*, 7 June, http://abcnews.go.com/Business/FunMoney/story?id=3250511&page=1 (accessed 19 August 2012).
Zeveloff, J. (2012) 'Look how much more expensive luxury items got in China this Year', *Business Insider*, 5 July, www.businessinsider.com/luxury-consumer-price-index-in-china-2012-9?op=1#ixzz25iHYZPro (accessed 7 May 2013).

Chapter 7

The ease of mobility

Shamus Rahman Khan

In this chapter I argue that there has been a shift in the culture of the elite and that this change is associated with a greater physical mobility of elites. I call this change "from entitlement to privilege" and associate privilege with "ease," a developed capacity to navigate a diverse range of social institutions. "Elite space" – sequestered and removed from the view and access of others – still exists. But elite culture has shifted in important ways. Elites think of themselves not as a class with particularly lineages, institutions, and associations, but instead as a collection of talented individuals who have a unique capacity to navigate our world; for the elite this capacity explains their position, and not the social trappings of class. As such, the world is more open, more flat, ready to be seized by "talented individuals." This cultural shift makes the world more legible, and more open for elite actors.

I develop this argument by overviewing shifts in elite relationships to culture drawing upon research that has argued that elites have moved from being "snobs" to become "omnivores." This argument suggests that elites have moved from using particular cultural distinctions to define themselves to suggesting that they select those cultural traits that are of greatest interest to them. Next I draw upon some of my own earlier research (Khan 2011) to outline what it means to "embody privilege." I argue that such an embodiment results in a greater capacity to be physically mobile and to negotiate new spaces and experiences. The combination of these two elements leads to my conclusion: that the physical embodiment of ease by those who embody privilege allows for the perpetuating of inequality insofar as such an embodiment is a social product that emerges through experiences that are costly to acquire but appear a natural outcome of individual-level differences.

Elite relationships to culture

Pierre Bourdieu formulated his theory of cultural capital and cultural reproduction utilizing the social structure of twentieth-century France

(1984). Bourdieu argued that we use culture to signal who we are. And that signaling can serve as a resource. Interactions having the "right" cultural traits – those valued by others within the interaction – can result in either greater felicity of communication or favorable treatment. Such cultural traits can also result in the drawing of symbolic boundaries (Lamont 1994). Such boundaries help define group belonging, within which resources are shared, made available, or excluded. As such, culture distinctions are not just markers of social position; they help produce such positions. And central to such cultural distinctions are the boundaries which either include or exclude.

However, research has increasingly shown the ways in which social structure and, particularly, the composition and practices of the elite are more fluid and porous. Take elite institutions. At my own university, Columbia, women were once banned from admission and today they make up more than half the university. Not long ago minority groups were all but excluded. Black students used to make up just 0.8 percent of the student body; today they are 13 percent – their overall percentage in the nation as a whole. In fact, Columbia is today a majority minority institution, meaning that less than half the student body is white. This transformation is more than just window-dressing. It represents a radical transformation of an elite space.

And it is not just institutions that have been transformed. Look at the musical (cultural) tastes of Americans today. Some people have narrow tastes, mostly liking single genres such as classical or heavy metal. Others seem far more eclectic, their collections filled with hip-hop and jazz, country and classical, blues and rock. While people themselves think of such differences as a matter of individual choice and expression, they are largely explained by social background. And increasingly, poorer people are much more likely to have singular or "limited" tastes. The rich, by contrast, are the most inclusive (Bryson 1996; Goldberg 2011).

We would see a similar pattern if we looked at other kinds of cultural consumption. The restaurants cherished by upper class New Yorkers range enormously. Restaurants that cost $1,000 per person are on the list, but so too is a cheap "authentic" Szechuan spot in Queens, a local hotdog stand, and a favorite place for a slice of New York pizza. Sociologists have a name for this. Elites are not "highbrow snobs" but instead "cultural omnivores" (Peterson and Kern 1996).

The patterns I have outlined in my own institution are part of a much broader trend of omnivorousness in the culture of our elite. Gone are the Jewish quotas that kept talented young men and women out of elite high schools and colleges; inclusion is now an affirmative practice (Espenshade and Radford 2009; Karabel 2005). "Diverse" popular programming is a mainstay of every museum. Snobbery and exclusion seem not so much constructed by the elite as confronted by them.

This is not a case of American exceptionalism. That is, it is simply not true, as some have argued, that Bourdieu's France cannot be found in the annals of American history. For example, in 1882, one of the richest men in the world, William Vanderbilt, could not gain access to the 18 coveted boxes at the New York Academy of Music. So he offered $30,000 for one (Beckert 2001: 247). Vanderbilt was a representation of new wealth and to the old families occupying these seats his attempts buy a place reserved by birthright was incredibly crass. Money may be king in New York. But not everything could be bought.

Or so it seemed. Upon his bid being rejected Vanderbilt joined the Goulds, Rockefellers, Morgans, and Whitneys and founded the Metropolitan Opera House Company. With 122 private boxes they had plenty of space for the growing elite of the city. They were even able to accommodate the 18 "first families" who lost their boxes as their old exclusionary opera house shut a few years later.

On the one hand, these new elites sought to supplant the old powerful families from their long-held seats. But on the other, they built a new temple of power on the very foundations of the old. New elites were often conservative in their tastes – building mansions that emulated those of European aristocrats, buying up European art, building shrines to European music.

In his history of the Gilded Age, Sven Beckert argues that this era helped consolidate the American Bourgeoisie. The old families of New York formed a kind of elite caste defined by their lineage, and as such they were not threatened by the fact that they shared many of the same tastes as common men. Through much of the nineteenth century, cultural differences between elites and the rest were not so great. Shakespeare and Opera held mass appeal. To attend an evening's concert at the New York Academy of Music might mean hearing Verdi, but also some church music and vaudeville-esque interludes by popular comedians (Levine 1990).

Gilded Age robber barons joining the elite forced a change. As access to elite status became less limited through family ties and more open to men of new wealth, New Yorkers found a new mechanism of social closure, creating a new exclusive culture that was distinct from that of the common American. The result of the rise of the new elite was something far more elitist: through snobbery elites became a class. They developed a shared culture and sensibility. They also shared common enemies.

The Rockefellers and Morgans were not the only "new men" on the scene. Others were pouring into Lower Manhattan. Elites feared the eight million rabble which flowed ashore between 1855 and 1890. Elites moved uptown. Among their mansions they built the Park Avenue Armory in 1880, "defensible from all points against mobs" (Beckert 2001). Their new neighborhood was ready for class warfare. Many sent children away to boarding schools to escape the corruptions of the city (Beisel 1998; McLachlan 1970).

Elites built moats and fences not just around neighborhoods, but also around cultural artifacts. The Metropolitan Opera made cultural performances more "pure," dropping the vaudeville. High ticket prices made the popular music of Verdi less accessible; soon it was the rich and not the rest who enjoyed this music (Levine 1990). Even great public institutions like the Metropolitan Museum of Art were only nominally so. Far from the homes of workers and with security that insured correct behavior and dress, the fine art that had once circulated among the hands of workers on postcard replications (albeit often as pornography) was limited to an imposing building only "respectable" New Yorkers would enter (Beisel 1998).

This was the birth of an upper class; its own schools, clubs, and cultural artifacts that made it quite distinct from other Americans. In short, elites constructed and understood themselves as a "class" – not as individuals. And as such, elite mobility was comparatively limited. Elites had their spaces in the city. In New York this was the Upper East Side and a series of neighborhoods on the Island of Manhattan. Large parts of Brooklyn were a different world – one populated by migrants who were to be avoided (and not visited upon a culinary adventure). The working classes moved through their own neighborhoods and were comparatively excluded from elite neighborhoods, lest they need to visit them to work.

Some may exclaim about how far we've come. Our modern omnivores have filled in the moats and torn down the fences. And that is particularly true if you talk to the elite. They will tell you that, with exclusion and snobbery a relic, the world is available for the most talented to take advantage of. Read Thomas Friedman and this is exactly the story you will hear (2005). To talk of "elite culture," it seems, is to talk of something quaint, something old, and something anti-American and anti-democratic. Whereas the old elites used their culture to make explicit the differences between themselves and the rest, today, elites suggest their culture is simply an expression of their talents. They are open-minded, creative, ready-to-pounce-on-an-opportunity individuals.

But looking at the omnivore, scholars have generated a far different argument. The elite act as if they do not have anything resembling "a culture." Unlike the shared class character of Gilded Age elites, omnivores seem highly distinct and their tastes appear as individual expression. Instead of liking things such as opera because that's just what people of your class like, the omnivore likes what he likes because it is an expression of a distinct self. Perhaps liking a range of things explains why elites are elite, and not the other way around.

By contrast, those who have exclusive tastes today – middle-class and poorer America – are subject to disdain. If the world is open and you don't take advantage of it, then you're simply limited and closed-minded. Perhaps it's these attributes that explain your incapacity to succeed.

And so I would argue that elite culture today is a culture of "individual self-cultivation." Yet there is something pernicious about this presentation of self. The narrative of openness and talent obscures the truth of the American experience. Talents are costly to develop – the research I draw upon comes from a school that spends over $80,000 educating high school students; the average high school spends about one tenth of that. Our American refusal to socialize such educational costs means that talents are not individual capacities, but produced on the basis of economic background. State support for public goods has given way to state support for private provision through markets; such markets have exacerbated inequalities.

If we look at who makes up the "most talented" members of society we see that they are very likely to be the children of the already advantaged. Such trends appear to be getting worse. America has less mobility than almost any other industrial society; one of the best predictors of being an elite today is whether or not your parents were elites (Corcoran 1995; Kopczuk et al. 2010; Mazumder 2005; Solon 1992). And the American inequality and mobility trends may be warning signs for other nations, particularly if market provision of goods are strongly favored as social policies (Atkinson and Piketty 2007; 2010).

We might ask, if the world is a meritocracy of talent, then why are so many of the talented children of the wealthy? Because society has recessed in the minds of the elite; if anything, it is a producer of social problems. To the elite, society created the biases of old institutions – racism, sexism, exclusion. The resulting view is one where society must be as benign as possible, sitting in the background as we play out our lives in a flat world. And the result of such a stance is a new efficiency: the market. And so we have a seemingly ingenious move. We can blame social problems on the processes whereby we thought in terms of collectivities. With such barriers removed, market equality can take over.

Markets allow elites to limit investments in all by undermining public goods and shared, socialized resource allocations. This allows them to increase their own advantage by deploying their economic spoils in markets; they receive returns to these investments, while those without resources to invest are left behind. The result is less equality and more immobility. The elite story about the triumph of the individual with diverse talents is a myth. In suggesting that it is their work and not their wealth, that it is their talents and not their lineage, elites effectively blame inequality on those whom our democratic promise has failed. And their ease has been central to their capacity to navigate a flat world – ease that makes them mobile through space and helps blame those locked in place through impressions of their own failures.

What is ease?

Through an ethnography of St. Paul's School, one of the most elite boarding schools in the world (which I attended from 1993 to 1996 and to which I returned to study in 2005), I argue that the young elite students at St. Paul's cultivate a sense of how to carry themselves, and at its core this practice of privilege is ease: feeling comfortable in just about any social situation. It is from this fieldwork that I developed the argument above. In classrooms students are asked to think about both *Beowulf* and *Jaws*. Outside the classroom they listen to classical music and hip-hop. Rather than mobilizing what we might think of as "elite knowledge" to mark themselves as distinct – epic poetry, fine art and music, classical learning – the new elite learn these and everything else. Embracing the open society, they display a kind of radical egalitarianism in their tastes. Privilege is not an attempt to construct boundaries around knowledge and protect such knowledge as a resource. Instead, students display a kind of omnivorousness. Ironically, exclusivity marks the losers in the hierarchical, open society. From this perspective, inequality is explained not by the practices of the elite but instead by the character of the disadvantaged. Their limited (exclusive) knowledge, tastes, and dispositions mean they have not seized upon the fruits of our newly open world.

This elite ease is also an embodied interactional resource. In looking at seemingly mundane acts of everyday life – from eating meals to dancing and dating – I show how privilege becomes inscribed upon the bodies of students and how students are able to display their privilege through their interactions. In being embodied, privilege is not seen as a product of differences in opportunities but instead as a skill, talent, capacity – "who you are." Students from St. Paul's appear to naturally have what it takes to be successful. This helps hide durable inequality by naturalizing socially produced distinctions.

To see the historical roots of ease, I return to the case of the French. And again there is no better guide to the contemporary French elite than the social scientist Pierre Bourdieu. My own work and ideas are inspired by Bourdieu, who is similarly fascinated by the "Inheritors" – those at the top of the French educational system, the young men and women who are on a path to success in the French economy (1996). Their success, it seems, is preordained, despite our rapidly changing world.

His questions are much the same as those from my own work: What do schools do, how do they do it, and how do the advantaged fare within systems of schooling that are increasingly concerned with eliminating such advantages and being "fair"? How is it that elites manage to navigate a changing world economy? How is it, when there is no longer a nobility where status can be legitimately inherited – indeed, where such a notion is actively challenged – that elites still seem to be a kind of "nobility," transferring their position from one generation to the next? How is it, in short, that as the world around us seems to change, *who elites are* seems to stay the same?

Looking at the Grandes Ecoles – France's elite public schools – two decades after the protest movements of 1968 which were supposed to have changed the world, Bourdieu asked what, if anything, had changed in these educational institutions (1996). After the calls for revolution, how was the new world different from the old? In France, the famous student and worker protests in May 1968 had been aimed in part at these elite schools. On the one hand they were seen as publicly funded institutions for the elite. On the other, they were argued to be indifferent to educating their students in anything other than a conservative morality. What Bourdieu found led him to marvel at how things seemed to be the same. The elite still managed to get into these schools at astonishingly high rates and outperform other students within them. And though the Grandes Ecoles had adopted the language of 1968 – merit, openness, relevance – Bourdieu found that in fact they were still public institutions for the "nobility." How could this be? In France, it is a truth widely recognized that the nation was remade after 1968. But Bourdieu's findings suggested that among the elite, this was a fiction. The nobility still had their systematic advantages.

Educational institutions have organizational logics that determine what good work looks like, what kind of work is valued, and what kind of qualities students should have. After 1968, these standards were no longer supposed to favor the nobility. They were replaced by impersonal and objective standards, highlighting "what it takes" to be a good student, scholar, and even public citizen. Yet Bourdieu found that the logic of this "new" institutional organization still mirrored the dispositions of the nobility. Put simply, the rules of the game still matched the ways in which elite actors play the game. "Impersonal fairness" was a sham. The explanation rests on the continued ease that the nobility feel within elite schools – what Bourdieu thinks of as a correspondence between one's *habitus* and the expectations of an institution.

Thus, when, in the indefinable nuances that define "ease" or "natural" talent, we think we recognize behavior or ways of speaking considered authentically "cultured" because they bear no mark of the effort and no trace of the work that go into their acquisition, we are really referring to a *particular mode of acquisition*: what we call ease is the privilege of those who, having imperceptibly acquired their culture through a gradual familiarization in the bosom of the family, have academic culture as their native culture and can maintain a familiar rapport with it that implies the unconsciousness of its acquisition.

Why, then, has the hierarchy stayed the same in the Grandes Ecoles and among French society more generally? Why are the elite still overrepresented within these institutions and more likely to be successful within them? Because throughout their lives before entering such institutions they have developed dispositions that will advantage them. They feel at home within the institutions that reward them for exactly the type of behavior that is already "native" to them. And the result is even more insidious than it had been in the past because today, unlike years ago, the standards are argued not to advantage anyone. The winners don't have the odds stacked in their favor. They simply have what it takes.

Does this explanation work for the United States? The idea of ease has a lot of explanatory power. But its combination with the frames of hard work and merit generates a uniquely American elite. At the school I studied the students who enter the school with the presumption of ease are aggressively confronted and challenged. Ease is not simply inherited from experiences with families; it is made in interactions at the school. Daily life at St. Paul's is an education unto itself, and presumptuous displays without such experience are met harshly.

In today's age of free, accessible information, knowledge *about the world* is not a particularly easy resource to protect – nearly anyone can learn about Plato, or classical music, or what wine to order with dinner. And after the social movements of the last century, excluding people from such knowledge is no longer acceptable. However, knowledge of how to carry oneself *within the world* is a much more challenging resource to acquire. So eating that meal – ironically, the most common of things that we do everyday – is more challenging than knowing what to order. The latter requires cognitive knowledge that can be learned by anyone; the former requires corporeal knowledge that is developed through experiences within particular settings. The distinction is between learning rules, which are easy, and learning practices, which are far more challenging, as they require living the relations in question. The nearly ingenious trick is that the mark of privilege, corporeal ease, is anything but easy to produce. What appears a natural, simple quality is actually learned through repeated experiences in elite institutions. The result is a near invisible barrier. The apparent easiness of these characteristics implies that if someone doesn't know how to embody ease, it is somehow *their own fault* – they do not naturally have what it takes. This allows for inequitable outcomes to be understood not as the result of the odds being stacked in the favor of some but as something that simply "happens."

This sense of corporeality I take from others as well. Michel Foucault argued that "the body is also directly involved in a political field, power relations have an immediate hold upon it; they invest it, market it, train it, torture it, force it to carry out tasks, to perform ceremonies, to emit signs." Foucault thinks of this as "the political technology of the body," where the effects of such a technology can be attributed to "dispositions, manoeuvres, tactics, techniques, functionings" (1995: 26). In short, our bodies are expressions of the larger power relations of society, and each act of the body works to express itself relative to its own position within these power relations. In a similar vein, taking issue with the Freudian social psychological accounts of how we learn about the world and act within it, Bourdieu argues that social injunctions are not things we "learn" in the mind – they are imprinted not upon some unobservable "super-ego" but on a corporeal "memory pad." Our experiences of the world are inscribed upon the body:

> We learn bodily. The social order inscribes itself in bodies through this permanent confrontation, which may be more or less dramatic but is always marked by affectivity and, more precisely, by affective transactions with the environment.... The most serious social injunctions are addressed not to the intellect, but to the body, treated as a "memory pad."
>
> (Bourdieu 2000: 141)

Our social knowledge is not simply some cognitive framework we are taught but a corporeal inscription. By observing the body within the world we can see far more than the simple physicality of any one actor; instead we can see "the whole structure ... at the heart of the interaction" (Bourdieu 2001: 63).

A crucial part of being an elite, across time and place, is displaying the right corporeal marks of belonging. But the content of these marks varies. And again, the trick of such disciplining and marks is that this social inscription appears as the natural, distinctive, particular quality of each individual student instead of a social product that helps further durability of inequality.

What marks elites as elites is not a singular point of view or purpose but rather their capacity to pick, choose, combine, and consume a wide gamut of the social strata. The "highbrow snob" is almost dead. In its place is a cosmopolitan elite that freely consumes high and low culture, and everything in between. The new adolescent elite listen to classical and to rap; they eat at fine restaurants and at diners. They are at ease everywhere in the world. We even seem to demand this omnivorousness pluralism of our elite. We don't want a patrician president; we want a man who knows how to act around the Queen of England but is just as comfortable sitting in a lawn chair holding a beer summit.

Today's elites share not just a cultural propensity to be omnivorous but also a capacity to do and appreciate many things. They have the time and resources to explore broadly, cultivating not a class character but an individual one – their tastes are particular to them, not defined by the symbolic boundaries of their group (so they think). Further, this picking and choosing is not just in how elites approach the world of culture and tastes but also in how they constitute themselves – their group is no longer narrow and exclusive but wide and varied. From this perspective, the distinction between the elite and the marginalized is that it is now the marginalized whose tastes are limited; they are closed-minded, they exclude anything that is unknown. And elites are mobile through the world – with a drive not to exclude, but to include (for they've benefited terribly by the "inclusion of the market").

This is not to say that the distinctions between social classes are disappearing; rather, the class divide is appearing differently. As pressures to open the elite have increased in the last 50 years, so have the cultural practices of the elite. Elites have incorporated some of the cultural attributes and tastes of those they had previously excluded. Yet this new practice – omnivorous consumption – is itself a symbolic marker. Omnivorous consumption develops within elites a sense of indifference, or an ease of position. Following the classical sociologist Max Weber (1992), I think of privilege as a "mark" – something that the privileged display to one another and to the disadvantaged. And through the display of these marks, the privileged seem to say, in response to the disadvantaged, "It is your own closed-mindedness, your own choices to not take advantage of this new open world, your own lack of interest that explains your position and not durable inequalities." The fact that some of us have this mark (and most of us don't) is not a product of inequality – we all have access to knowledge. But from the perspective of elites, their personal qualities and characters *produce* inequality within the necessary hierarchies that define our human lives.

The view of the world that students from St. Paul's come away with is one wherein the world is defined by its possibility, not its constraints. Thinking of the world as a space of possibility is consistent with a meritocratic frame: the world is yours; all that is required is hard work and talent. Students believe that they work extremely hard and they are exceptionally talented. While I would not characterize students as working hard – as they often do not really do their work – they are certainly busy. This busyness presents the appearance and feel of hard work.

This vision of self and the world – both inculcated by the school and eagerly promoted by the students – has important ramifications. The attitude that the world is perpetually available – and that you are exceptionally capable – goes beyond the simple frame of meritocracy. The world and its innumerable possibilities is a space one can and should navigate with ease. This ease is an essential elite posture, and it often manifests as an indifference to the remarkable opportunities granted them. These students see the extraordinary as everyday. Students can throw stones at a priceless sculpture (as they do to an Alexander Calder). When thinking about a trip to the Metropolitan Opera in New York, where they are flown from New Hampshire for a daytrip, the best answer they can give to whether or not it was enjoyable is "I guess." In their indifference, these students are, from their perspective, cultural egalitarians. They watch Jerry Springer, listen to hip-hop, go to the opera, and are equally comfortable dressed formally for a seated meal and as "pimps and hos" at a school dance. They treat jumping on a plane to go to the Met Opera as an everyday affair, like walking to the local coffee shop to hear a new singer-songwriter.

What St. Paul's is teaching is a style of *learning* that quickly becomes a style of *living* – with an emphasis on ways of relating and making connections rather than with a deep engagement with ideas and texts. It is no surprise, within this pedagogical model, that an indifference – not just toward high literature but toward many of life's opportunities – is the result. This ease of life is not just a mark of privilege. It is also a mark of protection. For if the elite truly embraced hard work, they could be outworked. Ease is both an obscure thing and hard for the rising classes to master. They must work hard to achieve, and it is nearly impossible for this hard work not to leave its mark on them. The advantaged have embraced the accoutrements of the open society with their omnivorousness. But through their marks of ease, they have found ways to limit advancement within such openness, protecting their positions.

Embodiment is a fancy word for a simple idea: we carry our experiences with us. Our time in the world becomes imprinted on our bodies themselves. Time in elite spaces matters, and by definition elite spaces are ones that are exclusive. The importance to embodiment is that once social experiences become embodied, they begin to seem natural. It's just how you carry yourself. We all have to act in some way; your embodiment is yours. The particular form of embodiment of the new elite is ease. This ease is enormously wide-ranging. As they have integrated those who have been excluded, the elite have adapted many of the cultural markers they previously shunned. And so the new elite are at ease in a wide range of areas.

Though the elite have been opened, and have opened themselves to the world, the world has not opened to all. Access is not the same as integration. But what is crucial is that no one is explicitly excluded. The effect is to blame non-elites for their lack of interest. As we have seen, the result of this logic is damning. The distinction between elites and the rest of us appears to be a choice. It is cosmopolitanism that explains elite status to elites and closed-mindedness that explains those who choose not to participate. What matters are individual attributes and capacities, not durable inequalities. From this point of view, those who are not successful are not necessarily disadvantaged; they are simply those who have failed to seize the opportunities afforded by our new, open society. Elites, in embodying their costly experiences, simply seem to have what it takes.

The implications for mobility

Haven't elites always been at ease? Of course. But in this chapter I argue that the character of that ease matters. The elite refinement we read about in Victorian novels, for example, is a kind of ease in a social situation. But to look at such ease is to tell us that this space is an exclusive one, with elaborate rules whose mastery is a lifelong process at which many fail, particularly those who are not initiated at birth.

Such exclusivity comes at a price for these elites. For such a highly mannered quality means that its transferability is limited. To make fine distinctions only recognized within a tiny circle is to act in ways largely irrelevant to most social communities. Yes, you may have social power that allows you access. But you also have a mark of aristocracy that suggests you don't belong.

In my work I have argued that the mark of privilege is different. Mark Zuckerberg – himself a graduate of a school much like St. Paul's – may be worth billions, but he dresses as you might: in a t-shirt and jeans. He is not alone. Today Americans do not want a president who is patrician, we want one who can nimbly meet the Queen of England and, in the same month, have a beer with a working-class policeman at the White House.

To be privileged is to be different. But the differences are talents. Most important, the world is not made up of "separate spheres" – where the workers have their worlds and the rich their own and never the two shall meet. Indeed, the elite language of opportunity seeks to suggest that the world is available. There are resources everywhere – humans, ideas, materials, etc. And the task is to extract them, make the most of them, and create value through them. To do so requires being able to see such opportunities.

I have implied a deep connection with this posture to capitalism and a belief in markets. When the myths of capitalism became not simply a justification of inequality but instead something elites began to believe and hold themselves, their orientation shifted. For with exclusion come inefficiencies. And the difference between peoples is conditional not on heritage but instead on human capital. Embodying such a stance takes work. And it means a corporeal disposition of ease.

To move through the world, of course, requires an apparatus of support, backed in the last instance by force. While my work deals within the cultural sensibilities and frames of actors, we must not forget the tremendous importance of the material and structural. For the cultural apparatus requires such structural and material support to sustain itself (and vice versa). To be at ease across the world requires that one actually be safe across the world. This is a different kind of privilege, one no less important. And it has a kind of visibility, particularly to the disadvantaged. And it is the kind of privilege that makes blaming the victim more of a challenge. For unlike the corporeal ease of privilege, it has a legibility to almost all, except those who enjoy it.

References

Atkinson, A. B. and Piketty, T. (2007). *Top Incomes over the 20th Century.* Oxford: Oxford University Press.
Atkinson, A. B. and Piketty, T. (2010). *Top Incomes in Global Perspective.* Oxford: Oxford University Press.
Beckert, S. (2001). *The Monied Metropolis.* Cambridge: Cambridge University Press.
Beisel, N. (1998). *Imperiled Innocents.* Princeton: Princeton University Press.
Bourdieu, P. (1984). *Distinction.* Cambridge, MA: Harvard University Press.
Bourdieu, P. (1996). *The State Nobility.* Translated by R. Nice. Stanford: Stanford University Press.
Bourdieu, P. (2000). *Pascalian Meditations.* Translated by R. Nice. Stanford: Stanford University Press.
Bourdieu, P. (2001). *Masculine Domination.* Translated by R. Nice. Stanford: Stanford University Press.
Bryson, B. (1996). "'Anything But Heavy Metal': Symbolic Exclusion and Musical Dislikes." *American Sociological Review*, 61(5): 884–899.
Corcoran, M. (1995). "Rags to rags: poverty and mobility in the United States." *Annual Review of Sociology*, 21: 237–267.
Espenshade, T. and Radford. A. (2009). *No Longer Separate, Not Yet Equal.* Princeton: Princeton University Press.
Foucault, M. (1995). *Discipline and Punish.* New York: Vintage.
Friedman, T. (2005). *The World is Flat.* New York: Farrar, Straus and Giroux.
Goldberg, A. (2011). "Mapping Shared Understandings Using Relational Class Analysis: The Case of the Cultural Omnivore Reexamined." *American Journal of Sociology*, 116(5): 1397–1436.
Karabel. J. (2005). *The Chosen: The Hidden History of Admission and Exclusion at Harvard, Yale, and Princeton.* Boston: Houghton Mifflin.
Khan. S. R. 2011. *Privilege: The Making of an Adolescent Elite at St. Paul's School.* Princeton: Princeton University Press.
Kopczuk, W., Song, J., and Saez, E. (2010). "Earnings inequality and mobility in the United States: evidence from social security data since 1937." *Quarterly Journal of Economics*, 125(1): 91–128.
Lamont. M. (1994). *Money, Morals, Manners.* Chicago: University of Chicago Press.
Levine, L. (1990). *Highbrow/Lowbrow: The Emergence of Cultural Hierarchy in America.* Cambridge, MA: Harvard University Press.
McLachlan, J. (1970). *American Boarding Schools: A Historical Study.* New York: Charles Scribner's and Sons.
Mazumder, B. (2005). "Fortunate sons: new estimates of intergenerational mobility in the United States." *Review of Economic Statistics*, 87(2): 235–255.
Peterson, R. A. and Kern, R. M. (1996). "Changing Highbrow Taste: From Snob to Omnivore." *American Sociological Review*, 61: 900–907.
Solon, G. (1992). "Intergenerational income mobility in the United States." *American Economic Review*, 82: 393–408.
Weber, M. (1992). The Protestant Ethic and the Spirit of Capitalism. Translated by T. Parsons. London: Routledge.

Chapter 8

The uneven pragmatics of "affordable" luxury tourism in inland Yucatán (Mexico)

Matilde Córdoba Azcárate, Ana García de Fuentes and Juan Córdoba Ordóñez

Introduction

Tourism and the down-market movement of elite lifestyles and architectures

Contemporary leisure landscapes have been sharply impacted by the luxury fever that has accompanied the accumulation of wealth in the top tiers of the social ladder at a global scale since the late 1990s (Frank 2010). In their book *Mobile Lives*, Elliott and Urry (2010: 128) assess the widespread importance of elite casino capitalism lifestyles and architectures as exemplars of "developments that developers elsewhere ... seek to emulate." "What gets imagined and constructed at the select or elite," they argue, "then moves elsewhere; or indeed, the same development itself moves down-market" (Elliott and Urry 2010: 128). Tourism planning is a key actor in the down-market movement of elite lifestyles and architectures, and the proliferation of so-called "affordable" luxury hotels since late 2000 is a major example of this tendency (Frank 2011).

Affordable luxury hotels are those tourism developments that aim at "reaching the affluent, and global explorers" that are moved by the so-called "new luxury rules": smarter spending, customization, loyalty programs, authenticity, casual and intuitive stays. These are people who look for hotels that curate the destination experience, who seek out the invisible deal, who escape using the right credit card, who trust the power of marketing and, more importantly, who believe in the power of people (Perrin 2010). *Paradores* in Spain, *châteaux* in France, *Latin-style ranches* around and beyond Europe, or colonial *haciendas* in Latin America are good exemplars of these developments. All of these places promote the idea that you can feel like "you are actually super-rich"; they are sited in historical buildings, and proclaim to "give back" to the communities wherein they are located (Conde Nast Traveler 2009).

This chapter argues that the down-market movement of elite architectures and lifestyles through tourism developments such as the ones exemplified by affordable luxury hotels depend on the successful but controversial articulation of tourism planning practices with discourses of elite luxury consumption, sustainable development, social participation, and cultural heritage preservation practices. Few studies have been carried out to show how the above-mentioned articulations between elites, luxury, tourism, culture and development, are achieved in practice, and what their social, political, spatial and environmental consequences are. In this chapter, a detailed ethnographic account focused on the pragmatic articulation of luxury in a Mexican hacienda reveals that sometimes these connections result in dangerous processes of commodification and thematization of culture as well as in the reproduction of social and spatial segregation patterns. In so doing, it provides much-needed empirical material to explore how the actual down-market movement of elite lifestyles and architectures is achieved in practice and also asks: What are some of its implications?

The idea that luxury, or that a taste for luxury, can promote development is an old one. David Hume ([1757] 2006; 1985) and Adam Smith ([1776] 1976) underlined the crucial role that a taste for luxury played in the decline of feudalism and in the promotion of economic development in eighteenth-century Europe. For Hume, the improvement of trade and manufacture along with the emergence of Europe as a commercial society generated a series of changes that he described as "times of industry and refinement" (Hume [1758] 1985: 273). According to this author, luxury was mainly understood as something beyond necessity and convenience, as excess, as an abundant provision of means of comfort, ease and pleasure.[1] The introduction of attractive consumer manufactured goods along with a growing refinement of taste and the subsequent increase in luxury consumption were key to the decline in the power of feudal nobility and the economic development that led to the emergence of the modern estate (Hume [1757] 2006).

In the travel and tourism industries, luxury has been precisely conceived of as an economic resource that presupposes consumption and contributes to economic development per se (Rojek and Urry 1997: 2). Generally as a modality of cultural tourism, luxury tourism is closely tied to discourses of authenticity, exclusivity and elite conspicuous consumption (Park *et al.* 2010).

Increasingly popular among destinations of the Global South, indigenous luxury hotels are an example of tourist developments where these connections rule. The industry's largest luxury hotel operator, Starwood Hotels and Resorts, puts it in a straightforward way: "The idea of indigenous luxury provides a guiding philosophy for new additions to the [luxury] collection. Historic palaces, modern marvels, and exotic resorts all exemplify [this luxury]" (Starwood 2010). The *Haciendas* tourism development in inland Yucatán (Mexico) is one example of this collection of luxury enclaves, and the one that we will address in this chapter.

Setting the ethnographic scene: **The Haciendas project, crafting a distinctive Mexican Caribbean**

The Haciendas is the name given to a private project led by a well-known representative of the global elite – Roberto Hernández, former chairman of Grupo Financiero Banamex and one of the richest people in the world according to Forbes (2010). The *Haciendas* project has involved the acquisition of old *henequén*[2] haciendas and their transformation into 'affordable' luxury hotels in inland Yucatán. To date it is estimated that nearly 30 haciendas have been purchased in the region, although only five have been fully restored as such luxury hotels: Hacienda Temozón Sur, Hacienda Santa Rosa and Hacienda San José in the state of Yucatán; and Hacienda Uayamón and Hacienda Puerta Campeche in the neighboring state of Campeche. These five haciendas are known as *The Haciendas* and they have been taken as epitomes of Hernández tourism ventures in the region.

Still a small-scale form of tourism, the *Haciendas* project is nonetheless "geographically, thematically, economically and ideologically" already mediating other forms of tourism in Yucatán, as well as "showing evidence of dangerous monopolist practices" (Breglia 2009: 245). In fact, although there are other haciendas that have been privately restored and incorporated into mainstream tourism packages in Yucatán – mostly as hotels and spas, or just as restaurants – none of them has been explicitly marketed as a luxury resort.[3] Hacienda tourism therefore predominantly refers to *The Haciendas* and whenever the term is used – in the media, tourist brochures, informal conversations and so on – the association is straightforward. Such an early and direct connection provides strong evidence, as we will show, of the organization of culture around themed experiences available and affordable to all classes (Elliott and Urry 2010: 65).[4]

This chapter offers an in-depth ethnographical account of the pioneering transformation of Hacienda Temozón Sur, the first *henequén* hacienda transformed by Hernández into an "affordable" luxury hotel. As a hotel, Hacienda Temozón Sur has not yet appeared in the 2012 Golden List of the world's most luxurious hotels and it is not part of the itineraries of the richest sector of the Mexican population, for whom the Caribbean coast still is the major destination.[5] The Hacienda is, however, listed alongside 82 other hotels and well-known global elite developments as "Six Senses Resorts" and "Canouan Resorts Developments," in the *Conde Nast Traveler* list of 2012. As we will show, the transformation of Hacienda Temozón Sur into a guilt-free luxury resort is done through the reproduction of the elite lifestyle of the local oligarchy of Yucatán's *henequén* glory times. The reproduction of this historical elite lifestyle implies the recreation of the Hacienda as a cocooned, affluent, gated and glamorous space for tourism consumption. This recreation is done through a series of architectonical

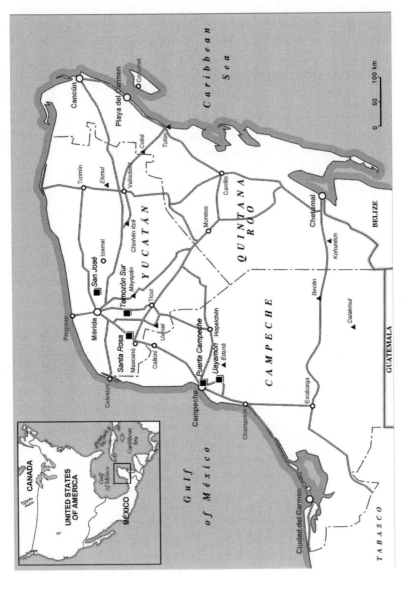

Figure 8.1 Location map of the Yucatán Peninsula and *The Haciendas* (source: Juan Córdoba Ordóñez).

arrangements, the aesthetization of the past, a specific ordering of nature, and a repertoire of staged and professionalized practices devoted to pamper tourists' senses. These material arrangements and social practices are discursively premised upon luxury consumption. The dependence upon enclosed architectures and professionalized encounters with the Other, as well as the reliance upon global corporations for community development ventures, detaches the Hacienda from the local and regional landscape of poverty and lack of opportunities that is typical of contemporary Yucatán (Córdoba Azcárate 2011).

Methodological notes

As others have previously demonstrated, ethnography is a fruitful method to gather first-hand knowledge of elite spaces (see Khan 2010; Wedel 2009). However, ethnography in these spaces is not an easy endeavor. In our case, information and access, to both data and the Hacienda, remained problematic even if it was a down-scale elite development. Physical access to the Hacienda was only possible upon request and managers always monitored our circulation within it.

The clientele of Hacienda Temozón Sur is mostly composed of wealthy European and Mexican middle and upper classes. Access to them is difficult as privacy policies impede opportunities to meet clients within the resort or to follow their tracks outside. The typically motorized experience of the place, always coming and going in private vans, minimizes casual encounters. The small-scale nature of this tourism development makes it difficult to talk anonymously to the fewer than 60 workers at the Hacienda, 94 percent of whom are inhabitants of the community of Temozón. These workers are subject to strict privacy rules, and their disruption for long conversations may result in labor sanctions. Managers and other workers typically monitor casual conversations and formal interviews. Statistical data are not widely available, and most of them account for basic tourism data produced by Starwood.

For these reasons, in our research the ethnographic emphasis has focused on the ways in which Hacienda Temozón Sur crafts a luxury experience for its clients, both materially and socially. Specifically, we have tried to understand by which precise means (material arrangements and practices) the hacienda emulates the lifestyles of the global elite and the socioeconomic and spatial consequences that this has had at regional and local scales. In so doing, and in line with the work of Beaverstock *et al.* (2004), this research aims to shed light on the importance of understanding the influential power of global elite mobile lives and spaces, if we are to generate more inclusive and socially just futures.

Haciendas: from *henequén* processing factories to abandonment and luxury tourist renewal

Henequén *and status-conscious haciendas*

Haciendas in Yucatán fit into the classical definition of a Latin American Hacienda provided by Wolf and Mintz:

> An agricultural estate operated by a dominant landowner ... and a dependent labor force, organized to supply a small-scale market by means of scarce capital in which the factors of production are employed not only for capital accumulation but also to support the status aspirations of the owner.
>
> (1957: 380)

In Yucatán, the small-scale market became a large international market through the industrialization and commercialization of *henequén*, the Mexican 'green gold' of the late nineteenth and early twentieth centuries and the region's monocrop agricultural system from the last quarter of the nineteenth century well into the mid 1970s.

In 1916, Yucatán had 1,100 Haciendas exclusively devoted to *henequén* processing. There were nearly 213,000 hectares under cultivation and Haciendas were producing and exporting over 200,000 tons of *henequén* a year, mainly to the United States (Fox 1961: 225; Villanueva 1990: 53). At this time, Hacienda Temozón Sur, in the inland municipality of Abalá, was one of the most important landholdings in the country with 6,600 hectares, 640 workers, and the largest *henequén* industrial equipment of the region. By 1920, the fiber comprised more than 95 percent of the region's exports and at the beginning of 1970 it still represented more than half of Yucatán's farmed land (Brannon and Baklanoff 1987; Wells 1985). Over 55 percent of the economically active population was at that time employed in the *henequén* industry (Baños 1996; OECD, 2007: 123).

Henequén haciendas were crucial in the region's sociopolitical organization and economic development. They were at the epicenter of the expansion of commerce and services and the major reason for the development of international and intraregional communication infrastructures (Garcia de Fuentes and Morales 2000). At the beginning of the last century, Yucatán was, with over 1,000 rail kilometers, the Mexican state with the biggest rail network. Most of the railway system was the basis for the haciendas' exchange of goods and people, and it had the unique characteristic of having been "mainly envisioned, constructed, managed and financed by local capitalists and workers" (Wells 1992: 161). Internationally, *henequén* processing placed the Peninsula in the global market, though it did so as a fragile and dependent development economy totally reliant on international, mostly North American, markets.

Haciendas are paradigmatic examples of how ownership of landed estates has been closely intertwined with elite status in Mexico (Van Young 2006). In Yucatán, they informed the formation and accumulation of the greatest part of personal fortunes. *Henequén* haciendas enforced a highly structured social system based on racial divisions and paternalistic relationships. As Van Young (2006: 20) put it, Haciendas were "economically capitalist but socially feudal" systems. Their social organization was composed of the *hacendados*, or landowners, mainly creoles – persons born and naturalized in Yucatán but of European origin – and the *peones* – land workers, mainly Maya *indígenas* – indigenous populations – and immigrant workers from Korea and other parts of México, mostly Yaqui *indígenas* from Sonora.

Neither *hacendados* nor *peones* were homogeneous social groups and they varied strongly internally according to their origins, cultural and racial backgrounds, commercial interests and ideological standards. Yet, for the purposes of this chapter, both collectives shared several characteristics that make it possible to conceive them as distinctive social groups (Ancona 1995). First, *hacendados* shared what Wells (1991) has defined as the "*hacendado* elite mentality." The *hacendado* elite mentality was guided by the principle that "no expense is too great," which was directly translated into sumptuous material consumption: ostentatious homes, ornate carriages, grandiose parties for *la gente decente de Mérida* (nice people from Mérida) and frequent trips to Europe (Wells 1991: 134–135). Second, *hacendados* had total control over the processes of production and distribution of the *henequén*. Third, they exercised severe political and repressive power over the *peones*; and fourth, *peones'* hard working conditions have been largely defined as states of helpless peonage or regimes of semi-slavery (Alston *et al.* 2009; Katz 1974).

Figure 8.2 Photographs at Hacienda Temozón Sur representing the wedding of a *hacendado* (left) and *peones* (right) (source: photograph by authors).

Each hacienda had its independent currency and payment system, financial control mechanisms and norms of social conduct. All of these were unilaterally established by *hacendados* and conformed to a debt–peonage labor system. *Hacendados* would pay a daily or weekly wage to *peones* in the hacienda's own currency or company scripts (*vales*) only valid in each hacienda's unique store, the *tienda de raya* (Ancona 1995). *Tiendas de raya* supplied basic goods and needs within each hacienda to *peones* and their families. *Tiendas de raya* used a system of hereditary debts which tangled together in a dependency relation both *peones* to particular *hacendados*, and *hacendados* to particular regional elites (Nickel 1996). The asymmetrical power relationship between *hacendados* and *peones* and the poor living and working conditions of most of the latter, made some haciendas, such as Temozón Sur, sites of ethnic and labor contestation (Castellanos 2010; Fallaw 1999).

Haciendas' architecture played a crucial role in organizing, sustaining and reinforcing this uneven social organization. Buildings and infrastructures were designed not only to maximize productivity but also to inscribe *hacendados*' power. For this purpose, haciendas were designed as spatially segmented and architecturally distinct population settlements and domestic units (Peniche Rivero, 1999). Although their composition varies across the region, there were a series of widespread regularities in their design which included: a *casa principal*, usually the largest building where the *hacendado* kept his living quarters and in which most of the administration took place; several Maya vernacular houses where resident *peones* lived, located within the gates of the hacienda's property; and then other major constructions under *hacendados*' administration and control. Among them, and besides the *tienda de raya*, the most important ones were the *casa de maquinas* or machine house, where the *henequén* processing took place; the *casa del mayordomo* where the foreman lived and where the administration took place when the *hacendado* was away; a *capilla* or chapel which stressed the importance of the hacienda as a population center; and many smaller buildings used as storage and animal shelters, as grain storerooms and stables.

Casas principales were generally constructed upon elevated basements and they normally kept to totally decontextualized architectonical styles. They were characterized by their highly decorative eclectic European styles which varied from baroque and rococo to neoclassical, Arabic and even Asiatic designs (Wytinsky *et al.* 2003). As Wells (1982: 224) put it, "looking to the far-off capitals of the western world for inspiration and design, the prosperous *henequeneros* built ornate palaces with marble pillars, intricately carved façades, and ostentatious stained-glass enclosed porticoes." *Casas principales* thus epitomized the particular elite lifestyle and mentality of the *hacendados* and they have become, as we are going to show, fundamental in *The Haciendas* project of renewal as luxury hotels.

Abandonment and elite tourist renewal

Yucatán's monopoly on the *henequén* market along with this social world of distinctions and architectonical display were strongly affected by the economic crisis of 1929 and then totally devastated by the introduction of synthetic fibers, especially nylon, in the global market in the late 1960s. These crises weakened the industry and led it to a vast contraction by the end of the 1970s (Garcia de Fuentes and Morales 2000). The state took close control of the industry, subsidizing first its initial phases of production and then creating Cordemex, a parastatal industry controlling all phases of production. By 1976 the state had gained total control over the production of the fiber (Villanueva 1990) at a time when half of the active population was still fully dependent on the *henequen*, which, moreover, still represented 60 percent of the region's agricultural production (Villanueva 1990).

State subsidies to *henequen* production remained until the 1990s and though they helped to maintain the region's economy during the huge depression of the early 1980s, they also allowed *hacendados* to remain in control of the fiber's commercialization until the very end of the industry. By providing *hacendados* with time and resources, the state gave them a

Figure 8.3 Abandoned Hacienda ex-*henequenera* Uayalcén, just a few kilometers away from Temozón Sur (source: photograph by authors).

wide margin to reorient their capital towards more profitable enterprises, mostly to developing a tourism industry on the Caribbean coast.

The creation of Cancún in 1974 by the federal government in the uninhabited marshlands of the Mexican Caribbean coast shifted the socio-economic balance of the peninsula from one monocrop to another: the sea, sun and sand, mass tourism (Córdoba et al. 2007; Torres 2002). In less than 30 years and through the massive impulse of public, private and corporate investments, the tourism industry in Cancún became the major economic force of the region. The service sector, nearly non-existent in 1970, by 2004 already represented 77 percent of the Peninsula's GDP (INEGI, 2005). By contrast, in the 1990s *henequén* represented less than 10 percent of the agricultural production of the peninsula (OECD 2007: 123).

The radical shift from *henequén* to tourism left haciendas in a state of complete abandonment, peasants dispossessed, and Yucatán's elites drastically reconfigured. Previously synonymous with being a *hacendado*, Yucatec elites soon disintegrated to be part of a bigger global heterogeneous group, strongly connected with international corporations. Within these new globalized elites, Ramírez (2008, 2012 personal communication) has differentiated three major groups. One group, composed of no more than ten businessmen, which managed to gain control of the three major economic sectors at a regional level (tourism, construction and commerce); a second group which has influential positions in major international and national corporations with regional interests as well as in service-oriented and automobile franchises and industries; and a third and wider group, composed of politicians closely associated with land speculation and real-estate development corporations at regional, national and international levels. The reconstruction of *henequén* haciendas as luxury hotels within *The Haciendas* project mainly involves this last group. The connections between political and economic national elites with this emergent form of affordable luxury tourism and their implications for regional development have not yet been studied. This is of foremost importance as *The Haciendas*' reconstruction not only shows the controversial connections among contemporary elite business practices and the tourism and development industries, but also helps to shed light on the actual ways in which these elites shape everyday spaces and practices by reinventing, in this case, elite past lifestyles and buildings.

Luxury and cultural tourism in The Haciendas ... *or just business as usual?*

Coinciding with a global wave of policies promoting alternative forms of tourism in the late 1990s, Hernández, with the partnership of Alejandro Patrón Laviada – brother of the former Yucatán governor Patricio Patrón Laviada – acquired a series of abandoned *henequén* haciendas in inland

Yucatán. They had the intention of turning them into exclusive hotels for global elites. For this purpose, they created a real estate business group, Grupo Plan, directed by a well-known Mexican architect, Luis Bosoms – Roberto Hernández's son-in-law – and formed a partnership with the US company Starwood's Luxury Collection.

The Haciendas have been restored under the auspices of Fomento Cultural Banamex, a non-profit branch of the Grupo Financiero Banamex created in 1970 as a direct response to cultural heritage global protection policies. Since 2000, Grupo Plan and the Luxury Collection have shared their administration and management. Each hotel and resort is designed to be "a distinct and cherished expression of its location; a portal to the destination's indigenous charms and treasures," the only way of living "unique, authentic experiences that evoke lasting, treasured memories" (Starwood 2010).

As part of the Luxury Collection, *The Haciendas* have been classified as a luxury variant of cultural tourism in the region (Secretaría de Fomento Turístico 2009). They are specifically advertised as "Premium Tourism" and "Grand Tourism" together with spas and golf sites. The creation by Grupo Plan, also in 2002, of the non-profit institution Fundación Haciendas en el Mundo Maya – directed by architect Bosoms' wife – marks an

Figure 8.4 Surroundings of the restored Hacienda Temozón Sur (source: photograph by authors).

inception point in this tourism venture. Through this institution, *The Haciendas* embrace the discursive referents of a sustainable and participatory cultural tourism development strategy for inland Maya communities. As they put it, their mission is to generate "viable, sustainable micro-regional development in the immediate surroundings of restored Haciendas" (The Haciendas, 2007). For this purpose, and in association with Fomento Cultural Banamex, the Fundación has set in motion a series of development projects in the communities in which they are located. These projects have been essential in the embellishment and tourism functionality of haciendas and not so much, as they claim to be, in the development of the communities where the haciendas are located. As Breglia highlights, hacienda tourism in Yucatán is the perfect example where "one small, well-connected, financially and politically powerful group of people are in control," weaving together cultural tourism, luxury and economic profitability (2009: 253). The next section explores how this weaving has taken place in practice and what are some of its consequences.

Crafting luxury in Hacienda Temozón Sur

Hacienda Temozón Sur is located in the village of Temozón Sur, in the municipality of Abalá, 40 kilometers away from Mérida, the state's capital. Abalá is a municipality with a high level of marginality (CONAPO 2005). Of its population, 57 percent (4,285 people) live in poverty, 17 percent of whom are officially classified as extreme poverty (CONEVAL 2010).

The Hacienda is specifically marketed by the Luxury Collection as a "luxury boutique hotel," "a superb residence in the Heart of the Yucatán Peninsula which recreates the belle époque of the Mexican southeast" and which in so doing "creates opportunities for locals who would never have had the chance ... to earn a living in rural Yucatán" after the *henequén* crisis (The Haciendas, 2007).

The transformation of the Hacienda into a luxury tourist enclave is discursively and institutionally legitimized, by claiming the inherent importance of haciendas as cultural heritage for Yucatán's history. In practice, however, reconstruction processes have privileged the relationship between the hacienda and the elite status aspirations of *hacendados*, leaving out, among other things, the history of these sites as contentious scenarios of asymmetrical labor and power relations. Specifically, the production of luxury at Hacienda Temozón Sur has required a selective recovery of the hacienda's architectonical heritage, a specific ordering of nature and secluded host–guest encounters.

Selective restoration and re-functionalization of architectures

Material practices, writes David Harvey, "instantiate and objectify human desires in the material world, not only through the reproduction of self and bodily being but also through modifications of surrounding environments" (1996: 79). One of the ways luxury is achieved and signified at the Hacienda is precisely through the re-functionalization of architectures and the aesthetic display of objects linked to the *hacendado*'s elite lifestyle. These are material practices that aim to instantiate and objectify tourists' desires through the reproduction of a European self and the modification of a colonial environment for tourism consumption.

This process of restoration has materially anchored the Hacienda's history to a golden era that has little resemblance with its past as a non-egalitarian, quasi-feudal socioeconomic system of production. This process of restoration has created the Hacienda as a romanticized scenario or stage in which tourists' experiences and imaginaries are univocally equated to those of the *hacendado*. This romanticized stage is composed of three interrelated elements: a staged and gated entrance; the equation of the Hacienda with the *casa principal* at the expense of other spaces; and the museification of the *hacendado*'s everyday objects in adjacent architectures and spaces. We explore each of these elements in what follows.

Hacienda Temozón Sur is a gated community. Gating is a direct result of the Hacienda's marketing as a secluded, safe, glamorous space for the jet set and global elites (Beaverstock *et al.* 2004; Beaverstock and Faulconbridge and Sheller in this volume). In this marketing, the Hacienda appeals to its unique global position as being home for such guests as former US presidents Clinton and Bush and Mexican president Calderón, as well as many other celebrities including the singer Shakira. These personalities access the place either through its private heliport or using chauffeur-driven vans. Most of the Hacienda's guests, mainly middle and upper classes from Europe and Mexico, do not, however, enjoy such privileges. These clients normally access the place driving their own rented cars, which implies driving a few kilometers in the village of Temozón Sur and, mostly, getting lost. With this in mind, in the process of restoration for luxury tourism, Grupo Plan designed and built an idyllic Mayan village just outside the hacienda's *casa principal*. This village forms a one-kilometer avenue of polished vernacular Mayan façades, uniformly painted in white and red, matching the façade of the *casa principal* of Temozón Sur. These vernacular houses are in fact rented spaces where fewer than ten women, dressed in traditional Mayan outfits, work at several handicrafts including *henequén* fibers, broidery, soaps, candles and silver that are later purchased as luxury gifts by the Hacienda's guests in the Hacienda's shop.

Figure 8.5 Gated entrance to Hacienda Temozón Sur (source: photograph by authors).

The sight of this scenario provides tourists with a first impression of a homogeneous and clean community harmonically working for the Hacienda. This vision encourages them in a sort of pilgrimage to an idealized past in which the Hacienda was the main economic driving source for the community's development. Outside this staged space, the rest of the 180 houses in the village of Temozón Sur and more than 1,400 in Abalá (INEGI 2010) remain poor constructions offering the typical contemporary rural landscape of Yucatán: a mixture of poor Mayan huts, concrete houses and makeshift housing strongly decorated with global icons and regional political propaganda and lacking basic services such as potable water or electricity. According to CONEVAL (2010), 88 per cent of the population in Abalá still lacks access to main basic services at home.

The gated construction and the selective and staged enactment of the immediate social surroundings of the Hacienda together with the objectification of women's development help to maintain the Hacienda's present reality as a culturally aware "superb oasis of luxury and relaxation" where references to an immediate social context in need of further development are obliterated (The Haciendas 2007). This selective enactment of the social continues inside the Hacienda, which is designed to enable guests to live as "in the 19th century, but still receiving high-end luxury collection" (Yucatan Today 2009). The idea, according to the general manager, was "to restore original designs, like paintings, decorations, furniture but drawing a line where the historical part ends and the luxury experience begins." In practice, this line has been inscribed by erasing all references to the Hacienda's past as a productive space with a highly functional distribution of buildings and spaces.

The *casa principal* has been the major target in the conversion of the Hacienda into a luxury hotel. This selective restoration involves some historical problems if considering how the *casa principal* was and still is perceived by the local population.

At every hacienda, the *casa principal* contrasted with vernacular Mayan houses which are highly functional and totally dependent in their design on climate conditions (Rodríguez Viqueira and Fuentes Freixanet 2006). Contrary to the extravagant styles and imported materials of construction of *casas principales*, vernacular houses have an elliptic structure with walls made of mud (adobe) or limestone and roofs covered with wooden poles and palm tree leaves. The architectonic contrast between ostentation and functionality and environmental adequacy was a deliberate and visible one during the *henequén* times. It materially re-instantiated the social, racial and economic distance between *hacendados* and Maya indigenous people employed as *peones*. Through restoration works the *casa principal* at Hacienda Temozón Sur has been transformed into a 28-room retreat. The *casa principal* has been carefully painted with its traditional colors, a red wash, whites and yellows. Original materials, like iron, stone and wood, have been maintained for major visible structures and furniture and decoration in common areas, and rooms recreate at first glance the French style of the Hacienda's former owners. Old European furniture has been imported and where possible preserved and put into new usages – for example the old pharmaceutical cabinets now transformed into mini bars or tourist bookshelves – and all rooms have been decorated with European furniture and Renaissance-style paintings. These European artifacts were representative of luxury and marked status. Today, they provide tourists with the taste of inhabiting a European palace in the middle of tropical Yucatán, with a romanticized and de-contextualized image of home from abroad. The arrangement of colors, furniture and paintings in this European fashion is crucial to mark the continuity of the place with the *hacendado*'s European aspirations through the equation of elite tourists' experiences and imaginaries with those of the *hacendado*.

The rest of the buildings within the Hacienda have also been re-functionalized and aesthetized to serve tourism consumption purposes. The Old Machinery House, for example, has been converted into a museum space in which restored everyday objects are exhibited together with a collection of black and white images of the *hacendado*'s private

Figure 8.6 Panoramic view of the *casa principal* from inside Hacienda Temozón Sur (source: photograph by authors).

albums. The objects and images collected and stored in this site almost exclusively portray the everyday life of luxury and amenities around the *hacendado* and his family, scarcely showing the hard work done by *peones* at the haciendas. Images show, for example, family celebrations as weddings and christening rituals, the *hacendado* dealing with paperwork in his office, his frequent travels to Europe or the United States, or gentlemen's meetings at the *casa principal*. In all of these pictures the *hacendado* and those around him wear European clothing and accessories. Objects on display, such as wagons, bicycles, ladies' umbrellas or babies' toys, reveal the luxuries around the *hacendado*'s life while leaving out the Hacienda as a highly non-egalitarian socioeconomic system. Those spaces that were used for drying and dying the *henequén*, or for storage and animals, have been transformed into tennis courts, jogging tracks, swimming pools and conference rooms.

By creating these leisure stages for tourists a very selective link with Yucatán's past is manufactured. The result is a bucolic image of the inland Caribbean for tourism consumption in which the past is rewritten to conform to the *hacendado*'s privileged and elite lifestyle. In this image, hard working conditions and a highly non-egalitarian society are veiled and the tourist's experiences are equated to the *hacendado*'s privileged life. The conflictive nature of the *henequén* times is abstracted and Yucatán history narrated from a reductive point of view. This point of view, as we will see in the next section, is furthered through a very particular ordering of nature as gardens.

A European craftsmanship of nature

Hacienda Temozón Sur is a clear example of how gardens are "forms of material culture inscribing affluence and power, legitimating social stations made problematic by economic change" (Mukerji 1994: 440).

Following the formal gardening style of the Palace of Versailles, the 37 hectares of the Hacienda's gardens have been constructed according to mathematical formulas, where geometry, monumentality, perspective and the controlled movement of bodies are the rules. Panoramic visions from the *casa principal* over adjacent buildings are secured by respecting the traditional elevated structure of this building as well as by the delineation of symmetric paved pathways that have the *casa principal* as their center of reference. The elevated disposition and the careful layouts of pathways clearly confirmed the centralized power of the *hacendado* over *peones* as it confirmed the power of absolutist kings over populations (Mukerji 1994: 440). While an elevated structure allows a panoptical control over spaces and activities, careful layouts prevent disordered movements around the hacienda. These dispositions secure for tourists the control over the movement of those who cater for them and the vision of a perfect environment in which the tropical forest is made present, preserving all its exuberance but without all its annoyances. For this latter purpose ten gardeners collect leaves and other organic residuals daily; birds are kept in cages, exotic plants in flowerpots, and tropical insects are kept away through daily fumigation. A botanical garden is maintained in which the rhythmic sound of water in fountains and artificial pools embraces clients as they walk by. Carefully planned fresh shadows are maintained all around the gardens and clients are able to read, in English and Mayan, the labels of several of the most important botanical plants collected by Grupo Plan and later sold at local workshops by Fundación Haciendas del Mundo Maya.

This transformation of nature at Hacienda Temozón Sur contrasts with a contemporary context of hectares of abandoned *henequén* fields, deforestation and an increasingly intractable waste problem. According to the Yucatán Urban Development and Environment Secretary, Yucatán lost more than one million hectares of forestland between 1976 and 2000. Far from the carefully crafted exuberance of tropical vegetation inside the Hacienda's gates, its surroundings present a landscape subjected to strong deforestation and its associated problems of erosion and desertification (Lutz *et al.* 2000). Abandoned lands in which *henequén* used to grow have been transformed into disordered tropical jungles, normally growing as

Figure 8.7 Gardeners working at Hacienda Temozón Sur (source: photograph by authors).

secondary forests and used for the subsistence production of maize through the use of a slash-and-burn system (*roza, tumba, quema*), with its controversial ecological impacts. Besides, the generalization of illegal waste dumps and land filling evince serious waste management problems and contaminate potable water. By keeping all these elements at a prudential distance the carefully manicured tropical nature of the Hacienda reifies it as a cocooned, sanitized and gated space.

The material arrangement of buildings and the craftsmanship of nature that we have explored in this section show how the accomplishment of luxury at Hacienda Temozón Sur demands the articulation of an aestheticized space which detaches the Hacienda from the historical, social and environmental past and present reality of the peninsula. This aestheticized space is one of a distinctive Caribbean also characterized by a sensory and secluded engagement with the Other.

A sensory and secluded engagement with the Other

Macdonald and Fyfe (1996) have studied how the power and efficacy of architectural spaces as material metaphors are inseparable from bodily, sensory engagement with particular places. This is precisely what tourism literature has recently stressed when observing how bodily senses like touch and smell are important elements accompanying the visual in making sense of tourist places and experiences (Crouch and Desforges 2003). In fact, the development and organizing of sensory experiences regarding taste and touch are crucial in the accomplishment of a taste of elite lifestyles in *The Haciendas*.

Specifically, at Hacienda Temozón Sur, the taste of an elite lifestyle is accomplished by pampering clients' senses through personalized attention, the generation of unique flavors, and the practice of therapeutic body massages. These practices involve adapting and adjusting workers' spatial movements to clients' requirements. These adjustments are based on the disciplining of bodies and the performance of a highly touristic choreographic space in which, as Edensor puts it, "bodies are tutored in 'appropriate' ways" (1998: 106). These practices demand highly professionalized workers and the conditioning of selective atmospheres.

During their stay at the Hacienda, clients are surrounded by well-trained, English-speaking, indigenous Maya waiters and maids. Women are dressed in impeccable traditional Maya clothes while men are dressed in plain brown uniforms. All of them, mostly of Mayan origin, are under the direction of a permanent manager, normally of foreign origin, who is directly employed by Starwood Luxury Collection to be in charge of the Hacienda. Employees offer guests a personalized service which includes the possibility of having the same persons attending to their needs or elaborating their own timetables of lunches, dinners and activities.[6]

The disciplining of the bodies of those who cater for tourists and the development and organization of etiquette are most visible at the Hacienda's restaurant. Waiters have been trained in how and when to address clients: uniforms with their names on are worn, corporeal distances are carefully observed, language and gestures controlled, excessive talk forbidden, and a careful attention to filling glasses, lighting cigarettes or accommodating chairs is displayed. The waiters and the maître d' are under the constant surveillance of the manager who, playing the role of the traditional foreman, observes, controls and constantly corrects their interactions with clients. Clients, on their part, know that they should dress properly and display a complete array of good table manners. They expect careful attention and demand it, sometimes with just a look, if the service is not up to their standards.

This presentation of the self takes place in a space where the production and presentation of unique food flavors has become a dominant leitmotif. The most popular Maya dishes and traditional ingredients are cooked by an internationally recognized Mexican chef who is listed as one of the 30 Mexican celebrity chefs educated in Michelin's and Ferran Adriá of El Bulli's philosophies.[7] It is not by chance that *The Haciendas* have turned to gastronomy as a way to differentiate themselves from other forms of tourism alternatives and that they have turned to fusion cuisine as a way to achieve it. Gastronomy offers a major element in tourists' search for social distinction (Molz 2007). The main specialty of the Hacienda Temozón Sur restaurant is the fusion between Yucatec and international, mostly French cuisines. This fusion of foods aims to generate a unique flavor of Yucatán in the privileged palates of those able to eat there. This is a distinctive Yucatán that appeals to clients with a desire and the economic means to travel the region differently. Here, meat is accompanied with imported wine, fish is offered and cooked with elaborated European condiments, chocolate and orange desserts take the place of chili fruits, and fresh bread combines with traditional tortillas. In contrast to this, food consumption in Yucatán has to be understood in terms of what Leatherman and Goodman have termed the "coca-colonization" of the Yucatec Mayan diet (2005). This process of coca-colonization refers to the increasing consumption of commercialized processed foods and calorie-intensive but nutrient-poor snack foods and beverages in inland Mayan communities and which these authors interpret as a major disruption caused by tourism in the region. This widespread diet is closely associated with two of the major health problems in the region, diabetes and obesity, and it is in sharp contrast with those authenticity claims of encountering the cultural "Other" through food consumption that the Hacienda offers.

Along with the generation of unique flavors, the offer of "traditional" treatments is the other most relevant practice to pamper the self in

Hacienda Temozón Sur. These treatments typically consist of body massages designed to revitalize, energize and purify the self. Massages are done in artificially created atmospheres, either at the new spa or at the Mayan *cenote*,[8] specifically renamed, the "cave spa" of the community. These spaces have been carefully designed to preserve privacy, solitude and silence and hence to seclude clients' selves from their immediate surroundings. A group of six local indigenous women working for the Hacienda under the label of ancient Maya *sobadoras* are in charge of massages. These women have been trained by Grupo Plan as professional therapists in an effort to "bring Mayan wisdom and tradition" to the Hacienda's guests "while helping Mayan families in their daily sustainability" (The Haciendas 2007). However, *sobadoras* can hardly earn a living through their work, barely reaching the daily minimum wage of 60 Mexican pesos (personal interview, 2012). Moreover, this practice has also required the re-signification of the active work of rural Maya midwifes (*parteras*) and healers (*sobadoras*) for tourism consumption. In so doing, the *sobada* has lost its traditional meaning and symbolism as a practice performed by old expert rural women to help women in labor and has become a practice performed by trained young professionals and directed to tourists' inner selves; a sort of self-indulgent practice which advocates the isolation,

Figure 8.8 Waiters catering for tourists at Hacienda Temozón Sur (source: photograph by authors).

shelter and exclusive treatment of tourists' selves in a very similar fashion to Western spas and old-style seaside resorts.

By interacting with a well-trained, educated, professional and disciplined team of workers, clients are submerged into a timeless elite microclimate in which rural Yucatán's traditions as well as its lack of opportunities remain very much veiled. European tastes in gardening and food consumption practices, as well as a careful attention to tourists' selves, are performed in Hacienda Temozón Sur as practices through which both a luxury is accomplished and a connection with the *hacendado*'s elite mentality is enabled.

Conclusions

The transformation of Hacienda Temozón Sur into an "affordable" luxury hotel is a privileged example of the materialization of *bourgeois utopias* (Fishman 1987), as sealed-off places of leisured living and conspicuous consumption with little impact on surrounding communities. It exemplifies how specific tourism developments are being disembedded from regional and local territories to be repackaged and connected to mobile global elite flows (Sheller 2009). Specifically, this case has offered the opportunity to study how elite lifestyles and architectures premised upon luxury consumption move down-market through concrete social practices and material arrangements. It has shown how these arrangements and practices are informed by contemporary Mexican elite business practices and how they delimit exclusive spaces in which some elements are made present – for example an ordered nature, an aestheticized past, sublimated culinary experiences – while others are excluded or abstracted – for instance poverty or a non-egalitarian past.

The transformation of Hacienda Temozón Sur into an "affordable" luxury hotel has worked by disguising the reality of social inequalities and spatial segregation typical of both the *henequén* era and of contemporary Yucatán in discourses of heritage valorization, sustainability and local participation. The reason behind this abstraction is that as we have seen, the emulation of elite lifestyles needed for the hotel to qualify as a luxury hotel in the tourism industry has required the selective socio-material and practical organization of exclusive, aestheticized spaces based on the culture and values of the oligarchy formed during *henequén* glory times.

The Hacienda's restoration project exemplifies the tendency in heritage management practices to objectify places by focusing more on architectures and objects rather than on communities and thus attributing inherent cultural values and significance to these things (Smith 2006). It illustrates how, as a consequence, "culture is substantialized and abstracted from its uses, becoming something material available to conservation" (Byrne 2008: 159) and therefore consumption, and how, in addition, certain heritage management practices and the tourism industry work together to enact a specific past. Moreover, and despite their discourses of community participation and local engagement, *The Haciendas*' luxury inclination has proved to be still distant from cultural tourism's philosophy of encountering the Other and broader community development (Crouch 1999). Despite positive reviews about their capacity to generate local engagement (Ashley *et al.* 2007) the reality is that fewer than 60 people out of the 5,976 inhabitants of the municipality of Abalá, that is, less than 1 percent, are directly employed by the Hacienda, none of them occupying management positions which are planned according to the international needs and demands of Starwood's Luxury Collection. Besides, the Hacienda's specialization in the luxury tourism niche market, and the demand for professionalized workers, has set in motion specific training programs, such as English, computer skills, embroidery or hospitality skills courses which, although highly functional for the Hacienda, have very little impact for the wider community as development tools.

The ethnographic account of the material assemblages and social practices through which elite lifestyles and architectures are emulated has contributed to better understandings of how global elites re-shape consumption patterns and what some of the consequences may be. Other ethnographic accounts of the pragmatics involved in such emulations would greatly enrich and benefit the discussion that has been opened here.

Acknowledgments

Research conducted for this chapter is part of the project *Tourism imaginaries and mobilities in times of crisis* (Ref. CSO2011–26527) sponsored by the Spanish Ministry of Science and Innovation National Research Plan (2012–2015). The authors would like to specially thank Manuel Xool, Gabriela Fierro, Fernando Domínguez Rubio and Luis A. Ramírez for their precious and insightful thoughts as well as for their support during fieldwork. We also wish to thank Javier Caletrío and Thomas Birtchnell for their support and their dedication to this book as well as those who made possible this research back in Mérida and Temozón Sur.

Notes

1 See Brewer (1998) for a detailed discussion of luxury and economic development.
2 *Henequén* (*Agave fourcroydes*) is an agave plant similar to sisal and whose development in Yucatán was linked to the production of sisal-fiber ropes in unique industrial quantities for exportation mostly to the United States.
3 For a complete list of restored Haciendas in the region, see Yucatan Today (2009).

4 Using special discount packages, the cheapest night at one of Hernandez' Haciendas can be booked at US$250, the most expensive of all options being to close the entire retreat (28 rooms) for oneself (October 2012).
5 Hotels at Los Cabos in the Cortes Sea and Riviera Maya off the Caribbean are the only places in Mexico ranked in the *Conde Nast Traveler* 2012 Gold List.
6 See Bakker (2005) for a discussion on luxury and tailor-made holidays.
7 The Hacienda's chef has also been the recent personal chef of foreign presidents in their official visits to Mexico (http://2012.cancunwinefoodfest.com/personalities-details/7/Bravo+Christian.html, last accessed 6 May 2013).
8 *Cenotes* are naturally formed water sinkholes mostly extending below sea level and characteristic of the Yucatán Peninsula.

References

Alston, L. J. Mattiace, S. and Nonnenmacher, T. (2009) "Coercion, Culture, and Contracts: Labor and Debt on Henequen Haciendas in Yucatan, México, 1870–1915," *The Journal of Economic History*, 69: 104–137.

Ancona Riestra, R. (Coord.) (1995) *Arquitectura de las Haciendas Henequeneras*. Mérida, México: Universidad Autonóma de Yucatán.

Ashley, C., De Brine, P., Lehr, A. and Wilde, H. (2007) "The role of the tourism sector in expanding economic opportunity." Corporate Social responsibility Initiative Report No. 23. Cambridge, MA: Kennedy School of Government, Harvard University.

Bakker, M. (2005) *Luxury and Tailor-made Holidays, Travel and Tourism Analyst*, Chicago: Mintel International.

Baños, O. (1996) *Neoliberalismo, reorganización y subsistencia rural: el caso de la zona henequenera de Yucatán, 1980–1992*. Mérida, México: Universidad Autónoma de Yucatán.

Beaverstock, J. V., Hubbard, P. and Short, J. R. (2004) "Getting away with it? Exposing the geographies of the super-rich," *Geoforum* 35: 401–407.

Brannon, J. and Baklanoff E. N. (1987) *Agrarian Reform and Public enterprise in México: The political economy of Yucatan's Henequen Industry*. Tuscaloosa, AL: University of Alabama Press.

Breglia, L. (2009) "Hacienda hotels and other ironies of luxury in Yucatan, México," in Baud, M. and Ypeij, A. (eds.) *Cultural tourism in Latin America: the politics of space and imagery*, Cedla Latin American Studies Vol. 26, The Netherlands: Brill, pp. 245–262.

Brewer, A. (1998) "Luxury and Economic Development: David Hume and Adam Smith," *Scottish Journal of Political Economy* 45(1): 78–98.

Byrne, D. (2008) "Heritage as social action," in Fairclough, G., Harrison, R., Schofield, J. and Jameson, J. (eds.) *The Heritage Reader*. London and New York: Routledge.

Castellanos, M. B. (2010) "Don Teo's expulsion: property regimes, moral economies and Ejido reform," *The Journal of Latin American and Caribbean Anthropology* 15(1): 144–169.

Conde Nast Traveler (2012) "Gold List 2012." At: www.cntraveler.com/gold-list/2012/2012-gold-list-the-worlds-best-places-to-stay#slide=1 (last Accessed 5 October 2012).

Conde Nast Traveler (2009) "Yes We Can! Eight Great Trips That Give Back." At: www.cntraveler.com/ecotourism/2009/05/Yes-We-Can-Eight-Great-Trips-That-Give-Back (last accessed 5 October 2012).

Consejo Nacional de Evaluación de la Política de Desarrollo Social (CONEVAL) (2010) *Indicadores de carencia social por municipio.* Abalá, México: CONEVAL.

Consejo Nacional de Población (CONAPO) (2005) *Estimaciones con base en el II Conteo de Población y Vivienda.* México: CONAPO.

Córdoba Azcárate, M. (2011) "'Thanks God, this is not Cancún!' Alternative Tourism Imaginaries in Yucatán (México)," *Journal of Tourism and Cultural Change* 9(3): 183–200.

Córdoba Ordóñez, J., Córdoba Azcárate, M., Gago, C. and Serrano Cambronero, M. (2007) "Turismo y desarrollo: la eterna controversia desde el caso de Cancún (Quintana Roo, México)," in García Ballesteros, A. and García Amaral, M. L. (eds.). *Un mundo de ciudades. Procesos de urbanización en México en tiempos de la globalización.* Barcelona: GeoForum, pp. 180–210.

Crouch, D. (ed.) (1999) *Leisure/Tourism Geographies.* London: Routledge.

Crouch, D. and Desforges, L. (2003) "The Sensuous in the Tourist Encounter. Introduction: The Power of the Body in Tourist Studies," *Tourist Studies* 3(1): 5–22.

Edensor, T. (1998) *Tourists at the Taj: performance and meaning at a symbolic site.* London and New York: Routledge.

Elliott, A. and Urry, J. (2010) *Mobile Lives.* New York: Routledge.

Fallaw, B. (1999) "The Southeast Was Red: Left-State Alliances and Popular Mobilizations in Yucatán, 1930–1940," *Social Science History* 23(2): 241–268.

Fishman, R. (1987) *Bourgeois Utopias: The Rise and Fall of Suburbia.* New York: Basic Books.

Forbes (2010) "The World's Billionares: #828 Roberto Hernandez Ramirez." At: www.forbes.com/lists/2010/10/billionaires-2010_Roberto-Hernandez-Ramirez_CQOG.html (last accessed 5 October 2012).

Fox, D. (1961) "Henequén in Yucatan: A Mexican fibre crop," *Transactions and Papers Institute of British Geographers* 29: 215–229.

Frank, R. H. (2010) *Luxury Fever: Weighing the cost of excess.* Princeton, NJ: Princeton University Press.

Frank, R. H. (2011) *The High-Beta Rich: How the Manic Wealthy Will Take Us to the Next Boom, Bubble, and Bust.* New York: Crown Business.

García de Fuentes, A. and Morales, J. (2000) "Dinámica regional de Yucatán 1980–2000," *Investigaciones Geográficas,* Boletín del Instituto de Geografía, Universidad Autónoma de México, Núm. 42: 157–172.

Haciendas, The (2007) *Hacienda Temozón Sur. Community.* At: www.haciendasMéxico.com/Temozon/community.php (last accessed 5 October 2012).

Harvey, D. (1996) *Justice, Nature and the Geography of Difference.* Oxford: Blackwell.

Hume, D. ([1757] 2006) "Of the standard of taste," in Hume, D. (2006) *Essays Moral, Political and Literary.* Oxford: Oxford University Press, pp. 231–257.

Hume, D ([1758] 1985) *Essays Moral, Political, and Literary,* ed. E. Miller. Indianapolis: Liberty Classics.

Instituto Nacional de Estadística Geografía e Informática (INEGI) (2005) *Anuario Estadístico de Yucatán.* Aguascalientes, México: INEGI.

Instituto Nacional de Estadística Geografía e Informática (INEGI) (2010) *Anuario Estadístico de Yucatán.* Aguascalientes, México: INEGI.

Katz, F. (1974) "Labor conditions on Haciendas in Porfirian México: some trends and tendencies," *The Hispanic American Historical Review* 54(1): 1–47.

Khan, R. S (2010) *Privilege: the making of an adolescent elite at St. Paul's School*. Princeton: Princeton University Press.

Leatherman, T. L. and Goodman, A, (2005) "Coca-colonization of diets in Yucatán," *Social Sciences Medicine* 61(4): 833–846.

Lutz, W., Prieto, L. and Sanderson, W. (eds.) (2000) *Population, Development, and Environment on the Yucatán Peninsula: From Ancient Maya to 2030*. Research Report. International Institute for Applied Systems Analysis. At: www.iiasa.ac.at/Admin/PUB/Documents/RR-00-014.pdf (last accessed 5 October 2012).

Macdonald, S. and Fyfe, G. (eds.) (1996) *Theorizing Museums*. Oxford: Blackwell.

Molz, J. G (2007) "Eating Difference: The Cosmopolitan Mobilities of Culinary Tourism," *Space and Culture* 10(1): 77–93.

Mukerji, C. (1994) "Reading and writing with nature: a materialist approach to French formal gardens," in Brewer, J. and Porter, R. (eds.) *Consumption and the World of Goods*. London: Routledge, pp. 439–461.

Nickel, H. (1996) *Morfología Social de la Hacienda Mexicana*. México City: Fondo de Cultura Económica.

Organization for Economic and Co-operation Development (OECD) (2007) *Territorial Reviews: Yucatan, México*. OECD Publishing. At: http://browse.oecdbookshop.org/oecd/pdfs/free/0407081e.pdf (last accessed 5 October 2012).

Park, K. S, Reisinger, Y. and Noh, E. H. (2010) "Luxury Shopping in Tourism," *International Journal of Tourism Research* 12: 164–178.

Peniche Rivero, P. (1999) "La comunidad doméstica de la hacienda henequenera en Yucatán, México, 1870–1950," *Mexican Studies* 15(1): 1–33.

Perrin, W. (2010) "Luxury's 10 New Rules," *Conde Nast Traveler*. At: www.cntraveler.com/features/2010/12/Luxury-s-10-New-Rules (last accessed 5 October 2012).

Ramírez, L. A. (2008) "A wheel of fortune, Yucatan´s entrepreneurial elite from the revolution to globalization," in Baklanoff, E. N. and Mosseley, E. H. (eds.), *Yucatán in an Era of Globalization*. Tuscaloosa: University of Alabama Press, pp. 69–91.

Rodríguez Viqueira, M. and Fuentes Freixanet, V. (2006) "Traditional Mayan Architecture According to Latitude and Altitude." The 23rd Conference on Passive and Low Energy Architecture, Geneva, Switzerland, 6–8 September 2006. At: www.cuepe.ch/html/plea2006/Vol1/PLEA2006_PAPER631.pdf (last accessed 5 October 20120.

Rojek, C. and Urry, J. (1997) *Touring Cultures*. London: Routledge.

Secretaría de Fomento Turístico (2009) Yucatan: Land of Wonders. Haciendas. At: www.yucatan.gob.mx/menu/?id=haciendas (last accessed 6 May 2013).

Sheller, M. (2009) "Infrastructures of the imagined island: software, mobilities, and the architecture of Caribbean paradise," *Environment and Planning A* 41(6): 1386–1403.

Smith, A. ([1776] 1976) *An Inquiry into the Nature and Causes of the Wealth of Nations*, eds. R. Campbell, A. Skinner and W. Todd. The Glasgow Edition of the Works and Correspondence of Adam Smith. Oxford: Oxford University Press.

Smith, L. J. (2006) *The Uses of Heritage*. London: Routledge.

Starwood Hotels and Resorts Worldwide (2010) *The Luxury Collection Story. History and Heritage*. At: www.starwoodhotels.com/luxury/about/detail.html?section=about

&category=history_heritage&parentCategory=about (last accessed 5 October 2012).
Torres, R. (2002) "Cancun's tourism development from a Fordist spectrum of analysis," *Tourist Studies* 2: 87–116.
Van Young, E. (2006) *Hacienda and Market in Eighteenth-Century Mexico: The Rural Economy of the Guadalajara Region, 1675–1810.* Lanham, MD: Rowman and Littlefield.
Villanueva Mukul, E. (1990) *La formación de regiones en la agricultura. El caso de Yucatán.* Mérida, Yucatán: Maldonado Editores.
Wedel, J. R. (2009) *Shadow Elite: How the world's new power brokers undermine democracy, government, and the free market.* New York: Basic Books.
Wells, A. (1982) "Family elites in a boom-and-bust economy: The Molinas and Peóns of Porfirian Yucatan," *The Hispanic American Historical Review* 62(2): 224–253.
Wells, A. (1985) *Yucatan's Gilded Age: Haciendas, Henequen, and International Harvester, 1860–1915.* Albuquerque: University of New Mexico Press.
Wells, A. (1991) "From Hacienda to Plantation: the transformation of Santo Domingo Xcuyum," in Brannon, J. and Gilbert, J. (eds.) *Land, Labor and Capital in Modern Yucatan. Essays in regional history and political economy.* Tuscaloosa: The University of Alabama Press, pp. 112–142.
Wells, A. (1992) "All in the family: railroads and henequen monoculture in Yucatan," *The Hispanic American Historical Review* 72 (2): 159–209.
Witynski, K., Carr, J. P. and Scott Mitchell, W. (2003) *The New Hacienda.* Salt Lake City: Gibbs Smith.
Wolf, E. and Mintz, S. (1957) "Haciendas and plantations in middle America and the Antilles," *Social and Economic Studies* 6: 380–412.
Yucatan Today (2009) "Hacienda Hotels??" *Yucatán Today, the Tourist Guide.* At: www.yucatantoday.com/en/topics/haciendas-yucatan (last accessed 6 May 2013).

Chapter 9

Visible–invisible
The social semiotics of labour in luxury tourism

Crispin Thurlow and Adam Jaworski

> The global culture industry ... is less a matter of the base determining the superstructure than the cultural superstructure collapsing, as it were, into the material base. Hence goods become informational, work becomes affective, property becomes intellectual and the economy more generally becomes cultural.... The image, previously separated in the superstructure, is thingified, it becomes matter-image.
>
> (Lash and Lury 2007: 7)

Introduction

The material and symbolic economies of tourism play out in particularly complex, imbricated ways. Just as social status often dictates access to spatial mobilities, the elite mobilities of tourism offer themselves as both indicators of, and resources for, performing social status. In other words, it is privileged people who can afford to travel for pleasure, and it is these same people who are able to perform their privilege by talking about their travels. This is true of all tourism, even though there are inevitable 'hierarchies' of destinations affording different levels of symbolic capital to different people: think Marbella versus Marakesh versus Mustique. (The cachet of any destination is, of course, always relative to the traveller's social context.) Different modes of tourism, too, are weighted differently in the travel-by-choice marketplace; in this regard, one might think of the variable cachet of 'package holidays', 'eco-tourism', 'cultural tourism', and the kind of super-elite tourism often staged as 'luxury travel'. In practice, the material practices of these different ways of travelling are not always easily distinguished; more often than not, the difference is either in the eye of the beholder or in the creative mythologizing of the marketer. As scholars of super-elite travel (as opposed to super-elite travellers ourselves), we find this to be particularly true of *luxury travel*, where marketers are unavoidably caught up with defining and somehow producing intangible, vague notions like 'elite', 'status', 'special attention' and, perhaps the most nebulous of all, 'luxury'. So much of what is actually produced in luxury tourism remains at the level of the symbolic rather than the material, in the image (or imagination) rather than the reality. And this is why luxury tourism, in particular, is an ideal site for tracing the kind of large-scale cultural shift described by Scott Lash and Celia Lury in the quote above.

In a world where images are increasingly 'thingified', the line between material processes and symbolic practices becomes more blurred or complicated. Within the social sciences, therefore, new methodologies are coming to the fore which take as their starting point the materiality and constitutive power of communication. Social semiotics is one such approach (see, for example, Kress and van Leeuwen 2001; van Leeuwen 2005). Where critical discourse analysis typically attends to the political economies of language (e.g. Fairclough 2003), social semiotics adopts a more multimodal approach focusing on the ideological workings and *affordances* (Kress 2010) of speech and writing (rather than the abstract idea of 'language') alongside visual discourses and other nonverbal resources. Rooted in principles of semiotics, semiology and iconography, social semioticians share a primary concern for elements of signification, connotative/cultural meanings and historical contexts (see Thurlow and Aiello 2007, for more on this). Social semioticians, however, look to *extend* these interests by viewing all semiosis as social action embedded in larger economic and cultural practices. Social semiotics therefore looks not only to relate texts to contexts, but also to speculate on related social tendencies and their political implications, recognizing that 'the signs of articulation' (Kress and Van Leeuwen 2001: 41) in any text form the basis for later articulations of the same ideological discourses into other texts. In other words, and just like critical discourse analysis, social semiotics shares a concern for understanding the ways textual or communicative practices are implicated in broader social processes and structural inequalities.

In this vein, our own work has sought to understand current (re)formulations of class status by examining the performative logics of luxury in the context of *super-elite* travel (e.g. Thurlow and Jaworski 2006, 2010; Jaworski and Thurlow 2009). Through the analytic lenses of critical discourse studies and social semiotics, we have been documenting some of the linguistic, visual, spatial and material resources commonly deployed in the elitist performances of individuals and in the stylizations of elitism by marketers and other commercial agents. Our concern throughout is to address the way elite status (and privilege) is a situated, interactional process rather than an essentially fixed, individualized attribute or social category (see also Bourdieu 1984; Sherman 2007). What an approach like ours is able to demonstrate is that elitism is more than simply a material or economic reality; it is also an aspirational ideal in relation to which all consumer-citizens, regardless of their wealth or power, are constantly persuaded and taught to position themselves. Indeed, the spaces of luxury travel are invariably populated not so much by the super-rich as they are by 'wannabes' and 'trip-of-a-lifetime' tourists. (The truly elite – the so-called 1%-ers – have already moved on and are sequestered in privately owned, tightly managed, rigorously policed locations beyond our reach.) Herein lies the symbolic power of luxury marketing: it not only sells visions of super-elite travel but (re-)envisions markers of social status and class privilege that 'trickle down' into other modes of travel and that bleed into other domains of life.

Set against this backdrop, our visual essay here considers one important dimension in the semiotic landscape (see Jaworski and Thurlow, 2010) of super-elite travel: the performance of what we are calling *visible–invisible labour*. Specifically, we highlight some of the common strategies used to represent and produce luxury service by drawing on the glossy rhetoric of advertisers as well as our own ethnographic fieldwork which engaged four exemplary modes of luxury travel: *global elite* (the Burj al Arab Hotel, Dubai), *retro elite* (the Simplon Orient Express, Venice to London), *egalitarian elite* (the Bellagio Hotel, Las Vegas) and *imperial elite* (Phinda Private Game Reserve, South Africa).[1] Each of these elite (or super-elite) mobilities promotes itself as the height of contemporary luxury and each represents a (re)mythologization of distinction, desirability and status. What emerges from our broader analysis is a number of organizing principles that delineate the interactional orders of super-elite mobility and that illustrate how luxury and privilege are currently being imagined and re-imagined (see Thurlow and Jaworski 2012). In the current chapter, however, we want to extend our analysis of just one of these principles: the deployment of visible–invisible labour. Typically, we find that the discursive performance of luxury demands a seemingly oxymoronic staging of labour. On the one hand, the results of intensive labour must be in evidence everywhere in order to manifest the tricky rhetorics of 'recognition', 'personal attention', 'tailored service' and so on. Simultaneously, however, the disturbances and discomforts of labouring must be sealed off – or concealed – from the luxury traveller so as to complete the illusion of order, control and ease.

For the sake of analytical convenience, we have organized our visual essay into three deceptively neat parts. We first centre the visual production or visualization of *invisble labour* (Part 1) and then turn to the ways workers and their work are often spectacularized as *visible labour* (Part 2). It is a fact of capitalist production that the sources, material conditions and embodied practices of labouring are almost always concealed from (or obscured for) those who consume its products. To some extent, it is this which explains the unseen hands behind immaculate lawns, carefully raked beaches, neatly ordered rows of chairs and loungers, and regimentally assembled flower arrangements. Nonetheless, there are times when labour and, more specifically, labourers come to the fore. If labourers are displayed – in adverts or acts of service – this is usually for particular effect, as with the arch-performances of a uniformed, dedicated butler or a named chef or concierge. In both these cases, visibility/invisibility is always semiotically and politically slippery; while the products of labour are usually everywhere, labourers are absent, and when workers are on display, the real work they do is cosmetically rendered for aesthetic purposes. In its performance of luxury, super-elite tourism is particularly caught up in this dynamic and appears to switch back and forth between the visible and the invisible. In addition, however, it also capitalizes on a range of semiotic resources and design techniques to organize and promote its unique version of *visible–invisible labour* (Part 3). It seems that luxury tourism wants to have its cake and eat it. How else is one to produce a sense of 'special attention', 'recognition' and 'tailored service' at the same time as staging 'discretion', 'privacy' and 'relaxation' in meaningful ways. In advertising, therefore, we find labour semioticized in ways that skillfully highlight the work but not the workers: for example, through the use of blurring, decentring, disembedding, desaturation and the metonymic reduction of workers (e.g. white gloves). It is here, too, that the haute cuisine styling of food serves as a useful resource for expressing maximum labour, minimum disturbance; like ducks on water, elaborate platters glide smoothly into view, concealing beneath the surface (or below deck) the intensity of effort required for their preparation. On the ground, our ethnographic encounters reveal the ways these glossy mythologies are *sometimes* resemioticized and/or materialized.

Part 1: invisible labour

> It is only by being exchanged that the products of labour acquire, as values, one uniform social status, distinct from their varied forms of existence as objects of utility.... It is value that converts every product into a social hieroglyphic.
>
> (Marx 1976 [1867]: 167)

Figure 9.1 The logic of luxury dictates that hotel guests should be surrounded by an abundance of scarce resources. In the desert-based hotels of Dubai and Las Vegas fresh water is not to be found just in taps, power showers, over-sized bath tubs and private jacuzzis, but also in fountains, waterfalls, canals, artificial lakes, outdoor 'air-conditioning' vapourisers and aquaparks. In this 'seven-star' hotel, the prosaic act of washing our hands gets a celebratory, spectacular spin: bouquets of white lilies on either side of the wash basins, rose petals precariously balanced on the rim of the Hermès toiletries tray, and two carefully but improbably stacked pyramids of hand towels (Figure 9.1). All this arranged by an unseen hand. Although we suspect the hand belongs to a uniformed attendant who

180 C. Thurlow and A. Jaworski

Figure 9.1 Beach changing room, Burj al Arab Hotel, Dubai.

follows us constantly (but discreetly) to remove any sign of our presence in the changing room.

Figure 9.2 Once again, we find a floral staging of luxury. As poignant markers of the ephemeral landscapes and excesses of luxury, flowers must be constantly rearranged and replenished. Here, indeed, we find an excessive performance of arrangement: every stem, stick and bud pointedly trimmed and positioned by another unseen hand. For the most part, the product of luxury labour must be evident – conspicuously so for conspicuous consumption – but the act of labour and/or the labourers themselves must not. To push Marx (quoted above) a little further, luxury labour thus appears more holographic than hieroglyphic.

Figure 9.3 Beyond the tightly policed gambling spaces, the hotel falls quieter and quieter into the middle of the night. We had been struck during the day to see back-stage staff (as opposed to front-stage workers like receptionists) emerge from behind seamlessly hidden doorways in the corridors, through back entrances, and out of service lifts behind concealed doors. Reminiscent of Victorian bell pulls in aristocratic or well-to-do houses, service workers are kept out of sight but always on hand; points of (unwanted) contact between the servers and the served kept always to a minimum. In our suites (aka rooms) the turn-up and turn-down services – and the tying of laces in our spare pairs of shoes – are

Figure 9.2 The lobby, Bellagio Hotel, Las Vegas, USA.

Figure 9.3 A corridor, Bellagio Hotel, Las Vegas, USA.

always performed out of sight, just as the polishing of the lobby floor happens in the dead of night while most guests are asleep.

Figure 9.4 Of course labour does eventually emerge and can be seen from time to time. The question of visibility is, however, not simply one of presence or absence, but also one of awareness – as this incidental encounter reminds us. With its proudly touted ratio of seven staff to every guest, our 'seven-star' hotel is saturated with labour. What doesn't happen behind the scenes typically happens outside the attentional frame of guests. Unattended attention. Round-the-clock cleaners camouflaged with their surroundings, wearing immaculate uniforms trimmed with Arabesque design motifs akin to those on the walls, floors and furniture. Consistently avoiding eye contact and interaction with guests and day-trippers who've come to photograph the lobbies.

Part 2: visible labour

> The commodification of difference promotes paradigms of consumption wherein whatever difference the Other inhabits is eradicated, via exchange, by a consumer cannibalism that not only displaces the Other but denies the significance of the Other's history through a process of decontextualization.
>
> (hooks 1992: 31)

Figure 9.4 First-floor atrium, Burj al Arab Hotel, Dubai.

The social semiotics of labour   183

Figure 9.5 Just one more chore for one of the stewards (each carriage has one): posing for photographs with the passengers during a short stop at Innsbruck. A deferential staging of 'upstairs–downstairs' and a ceremonial display of service. Echoed metonymically through the uniform, the steward's labour is thus resemioticized and recommodified as a sanitised 'take-away' image of service for the passengers. A seemingly effortless, all-smiles and neatly orchestrated routine for memorializing a 'once-in-a-lifetime' experience of time travel and 'good old-fashioned' service. By enacting this highly stylized service moment – with its display of emotional labour (Hochschild 1983) – the steward has notched up a few more euros for the tip awaiting him at the end of the journey.

Figure 9.6 In a number of key ways the mediatized, corporate imaginary and the situated practices of luxury labour are at odds with each other. We are struck, for example, by the apparent white-washing of workers in a lot of advertising, whereby the human geographies and political economies of service are often disingenuously erased (see bell hooks quoted above). Where whiteness is projected everywhere as a marker a luxury (from white towels to White workers), the reality is that 'people of colour' are often doing the back-stage work. Unless it is for some spectacular effect (e.g. the Singapore Girl, the turbaned chauffeur, or the beaming porter in our commercial examples online) where alterity is recontextualized as a marker of exoticity and Orientalized deference. Speaking of which…

Figure 9.5 The Orient Express, Innsbruck station.

Figure 9.6 Kitchen car, the Orient Express.

Figure 9.7 In two days of coming and going, we did not open our own door once. Our designated butler, Peter (not his real name) or one of his two colleagues was always there waiting for us. He waited, we were waited upon. Constantly working to sustain our sense of entitlement. When he was not leaping up to greet us, Peter sat behind the computer at his desk. From this computer, he could see the photos of us scanned from our passports so that all front-stage staff could greet us by name. Here, too, were logged guests' preferences (expressed or somehow discernible): our dietary requirements, our rising times, the fruit we ate from the bowl in our room, the pillows we had chosen from the menu of twelve. Throughout the hotel we were recognized, greeted and catered to according to these 'needs'. Between tailored service and surveillance, however, a disconcertingly fine line emerges.

Figure 9.8 In another moment of 'genesis amnesia' (Bourdieu 1977), the colonial histories and post-apartheid geographies of South Africa are ostensibly (and ostentatiously) set aside to make space for a 'sundowners at Happy Valley' experience. Only this time it is pre-breakfast refreshments served 'in the bush' by two Zulu rangers during an early morning game ride. The elephant gun (foreground) is exchanged momentarily for a thermos, a tea caddy and freshly cooked biscuits. Luxury tourism seems particularly inclined to resemiotize and re-exoticize forms of categorization

Figure 9.7 Twentieth floor, Burj al Arab hotel, Dubai.

Figure 9.8 Morning ride, Phinda Private Game Lodge, South Africa.

long inscribed in the construction and legitimization of inequality. Labour also accrues its cachet or symbolic value through the improbability of its location: here, the staging of order in the midst of nature's disorder.

Part 3: visible-invisible labour

> At stake ... is not only the production of inequality through the appropriation of labor effort but also workers' and clients' unequal entitlement to material and emotional resources.... Customized service indicates to guests that they are unique and deserving individuals.
>
> (Sherman 2007: 259–261)

Figure 9.9 Along with the fraught decision about which model of Rolls-Royce to choose for the airport transfer, this meal was possibly our most decadent moment. (We were guests of the hotel management.) The haute cuisine styling of our food was everywhere, starting with the flecks of gold leaf that conspicuously (we were told to notice them) adorned 'snacks' served in our room. As a central feature or resource in the semiotic production of luxury, the staging of food is a marker of distinction and good taste. And being let in on the 'secrets' of the trade (i.e. having the food constantly narrated to us) merely reinscribes the elitist stance (cf. Jaworski and Thurlow 2009) of staff as they seek to perform customized service (see Sherman, quote above).

Figure 9.9 Lunch, Burj al Arab Hotel, Dubai.

The social semiotics of labour 187

Figure 9.10 And these culinary spectacles – like many other luxury markers – circulate across the *global semioscape* (Thurlow and Aiello 2007) of luxury tourism. Thus, to the improbability of sculptured fruit in the desert landscape of Dubai, we add this moment of 'tailored' fruit in the bush of South Africa. Following the lead of Ian Cook and Philip Crang (1996), we witness how the haute cuisine styling of luxury food renders labour relations both visible and invisible in a kind of triple commodity fetish. All this food is grown somewhere else, picked somewhere else, transported from somewhere else. It is, of course, also washed, sliced and delicately arranged somewhere else. Out of sight, out of mind. Once again, we also see here the luxury-producing juxtaposition of order and disorder.

Figure 9.11 Suspended metaphorically mid-air on the twentieth floor, we are inside and outside, yet completely protected from the elements and the gaze of window cleaners, literally suspended in the air and cleaning our windows in the sweltering heat. This is our climate-controlled panopticon, our enclavic refuge. The one-way glass that empowers us and liberates us from unwanted attention is oddly reminiscent of the more sinister, voyeuristic powers of interrogation rooms, security guards' quarters and CCTV control rooms. Safely inside our Club Suite, however, we are invited to be masters of all we survey (cf. Pratt 1992).

Figure 9.10 Breakfast, Phinda Private Game Reserve, South Africa.

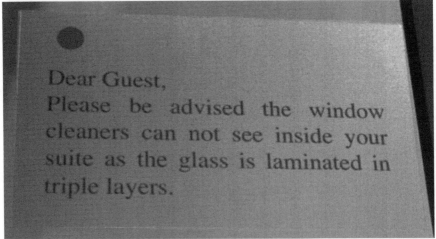

Figure 9.11 The Burj al Arab, Dubai.

Figure 9.12 Back to the beach! Here we are introduced to the height of technologies designed to minimise unwanted attention from staff and to maximise our sense of control: a red flag and a blue flag. Slot the red flag into its special holder and you are left undisturbed; raise the blue flag and one of the four bar staff will come to take your order. (No need for us to get up and walk across the searingly hot, but thankfully carpeted, sand

Figure 9.12 The beach, Burj al Arab, Dubai.

to the bar.) It seems that the coming and going of labour – the rendering of it as visible and invisible – is a way to exercise (or stage) the kind of control and orderliness that is yet another organizing principle of luxury tourism.

Conclusion

In the way of a conclusion, we want to refer to just two more images – one corporate and one ethnographic – starting with the striking visualization of space and class status in an advertisement from Cathay Pacific (please see our accompanying resource at http://faculty.washington.edu/thurlow/labour.pdf). This advert is pointed in its gendering and racializing of the three classes: a female passenger is used to embody economy travel where male passengers embody business and first class travel; phenotypically East Asian passengers stand in for economy class and business class while a phenotypically European or Middle Eastern passenger occupies the role of first class. We draw attention in particular, however, to the strategic deployment of labour/ers as a semiotic performance of distinction and super-elite (i.e. first class) status. The multimodal accomplishment of this advert obviously relies on its verbal copy, which deepens the rhetoric and also takes us a little closer to the underlying logics of luxury labour/ing.

Extract X: The world really does revolve around you
When we decided to upgrade our First Class, Business Class and Economy Class cabins, we turned to the people who fly them. The result is a new level of personal space, individual privacy and attention to those all-important details. Because at Cathay Pacific, your needs always come first.

…

New First Class
Just the right amount of personal attention, interaction and privacy.

New Business Class
A cosy retreat where one button takes you to a fully flat bed.

New Economy Class
A new shell seat protects your space, with entertainment on demand.

Consistent with the broader semiotic landscape we have been mapping in this visual essay, the revamped first class cabin relies on a service spectacle not unlike the one for Singapore Airlines (also in our online examples). Two decentred and dimly lit female flight attendants bend towards the spotlighted passenger who himself is somehow upstaged by the elaborately staged plate of food being set before him. The legend beneath the image confirms the double-bind that organizes the social semiotics of luxury labour: the balancing of 'personal attention' with 'privacy'. Once again, we also witness the role of food in the visualization of super-elite travel; as such, we see labour being simultaneously but strategically foregrounded and backgrounded. The front-stage display of labourers – in terms of both the diegetic experience of the first class passenger (e.g. being served by two people at once) and the contrastive design of the advert (e.g. the absence of attendants in business and economy) – fully conceals the kind of labour that makes airline meals possible (i.e. from crop workers to catering staff) while only partially obscuring the haute cuisine labour that will have happened moments earlier in the aeroplane's galley.

Figure 9.13 Just as there are unseen hands attending to the meticulous details of every spectacular haute cuisine platter, there appear to be hotel workers trailing every tourist in order to fold their toilet paper into fresh, crisp points. Which brings us nicely to our last ethnographic image as a case in point (next page). We are told that this is partly a practical intervention to demonstrate that the bathroom has been 'serviced'. Inevitably, it is also a performance of attention – not only to detail but also to customer care. With its gleaming brass cover and embossed, bejewelled wall mount, we recognize the image here to show no ordinary toilet roll. This is a Burj al Arab toilet roll in one of the two bathrooms of a 3,500- square-foot suite costing $4,000 a night. Just as the linguistic never exists in isolation from other semiotic resources, there is no neat line to be drawn between the symbolic and the material, between the utilitarian and the aesthetic. By the same token, and as we suggested above, the matter of visibility/invisibility is not necessarily a literal or absolute one.

This particular rhetorical/marketing tactic is also one that circulates widely across the semiotic landscape of luxury tourism and one which has quickly made its way into general practice. (We found the same thing happening in each of our research sites and have noticed how the same practice occurs in the kinds of ordinary hotels we normally get to stay in.) Indeed, in the *global semioscape* (Thurlow and Aiello 2007) of luxury travel, we find a plethora of semiotic items and practices circulating in more informal, often unnoticeable ways – like the hand-crafted fruit platters in Figures 9.9 and 9.10. It is in this way that the symbolic orders of super-elite travel ripple outwards across a more extensive landscape, hailing a wider demographic and establishing much more far-reaching aesthetic and social agendas. Just as some people 'learn to labour' (Willis 1981), others are schooled in the ways of being served. Some train to wait while others learn to be waited upon. And the way that labour/ing is imagined in luxury travel is not only normative in its visualization of certain practices, certain bodies, certain interactions; these visual performances also materialize and normalize the very notion of luxury itself. We must all of us be constantly taught to recognize luxury – to know what it looks like – but we must also be taught to desire it in the first place.

Figure 9.13

Acknowledgements

This chapter emerged from a larger project titled *Elite Mobilities: The Discursive Production of Luxury and Privilege* supported by a research grant fellowship awarded to Crispin by the University of Washington's Royalty Research Fund and the Simpson Center for the Humanities. For their on-the-ground support, we thank the Head of Public Relations at the Burj al Arab and the Train Manager of the Orient Express.

Note

1 Due to publishers' restrictions, we were not able to reproduce the corporate images in this version of the paper. We have, however, made them available online at http://faculty.washington.edu/thurlow/labour.pdf. All images reproduced here are our own and come from ethnographic fieldwork conducted in the summer of 2007. Most indicators suggest that the luxury travel market remains largely undaunted by the so-called global economic crisis (*The Economist* 2012).

References

Bourdieu, P. (1977). *Outline of a Theory of Practice* [trans. R. Nice]. Cambridge: Cambridge University Press.
Bourdieu, P. (1984). *Distinction: A Social Critique of the Judgement of Taste* [trans. R. Nice]. Cambridge, MA.: Harvard University Press.
Cook, I. and Crang, P. (1996). The world on a plate: Culinary culture, displacement and geographical knowledges. *Journal of Material Culture*, 1(2), 131–153.
Economist, The (2012). Gulliver: 'A golden age in luxury travel?' 30 April, available online at www.economist.com/blogs/gulliver/2012/04/income-inequality-and-luxury-travel (accessed 2 May 2013)
Fairclough, N. (2003). *Analysing Discourse: Textual Analysis for Social Research*. London and New York: Routledge.
Hochschild, A. R. (1983). *The Managed Heart: Commercialization of Human Feeling*. Berkeley, CA: University of California Press.
hooks, b. (1992). Eating the other: Desire and resistance. In *Black Looks: Race and Representation* (pp. 21–39). Boston: South End Press.
Jaworski, A. and Thurlow, C. (2009). Talking an elitist stance: Ideology and the discursive production of social distinction. In A. Jaffee (ed.), *Perspectives on Stance* (pp. 195–226). New York: Oxford University Press.
Jaworski, A. and Thurlow, C. (2010). Introducing semiotic landscapes. In A. Jaworski and C. Thurlow (eds), *Semiotic Landscapes: Image, Text, Space* (pp. 1–40). London: Continuum.
Kress, G. (2010). *Multimodality: A Social Semiotic Approach to Contemporary Communication*. London: Routledge.
Kress, G. and van Leeuwen, T. (2001). *Multimodal Discourse: The Modes and Media of Contemporary Communication*. London: Arnold.
Lash, S. and Lury, C. (2007). *Global Culture Industry: The Mediation of Things*. Cambridge: Polity.

Marx, K. (1976). *Capital*, Vol. 1. New York: Vintage [originally published in 1867].

Pratt, M.-L. (1992). *Imperial Eyes: Travel Writing and Transculturation*. London: Routledge.

Sherman, R. (2007). *Class Acts: Service and Inequality in Luxury Hotels*. Berkeley: University of California Press.

Thurlow, C. and Aiello, G. (2007). National pride, global capital: A social semiotic analysis of transnational visual branding in the airline industry. *Visual Communication*, 6(3), 305–344.

Thurlow, C. and Jaworski, A. (2006). The alchemy of the upwardly mobile: Symbolic capital and the stylization of elites in frequent-flyer programmes. *Discourse & Society*, 17(1), 131–167.

Thurlow, C. and Jaworski, A. (2010). Silence is golden: The 'anti-communicational' linguascape of super-elite mobilities. In A. Jaworski and C. Thurlow (eds), *Semiotic Landscapes: Image, Text, Space* (pp. 187–218). London: Continuum.

Thurlow, C. and Jaworski, A. (2012). Elite mobilities: The semiotic landscapes of luxury and privilege. *Social Semiotics*, 22(5), 487–516.

Van Leeuwen, T. (2005). *Introducing Social Semiotics*. London and New York: Routledge.

Willis, P. (1981). *Learning to Labor: How Working Class Kids Get Working Class Jobs*. New York: Columbia University Press.

Chapter 10

'This is not me'

Conspicuous consumption and the travel aspirations of the European middle classes

Javier Caletrío

Introduction

> It is among the highest leisure class, who have no superiors and few peers, that decorum finds its fullest and maturest expression; and it is this highest class also that gives decorum that definitive formulation which serves as a canon of conduct for the classes beneath. And here also the code is most obviously a code of status ...
> (Veblen [1899] 2005: 30)

Over the last two decades, signs of conspicuous consumption have proliferated in global cities and privileged playgrounds. An expanding network of mega-yachts, private islands, ultra-expensive mansions, luxury hotels, and exclusive restaurants and country clubs has become the stage where global elites display their growing wealth. Such displays of excess have reverberated beyond specific locales through a global media bringing amplified images of shining luxury, distinction and privilege to every neighbourhood of every city, from the dusty slums in Nairobi to the overcrowded high-rises of Chongqing. In a world of dwindling natural resources and growing environmental crises, concerns about the seductive power of those images to suggest 'a canon of conduct for the classes beneath' (Veblen [1899] 2005: 30) and stoke consumption desires are being echoed in academic calls for a resurgence of elite studies and a more systematic and sustained focus on the super-rich (Savage and Williams 2008). Featherstone observes that:

> The ... point to note about the growth in the number of billionaires is the example they set for consumer culture lifestyles.... It has been argued that today, as the pull of place and local status hierarchies diminish, the visibility of luxury in the media becomes a more potent reference point for people. Certainly the lifestyles of the rich and upper-middle classes attract attention with television providing endless programmes which revolve around the improvement and furnishing of a stylish home, purchase of a second home, holiday planning, cars,

fashion, celebrity events, etc. The programmes endeavour to strike a balance between the interest in the lifestyles of celebrities, the new rich and the upper-middle class, and the endeavours of 'ordinary people', who seek improvement and transformation on a tight budget.

(Featherstone [1991] 2007: xx)

In a similar vein, Elliott and Urry justify a sustained focus on the mobile lives of the rich, whom they refer to as 'globals', by noting that:

the ultramobile way of living charted by globals remains a form of life conducted by only a minuscule elite (by percentage of global population). Nevertheless, it is the mobile lifestyles of the globals that are held up as a normative ideal in popular culture and the media, and in turn mimicked by many other people.

(Elliott and Urry 2010: 82)

Writing more specifically about the playgrounds of the super-rich, Elliott and Urry add:

Some might argue that this kind of elite casino capitalism only pertains to a small sector of the world's consumers, to the super-rich globals.... Hence it is not of wider social, economic and political significance. Thus we are overstating their importance. But for various reasons ... this is not, we think, true at all. First, this kind of places establish exemplars of development that developers elsewhere then seek to emulate and to produce mass-market versions of such places of excess, including theme restaurants, down-market resorts and suburban shopping malls. So what gets imagined and constructed at the select or elite end then moves elsewhere; or indeed, the same development itself moves downmarket, as some suggest is currently happening in Dubai.

(Elliott and Urry 2010: 128)

The aim of this chapter is to analyse this relationship between the rich and the middle classes, to examine whether the lives and places of the elite really do serve as a 'canon of conduct for the classes beneath' (Veblen [1899] 2005: 30). It does so by focusing on how conspicuous consumption shapes notions of normalcy and excess in travel patterns. Drawing on semi-structured interviews conducted in the Spanish Mediterranean with 92 EU nationals, the chapter argues that, for the majority, aspirations to travel for leisure seem to be inspired, not so much by the elite seclusion of first-class lounges, private islands, mega-yachts, and luxury hotels, but by a cosmopolitan ideal of a world of democratized mobility pervasively conveyed through global media. Research presented in this chapter suggests that travel for leisure is highly valued and desired as forming part of consumer and citizenship rights. Travel for leisure also emerges as one of the last issues people would want to give up in order to reduce carbon emissions, but the influence of the elites in this matter is absent. One may correctly argue, however, that the proliferation of images of wealth, excess and privilege may be shaping consumption patterns in subtler ways, by marginally shifting thresholds of normalcy and 'naturalness' in travel styles and landscape aesthetics. These subtler shifts in affective dispositions and forms of classification are better identified and adequately described through long-term research involving a combination of methods and data. The limitations of using only semi-structured interviews to capture the way that the glamour, myths and ideologies of travel operate (especially at the level of the unconscious) are obvious (Thrift 2007). The accounts presented here are, nonetheless, still valid to broaden the terms by which the discussion about the role of elites in consumer culture is taking place and to identify issues deserving further attention.

The Mediterranean, the rich and the rest

Holidays and travel aspirations often involve contested ideas of 'the good life'. Since the beginning of the nineteenth century, the Mediterranean has occupied a privileged position in the European imagination as a desired place of escape, leisure and more natural forms of living (Pemble 1987; Littlewood 1999). First accessible only to the upper classes, the Mediterranean received an influx of less wealthy groups following a gradual downward expansion of travel rights, practices and conventions (Pemble 1987; Cirer 2004, 2009). This culminated in the era of mass tourism that characterizes the region today and that has given way to a heterogeneous landscape of popular and exclusive resorts sitting cheek by jowl (Blume 1992), spaces exemplifying different notions of taste and distinction and showing differential accessibility and connectivity to global flows in a manner that Graham and Marvin (2001) describe as 'splintering urbanism'. Clearly demarcated islands of secluded exclusivity and spaces of conviviality coexist with more ambivalent spaces where the rich and the rest come face to face, such as in the marinas of Antibes, Ibiza, Puerto Banús and Porto Cervo. This array of landscapes routinely travels through the media, reaching distant audiences. Promotion campaigns for Limassol or Benidorm in women's magazines or the Paris Metro overlap with TV news coverage of the Cannes film festival, the new perfume advert set in Capri or the latest celebrity scandal in Costa Esmeralda.

Fieldwork

The research presented here was conducted in a middle-class resort and an urban beach, neither of which is frequented by elites. Discussions about travel aspirations were, however, facilitated by a set of 25 photographs of different tourist landscapes in the Mediterranean and different modes of transport including expensive cars and yachts, a biz-jet, a ferry, a bicycle and an EasyJet plane. Tourist landscapes included high-rises and crowded beaches (e.g. Benidorm, Gandia), 'unspoilt beaches' (Formentera), villa landscapes (Moraira, Dénia, Jávea), and luxury villas with yachts. Some photographs were mine and others had been taken from online and printed travel and women's magazines and an economic weekly. Interviewees were shown the photographs and asked about their feelings when seeing images of rich people and luxury in the media.

Data was collected through semi-structured interviews conducted in the summer of 2011 with young European nationals aged between 17 and 35. The focus on this particular age group in exploring the potential tensions between the desire for a mobile life and concerns for the environment is justified by a generally higher level of mobility (both physically and virtually) and greater levels of environmental concern than are found among other sectors of the population (Pew 2009; Callejo-Gallego *et al.* 2004). A total of 44 interviews with 92 people were conducted during July and the first week of August 2011. Research was conducted in Benicàssim – a seaside resort north of Valencia – during an indie music festival popular among British university students (20 interviews involving 44 people), and the Malvarrosa beach in the city of Valencia (24 interviews involving 48 people). Interviewees were Spanish (46), British (35) and from other EU countries (11). Most interviewees were university students while 37 were working and three were unemployed. In total, 69 interviewees already had or were studying for a university degree.

Showing detachment from the lives of the rich

Following the financial crash of 2008, British media fuelled a debate about the rich. Conversely, in Spain, such levels of contempt towards the rich did not penetrate the media until 2012. In this context, during the interviews I was expecting two dominant responses, one corroborating the observations made by social commentators about the desire to emulate the wealthy, and another of anger and resentment, reflecting the increasingly critical mood, at least in the British media against bankers and other high-earners since the 2008 financial crash. The findings, however, were somewhat different. Responses given by the interviewees ranged widely but can be broadly grouped in two sets exemplified by the quotes below.

Response type 1:

> I think lucky buggers! Lucky them! ... But it doesn't raise any strong feelings. It is not my lifestyle. It is just how they live. They have the money and they live that way.... If I had the money I would do the same.
>
> (University student, 21, Manchester)

Response type 2:

> I've been in Ibiza and I've seen those big yachts. I didn't really make much of it. I saw it and said 'that's a big yacht', but that's it. That is not my style. That is not something that interests me. Call it indifference if you want.
>
> (Schoolteacher, 27, Valencia)

These responses differ in their disposition to emulate the rich but both share a sense of detachment. The first corroborates partly what has long been noted by sociologists about the seductive power of the elites and was replicated by roughly a quarter (22 out of 92) of the interviewees. The second, subscribed to by roughly three-quarters of the respondents, describes luxury holidays as something 'uninteresting', 'unnatural' or 'ostentatious', which 'has no resonance with my way of living', something that, as in the quote below, people feel aloof from or cannot, and do not want to, identify with:

> This is all about money. This is not me. This is not my style. I have nothing to do with this. The type of trips I do is not ostentatious. What seems good to me is to socialize with people. What I try to do with the few holidays I have is to see places. Indeed we travel little and when we travel abroad it is always to those European cities you have to see at least once in your life.
>
> (Nurse, 32, Valencia)

The rest of the chapter focuses on this second group of interviewees, those who express no interest in emulating the rich, asking what these accounts of a sense of detachment suggest about the relationship between everyday people and the high-earners. At first glance, such responses may appear feigned, with people pretending to be indifferent, something feasible at a time of crisis in Europe where it is politically incorrect to express a desire to be rich. Also, envy is widely seen as a low motive and it is reasonable to assume that interviewees would mask their feelings (Sayer 2005: 149). In a similar vein, Jon Elster (1983) has described how people stop or pretend to stop desiring what they cannot achieve, such as in Aesop's fable of the fox and the grapes, in which the fox pretends not to care for the grapes that he cannot have, by telling himself that the grapes are in any case sour. Bourdieu's ([1979] 1986) theory of the judgement of taste may be read along these lines by assuming that interviewees participate in classificatory struggles aimed at devaluing or delegitimizing the kind of capital they lack, in this case financial capital. This would be the case of, first, the working class describing its relatively austere holidays as a more dignified way of spending their leisure time, or, second, the educated middle class presenting its more ascetic holidays focused on learning and self-development as an ethically and aesthetically superior form of travelling. Their efforts at building symbolic boundaries between them and the rich would be expressed as indifference towards excess and extravagance. This first reading presumes an attempt to present as a choice what would in fact be a lack of access to goods and recognition derived from their position in the social ladder.

An alternative interpretation holds that interviewees are expressing genuine indifference. Andrew Sayer notes:

> People's normative concerns in relation to class go beyond the unequal distribution of material goods and recognition and respect, to questions of just what is good in terms of ways of life, practices, objects, behaviours and types of character that people see as desirable.... Some may want mainly the goods that the dominant groups monopolize, others may care most about different kinds of goods. I shall argue that we cannot understand these struggles purely in terms of Hobbesian pursuit of advantage in terms of economic, cultural and social capital, as argued by Pierre Bourdieu. Although achieving these goods may bring power, recognition and perhaps envy, actors may pursue them for their own value too. The struggles are not merely for power and status but are about how to live.
>
> (Sayer 2005: 3)

In light of Sayer's account one could interpret some of the responses as reflecting an aspiration to a good life founded on restraint and moderation. Travelling can be seen here as a way of cultivating a more democratic or cosmopolitan outlook, not through ostentation, but through conviviality and being part of a wider collective. Yet this stance is contested, with an alternative reading seeing detachment as reflecting a wider process of disaffection from or disengagement with others that, according to the political scientist Robert Putnam (2000), characterizes societies in the rich North. Indifference towards the conspicuous lives of the rich is an expression of the state of 'hibernation' from public life which increasing numbers of people slide into.

Detachment

These diverse analyses provide valuable insights into possible ways of understanding how the rich are related to. However, it is the justification that interviewees provided which suggests that, at least at an explicit level, the super-rich do not act as a reference group in tourists' accounts of their holidays. Conversing about luxury holidays, middle-class tourists described the rich as a remote reality, 'a different world', 'a different universe'. But beyond the acknowledgement of unbridgeable economic rifts and unaffordable lifestyles, indifference remained a constant in most interviews.

> RESPONDENT: These images are all about luxury, money, waste, extravagance. This seems to me unachievable. Well, that's not the right word, because that would imply that I aspire to have that. But this is not the case. It is not something I aspire to. The right word is unreal...
> JAVIER CALETRÍO: Is this unfair?
> R: No, I don't think it is unfair. Since I don't desire that lifestyle, I don't want to have it and therefore I don't think it is unfair. Everyone seeks what she likes. Good luck to them with their lifestyle. [...]
> JC: Would you say this is obscene?
> R: I would rather say eccentric.
>
> (Journalist, 30, Madrid)

This interviewee tries to convey an economic and social distance from the lives of the rich and stresses the magnitude of such distance by describing their travel styles as unreal. Such distance is both reflected in, and maintained or reinforced by, her reluctance to engage with the lifestyle of the rich, not even as something to criticize, let alone as an aspiration – she declines to judge their lifestyle as obscene and instead prefers the more neutral term 'eccentric'. My explicit question about whether she considers the style of the rich as obscene was prompted by the recurring indifference that pervaded most responses and the lack of critical views about rising inequalities. A written transcription of the interviews sadly cannot convey the blasé or déjà vu attitude that infused tourists views on the rich, conveyed by their voice tone and body language. This may seem surprising in the context of crisis. In order to ascertain more precise comments, I referred to an earlier interview in which a respondent had described those photos of luxury as 'obscene'. The overwhelming response, however, was that obscene was too strong a word and those photos did little to provoke strong feelings. Interviewees would often refer to everyone's right and freedom to spend one's wealth as one wishes, suggesting either that current levels of inequality are fair or a lack of agency so deep that it takes inequality as a natural fact, as the following quote suggests:

JC: Someone told me he thought this was rather obscene.
R: No, it is not obscene. They are just enjoying themselves. Kate Moss, she's just enjoying herself. She has the money, she can do it.
JC: During the crisis the media back in England has been critical of bankers and rich people, arguing that they should not be paid that much. Are you aware of this? Is this something you relate to luxury when you see these images?
R: Yes, you kind of relate to those things, but I don't have much information about it. Maybe if I had I would feel more strongly about it. Just one person cannot do much about it. And besides this, Kate Moss is just spending her own money.
JC: Is it fair? I mean would you say these inequalities are fair?
R: Well, it is just life. That is how things are. Is it fair? I think it is luck.

(Graphic designer, 22, Newcastle)

This young woman reveals a reluctance to evaluate the lifestyles of the rich and describes the model Kate Moss as simply enjoying a life she can afford. After all, she argues, it is her own money. Further, the interviewee refers to these inequalities as a natural facet of life. A similar sentiment is again expressed in the following quote:

R: We don't associate with that.... That is actually quite ostentatious.
JC: Ostentatious? Do you mean you disapprove of it?
R: Not necessarily. It is just that I am not interested on that. If they have the money and want to do it, fine. After all it's their own choice. [...]
JC: This morning someone told me it is obscene.
R: Not really. It is just something you relate to royalty and celebrities. It is not related to the common man. I'd like to have more money but I'd travel more and to more distant places rather than doing that ostentation.

(Advertising executive, 23, London)

This reluctance to judge the lifestyles of the rich does not preclude disliking exuberant displays of wealth or feeling pity for them. Some interviewees had seen the rich in yachts at close range in places like Marbella or Ibiza, but such physical proximity did not generate desires to emulate their consumption patterns. Instead it inspired pity. Interviewees would describe the rich as unhappy people, living boring lives, without real friends and in need of recognition through extravagant consumption. Some regarded their visit to places like Puerto Banús, the marina in Marbella (Spain), as akin to visiting the zoo where exotic creatures can be seen at close quarters. Rather than admiration, interviewees expressed uneasiness and felt out of place.

R: When I see images like this I say 'I wish I could also enjoy that.' The first reaction is that, you know, 'I wish I could have that.' But you also think those are not the kind of things that are going to make you happy. You also think you would not feel comfortable there. They are not the kind of people I would approach to talk. And they would probably not accept me. That's something you feel when you are in places like Puerto Banús in Marbella. Moreover, I'd not like to spend my holidays on a boat. I rather visit rural places, small interesting places.

(University students, 18 and 20, Exeter)

JC: Someone I interviewed recently described this as obscene.
R: Well, I would not use that word. The thing is that we already know that there are rich and poor people in the world. It's not something new.... I've been in Puerto Banús. You feel out of place there. Those huge yachts ... I was feeling sorry for them. I don't think that will give them happiness.

(Marketing consultant, 29, Valencia)

R: I wouldn't say it is obscene, but at the same time I don't feel envy either. It's just not my cup of tea.... I've been in Marbella. You instantly know it is a rich place, that you don't fit there. I don't personally like it but I don't feel jealous. It's not appealing to me.

(University student, 20, Galloway, Ireland)

Justifying indifference

Interviewees justified this blasé attitude in different ways. Some argued that there is also extreme poverty in the world and that extreme wealth should not necessarily make them feel any different, while others observed that these inequalities are not new and therefore they are not something they should be especially concerned about now.[1]

R: To be honest this doesn't appeal to me and I don't give much thought to it because of the money. I'd never have the money to do that. Also it looks boring to be all day on a boat. I'd rather see places.
JC: Would you say this is obscene?
R: I wouldn't go that far. I don't have strong feelings about it. I've never experienced that so I wouldn't know how it is. It is just something I can't relate to...
JC: Would you say it is unfair?
R: I wouldn't say it is unfair. It is part of life. The same applies to many situations. Poor people in Africa never go on holidays and we have holidays every year. Is that fair?

(University student, 21, Madrid)

Both the extreme wealth of billionaires and the extreme poverty of people dying in Africa appear as different, and yet strangely similar, realities which one cannot reach or meaningfully engage with, neither as issues to change nor improve nor, in the case of luxury, as things to imitate – there is a total lack of agency. When respondents did choose to be more negative, this was based on an inappropriate or extravagant display of privilege and wealth at a time of crisis than feelings of unfairness.

> No, I don't think it is unfair. I think it is inappropriate, I think it is ostentatious. There are people who cannot pay the mortgage and then you see these people having this lifestyle. You don't need all that to live well. The important thing in life is to have health and find a balance between health, your loved ones and work. This is enough to have a good, normal life.
>
> (Journalist, 31, Madrid)

Such accounts suggest that, for certain groups, the super-rich are less relevant as a reference group than literature on consumption and social stratification may suggest. Evidence supporting this emerged also when discussing with the interviewees their disposition to travel less or closer to home for environmental reasons. As in previous research conducted between 2008 and 2010 (Caletrío 2009), the concerted response was a resounding 'no'. But interestingly, even after having talked explicitly about the rich, only four people out of 92 mentioned this privileged group in relation to this issue and claimed, as the quote below illustrates, that anyone should be entitled to travel as much as the rich do:

> R: I travel once a year, but big corporations and celebrities travel a lot. Some people do it every day. It is therefore fair we can enjoy a holiday. You spend all year working and you deserve a time for joy. Maybe every person could have an allowance and once you use it you are taxed for your trips.
> JC: Is that something you would approve?
> R: The thing is that we don't travel much and in Europe distances are rather short. It is also important to see places and broaden your horizons.
>
> (Publishing assistant, 23, London)

A majority made implicit or explicit reference, not to the rich, but to their immediate social circles when assessing their travel patterns, which they considered to be reasonable.

> JC: Have you ever thought about travelling less or travelling closer to home for environmental reasons?

R: I don't travel abroad that often. I want to travel and see places and if other people do it, why shouldn't I? My friends travel more than I do.

JC: Do you mean if other people stop travelling or travel less you'd do it too?

R: No, I wouldn't do that. What I mean is that at home I make an effort. I use ecological washing liquid and recycle and therefore travel is my luxury.

(University student, 20, London)

Interviewees were aware of issues such as the impact of their lifestyles on the environment and this was also relevant when considering what constitutes a normal or excessive number of holidays.

The desirable life, excess and economic inequalities

'The desirable life', Elliott and Urry observe, 'is not only about money and possessions; it is about movement, the capacity to escape, to be elsewhere, especially in certain kinds of distinct, ambient place. Mobility status stands today for an addiction to power and pleasure' (Elliott and Urry 2010: 80). However, the accounts presented above suggest that it is the mere possibility to be on the move that everyday people treasure, rather than the luxuries, 'money and possessions' displayed through elite mobilities. The air of glamour surrounding the rich 'globals' seems to stem from their boundless mobility rather than the expensive ways in which their travelling is done. For the interviewees in this study, the meanings and experiences of mobility oscillate between a universal entitlement characterizing European societies and, within the wider context of national and global inequalities, a real luxury whose availability cannot be taken for granted. But there were few signs that tourists regard their travel patterns as excessive – most considered their travelling once or twice a year as the normal pattern and were aware that for many that still remains an aspiration. Within Spain, this opinion accurately reflects current patterns of travel. Drawing on official data, Garín and Moral (2011) note that since 1985 the population enjoying at least one holiday per year has never been higher than 50 per cent. More specifically, in 2010 the active population without holidays was 51.3 per cent. Partly because of economic constraints but also due to cultural factors the population that travels abroad annually is limited. In the period from 1999 to 2002 this was 8.5 to 9.7 per cent and in 2009 the figure was 7 per cent.[2] According to Garín and Moral, 48 per cent of the population has never been abroad (though this seems to be declining: in 2006 the figure was 44 per cent), 15 per cent has never been outside its own autonomous community, and 10 per cent has never been outside its own province. This situation is closely related to economic inequalities, with the top 20 per cent of the population being responsible for 80 per cent of the leisure-related journeys (Santana-Turégano and Rodríguez-González 2011).

Concluding remarks

Travel for leisure evokes 'the good life' and is a highly valued practice amongst European middle classes, one that few are willing to limit on environmental grounds. While acknowledging that, even in the age of low-cost consumption, time and money to travel are not always available, those in the lower ranks of the social ladder still evoke the *possibility* to see certain places, 'places one has to visit at least once in your life', as an essential element of a social contract. No doubt the media is central in shaping such expectations and Zukin's words, written twenty years ago, resonate more strongly in today's Information Age:

> The domestication of fantasy in visual consumption is inseparable from centralized structures of economic power. Just as the earlier power of the state illuminated public space – the streets – by artificial light, so the economic power of CBS, Sony and the Disney Company illuminates private space at home by electronic images. With the means of consumption so diffused, communication of these images becomes a way of controlling both knowledge and imagination, a form of corporate social control over technology and symbolic expressions of power.
>
> (Zukin 1993: 221)

However, images of conspicuous consumption may not domesticate fantasy, shape affective dispositions and inflame desires and aspirations in the straightforward manner presumed by some sociological accounts. Such accounts tend to overlook instances in which such images are contested or simply ignored in favour of being like 'everyone else' rather than like those at the very top of the social ladder (Savage *et al.* 2005). In this respect, research presented here suggests that the discourse of tourism and global citizenship, with their emphasis on learning and self-development as a universal right (Urry 1995; Rojek 1998) is instrumental in articulating expectations about travelling. Obviously this should not be taken naively as a more positive expression of consumer cultures. Such discourse of global citizenship is mobilized in different ways by different actors, from human rights advocacy groups to environmental NGOs, and yet also by global corporations. Images suggesting the idea of a global village of cosmopolitan belonging, home to an emerging global civil society unified in diversity, constitute a favoured language through which corporations, especially in the transport, communication and IT sectors, project and seek to justify their global reach (Goldman and Papson 2011).

Despite the claims of this chapter, I am not arguing that elites exert no effect in shaping consumption patterns. Rather my argument is that we need to understand more clearly the ways in which this is happening. Claims about the emergence of a global class should not overstress its homogeneity (see Beaverstock and Faulconbridge in this volume) or prevent closer examination of the ways in which different elites in different parts of the world display their wealth. Crucially, neither must we allow this concept to distort the way in which everyday people in different groups within different societies engage with those conspicuous displays. Everyday people seem to discriminate between different expressions of wealth and distinction, and the rich are gaining legitimacy in new, subtler ways (see Khan 2011). Partly related to this is the way in which aesthetics of elite landscaped resorts are shifting the threshold of what everyday people accept as 'authentic' and 'natural' and what kinds of tourist are tacitly associated with such notions. In certain places in the north-west of the Mediterranean, shrinking and seemingly 'untouched', 'unspoiled', 'wild' or 'authentic' landscapes are increasingly associated with a world of privilege and excess, places and experiences which are distant and unattainable. Elite resorts increasingly seem to transpire a sense of ecology, while places of ecology increasingly seem fitted for elite aesthetics (Zukin 1993, Córdoba-Azcárate *et al.* this volume). This is not by any means a simple process and the dynamics at play here are complex. If anything, these are highly contested landscapes, as suggested by some of the accounts above or by looking more closely at environmental politics in Mallorca, Sardinia or Corsica. Everyday people do show reflexivity about the moral poverty of many of these expressions of excess. Yet at the same time it is some styles of being a tourist and not others that are tolerated or accepted with apparent indifference. An expected but, nonetheless, still disturbing finding is that interviewees only showed strong feelings towards images of 'mass tourism' – regarded as another type of 'excess' – such as busy beaches in Benidorm. Interestingly these were the only travel styles and tourist resorts that interviewees felt entitled to judge and condemn. It was the 'excess' of the less wealthy that received condemnation while the excess of the few was dispassionately tolerated. Once more, as in so many instances, the charming ease of the elites seemed to let them get away with it.

Notes

1 Although some people were mindful of a growing polarization of wealth – this was the case of the less well off who feel their relative situation is getting worse as a result of the crisis – at the time of conducting this research (July and August of 2011) most interviewees were oblivious of, or not especially concerned about, growing inequality.

2 This has to do with a tradition of spending holidays in the countryside hosted by relatives, or on a nearby beach, in which case going abroad does not seem like a sensible option given the good climate and quality of holiday places nearby.

References

Blume, M. (1992) *Côte d'Azur: Inventing the French Riviera*. London, Thames and Hudson.
Bourdieu, P. ([1979] 1986) *Distinction*. London, Routledge.
Caletrío, J. (2009) '*Veraneo en la playa*': Belonging and the familiar in Mediterranean mass tourism. In P. Obrador, M. Crang and P. Travlou (eds) *Cultures of Mass Tourism: Doing the Mediterranean in the Age of Banal Mobilities*. London, Ashgate.
Callejo-Gallego, J., Gutiérrez Brito, J. and Viedma-Rojas, A. (2004) *Transformaciones de la Demanda Turística Española: Apuntes Prácticos*. Madrid, Editorial Centre de Estudios Ramón Areces.
Cirer, J. C. (2004) *De la fonda a l'hotel: la gènesi d'una economia turística*. Mallorca, Documenta Balear.
Cirer, J. C. (2009) *La invenció del turismo de masses a Mallorca*. Mallorca, Documenta Balear.
Elliott, A. and Urry, J. (2010) *Mobile Lives*. Oxford, Routledge.
Elster, J. (1983) *Sour Grapes: Studies in the Subversion of Rationality*. Cambridge, Cambridge University Press.
Featherstone, M. ([1991] 2007) *Consumer Culture and Postmodernism* (2nd ed.). London, Sage.
Garín, T. and Moral, M. J. (2011) *Comportamiento Turístico de los Residentes en España*. Madrid, Fundación de las Cajas de Ahorros.
Goldman, R. and Papson, S. (2011) *Landscapes of Capital*. Cambirdge, Polity.
Graham, S. and Marvin, S. (2001) *Splittering Urbanism*. London, Routledge.
Khan, S. (2011) *Privilege: The Making of an Adolescent Elite at St. Paul's School*. Princeton, Princeton University Press.
Littlewood, I. (1999) *Sultry Climates: Travel and Sex since the Grand Tour*. London, John Murray.
Pemble, J. (1987) *The Mediterranean Passion*. Oxford, Claredon.
Pew Research (2009) Global Warming Seen as a Major Problem Around the World: Less Concern in the U.S., China and Russia. Pew Research, 2 December. Retrieved from www.pewglobal.org/2009/12/02/global-warming-seen-as-a-major-problem-around-the-world-less-concern-in-the-us-china-and-russia on 13 May 2013.
Putnam, R. (2000) *Bowling Alone*. New York, Simon & Schuster.
Rojek, C. (1998) Tourism and citizenship. *International Journal of Cultural Policy* 4(2): 291–310.
Santana-Turégano, M. A. and Rodríguez-González, P. (2011) *La polarización en el consumo turístico de los españoles*. Retrieved from www.fes-web.org/uploads/files/modules/congress/10/grupos-trabajo/ponencias/857.pdf on 12 November 2012.
Savage, M. and Williams, K. (eds.) (2008) *Remembering Elites*. Oxford, Blackwell.
Savage, M., Bagnall, G. and Longhurst, B. (2005) *Globalization and Belonging*. London, Sage.

Sayer, A. (2005) *The Moral Significance of Class*. Cambridge, Cambridge University Press.
Thrift, N. (2007) *Non-Representational Theory*. London, Routledge.
Urry, J. (1995) *Consuming Places*. London, Routledge.
Veblen, T. ([1889] 2005) *Conspicuous Consumption*. London, Penguin.
Zukin, S. (1993) *Landscapes of Power*. Berkeley, University of California Press.

Chapter 11

Tracing the super-rich and their mobilities in a Scandinavian welfare state

Malene Freudendal-Pedersen

The super-rich are not an everyday topic in Denmark, neither in the media nor in research. Looking at a list presenting the ten richest people in Denmark, most Danes would not be able to identify any faces or stories from gossip magazines. The Danish super-rich live a quiet, sheltered life. Interestingly though, their mobilities would definitely be one of the first things that come to mind as being central to the few stories that do emerge, such as big cars, private jets, secluded holiday resorts and consumption of foreign commodities.

Initially the research question for this chapter was: "Are the mobilities of the super-rich in Denmark performed differently and at a larger scale than within the remaining population?" Through bibliographic research, research on newspaper articles and other media, statistical research, and the use of blogs as well as informal talks with colleagues, I realized I would not be able to fully answer this question. Beaverstock *et al.* pointed out in 2004 that there seems to exist a "silence" around the super-rich, and this is also very much the case in Denmark. Despite this silence some research has been done on the super-rich in other countries (see for instance Savage and Williams 2008; Wedel 2009) and there is convergence between the super-rich in Denmark and other places, since part of their highly consuming hyper-mobile lifestyle means interacting in closed global circles. Still I found this "silence" very interesting and, at least in Denmark, it seems to be related to the notion of equality embedded within the concept of the welfare state. Also it seemed to be part of the answer to the lack of empirical data in relation to the mobilities of the super-rich in Denmark. Thereby the question of "why the super-rich and their mobilities are more or less absent in Danish research and the public mind" became an important question for this chapter. Additionally the chapter answers part of the question concerning the actual mobilities performed and lived by the super-rich.

The first part of the chapter is a theoretical discussion on the ideas of equality and class in Denmark, supplemented with statistics on mobilities, economics and class differences. The second part tracks the super-rich and their mobilities through public statistics and newspaper articles. It turned out that most facts and discussions about the super-rich were to be found in particular in the conservative newspaper *Børsen* (Stock Exchange). Finally, before the concluding remarks, I will give some empirical examples from a rich (but not super-rich) executive and a bodyguard, whom I interviewed about their professional relations with the super-rich.

Place

When travelling outside Europe it is not unusual to meet people who have never heard of Denmark, and some even think it is a city in The Netherlands or Germany. Denmark is a small country with only 5.5 million inhabitants and a labor force of about 2.9 million. The Nordic tradition of the welfare state is social citizenship with the right to a minimum level of economic prosperity. Denmark has the fourth highest ratio of tertiary degree holders in the world and the GDP per hour worked was the 13th highest in 2009 (Unesco 2009). According to the World Bank, Denmark has the world's lowest level of income inequality, a point I will examine critically later in this chapter, as well as the world's highest minimum wage (IMF 2010). Compared to other countries in the EU, Denmark has a low unemployment rate – 6.3 percent in June 2012 – and so far a relatively stable economy, despite the European crisis in the economy. The car is the most popular mode of transport in Denmark. 57 percent of all trips and 74 percent of all kilometers traveled are by private car. No less than 84 percent of all Danish people have access to at minimum one car per household and 87 percent of Danish people above 18 years old have a driver's license. Of all trips made in Denmark 43 per cent are leisure trips and a large number of trips are below two kilometers. Men drive 32 per cent more than women do and people in the rural districts drive more than people in the city (DTU Transport 2012). All in all Denmark is a wealthy country with a high and constantly growing car dependency. Throughout the 1960s and 1970s single-family housing and private cars were the main ideals in planning. Also, in relation to information and communications technology (ICT), Denmark has a high sufficiency level. In the period from April to June 2012 97 percent of Danes between 16 and 74 used a mobile phone or a smartphone: 89 percent used such devices to text, 55 percent accessed the internet, 41 percent used them for navigation and 39 percent downloaded applications (Statistics Denmark 2012). Only 6 percent of Danes between 16 and 74 have never used the internet, and the non-users are primarily found in the group of people above 65. The most frequent activity on the internet is emails (86 percent), internet banking (79 percent) and online news (73 percent). Also playing games and listening to music (53 percent) as well as using Facebook and writing blogs (48 percent) are quite frequent (Statistics Denmark 2012). I could go on with the numbers showing the high level of mobilities performed and lived in Denmark, but the scope of this chapter is not solely about the mobilities of the Danish population but the mobilities of the super-rich in Denmark, and that turns out to be trickier, something I will return to later.

Class and the Danish welfare system

Generally speaking, the Nordic welfare system is based upon the idea that the broadest shoulders should carry the heaviest burdens and that everybody, no matter their income, should have the right to education and health benefits. The Danish government gets much of its revenue by taxing personal income (also, those with no job have an income in terms of unemployment benefits). The tax system is progressive and Denmark has one of the highest levels of taxation in the world. Compared to other countries registration tax for car ownership is very high and buying a car is quite expensive. Roads are toll-free except for the bridge between Seeland and Fyn, and when you drive your car to work you get a tax deduction. The overall idea is that the more flexible the workforce the more flexible the labor market: people are more willing to move. Taxation thus benefits mobilities.

The taxation system pays, among other things, for unemployment benefits, free education, free medical help, free elderly care and low pricing on childcare. Because of this the Gini coefficient in Denmark is very low (Statistics Denmark 2011). This is not to say that inequalities do not exist in Denmark; they do and they are increasing. In 2009, 10 percent of the poorest people have experienced an average annual negative growth of 0.9 percent in their income, and yet 10 percent of the richest people have experienced an average annual growth of 3.3 percent. The richest 10 percent dispose of 64 percent of the wealth (Socialpolitisk Forening and CASA 2010). Nevertheless, it seems to be a common understanding in Denmark that we are all middle class, even if an increasing amount of the Danish population thinks the wealth inequality is too big (Socialpolitisk Forening and CASA 2010). The "Occupy Wall Street" equivalent, "Occupy Denmark," had its first demonstration in October 2011 and discussions on wealth, consumption and environmental effects have taken up an increasing amount of space in the media.

A large amount of research about income distribution in relation to the poorest in society has been done in Denmark (E. J. Hansen 1989; F. K. Hansen 2004; Bak 2004; Larsen 2004). Research shows that the number of poor people in Denmark is increasing and is estimated to be around four percent of the population (Hansen 2011). Research undertaken on the super-rich is on the other hand non-existent.

A few studies have been done on the upper class. Stine Thidemann Faber's (2008) PhD thesis "In Pursuit of Class" is a study of social class on a micro level and uses qualitative interviews with women to focus on class and gender. It explores how class has significance for how women experience and perceive themselves and others, as well as their perceptions of opportunities accessible to them. In Faber's interviews, social differences are initially rejected, muffled and underplayed, but the women do in fact discuss social differences, although the word "class" is never used. This distancing from others is communicated mainly in terms of moral reservations and moral condemnation when the women indirectly refer to people who think, act or prioritize differently. As Faber herself said about her work in a newspaper interview:

> I think it's because we have an ideal of equality in Denmark. In addition, as the middle class has grown in size, many researchers believe that talking about class is outdated. Today ethnicity is the dominant issue. But it may well be problematic that the class issue is not at all articulated, as in that way many aspects of our society will not be illuminated. It is as if we are trying to push social inequality away and instead individualize social problems.
> (Engstrøm 2009, my translation)

The equality issue

As early as 1984 (reprinted in 2002) Marianne Gullestad, a Norwegian sociologist, formulated the idea of the Nordic equality ideal in her book *Kitchen Table Society*. This issue has continued to be present in Gullestad's work. According to Gullestad, people in the Nordic countries are in particular characterized by the idea that all are equal, and therefore the majority of people prefer not to talk about inequality. This understanding is related to a particular way of acting, a form of social tactics, where people just claim to be equal with each other. Gullestad argues that this leads to a specific form of interaction: "Where people have things in common it is highlighted, and that which separates them is tactfully kept as far as possible out of sight" (Gullestad 2001: 35, my translation). One of the few examples I can come up with in relation to the direct reference of equality in Denmark is, oddly enough, when the conservatives argue against congestion charging. Here they use the equality issue as an argument as to why congestion charging is not a good idea, since those with less money will suffer the most. I guess it goes without saying that this is not their most common line of argument.

When people evade talking about class or social differences this is not just about tact and good manners, but also about how class differences and differences between the sexes are in direct conflict with Nordic people's understanding of themselves. In a country like Denmark, wanting to represent a modern and equal society, it is simply not ideologically correct to articulate social, economic or cultural differences (Faber 2008: 99). As I showed earlier, men drive 32 percent more than women in Denmark, but gendered mobilities fall into the same category as class, and are seldom articulated in either the media or research.

> The equality mindset means that class differences and other differences in lifestyle fade away as unfortunate results of confusing and complex processes. For this reason, these differences are a particularly sensitive subject. They are present all the time, individuals at all times pay more or less conscious attention to them, but would rather not talk about them. When in fact talking about them, they are handled carefully and often made into questions about opinion and taste or formulated as moral condemnation.
> (Gullestad 2002: 75, my translation)

This is in line with Sayer's (2005) discussion of the "moral significance of class," where he argues that the concept of class makes us feel uncomfortable, both as researchers and as individuals interacting and communicating. Contemporary culture is in denial about class because it is embarrassing to acknowledge it. This is so even if class (when not considering material wealth) affects relationships, practices, the esteem and respect of others and hence our sense of self-worth. Even if class is often blatantly obvious we ignore it when discomfort is inherent in the concept of class, because class leads to inequality and thus lacks its own legitimacy (Sayer 2005: 4). We are born with different resources and opportunities, tangible and intangible, which both limits and enables our access to relationships and experiences. It becomes painful, since class, in addition to posing an unequal distribution of material goods, is also about the struggle for the definition of what is good – the good life, good interpersonal skills etc. Morality should be understood as the question of whether we understand and feel actions to be good or bad, and how we think and feel we should treat others and others should treat us. Thus the moral significance of class and the reason why class struggle still exists is because it becomes a struggle for the definition of the good life between classes. We constantly exercise a moral assessment of others and put them into classes more or less unconsciously because we judge each other aesthetically, performatively and morally (Sayer 2005: 142). Savage (2000) also underlines people's needs to be part of "normality":

> The idea of class means something to people, even where the replies are hesitant. Crucially, rather than evoking a sense of belonging to a collective group, it invokes a sense of differentiation from others.

> In most cases it means they are not one of the privileged who have it easy, nor are they one of those at the bottom who are morally suspect. People's sense of self-identity is linked to a claim of "ordinariness" or "normality", which operates as a double reaction against both above and below.
>
> (Savage 2000: 115)

But as Savage also rightly points out, the idea of "ordinariness" needs to be contrasted with something else in order to be given substance and thus the idioms and discourses of class are "smuggled back into people's thinking" (Savage 2000: 117). Still the more "pleasant" notion is the concept of equality that seems to be based on the idea that a society purged of social inequality is a just society, because it does not restrict the life chances of others (Hansen 1992). The idea of equal worth plays a central role in the personal relationships between people and how comfortable they feel in a situation (Sayer 2005). Gullestad (1984/2002) argues that baseline social and cultural differences are not openly acknowledged, but instead characterized by social life and togetherness in more indirect and subtle ways. The similarity with others, such as the establishment of sociality and culture, is used in Scandinavia as a way for people to create and confirm themselves. Ideals of equality imply that it is problematic when people are perceived differently and hence it is a minority who emphasize or make underlying contradictions and inequities explicit (Gullestad 1984/2002). The unease of openly perceiving oneself as significantly different from others is, it seems, quite a common result of research on class as Kelley and Evans describe it in a study of six western democracies: "Rich and poor, well-educated and poorly educated, high-status and low-status, all see themselves near the middle of the class system, rarely at the top or bottom" (Kelley and Evans 1995: 166) (see also Savage 2000; Savage *et al.* 2001; Devine 2005).

A hunch about the super-rich and their power

A Master's thesis in sociology undertaken at Copenhagen University by Ellersgaard and Larsen (2010) tried to confront the non-disclosure of class in Denmark and get a bit closer to the super-rich in Denmark. The thesis "The companies' men – Danish top executives' collective biographies" centers on chief executives in Denmark. It opens with the statement that within Danish sociology:

> the concept of elite [is] almost non-existent. And when the term is used, such as during power studies, it does so with awe, far from showing the research community from its most courageous and controversial side. Maybe this is because people through the study of elites

cannot hide themselves? Those studied have the resources to actively identify errors and shortcomings of the research and take a stand on the definition of social reality. This thesis is an attempt to break with sociology's fear of contact with the groups where power is concentrated.

(Ellersgaard and Larsen 2010, my translation)

The reluctance to deal with the upper class is supported by Savage and Williams who state that '...those who control money are establishing themselves as central social and political agents, who can also embed themselves in wider circuits of power' (2008: 9). Ellersgaard and Larsen's work is primarily based on publicly available information on 82 chief executives in Denmark and illuminates how power is concentrated within specific education, classes and history. It provides a picture of where power is concentrated within the business community but also briefly touches on the remaining parts of lives lived. What we learn about their lives is that they all have stay-at-home wives who early in their lives gave up their own careers and had a stable marriage with many children. In addition we learn that chief executives' interests are centered on golf, sailing and cultural events like opera and that they are consumers of global high-end brands and goods. It is clear from the description of their working lives, connections and power relations that the "companies' men" are part of a specific, highly mobile group of people.

> One of the most striking developments in present-day capitalism is the increasing number of highly paid financial intermediaries whose role is not the executive management of "men and things" within corporate hierarchies but the switching or servicing of the flows of money through market trading and corporate deals whose profits greatly increase the number of working rich.
>
> (Savage and Williams 2008: 10)

Ellersgaard and Larsens's research demonstrates that differences exist but also that an unwillingness, or maybe more accurately a fear, exists in relation to examining elites. Why this unwillingness or fear exists is not within the scope of this chapter but it seems that one obvious place to start this discussion would be the increasing pressure on universities to get research funding from places where the power elite hold influence.

The super-rich in Denmark

Earlier I mentioned that the Gini coefficient in Denmark is very low and this is primarily because our social security system ensures everybody has an income. The average family income in Denmark is approximately

€50,600 a year. Rudersdal municipality, 20 kilometers north of Copenhagen, has the highest average (€58,893 a year) and the biggest concentration of rich people and large estates. Car ownership is very high, even if the city has a high share of public transport with fast connections to Copenhagen. The lowest average, amounting to €31,506 a year, is in Copenhagen municipality, which has the largest amount of poor people and social housing (Statistics Denmark 2011). This supports the Gini coefficient showing that Denmark has very high levels of equality in terms of income (wages also includes social security). What the Gini coefficient does not reveal, however, is the value of real property and stocks, and factoring in these assets would create quite a different picture. Ellersgaard and Larsen (2010) also encounter this problem in their attempt to clarify the economic capital of the chief executives (capital understood along Bourdieu's lines (1984)). The only data available is about wages. Ellersgaard and Larsen estimate that adding the value of cars, yachts and the overall value of property investments would create a different picture, as one of the chief executives, for instance, owns a holiday home at an estimated value of €6 million (2010: 164–165).

Throughout the nineties Denmark had a large increase in housing prices and for those investing in stock there have been large returns. The 50 largest fortunes in Denmark have a value of $75 billion and the owners of these fortunes also own the businesses most significant for the Danish economy (Hansen 2008). Similarly, the number of dollar millionaires grew from 36,000 to 44,500 in just one year (Capgemini and Merrill Lynch 2011). There are eight US-dollar millionaires in Denmark for every 1,000 inhabitants, almost on par with the United States, which has ten US-dollar millionaires per 1,000 inhabitants. In Sweden the figure is down to six, while Norway can boast having 17. However, exactly how many ultra-rich people there are in Denmark is unclear since there is a custom of keeping quiet about personal wealth and there is no official list.

Forbes' 2011 annual list of the richest people in the world included three Danes. These three are all affiliated with, or owners of, some of the biggest cooperation's in Denmark: Lego, Jysk and Coloplast. Interestingly Maersk Mc-Kinney Moller, who had the highest place on the newspaper *Berlingske*'s list of Denmark's 50 richest, is not included. His estimated fortune was €16 billion, based on a review of ownership and financial figures (Maersk McKinney Møller died recently and his daughter took over the firm). In an article from the Danish TV2 online a financial business commentator explains how Maersk was not included on the Forbes list when he actually earned more than the other three put together: "Part of Maersk's property is located in funds abroad in places where you cannot determine their value." By doing so the money is no longer "part" of his private fortune and Forbes' list is based on information on private wealth (Nikolajeva 2011). The financial business commentator also believes that there may be another explanation as to why Maersk was not on the prestigious list: "Maersk has always done his best to keep the size of his fortune a secret, and he can do this in accordance with Danish law. That is why assessing his fortune will always be an estimate" (Nikolajeva 2011). Private fortunes are not public in Denmark and it seems no one really knows how big the ship-owner's personal assets were.

It is no secret to the Danish public that Maersk had a lot of influence and power. He had close connections to the royal family as well as the top politicians in Denmark. One of the most public discussed issues was his "gift" to Copenhagen – a new opera house built on the harbor front, opposite one of his earlier gifts to Copenhagen, the "Amalie Garden." The Amalie Garden was built in 1983 and was met with a lot of criticism for not being for the people of Copenhagen. Some of the same critique has been aimed at the opera house. It is known that Maersk interfered with the architect's work and decided on the esthetic expression against the architect's will. The big issue was the windows: Maersk did not want people to be able to glance at the opera guests from the outside so today the view is designed to display from the inside out. Another interesting issue in relations to this "gift" is mobility. The opera house is built on the Copenhagen harbor front, which was redeveloped throughout the 2010s in line with harbor fronts in a large number of other cities around the world. The opera house is located on an old site for shipbuilding and has two old cranes servicing a dry dock. Before the construction of the opera house, the location came to be a very important leisure space for Copenhageners, with restaurants, bars, sports and cultural events. The location has a magnificent view of the harbor and it is one of the best places in the city to watch the sun set. Maersk planned to tear down the cranes to build parking facilities; unfortunately for him they became listed buildings before he was able to realize his plans so he had to build the parking facilities around the cranes. Today, instead of being a place for people to sit and enjoy the sunset over Copenhagen harbor it is, most of the time, empty asphalt, a non-space facilitating the richest people's need to use their cars. The opera house is accessible using public transport, as the bus gets one very close and the Metro requires only a ten-minute walk. Another possibility is using a bike that can be parked at the rear of the opera house close to the personnel entrance. Transforming this place along the harbor into a parking lot with a view was essential in order for the rich to be able to drive as close as possible to the entrance of the opera house.

It is clear from this example that there is a group of super-rich people in Denmark, but also significant is how little we actually know about them. There is a common understanding that we are more or less alike, even if we know there is a difference. Gender and class do not fit well with the Nordic idea of equality even if it is safe to say that both Norway and Sweden are more articulate about these issues than Denmark.

Mobilities of the super-rich

It will probably not come as a surprise, but car statistics in Denmark show that there is a correlation between where the rich people live and the number of cars bought. The average CO_2 emissions for the 10 percent richest families in Denmark is 6.3 tons; the poorest 10 percent's average CO_2 emissions average is 3.3 tons. A large amount comes from petroleum and diesel producing 2.6 tons' CO_2 emission for the 10 percent richest and 0.9 tons' CO_2 emission for the poorest 10 percent (Arbejderbevægelsens Erhvervsråd 2010). This does, however, only tell us something about the richest 10 percent of the Danish population.

To get a bit closer to the super-rich we turn to a story in one of the major Danish newspapers, *Politikken*. Here, Kristoffer Sundberg from JoinJetit (a firm selling and chartering private jets) says that Denmark is a good market for private airplanes similar to Great Britain and Switzerland. Denmark is considered as one of the future markets, says Sundberg: "For the private buyer, it's perhaps that they have bought the big house and dream car and what's next?" (Theils 2011). Claus Lassen, who has done extensive research on aeromobilities in Denmark, also underlines the major increase in private jets. Lassen explains how new airports in Denmark emerge based on private and company jets. While he has not published anything on this yet, it is one of the interesting side stories to appear from his work. It is not just about having a new accessory, but also about the ability to move faster when speed becomes one of the biggest stratifiers in late modern lives (Bauman 1998; Elliott and Urry 2010). Similarly, Hasler describes how the end of the Cold War has had a big significance in opening up the global market for even greater benefits for the super-rich:

> Now ... the rich are free: free to move their money around the world.... The super-rich are also free to move themselves. Although still less mobile than their money, they too are becoming less rooted, moving easily between many different locations.
>
> (Hasler 2000: 2–3)

Data on the mobilities of the super-rich can also be found in the Danish National Travel Survey (TU), which is a joint venture between the Danish State, local authorities and transport operators, including the Department of Transport at the Danish Technical University (DTU). The survey is conducted by DTU Transport with a subcontractor using telephone interviews. The survey has existed since 1975 and from 1992 onwards the survey has been undertaken yearly, except for the years 2004 and 2005. Normally, the survey consists of approximately 13,000 interviews per year, but between 2009 and 2011 the sample was doubled. Interviews are carried out daily around the year, in a combination of web interviews (20 percent) and telephone interviews (80 percent). According to Hjalmer Christensen at the DTU, who kindly helped me pull numbers on the super-rich out of the Danish transport survey data, the conclusion is that in a Danish context we cannot talk about a special transportation picture for the super-rich. There is a strong correlation between income and transport up to a personal income of about €67,000. Above this it is difficult to see any further connection. Also Hjalmer Christensen pointed out that the differences between the three upper income groups (i.e., the super-rich) have a large statistical uncertainty, while the extracts from the four or five lowest income groups must be considered quite valid. From the transport data you can find relations between a decline in walking, biking and public transport and increasing income. All in all this does not provide any clear picture of the mobilities of the super-rich, but it does give an indication that their transport is privatized and not public. This is sustained when searching on *Infomedia* (the national Danish database for newspaper articles) with the words "upper class" and "consumption." The majority of articles appearing are about new luxury cars, and even if the subject is on cocaine use, or playing golf, the mode of mobility is mentioned (cars or planes).

A story about the mobilities of the super-rich

To understand why in the TU data there is no indication, for instance, that the super-rich in Denmark drive more, even if part of it is because of the very small sample, I decided to interview a bodyguard. Through this conversation I was hoping to get an overview of how much of the mobility of the super-rich might be hidden in this service. According to him, not many Danish people have bodyguards and when in fact they use this service it is paid for through their company:

> Only very few super-rich in Denmark are afraid that their kids might get kidnapped; this is not something we consider a threat in Denmark. The major security risks in Denmark come from the line of work the parents have, for instance people working for the weapons industry.

Their major work in the company was transporting and safeguarding big company and industrial events. On the assignments related to protecting a family unit, one of their jobs was transporting kids to and from school:

> In a stressful everyday life everything becomes easier for the parents when they do not have to take their kids to and from school. The nanny takes care of the practical stuff and then we drive them so the parents can focus on themselves.

This might explain why the super-rich seem to have had a small decline in car driving. Commuting in Denmark only accounts for 35 percent of all journeys and when someone else performs the remaining everyday life mobilities of the super-rich it doesn't show up in the statistics. The national Danish travel survey questionnaire is related solely to the transport conducted by the interviewee.

What I found really interesting was the bodyguard's descriptions of their duties when the family wanted to go on a family outing:

> The family wants to be alone so they drive in their own car and we follow behind in another car. Our job is of course to protect them, but more important we have a heart starter and a first aid kit in the car because people know that the biggest risk for them is driving on a highway.

Everyday life is always located in specific places where things like day-care, grocery shopping, school and so on need to be handled. And living in a world with other people means risks – especially when it entails one of today's most deadly technologies, the automobile. What money can offer is fast help but it can never remove the biggest threat of the unintended consequences of everybody wanting more mobility. The super-rich can live their protected lives on the move, escaping on their way to elsewhere, but the potential risks and fixations in place are ever present, unless they have no personal commitments whatsoever. As Elliott and Urry describe in their book *Mobile Lives* (2010), with an informant who strives for distance from locality relentlessly orientated towards an elsewhere, there is a mobile elite of people changing places whenever they feel like it, escaping the risks and consequences of their way of living. This striving is lived as a series of exits from local situations demanding degrees of attachment and commitment (Elliott and Urry 2010: 79). The life of these mobile elites is not only about money and possessions, "it is about movement, the capacity to escape, to be elsewhere, especially in certain kinds of distinct, ambient place" (Elliott and Urry 2010: 80). Simultaneously, this hypermobility can be seen as an attempt to master an otherwise unsettling and dangerous world. This point is also made by Beck (1992) in *Risk Society*, where he points out how this is unobtainable because of what he calls the boomerang effect. In a risk society this is related to environmental crises always having global effects that will eventually catch up with you wherever you go. Future research on everyday life practices of super-rich families could potentially produce some interesting insights on how this exit from local situations is never possible when there are emotional attachments involved.

From high mobilities to less mobility

My second interview was with a rich (but not super-rich) executive who used to live a highly mobile life. He is the closest I have so far managed to get to the upper class in Denmark, and my entrance into this world was facilitated by his desire to tell me about his new business, which is introducing electrical cars into Denmark based on the idea of access instead of ownership. While contemplatively looking into his cup of coffee he conceded the point: "Implementing the idea of access instead of ownership is not aimed at the rich; they want the ultimate freedom and flexibility of their private car; this idea is for the middle class and the poor."

I interviewed him at an expensive address in the middle of Copenhagen and it became a long talk about his passion for electric cars, more precisely the newest Tesla model and all of its advantages. He himself preferred the new family model, he explained, but because of long waiting times he "had been forced" to buy the sports car instead, costing €100,000 upwards. He commutes to work in it every morning, since it is a "direct commercial" for his aspiring business.

> I think this is the right moment to try this business. I have set aside a specific amount of money giving me three years to make this business a success. Because of the big attention to the CSR [corporate social responsibility] bottom line, companies today willingly discuss sustainable mobility, but I don't think it influences their everyday mobilities.

The executive has a long-standing experience with a highly mobile life, and he is starting this new business in the late part of his working life. Throughout his working life so far, he has had several chief executive jobs in different parts of Europe while having a wife and two children in Denmark. He organized this life by flying home most weekends and the family visited him on holidays. Initially, he took his family with him, but the kids were unhappy about the changing environments and schools. After 20 years of living this way, he decided to move back to Denmark (now with grown-up kids and an ex-wife) with "enough" money to start pursuing what he felt was the right thing, a firm that within three years has introduced the electric car to Denmark:

> The main idea is to make a range of different services organized through ICT, such as electric taxis, electric shared cars, electric company cars and so on. Today everybody has a smartphone so they can use this to make last-minute mobility decisions when they need them. It doesn't need to be planned. The whole idea is that people can have access when the need it.

When asked who this transformation is aimed at he immediately acknowledges that it is not for the rich, since he does not think that they are willing to engage in systems of access instead of ownership:

> I know a lot of these people and they want their own car, they also want their own plane. I don't mind travelling on business class because it is faster to get through the airport. But a lot of them don't want that because it is not as flexible, you still have timetables and lining up in queues.

Today the executive travels around the world working on introducing and selling this system of flexible, efficient and suitable mobilities, organized through applications and web-based systems. He himself owns his own car and believes that others with "enough" do not want to share mobility with anybody. When asked if he thinks that it is fair that the super-rich do not have to think about sustainable mobility the answer is: "This is just how it is always going to be, no need to think about whether it is fair, they won't have to be part of this, they can say no and nobody can do anything about it."

Concluding remarks

There is without doubt a group of super-rich people in Denmark. Estimating the total number is difficult due to the fact that most of them live quiet lives, investing their fortunes in more or less invisible ways. My first research question was to investigate if the mobilities of the super-rich in Denmark were performed differently and at a larger scale than within the remaining population. What we can see is that their car ownership is larger, and it seems that flying is increasingly done with private jets. In addition we know that public transport and biking is not part of their mobilities routine. Even if Denmark is very well documented on everyday activities, it is still very difficult to find out anything about the everyday practices and routines of the super-rich. This might be because many of the "normal" everyday activities are in fact not done by themselves but by employees and thus their activities do not show up in the different statistics. Where a middle-class family's father would have to describe his mobility patterns involving work, leisure, shopping and chauffeuring children, the super-rich father would only have his job and own personal leisure activity patterns to list.

The super-rich in Denmark live in very discrete, closed, globalized circles, and this leads directly to my second research question on why the super-rich and their mobilities are more or less absent in Danish research and the public consciousness. The equality ideal permeating Danish society makes it hard to learn anything about the super-rich. This idea goes a long way back into the Danish self-understanding. As long ago as 1820, theologian and politician N. F. S. Grundtvig (1783–1872), a veritable institution in Danish spirit and social life, wrote a very famous poem, "Even higher mountains." The famous phrase "within wealth we have gone far, when few have too much and fewer too little" stands today as an important statement for public distribution policies, and it constitutes a general consensus in the Danish perception of self. This ideal of equality also permeates the available public statistics where we never get closer than to the richest 10 percent in Denmark. In many ways it seems those closest to confronting the issue of the super-rich are a small group of journalists, authors and filmmakers, and we can only ask ourselves whether their stories are close to reality or mostly fiction. The rich appearing in newspaper articles or gossip magazines seem to a higher degree to be those aspiring to belong to the group of the super-rich, and within research and public statistics the super-rich are never extracted.

Interesting future research could include questions focusing on everyday life and the close relations that entails. Ellersgaard and Larsen's work shows that the majority of chief executives have immobile, stay-at-home wives in order to create the stability the hypermobile super-rich also want. There seems to be very little knowledge about the part of super-rich everyday life not related to working life. This could lead to some of the following research questions:

1 How is the lived everyday life of the super-rich impacted by risks in their dependency on both dwelling and mobility?
2 Are the mobilities of the super-rich more restricted since it seems certain possibilities are deselected?
3 Which kind of professionalized mobility services do the super-rich use to handle everyday activities?
4 To what degree are the hyper-mobile super-rich gendered, and does this differ from other groups in society?

Overall it would definitely be interesting to interview the super-rich families and see if their everyday life was that significantly different. More vacations, yes, more flying, yes, but on an everyday basis many Danish kids are transported to and from school in private cars, they have computers in their rooms and smartphones and they are dependent on friends, extracurricular activities and hobbies. The major difference might be that the super-rich will be the regional warlords in Dennis and Urry's (2009) future scenario. Those with enough money and power to control and own technologies like cars and planes unavailable to the rest of the population, always a step in front, having more mobility.

References

Arbejderbevægelsens Erhvervsråd (2010) *Det Opdelte Danmark – Fordeling og levevilkår 2010* [The Divided Denmark – Distribution and Living Conditions 2010], Copenhagen: The Economic Council of the Labor Movements.

Bak, C. K. (2004) Demokratisering og individualisering af fattigdommen? En kvantitativ og kvalitativ belysning af fattigdom i Danmark. [Democratization and individualization of poverty? A quantitative and qualitative illumination of poverty in Denmark], Copenhagen University, Department of Sociology.

Bauman, Z. (1998) *Globalization – The Human Consequences*, Cambridge: Polity Press.

Beaverstock, J., Hubbard, P. and Short, J. R. (2004) Getting away with it? Exposing the geographies of the Super-Rich, *Geoforum* 35: 401–407.

Beck, U. (1992) *Risk Society: Towards a new modernity*, London: Sage.

Bourdieu, P. (1984). *Distinction: A social critique of the judgement of taste*, Cambridge, MA: Harvard University Press.

Capgemini and Merrill Lynch (2011) *World Wealth Report 2011*, at www.ml.com/media/114235.pdf (accessed 11 December 2011).

Dennis, K. and Urry, J. (2009) *After The Car*, Cambridge: Polity Press.

Devine, F. (2005) Middle-class identities in the United States. In Devine, F., Savage, M., Scott, J. and Crompton, R. (eds.) *Rethinking Class: Culture, identities ad lifestyle*, New York: Palgrave Macmillan.

DTU Transport (2012) *Transportvaneundersøgelsen – Faktaark om biltransport I Danmark* [The Transport habits study – fact sheet on car transport in Denmark], Danish Technical University 06–2012-TU0611v1.

Ellersgaard, C. H. and Larsen, A. G. (2010) Firmaets mænd: De Danske topdirektørers kollektive biografi [The companies men – Danish top executives collective biography], Masters' thesis, Department of Sociology, Copenhagen University.

Elliott, A. and Urry, J. (2010) *Mobile Lives*, London: Routledge.

Engstrøm, L. (2009) Sociale klasser: Diskretion en selvfølge [Social classes: Discretion a matter of course], *Weekendavisen* 24 July, article id:e19b705c.

Faber, S. T. (2008) På jagt efter klasse [In pursuit of class], PhD thesis, Department of Sociology and Social Work, Aalborg University.

Gullestad, M. (1984/2002) *Kitchen Table Society*, Oslo: Universitetsforlaget.

Gullestad, M. (2001) Likhetens grenser [Limits to equality]. In Lien, M., Lidén, H. and Vike, H. (eds.) *Likhetens Paradokser. Antropologiske undersøkelser i det moderne Norge* [Equality paradoxes: anthropological studies in modern Norway], Oslo: Universitetsforlaget.

Gullestad, M. (2002) *Det norske sett med nye øyne* [The Norwegian seen with new eyes], Oslo: Universitetsforlaget.

Hansen, E. J. (1992) *Social Klasser og social ulighed* [Social Classes and Social Inequality]. In Andersen, H. (ed.) *Sociologi – en grundbog til et fag* [Sociology – a course textbook], Copenhagen: Hans Reitzels Forlag.

Hansen, E. J. (1989) *Fattigdom* [Poverty], Copenhagen: Socialforskningsinstituttet.

Hansen, F. K. (2004). Fattigdom og social udstødning [Poverty and social exclusion]. In Morten Ejernæs *et al.* (eds.) *Sociologi og Socialt arbejde* [Sociology and Social Work], Copenhagen: Danmarks Forvaltningshøjskole.

Hansen, F. K. (2011) *Indkomstoverførsler og ulighed* [Income transfers and social inequality], Copenhagen: CASA.

Hansen, M. K. (2008) Her er 50 danske diskrete milliardærer [Here are 50 Danish discrete millionaires], *Børsen* 11 January.

Hasler, S. (2000) *Super-rich: The Unjust New World of Global Capitalism*, New York: Palgrave Macmillan.

IMF (2010) *World Economic Outlook Database*, at www.imf.org/external/pubs/ft/weo/2010/02/weodata/index.aspx (accessed 23 August 2012).

Kelley, J. and Evans, M. (1995) Class and class conflict in six western nations, *American Sociological Review* 60(2): 157–178.

Larsen, J. E. (2004): Fattigdom og social eksklusion, Tendenser i Danmark over et kvart århundrede [Poverty and social exclusion, tendencies in Denmark over a quarter of a century], Copenhagen: Socialforskningsinstituttet Rapport no. 04: 27.

Nikolajeva, N (2011) Milliardær-liste: Ingen plads til Mærsk [The billionaire list: no room for Maersk], *TV2/Finans Online*, 10 March, artikel-id: e288d649.

Savage, M. (2000) *Class Analysis and Social Transformation*, Philadelphia: Open University Press.

Savage, M. and Williams, K. (2008) Elites: remembered in capitalism and forgotten by the social sciences. In Savage, M. and Williams, K. (eds.) *Remembering Elites*, Malden, MA: Blackwell, pp. 1–24.

Savage, M., Bagnall, G. and Longhurst, B. (2001) Ordinary, ambivalent and defensive: Class identities in the northwest of England, *Sociology*, 35(4): 875–892.

Sayer, A. (2005) *The Moral Significance of Class*, Cambridge: Cambridge University Press.

Socialpolitisk Forening and CASA (2010) *Social Årsrapport 2010* [Social Annual Report 2010], Copenhagen: Social Policy Association and Centre for Alternative Social Analysis.

Statistics Denmark (2011) *Statistisk Årbog 2011* [Statistical Yearbook 2011], Copenhagen: Statistics Denmark.

Statistics Denmark (2012) *NYT – fra Danmarks Statistik* [NEWS – from Statistics Denmark], 376, 20 July.

Theils, L. (2011) Danmark er et af europas største markeder for privatfly [Denmark is one of Europe's biggest markets for private airplanes], *Politiken* 15 June.

UNESCO (2009) *Global Education Digest 2009 – Comparing Education Statistics Across the World*, UNESCO Institute for Statistics.

Wedel, J. R. (2009) *Shadow Elites: How the World's new Power Brokers Undermine Democracy, Government, and the Free Market*, New York: Basic Books.

Chapter 12

The super-rich and offshore worlds

John Urry

Going offshore

All societies entail the movements of peoples and objects but capitalist societies seem to elevate the scale and impact of such movements to qualitatively new levels. Much social thought has described the continuous and restless movement that capitalism appears to initiate and regularise. The most innovative account of this is in *The Manifesto of the Communist Party*. Writing in 1848 Marx and Engels described how during just a century the bourgeoisie had created more colossal productive forces than had all preceding generations. The need for a constantly expanding market caused the bourgeoisie to chase over the surface of the globe, causing fixed, fast-frozen relations to be swept away. All that is solid melts into air.[1] Marx and Engels pointed to the increasing 'cosmopolitan character' of production and consumption during the nineteenth century.

Many analysts believe there is a massive ratcheting up of this borderlessness from the 1980s onwards, resulting in even less relevance of 'national borders' as power and movement have exponentially speeded up. Much academic and policy writing has emphasised that the contemporary world is more 'borderless' although some commentators have described how borderlessness was more true for corporate leaders, sports stars and professionals than for others.

Generally this movement of money, people, ideas, images, information and objects was viewed as economically, politically and culturally beneficial. Most aspects of contemporary societies were seen as being transformed through many elements of cosmopolitanism and borderlessness. Many changes, especially in the 'west', generated a 1990s 'global optimism'. Stiglitz talks of the 'roaring [nineteen] nineties'.[2] Having 'won' the Cold War the west set about making the rest of the world in its own global consumerist and borderless image. Choice proliferated as an astonishing array of food, products, places, services, friends, family and experiences became increasingly available, at least to those with income. The world was open if one lived, worked and consumed near the centre of this borderless world full of opportunities and choice. It seemed that this open, borderless world was here for ever with continued American dominance.

But this decade did not turn out to be the harbinger of a long-term, optimistic and borderless future. The 1990s was more a *fin de siècle*, of intense opulence and decadence combined with the anticipation of a doom-laden ending. And that ending came with the dramatic attack on the Twin Towers of the New York World Trade Center on September 11, 2001. This mediatised ending of the decadent 'roaring nineties' engendered many apocalyptic visions for the new century.[3] This dark agenda is captured in Bauman's later books which show there is much 'collateral damage' from 'liquid modernity' as the old century gave rise to the new.[4]

Many texts thus reveal that what flows across borders is not just consumer goods, experiences and new services. Also there are terrorists, environmental risks, trafficked women, drug runners, international criminals, outsourced work, slave traders, asylum seekers, property speculators, smuggled workers, financial risks and especially untaxed income. There is a dark side to borderlessness. From 2001 onwards it has become clear that there are many risks and hazards moving across borders, these risks fuel the imagination of other risks, and these real and imagined risks engender and legitimate new systems of surveillance. So rather than there being a general process of increased open movement across borders, a borderless world generates new borders and new secrets. Borderlessness generates borders and vice versa. New borders are regularly being created, policed and surveilled. So a borderless world is one of secrets.

The significance of such 'secret worlds' is seen in studies which show the huge amounts of money moving in and through secret 'tax havens'. There is an extensive offshoring of income and wealth so that taxation is escaped and resources to fund public or social infrastructures and services are much less than they could be. Offshoring involves the movement of resources, practices, peoples and monies from one national territory to another but hiding them within secrecy jurisdictions and moving them through routes which are wholly or partly hidden from view. Offshoring involves evading rules, laws, taxes, regulations or norms. It is all about rule-breaking, getting around rules in ways that are illegal, or go against the spirit of the law, or to use laws in one jurisdiction to undermine laws in another. Such rule-breaking is made possible by various new sociotechnical systems, of container-based cargo shipping; extensive air travel; the internet; huge amounts of car and lorry traffic; new electronic money transfer systems; the growth of taxation, legal and financial expertise oriented to avoiding national regulations; and the proliferation of many 'mobile lives' involving frequent movement across borders.

This offshoring world is dynamic, reorganising economic, social, political and material relations between societies and within them, as populations and states find that more and more resources, practices, peoples and monies are made or kept secret. The global order is the very opposite of a simply open world – it is one of concealment, of very many secret gardens we might say. This offshoring is bad for democracy and that is often its point. Brittain-Catlin summarises how in this secret realm 'the negative, dark spirit ... today pervades the offshore world and its network of secret paraphernalia and hidden practices that are so closely bound into the global economy'.[5]

'Tax dodging'[6]

Especially since the development of neo-liberalism in the later 1980s there has been an astonishing growth in the movement of finance and wealth to and through the sixty to seventy tax havens.[7] These tax havens, or 'treasure islands', include Switzerland, Jersey, Manhattan, Cayman Islands, Monaco, Panama, Dubai, Liechtenstein, Singapore, Hong Kong, Gibraltar, City of London and Delaware. The development of 'secrecy jurisdictions', or in France what are known as *'paradis fiscal'*, are core to the neo-liberalisation of the world economy. To be offshore is to be in paradise, by contrast with the high-state-high-tax life that is onerously experienced onshore. Tax havens are places of escape and freedom, a paradise of low taxes, wealth management, deregulation, secrecy and often nice beaches.

Roughly one-quarter of contemporary societies are tax havens. Many new havens have become major players over the past thirty years (Cayman Islands), many older financial centres have become partly havens (London), almost all major companies have offshore accounts/subsidiaries (83 per cent), more than half of world trade passes through such tax havens, almost all high net worth individuals possess offshore accounts enabling tax 'planning', and ninety-nine of Europe's 100 largest companies use offshore subsidiaries. As a consequence one-quarter to one-third of all global wealth is held 'offshore'.[8] And the scale of offshored money makes the world even more unequal than researchers previously imagined. Fewer than ten million people currently own a US$21 trillion offshore fortune, a sum equivalent to the combined GDPs of the United States and Japan, the first and third largest economies in the world.[9] This is the super-rich and almost all owe their fortunes in part at least to tax dodging.

The scale of offshored money has grown enormously, from US$11 billion in 1968 to US$385 billion in 1978, US$1 trillion in 1991, US$6 trillion in 1998, and US$21 trillion in 2010.[10] Conservative estimates indicate that offshoring has increased in money terms almost two thousandfold from US$11 billion to US$21 trillion since 1968. Thus, as Shaxson powerfully shows, 'offshore is how the world of power now works'.[11]

Central to an effective tax haven is the 'façade', which is physical, virtual and metaphorical.[12] A good tax haven possesses a façade that seemingly combines safety and secrecy, probity and privacy. As most commentators note, Switzerland is the most effective of façades, best able to assemble and sustain characteristics that stabilises an enduring façade. The best façades are long established with physical and symbolic signifiers of safety, secrecy, probity and privacy.

The respectable Swiss society sets the gold standard for such façades, providing what Shaxson terms a 'theatre of probity', especially developed during the nineteenth century. It is rare for a whole complex society, with in this case nearly eight million people, to constitute such a façade. This Swiss theatre or façade combines polite manners, multiple languages of business, careful paperwork, utter discretion, long-established banks and financial institutions, stable government, good public services, especially transportation, and the asking of no questions and hence no need to tell lies. The highly decentralised Canton system of government has engendered competition between them both to reduce taxation rates and to offer strict secrecy for their banks. In Switzerland, two-thirds of total taxes are levied by the cantons and they also wield other powers enabling them to compete for business by promising ever-greater levels of secrecy.[13]

For example, the small and sleepy Canton of Zug had been a poor farming region up to the 1960s but is now a key node within the wider tax haven of Switzerland. It possesses the highest concentration of US dollar millionaires and the widest wealth disparity within Switzerland. It hosts 30,000 corporations, including Foster Wheeler, Glencore, Thomson Reuters, Xstrata and Transocean. Many corporations merely have post boxes in the town's post office. The highest personal income tax is 22 per cent and companies pay an average of 15 per cent. Much of Zug is packed with very wealthy commodity traders, private-equity firms and divisions of big multinationals, occupying mostly low-rise, modern buildings near or next to Lake Zug.[14]

The good façade involves a singular assemblage of stability *and* mobility. The stability ensures that this is a place for business, that everyone trusts that money is safe, that companies can be formed and reformed with ease and security, that a person's word can be trusted, that there is a secured legal environment, and that banks do not go bust or get accused of fraud. The mobility ensures that money can move safely and securely in and out of the 'treasure island', and also that people can move in and out easily, safely and effectively. This necessitates both absolutely secure communications for monetary transactions and good transportation systems for intermittent visits by 'investors'. The good façade thus necessitates the appropriate combination of stability and mobility, as found for decades in Switzerland.

Other havens do not provide so effective a façade. Many offshore financial centres developed more recently, some encouraged by the United Kingdom, United States and related 'imperial' states. Many were essentially small and poor developing countries that in a post-colonial era were forced to forge a distinct economic position within the emerging global economy. This often came to consist of a development strategy centred upon 'low taxation and up-market tourism'. They achieved this through developing financial and legal expertise to attract flows of money avoiding or evading taxation rules and regulations. Such a development strategy made sense as these microstates took advantage of historic links with a 'host' major power and good transportation, since they were at the same time emerging tourist destinations. This engendered a kind of reverse dependency in which corporations and high net worth individuals in the rich North became dependent upon offshore financial centres.

There is no single definition of what counts as a tax haven, a category now bitterly fought over. Many secrecy jurisdictions seek to maintain the façade that they are simply a law-abiding offshore financial centre. But a brief visit to a centre's online marketing typically reveals text describing its attractiveness of minimal regulation, low tax and limited disclosure requirements to assist the minimising of tax payments. It seems that an offshore tax haven should not tax income, profits or inheritance; its banks should offer different currencies and operate online and not require personal visits; new accounts in the banks should require minimum documentation; there should be bank secrecy with no tax information exchange agreements with other countries (about forty havens have no such agreements); and it should be possible to open bank accounts using an 'anonymous bearer share corporation' so that people's names do not appear in any public registry or database.[15]

Many of these havens are microstates which have been able to deploy links to the former British Empire to establish or to guarantee their façade. Some successful tax havens are colonial outposts combining the façade of respectability of the City of London combined with limited tax gathering, lax regulation and unaccountable local politics. The City of London, which is itself governed in a peculiarly undemocratic fashion where corporations are electors, provides the appropriate façade for many treasure islands in what were poor developing societies. Runciman notes how 'depositors are happiest putting their money in locations that have the feel of a major jurisdiction like Britain without actually being subject to British rules and regulations (or British tax rates)'.[16]

Many such tax havens are islands (Cyprus) or a string of islands (Turks and Caicos Islands), or they are a small enclave within a larger entity (Gibraltar).[17] These 'microstates' enable the governance of finance, taxation, consumption, exclusion and security away from the gaze of much of the world's population. These havens are normally undemocratic and with a form of governance able to exclude those whose face does not fit. No one wants to speak out for fear of being ostracised in a small society since everyone knows everyone else. These havens are like 'goldfish bowls', where it is stated that if you do not like it here, you can leave![18] They are able to keep up the façade of 'respectability' that those moving large amounts of money offshore require. British Crown Dependencies (such as Jersey) or British Overseas Territories (such as the Cayman Islands) together account for approximately one-third of the global market in offshore financial services.[19]

The story of the Caymans is a good indicator of developments over the last forty or so years. This poor undeveloped set of islands was established as an offshore financial centre in 1967. It was supported in doing this by the UK Treasury and the Bank of England but opposed by the Inland Revenue. The most powerful person in the Caymans is the Governor, appointed by the Queen. He presides over a cabinet of local elected Caymanians. The Governor deals with important items of governance and makes all appointments of significant holders of power. This strange place where the National Anthem is 'God Save the Queen' has a population of only 10,000. And yet it has developed into the world's fifth largest financial centre with nearly $2 trillion on deposit and with 80,000 company registrations. And it seems to play a central role in the vast secret laundering of drugs monies, as evidenced in the HSBC scandal that erupted in July 2012.[20] Without the British façade, which is itself partially hidden from view, this treasure island would not exist and the malaria-bearing mosquitoes would once more run riot along its beaches.

Many microstates have become especially dependent upon these offshore financial activities. Offshore finance has become the dominant player in the local political economy and also within the local state. A good example of this is the British Virgin Islands, which established a new kind of international business company in 1984 and has prospered ever since with an astonishing 450,000 company registrations.[21]

In such cases offshore financial activities can crowd out manufacturing and in some cases service and tourist industries, as arguably happened in Jersey. Injunctions by the OECD or the G20 to limit tax dodging within such microstates need to address ways to assist these states to diversify away from the specialised offshore financial services upon which many have become dependent. These states have become locked into offshore. It is hard indeed for them to diversify, to re-skill the population, to acquire new knowledge-bases and to escape links with big banks that are clearly involved in money laundering the proceeds of crime on a vast scale.[22]

An extreme version of a microstate is the recently launched ship called *The World*. This residential cruise liner ship is like 'a luxury private island, a kind of free-floating, certainly isolated, but territorial property. Islands play an important role in fantasies of escape and control for celebrities and the super-affluent'.[23] *The World* roams the world's oceans on a semi-permanent basis. It is a fortress world detached from national jurisdictions, tax regimes, moral commitment to nations, local people and most limits upon consuming. *The World* is connected to modern informational networks being designed for permanent offshore living of high net worth individuals. Extreme wealth generates novel infrastructures of luxury, security and avoidance. Seven further 'ships' are now being planned, places to avoid the world while floating around on a kind of 'moving façade'.

In the case of 'British' territories key figures in the banks and governance structures are often knights or lords of the realm. These honours help to stabilize that territory's façade. A particularly notorious example of this was Allen Stanford, appointed a Knight Commander of the Order of the Nation of Antigua and Barbuda in 2006, although Texan. Developing a plausible façade through the British honours system meant that Stanford was able to generate one of the largest Ponzi schemes in history based in Antigua, where offshore banking only began in 1983. Stanford was subsequently indicted for a US$7 billion fraud, imprisoned for 110 years, and stripped of his knighthood, an increasingly common occurrence!

Contemporary Hong Kong is an interesting case. It now seems to function as an offshore territory for China similar to how it functioned for Britain before ownership was transferred to China in 1997. Chinese elites thus require their own offshore centre, governed at a distance and deploying a hybrid British and Chinese façade to conceal the scale of the tax avoidance/evasion passing through. Hong Kong is one of the world's 'top ten' tax havens according to a recent Christian Aid Report.[24]

Almost all major societies seem to 'house' within their sphere of influence one or more tax havens. This pattern includes China and the tax haven of Hong Kong, Portugal and Madeira, the Netherlands and the Netherlands Antilles, Britain and the Channel Islands, Italy and San Marino, the United States and Nevada and Delaware, Spain and the Canary Islands, many European countries and Liechtenstein and Luxemburg and so on. Many offshore territories operate through what has been called an 'extended statehood system' by which they are governed or extensively linked to, or protected by, a major state, such as the United States, UK, France, the Netherlands, China and so on.[25]

Thus major states engender and facilitate their own treasure islands, often with geographical ties or excellent transportation or symbolic links with their 'homeland'. Since the neo-liberalising of economies this tendency for 'housing' offshore tax havens by major economies has speeded up and has become central to the processes which engender increased economic inequalities. The colonial or post-colonial power is key to supporting or guaranteeing the façade of each tax haven. In a globalising world offshore banking is now huge business with much competition. Most financial elites within historically dominant societies have strong interests in constructing and sustaining their *own* treasure islands. In these havens their money and that of core corporations can be conveniently parked and moved offshore without publicity and scandal.

Until recently such convenient arrangements remained mainly secret; there were many 'complicitous silences'.[26] It was how business got done in a world where finance was in command. These havens have been essential to establishing the power of finance and the dictatorship of financial markets.

Too much finance

How did this offshore world come about? During the 1950s, and especially after the Suez debacle in 1956, the British Empire rapidly shrank. Less and less world trade was financed in sterling and more and more in US dollars. And a whole new market for finance came to be developed, often called the Eurodollar market. The recently nationalised Bank of England (1948) could have regulated this new market as it developed but it chose not to since it remained, even after nationalisation, the mouthpiece of private financial interests. There was thus a regulatory vacuum at the heart of this growing market, enabling a free 'offshore market' in finance to develop nominated in dollars rather than in sterling but located in a sense offshore and certainly not in the United States. This was the first time a major market for finance had developed where there was no physical exchange building and few rules and regulations. Neither American nor UK authorities regulated it. And it rapidly became the largest source of capital in the world.[27]

It originated in London but was offshore and hence established the potential offshoring of financial markets. The City of London thus transformed itself into an 'offshore island' and fourteen island states became British Overseas Territories, half of which were offshore tax havens. From these beginnings this Eurodollar market exploded during the 1960s and it helped to re-establish the power of the City and especially the Bank of England. Shaxson brings out the libertarian nature of the City, with the Governor of the Bank of England proclaiming in 1963 that 'exchange control is an infringement of the rights of the citizen'.[28] Even during the 1960s the stampede into this offshore market was making it increasingly difficult for states to develop national monetary policy. Policymakers in the United States were worried by the potential instability of this new market as such markets were unregulated.

Eurobonds were founded in 1963 and were unregulated bearer bonds with no record kept as to who actually owned them. The Eurobond market expanded greatly so that even by 1970 it was thought to be larger than the world's entire foreign exchange holdings. Such bonds could avoid taxation, with some analysts describing their significance as being as great as the invention of the banknote.[29]

Thus an offshore world developed that established the combined financial power of London and New York. The City of London was key, with long-established procedures thought to increase confidence, with much expertise especially in financing overseas investment, with it being less tied into powerful national industry, and most importantly with it being less regulated. Evans writes how the rise of Euromarkets 'meant the beginning of an important shift from international financial relations being conducted through the official channels of the Bretton Woods system towards the private markets of the Eurodollar system'.[30] Through the Eurobond market bankers were able to reconstruct financial power in which much debt was offshored. Shaxson describes how from the 1960s

> these island semi-colonies and other assorted satellites of London came into their own as offshore Euromarket booking centres: secretive and semi-fictional way stations on a path through accountants' workbooks, hidey-holes where the world's wealthiest individuals and corporations, especially banks, could park their money, tax free and in secrecy.[31]

Even in the 1980s this movement of money was in no way a response to the 'needs' of trade and investment. It was thought to be at least twenty times greater than what was required for financing international trade and new investment.[32]

One would thus imagine that money staying onshore is now the exception to the rule, suitable only for the 'little people' who still pay tax. In 2007 one-third of the UK's largest companies paid no taxes in the previous boom year.[33] Most big money is offshored, although offshore now includes most mainstream banks and financial institutions especially in the world's largest economies. Palan points out that through various regulatory changes there has been 'the embedding of offshore in the global political economy', a kind of mainstreaming such that going offshore need not literally mean going to a small island in the sun.[34] Shaxson describes how the United States is 'by a mile – the world's most important secrecy jurisdiction'.[35] In the little state of Delaware there is a single building which houses an unbelievable 217,000 companies, the largest and most unethical building in the world!

Moreover, money moved 'offshore' uses the same kinds of accounts, instruments and devices that are also deployed by money that is laundered, or corrupt, or criminal, or is financing terrorism. All these forms of mobile money can evade the generally weak forms of regulation that normally depends upon implementation by banks themselves. Thus poachers and gamekeepers are one and the same! Such banks are regularly found guilty of failing to prevent corrupt, laundered, terrorist and criminal money from moving through their accounts. The bank BCCI was a vast criminal conspiracy originally set up in 1972. It was only able to operate until 1991 because of offshoring possibilities which meant that no regulator could see the whole picture, although the astonishing weakness of the Bank of England's regulatory system was also to blame for its continuing as long as it did. During the 1990s the very respectable Bank of New York was a conduit for 'spinning' vast amounts of laundered Russian money so fast around the world that no one was able to catch it.[36]

In July 2012 the Senate Permanent Subcommittee on Investigations described how banking giant HSBC and its US affiliate exposed the US financial system to extensive money laundering, drug trafficking and terrorist financing. HSBC has 7,200 offices in more than eighty countries with 2011 profits of $22 billion; it may face fines of up to $1 billion, which indicates the exceptional scale of mobile and illegal money. This was an unambiguously systemic failure due to its poor anti-money laundering controls. The 330-page report especially detailed the significance of 'correspondent banking' where other agents acted on behalf of major banks. This proved to be a major conduit for illicit money flows, especially from vast Mexican drug empires. HSBC did not implement laws designed to prevent the laundering of drugs money occurring on this vast scale.

This world of offshoring generated the enormous shadow banking system and the imbalance between 'financialisation' and the 'real economy' which has become so significant over the past couple of decades. Almost all of the world economy is now 'financialised'.[37] By 2010 the total value of foreign currency transactions is US$955 trillion, which is more than fifteen times larger than world GDP, which is currently US$63 trillion.[38] These huge flows of finance redistribute income and rights away from the 'real economy'. It runs counter to a productive economy and society which is mostly made up of relatively small companies seeking to innovate with new products and related services. The world of offshore favours large corporations and the ultra wealthy – not small and medium-sized companies and the middle or working classes. The offshore world makes it hard for 'innovative minnows' to compete, and if they do prosper they are likely to become parts of multinational corporate bureaucracies whose income flows will be significantly offshored.[39]

Such an offshore world is key to the emergence of a significantly untaxed, ungovernable and out-of-control 'casino capitalism', much more like gambling than banking according to Roubini and Mehm.[40] Finance generates about 41 per cent of all operating profits in the United States, compared with 16 per cent around 1980, although accounting for less than 10 per cent of value added in the economy.[41]

Politics of taxation

Until very recently taxation was not an issue. It was more or less secret. Shaxson notes the insidious way in which, in the UK, 'serial tax avoiders are made knights of the realm.... Bit by bit, offshore's corrupted morality becomes accepted into our societies.'[42] The income and taxation of others had been regarded as private matters, not anyone else's business except one's accountant or lawyer. No one much knew how much (or little) major figures or corporations paid in tax; it was their business. One feature of celebrity lives was to be remunerated in ways which avoided paying too much tax. Likewise corporations often paid very small proportions of their profits in corporation-type tax, and this was not seen as a problem since it made more money available for 'investing' in the company concerned.

There has been a politics of taxation, often concerned with people refusing to pay taxes because they did not have the vote or because of objections to government policies including waging war.[43] During the 1970s tax was an issue as a taxpayer revolt in the United States helped Reagan's election to the US Presidency in 1980. This powerful politics of taxation, especially pioneered in California, involved passing Proposition 13 which limited property taxation and future tax rises through constitutional amendments which were then endorsed by the US Supreme Court.

But over the past decade the tax being paid by others has rapidly moved up the political agenda. There is almost always a 'tax' story running in the world's media and especially in the new media. The campaigning group UK Uncut helped to bring issues of tax onto the political and moral agenda through highlighting both individual and corporate tax 'dodging'. Hampton and Christensen report the flourishing of critical reports (by Oxfam on how tax havens contribute to global poverty), media stories (even in the pro-business *The Wall Street Journal* or *The Economist*), new campaigning NGOs (such as Offshore Watch), interventions by the World Social Forum (establishing a global campaign against tax havens), the increased role of the OECD (so as to curb 'unfair tax competition'), and the increased public identification and critique of corporations heavily heightened in tax evasion (such as Enron).[44] Much direct action, NGOs, official government reports and new activists have exposed and denigrated 'tax dodging'.[45]

UK Uncut has especially targeted as a 'scandal' the tax dodging by major UK-based companies such as Vodafone, Topshop, Boots, Goldman Sachs, Fortnum and Mason, Barclays, HSBC and RBS. Similarly, Occupy Wall Street campaigners in New York on tax day April 17, 2012 dressed in 'Tax Dodgers' uniforms protested against Bank of America, Wells Fargo, GE, Bain Capital and JP Morgan Chase. The Tax Justice Network opposes all mechanisms that enable owners and controllers of wealth to escape responsibilities to the societies upon which they and their wealth depend.[46] While the secrecy jurisdiction of Delaware proclaims that 'Delaware can protect you from politics', the Tax Justice Network tries to ensure that there can be no such protection, emphasising the importance of compliance, openness and transparency.

Thus in at least some countries it is now thought a matter of legitimate protest that companies and individuals pay low or zero amounts of taxation, that façades enable tax payments to be systemically avoided, and that others thus have to pay more or services are poorer that they really should be. Corporations and rich individuals increasingly are forced to defend their tax position, seeking a kind of 'taxwash' to keep the scandal-hungry media and protestors at bay.

Conclusion

This chapter has thus shown how the offshore system is an endlessly shifting ecosystem, with different concentrations of legal, financial and taxation expertise, diverse modes of secrecy and varied balances of what is legal and illegal. Offshore services were partly developed to avoid double taxation so that monies earned in one country were not taxed both in that country and in the country where the individual or corporation is based. But offshore banking has in fact enabled 'double non-taxation', often through so-called 'laddering' or salami-slicing to increase the secrecy and complexity of financial flows. It is often now impossible for authorities to see everything and this enables taxation to be systemically avoided. And offshore no longer has to be literally offshore from centres of economic power. Offshore is to be found everywhere. One company's onshore, we might say, is offshore for another. The loss of taxation from this offshoring world of finance is at a minimum estimate hundreds of billions of US dollars per annum.[47]

The money system thus has been turned into an object for capitalist speculation, no longer functional for industry and other services but in places becoming *the* economy itself. Mellor has described the development of a 'turbo-capitalism' where money is invested in financial assets to create more money. Shareholder value is dominant in such a principally offshored economy.[48] Most so-called investment by financial institutions is not investment at all but speculation in secondary markets. This is gambling against the future market position of companies, currencies and countries. By 2007 there were, for example, 10,000 hedge funds worldwide with a reported US$2.1 trillion of assets. These secondary markets further separate the ownership *and* the management of companies, a separation Keynes considered deeply problematic: 'the remoteness between ownership and operation … is an evil in the relations among men'.[49] And the development of offshore, with the scale of trading hundred times greater than the volume of trade, greatly escalates this chasm or remoteness between the ownership of companies and their operation, through what Keynes terms 'skilful evasions'.[50] Trading is for the sake of trading and where money can be made whether the market is falling or rising through automatic trading algorithms to hedge one's bets.

Thus capital within the contemporary world does not flow to where it is more 'productive' let alone most socially useful. Adair Turner, Chairman of the UK Financial Services Authority, argues that many products found in the financial centres of New York or London are 'socially useless'.[51] Finance often flows to where it is most secret, gets the lowest tax rates, can evade as many regulations and laws as possible and can move around the world finding ever laxer regulatory forms. It does not provide financial energy for the economy, just more income for the already obscenely rich individuals and corporations whose practices have fuelled many of the commodities and places examined elsewhere in this book.

Notes

1 Karl Marx and Friedrich Engels, *The Manifesto of the Communist Party* (Moscow: Foreign Languages, [1848] 1952), pp. 54–55.
2 Joseph Stiglitz, *Making Globalization Work* (Harmondsworth: Penguin, 2007).
3 The first of these doom-laden texts in the UK was published in 2003 by Martin Rees, President of the UK's Royal Society. See the provocatively titled *Our Final Century* (London: Arrow, 2003); and on 'catastrophism' John Urry, *Climate Change and Society* (Cambridge: Polity, 2011), ch. 2.
4 See for example, Zygmunt Bauman, *Liquid Love* (Cambridge: Polity, 2003); Zygmunt Bauman, *Collateral Damage: Social Inequalities in a Global Age* (Cambridge: Polity, 2011); Zygmunt Bauman and David Lyon, *Liquid Surveillance: A Conversation* (Cambridge: Polity, 2012).
5 William Brittain-Catlin, *Offshore. The Dark Side of Globalisation* (New York: Picador, 2005), p. 118.
6 The term 'dodging' is used to gloss the distinction between actions which are legal (avoidance) and those that are illegal (evasion), tarring them all with the same critical brush.
7 See the listing of tax havens based upon the index of financial secrecy: http://en.wikipedia.org/wiki/Financial_Secrecy_Index (accessed 28 January 2012).
8 http://en.wikipedia.org/wiki/List_of_countries_by_GDP_(nominal)#List (accessed 23 July 2012).
9 Tax Justice Network, 'Revealed: global super-rich has at least $21 trillion hidden in secret tax havens', 22 July 2012, www.taxjustice.net/cms/upload/pdf/The_Price_of_Offshore_Revisited_Presser_120722.pdf (accessed 23 July 2012).
10 Nicholas Shaxson, *Treasure Islands* (London: Bodley Head, 2011), pp. 7–10; Mark Hampton, John Christensen, 'A provocative dependence? The global financial system and small island tax havens', in Feargal Cochrane, Rosaleen Duffy and Jan Selby (eds) *Global Governance, Conflict and Resistance* (London: Palgrave, 2003); Tax Justice Network, 'Revealed: global super-rich has at least $21 trillion hidden in secret tax havens', op. cit. Estimates here are notoriously difficult and the figures quoted here are all said to be on the conservative side.
11 Shaxson, *Treasure Islands*, p. 7.
12 See Lee Hadnum, *The World's Best Tax Havens* (Kirkcaldy: Taxcafé, 2011), and www.taxhavens.biz (accessed July 4, 2012). Amazon, which itself avoids UK corporation tax through locating its headquarters in Luxembourg, reports that many customers purchase both Hadnum's book and that by Shaxson!
13 David Runciman, 'Didn't they notice?', *London Review of Books*, April 14, 2011, pp. 20–23; Shaxson, *Treasure Islands*, ch. 3. Robert Harris's novel *The Fear Factor*

captures the power and allure of the Swiss façade for establishing an innovative hedge fund in Geneva (London: Random House, 2011).
14 Deborah Ball, 'Tax haven's tax haven pays a price for success, *Wall Street Journal*, August 29, 2011, http://online.wsj.com/article/SB10001424053111904875404576528123989551738.html (accessed July 19, 2012).
15 See the *Offshore Law Directory* website at http://www.offshorelawdirectory.com (accessed May 13, 2013).
16 Runciman, 'Didn't they notice?', pp. 20–21.
17 See Mark Hampton and John Christensen, 'A provocative dependence? The global financial system and small island tax havens', in Feargal Cochrane, Rosaleen Duffy and Jan Selby (eds) *Global Governance, Conflict and Resistance* (London: Palgrave, 2003).
18 Runciman, 'Didn't they notice?', pp. 20–23.
19 *The Telegraph*, 'Tax haven activity "rife", despite G20 crackdown promise', October 4, 2011, www.telegraph.co.uk/finance/personalfinance/offshorefinance/8805988/Tax-haven-activity-rife-despite-G20-crackdown-promise-says-Tax-Justice-Network.html# (accessed July 4, 2012).
20 Shaxson, *Treasure Islands*, ch. 6; Carrick Mollenkamp, 'Senators doubtful as HSBC touts money-laundering fixes', *Reuters*, July 18, 2012, http://uk.reuters.com/article/2012/07/18/uk-hsbc-compliance-senate-idUKBRE86H03J20120718 (accessed July 23, 2012).
21 See Bill Maurer, *Recharting the Caribbean* (Ann Arbor: University of Michigan Press, 2000), ch. 8; BVI Incorporation, 'Other Advantages of BVI IBCs', www.bviincorporation.com/2/Other.Advantages/ (accessed 23 July 2012).
22 See Hampton and Christensen, 'A provocative dependence?'
23 Rowland Atkinson and Sarah Blandy, 'A picture of the floating world: grounding the secessionary affluence of the residential cruise liner', *Antipode*, 41: 92–110, p. 105.
24 *The Telegraph*, 'Tax haven activity "rife", despite G20 crackdown promise', op. cit.
25 Mimi Sheller, 'Infrastructures of the imagined island: software, mobilities, and the new architecture of cyberspatial paradise', *Environment and Planning A*, 2009, 41: 1386–1403.
26 Pierre Bourdieu, *The Logic of Practice* (Cambridge: Polity Press, 1990), p. 133.
27 Scott Lash and John Urry, *The End of Organized Capitalism* (Cambridge: Polity, 1987), pp. 202–209; Shaxson, *Treasure Islands*, ch. 5.
28 Shaxson, *Treasure Islands*, p. 90.
29 Shaxson, *Treasure Islands*, pp. 91–93.
30 Trevor Evans, 'Money makes the world go round', *Capital and Class*, 1985, 24: 99–124, 109; Warren Hogan and Ivor Pearce, *The Incredible Eurodollar* (London: Unwin, 1984); Lash and Urry, *The End of Organized Capitalism*, pp. 204–205.
31 Shaxson, *Treasure Islands*, p. 101.
32 Hogan and Pearce, *The Incredible Eurodollar*, pp. 158–160.
33 Shaxson, *Treasure Islands*, pp. 12–13.
34 Ronen Palan, *The Offshore World* (Ithaca: Cornell University Press, 2003), p. 135.
35 Shaxson, *Treasure Islands*, p. 146.
36 On money laundering, see Nick Kochan, *The Washing Machine* (London: Duckworth, 2006), especially ch. 2.
37 See Stiglitz, *Making Globalization Work*; Paul Krugman, *The Return of Depression Economics* (Harmondsworth: Penguin, 2008); George Soros, *The New Paradigm for Financial Markets* (London: Public Affairs Ltd, 2008).
38 Saskia Sassen, 'Too big to save: the end of financial capitalism', *Open Democracy News Analysis*, January 1, 2009.

39 Shaxson, *Treasure Islands*, pp. 190–191.
40 See Susan Strange, *Casino Capitalism* (Manchester: Manchester University Press, 1997); Nouriel Roubini and Stephen Mihm, *Crisis Economics* (London: Penguin, 2011), p. 231.
41 Kathleen Madigan, 'Like the phoenix, U.S. finance profits soar', *WSJ Blogs*, March 25, 2011, http://blogs.wsj.com/economics/2011/03/25/like-the-phoenix-u-s-finance-profits-soar (accessed January 4, 2012); *Spiegel Online*, 'Out of control: the destructive power of the financial markets', www.spiegel.de/international/business/out-of-control-the-destructive-power-of-the-financial-markets-a-781590.html (accessed July 28, 2012).
42 Shaxson, *Treasure Islands*, p. 31.
43 See David M. Gross (ed.), *We Won't Pay!: A Tax Resistance Reader* (CreateSpace 2008).
44 Hampton and Christensen, 'A provocative dependence?', p. 204.
45 See www.ukuncut.org.uk (accessed 27 January 2012).
46 Tax Justice Network, 'Tax havens cause poverty', www.taxjustice.net/cms/front_content.php?idcatart=2&lang=1 (accessed July 24, 2012).
47 Tax Justice Network, 'Revealed: global super-rich has at least $21 trillion hidden in secret tax havens', op. cit.
48 See ch. 4 in the excellent Mary Mellor, *The Future of Money* (London: Pluto, 2010).
49 John Maynard Keynes, 'National Self-Sufficiency', *The Yale Review*, 1933, 22: 755–769, p. 756.
50 John Maynard Keynes, *The General Theory of Employment, Interest and Money* (London: Macmillan, 1961 [1936]), p. 372.
51 *Spiegel Online*, 'Out of control', op. cit.

Chapter 13

Epilogue
The bodies, spaces and tempo of elite formations

Mimi Sheller

With the contributions to this volume on elite mobilities we are moving towards the study of not only the systems, spaces, and infrastructures of elite mobility, but also the more subtle ways in which mobility as practiced by the "super-rich" helps to performatively produce elite subjects, habitus, atmospheres, and temporalities. Alongside the significant role of aeromobility, we also see the ways in which other modalities of mobility are implicated in the production of differential spaces and temporalities, including, crucially, the offshore virtual mobility of capital and the imaginary discursive mobility of the places that support elite lifestyles such as private schools and luxury tourist sites. Elite mobilities bend time-space to their own gravitational pull, warping the lives of workers, the design of buildings, the rules of banking, the invisible hand of the market, and the territories of states.

These spaces and places of elite mobilities are supported, as Thurlow and Jaworski remind us, by precisely orchestrated forms of visible and invisible labour. Spatio-temporal fixes (Jessop 2006) that support elite formations can occur at many scales, whether as an unequal relation between service workers and the bodies of mobile elites, or extending out into the world through elite investments of capital, control over ideas via patents, or through mediatized spectacles of luxury consumption. As much as elite formations create great concentrations of wealth, of private property, and of cutting edge infrastructures of mobility, they lead ultimately to spectacular destruction of value in the excessive consumption of the "accursed share" (Sheller 2007). Mobilities research is indispensable to researching this kind of world shaping and the ways in which it unravels the worlds of others.

Empirically, we find that a super-privileged world of embodied practice has been carved out, and set apart from other everyday worlds, even as it courses through and enrols others. Distinct mobilities, with their associated ways of managing time and travel, and organizing capital and labour, are constitutive of this privileged world. Methodologically, we can begin to see the need for mixed mobile methods that will allow researchers access to these elite spaces and places, and to their behind-the-scenes production. The methods employed here range from tracking business patterns, wealth distributions, and social networks, to participant observation, interviews, discourse analysis, and visual and semiotic studies. In paying attention to both the flows of various kinds of movement and the moorings that keep things in place, as the new mobilities paradigm has called for (Hannam *et al.* 2006), a new approach emerges for the study of the enclaved, sometimes opaque and hidden practices of the super-rich, drawing new connections across various realms of mobile practice.

Beaverstock and Faulconbridge first introduce us to the different segments of the mobile elite, from the ultra-rich down to the very rich and the "merely" high net worth individual.[1] They remind us that mobility can be understood as a form of capital (Kaufmann *et al.* 2004), a social distinguisher (Nowicka 2006) and a meaningful practice (Cresswell 2006). Not just speed matters, but also flexibility, locational access, last-minute bookings, route choice, and all the other ways of managing scheduling through which "time and space [are] redefined." Budd refers to six key discourses – of comfort, convenience, speed, productivity, status, and flexibility – through which these elite mobilities are accomplished. Yet she notes too that "more attention should be paid both to the particularities of the kinds of services provided by the various companies servicing the mobility needs of the super-rich and to the way these companies construct meanings and competencies of mobility." In this epilogue I wish to round up some of what this collection has taught us about elite mobilities, and what avenues of future research it has opened up.

Elliott describes some of the lifestyle biographies of a new transnational corporate elite who depend on a combination of mobility systems, "from mobile phones and computer databases to yachts and private jets," that together support the "contemporary global experiences of great wealth, power and prestige." Through their network capital these "globals" shape their lives through practices consisting of "detached engagement; floating; speed; networked possibilities; distance from locality; and mapping of escape routes." In other words, there is a movement-space that the globals make as they create particular assemblages of mobility, which in turn shapes their subjectivities, their families, and their social milieux through networked possibilities. Elliott depicts how the rootless lives of the globals now entail "homes dotted throughout the world, endless business travel and family life restructured around episodic get-togethers, such that the old social coordinates divided firmly around work and home have somewhat evaporated." Extensive coordination is needed to manage such dispersed lifestyles, requiring network capital built on personalized and flexible systems of privileged mobility.

Khan crucially suggests that being at ease in this world is "an embodied interactional resource" of the super-wealthy, which "has been central to their capacity to navigate a flat world – ease that makes them mobile through space and helps blame those locked in place through impressions of their own failures." Thus the smoothness of elite air travel is an extension of the other kinds of ease of movement that elites are brought up and trained to expect. It extends from the home space, to private schools and leisure clubs, to luxury ground transport, to airport lounges, into the air, and finally to the luxury destination. It is not just a cocooned corridor through which the super-wealthy experience life, but almost a bodily forming of an elite pupa within the cocoon, one who emerges to sense himself as a lightly fluttering butterfly. Such elites might fly to the ends of the earth seeking out physical challenges and new bodily and sensory experiences, whether climbing Everest or taking a flight on Virgin Galactic, but they will never experience a body without ease.

Building on the observations of Thurlow and Jaworski, we might also ask of these smooth spaces of ease: Who does the labour to enable ease? How do personal staff, air crews, wives, nannies, chefs, trainers, cleaners, security guards, etc. move around with the rich? And how is the visibility and invisibility of such labour, including its clockwork movement in and out of place, necessary to the production of the illusion of easy ("frictionless") movement? Clearly the apparent ease of elite mobilities requires a great deal of work, and that work requires many other kinds of movement, pausing, waiting, stilled readiness. It also requires the just-in-time movement of luxury goods – caviar from Russia, single malt whisky from Scotland, Maine lobster, etc. – in a bizarre choreography of privileged consumption.

One of the places through which such elites affectively feel their own embodiment is in luxury resorts such *The Haciendas*, analysed by Córdoba Azcárate and her collaborators. They remind us of the "power and efficacy of architectural spaces as material metaphors [which] are inseparable from bodily, sensory engagement with particular places." Whether at home, in the corridors of air travel and yachting, or in the luxury destination, there is a "development and organizing of sensory experiences regarding taste and touch" which becomes "crucial in the accomplishment of a taste of elite lifestyles." This development and organization of sensory experience can occur within an architectural setting or within a vehicle, but also extends to surrounding landscapes through the organization of gardens, pathways, views, and roads; and in fact to entire islands and territories disembedded from regional belonging and repackaged and connected to the mobile global elite flows, which of course has consequences for the people who live and work in such places (Sheller 2009).

Elliott reminds us that "Implicated in all global mobile lives are various immobility regimes (Urry 2007)." Immobility regimes can range in scale from the stillness of a waiter waiting to be summoned, to the fixed capital invested in real estate, to the labour regimes that limit the mobility of workers across international borders. And of course the gender and racial formations implied within such stratified systems of (im)mobility need further exploration. How do gendered and racialized spaces get formed in and through the choreographies, architectures, and atmospheres of such disjunctive mobilities?

The high mobility of elites and their capital stands in sharp contrast to the lives of average people, which seem to be more fixed in place: "crucially, the private jets are an indication not only of super-wealth but of the highly mobile nature of globals themselves and of their money", Elliott argues, "shifting as they do between various countries and regions, tax regimes and legal systems, whilst living extraordinary sumptuous lifestyles well over and above even the highest standards of 'locals' living in territorially fixed societies." Yet such elite mobility also depends on creating places of stillness, pauses where the elite have the right to remain in place, and a kind of bubble of privilege in which they are suspended, even as 'locals' are forced to move out, to move back and forth, to move as if caught in a circular vortex.

Featherstone notes the unique spaces that cater to the super-rich, as they move between opportunities: "The possession of cars, jets and yachts offers the prospect of ultra-mobility, pleasurable and comfortable means of travel, leisure and escape, as people move between global cities and exclusive resorts." Being everywhere "greeted as cosmopolitan global citizens," property ownership is spread around the world for such families, and moving amongst multiple private spaces signifies the transnationally distributed elite, without an anchor to any single home. For such luxury consumers of space, the gated community is outdone by the private island, and it is these very spaces that researchers have the most difficulty in accessing. The study of elite mobilities will require methods to get inside the gates and onto the islands, to better understand how people and capital circulate amongst such enclaves, and to trace the building of material and electronic infrastructures that support them (including their environmental externalities).

At Exuma Cays in the Bahamas, for example, a 38-acre private island was for sale by Sothebys as "one of the most complete and luxurious private islands in the world"; it offered not only extensive luxury accommodations and staff housing, but also an "operations center" with "a freshwater treatment plant, island warehouse, elaborate power system, telephone and data systems, fuel systems, service vehicles, heliport and deep draft docks."[2] Access to such private operational and mobility services is key to the splintering of luxury space apart from more mundane everyday worlds. We need to develop better understandings of how such splintering of infrastructures of connectivity is achieved, how sovereignty is warped, how rules are bent, how capital is moved "offshore" through real-estate transactions, and how resources are corralled into private, secured micro-territories. To what extent do such micro-territories now outweigh state systems of control, proliferating through them like some unseen dark matter? Or is the relationship symbiotic? Is the dream of localized additive manufaturing, discussed by Birtchnell, Viry and Urry in terms of 3D printing, a manifestation of this emerging system of secessionist self-sovereignty?

Budd introduces some material details to the new "affluent infrastuctures" by which the "biz-jet" class "perform new strategies of mobility". Yet they remain frustratingly opaque. One would still like to know more about the sub-practices within these distinct segments, including more attention to varieties of ownership and access to private air travel. We need closer ethnographies of the fine-grained distinctions that are emerging amongst different fractions of the super-rich, which are often reflected in differentiated forms of mobility. In relation to air travel, for example, beyond purchasing a private jet there are possibilities for time-share, chartering, leasing, fractional ownership, and various kinds of service arrangement. These each involve different kinds of personal scheduling and flexibility, as well as different kinds of flexibility and circulation of capital, equipment, and service infrastructures.

Who, for example, chooses to purchase a $64.5 million Gulfstream Aerospace G650, with a speed of Mach .925 (faster than any civilian airplane), and cruising altitude of 51,000 feet? Alternatively, there is the more affordable $9 million Cessna CJ4, "largest and fastest in its class", which travels at speeds above 520 miles per hour, with a single pilot, and can go 2,100 miles without refueling. Yet if "ownership is not for everyone", as Gulfstream advertises, then another option is the Marquis Jet Card, which gives access to the NetJets "fractional aircraft fleet and infrastructure" at only "25 hours at a time with no long-term commitment." Other jet cards include Bombardier's Flexjet, which can gain one access to its new $18 million Learjet 85; JetSuite, which offers access to the fuel-efficient Phenom, a light four-seat Embraer jet; or jet pooling companies like Jumpjet, which allow several passengers to share a ride on busier routes.[3] For the merely rich, there is the Delta Air Elite Jet Card, which is "the only jet card with the ability to offer both private and commercial air travel access in one convenient account."[4] What are the embodied and social implications of each type of travel and what percentage of "high flyers" falls into each segment? What kinds of capital investment and business structure support each segment of elite air travel? Which is growing fastest?

These varied options suggest different ways of consuming elite air travel, for different segments of the wealthy. While some gain access to the more rarefied world of private jets either as owners or "fractional" owners, others resort to commercial airlines. Yet even first class air travel has distinctions within it. While a decline in standards has been noted in domestic first class travel in the United States, which is often offered as an upgrade to somewhat affluent frequent flyers, airlines like Cathay Pacific offer a "podlike cocoon with privacy screens and a seat with a massage function and four-way lumbar support that reclines to form a bed that is 6 feet 9 inches long" (which in early 2012 cost between $15,400 and $26,000 for flights from New York to Hong Kong).[5] As Budd notes, "it is the very ability to socially and spatially segregate one's self from the stresses and unpleasantness of normal routines of flying that is one of the primary attractions of business aviation."

Such cocooning and screening also bleeds over into the super-high-end luxury vacation market, where private islands, private yachts, and remote locations rule supreme. As with private jets, there is the option to rent a fraction of time, if full ownership seems too much of a commitment. For example, while noting that the ultra-rich seemed unaffected by the global recession in 2010, the *New York Times* Travel section carried an article on Caribbean luxury which included Calivigny Island off the coast of Grenada, which for $165,000 per night (more than double the 2010 price) offers a private 81-acre island, a 13,000-square-foot "beach house" with ten suites, and a 173-foot sailing yacht which could be chartered for an additional cost. The more affordable Falcon's Nest Villa at the Peter Island Resort and Spa in the British Virgin Islands even allows guests to request a no-fly zone above the resort, to keep away paparazzi.[6] A *Condé Nast Traveler* special section on the really rich notes that in order to avoid mingling with the masses the private jet set prefer "anyplace unreachable without a helicopter, boat, hydroplane, or all three."[7]

These deterritorialized spaces of high-security extreme access offer insulation from the outside world, which is comparable to the protections that Urry describes in relation to the enclaves of offshore capital, with the two often converging in the Caribbean microstates with "low taxation and up-market tourism." With their diverse modes of secrecy, hidden flows, avoidance and dodging, these safe enclaves are the spatial formation of elite mobilities as movement-space, in which the "good façade involves a singular assemblage of stability *and* mobility." Mobilities, it must be emphasized, are not just about moving people or goods from A to B – there are also financial mobilities, virtual mobilities and various imaginary mobilities that are combined into elite assemblages. Moving capital "offshore" is of course crucial to orchestrating many of these elite mobilities at the most global level, for as both Featherstone and Urry note, it involves the significant capacity to escape the state and its forms of regulation. Yet it is also part of a discursive imaginary of spatial isolation, the offshore as metaphor and semiotic index of elite mobility.

Within territorial states, too, there is a restructuring of space in relation to elite mobilities. While some have begun to note the emergence of airports as luxury duty-free shopping zones, unmoored from tax territory in order to serve the mobile super-rich, the new "affluent infrastructures" of aeromobility have further spatial effects. Business aircraft offer users the opportunity to perform new strategies of mobility (such as flying from smaller, less congested airports, greater time flexibility, and faster speed), but they also create new spatial fixes and enclaves in support of such mobility. In the so-called Piedmont Triad of North Carolina, for example, there is a spatial concentration of 160 aviation-related companies, including specialists in "maintenance, repair, and overhaul" (MRO) of aircraft, such as TIMCO Aviation Services, MRO operations for Cessna and the new $4.5 million HondaJet; "fixed-base operators", such as FedEx, which has one of its major cargo-sorting hubs here; and "original equipment manufacturers", such as B/E Aerospace, "the nation's largest designers and manufacturers of airline seats and interiors." Alongside these are specialist companies making advanced filtration systems, precision parts like landing gear, aerospace logistics, charter jet services, and the world headquarters for Honda Aircraft.[8] Thus an entire region is emerging that services the business jet class, and shapes the regional economy of the Piedmont Triad. Air space touches down on the ground, transforming economies and geographies. It is in such industries that rapid fabrication and prototyping technologies are also being worked into the industrial manufacturing and high-tech design sector.

Elite mobilities might also jump or bypass the frictions of travel, and string together distant sites in novel ways. Specialty travel agents stake their reputations on custom-designed itineraries, meeting the most unusual requests. Horchow Travel Services, for example, offers "private jet expeditions" that take in nine "legendary and unique islands – where indigenous traditions, endemic flora and fauna, and rarely-seen vistas have developed in splendid isolation, leaving us extraordinary natural and cultural wonders to discover". They base the merit of their trips, which range in price from $59,950 to $69,950 per person (double occupancy), on the claim that

> Throughout the journey, you will experience the ultimate in convenience, security, and service as you are whisked from one island to the next on our VIP-configured private jet, accompanied by an experienced expedition staff and world-class experts in ornithology, evolutionary ecology, and anthropology.[9]

Thus, as Budd says, business aviation "enable[s] users to bypass conventional forms of transport and timetabled spaces of flow and create personalised and bespoke geographies of movement." Some providers offer exclusive educational opportunities, and exposure to rarefied natures and cultures, curated in convenient island packages. Others offer to bring to life story-book fantasy (e.g., travel agency Based on a True Story, founded by British adventurer Niel Fox) or to create magic (e.g., private Bahamian island resort, Musha Cay, created by magician David Copperfield, whose motto is "whatever you dream can happen").[10] Here the powers of wealth and space-time bending re-shape the experience of reality into distorted fantastical shapes. Yet it remains to be theoretically and empirically unpacked what social and environmental impacts such one-off extraordinary fantasy realms have on those outside the ".01 percent".

With private jet travel, especially, and private islands where luxury foods are flown in and water resources monopolized, there may be devastating environmental impacts. There is a need, as Budd notes, "to quantify the environmental impact of business aviation operations at all stages of the service chain, from aircraft manufacture to disposal, and identify how best to improve the sector's environmental performance and help it adjust to an increasingly oil-scarce world." Yet we might ask tougher questions of such business operations than how they can adapt. How can they be controlled? How can they be reduced? Beyond the service chain and its direct ecological footprint, there are further direct impacts of these high-carbon lifestyles on wider geographies, including their relation to producing the greenhouse gases that contribute to climate change. Elite mobilities also produce and uphold the systems of global capitalism that drive contemporary geo-economies. As Elliott notes, "The emergence of a new transnational corporate elite ... is intricately interwoven with the formation of integrated global financial markets and interlocking information networks." Informational and financial mobilities are as crucial to the study of elite mobilities as are embodied practices and spatial analysis of forms of luxury and new modes of air travel.

Fast-moving global financial markets and information networks, and the capital-intensive performance of elite lifestyles that they enable, have wide-ranging social, spatial, economic, environmental, and political effects. Through transdisciplinary critically attuned mobilities research we can begin to unravel the complex systems that are concentrating vast wealth within a tiny apex of the global elites. Several areas remain to be examined in future research.

The first area concerns the political realm, and the ways in which elite mobilities as described here intersect and interact with state mobility regimes. At a certain point the system of private jets, aerospace economic regions, personalized travel and private security services intersects with hidden state practices such as secret renditions of prisoners on CIA flights, illicit arms shipments, and the use of drones for remote surveillance (Paglen 2006, 2009). Further research is needed on the penumbra of extra-territorial activity and "blank spots on the map" where the powers wielded by the super-rich converge with the powers of the secret state, each unaccountable to any kind of public scrutiny. Ruling elites are often the most "at ease" in this world of super-mobility, but they may also import their habits and practices of mobility into the repertoires of ruling.

Second, from the opposite direction there are the undertows of illicit mobilities within underground economies such as the narcoeconomy – what we might call narcomobilities. While illicit economies (such as weapons smuggling) sometimes involve state actors, they more typically involve extra-state actors whose access to wealth, and concern for secrecy, overlaps with the peformances and spaces of elite mobilities in the legal economy. In reality it may be difficult to untangle legal tax avoidance and illegal money laundering, or private jet vacations and private jet drug drops, and both may share the same Caribbean getaways, runways, and banks. We need to better understand how the criminal underworld thrives on the extra-territorial movement-spaces of elite mobilities.

Finally, there is a crucial environmental dimension that requires more research. While splintered island-enclaves might place offshore elites beyond the reach of state institutions and mechanisms of global governance, this does not place them beyond the reach of broken ecosystems, rising sea levels, tsunamis, or volcanic eruptions. If trips to the Moon or colonies on Mars seem within their reach, even "the globals" must ultimately reckon with the constraints of life on one shared Earth. Given their extensive power to shape time-space and control capital flows, a better grasp of the practiccs of elite mobility may help us to develop future scenarios by which to predict the timing and direction of transition technologies, the lock-in of destructive or adaptive processes, or the fragmentation of survivable regions of the globe and write-off of others. As we move beyond stable state-controlled territories, the mobile elites are perhaps harbingers of an age of offshore enclaves, self-provisioning, and flexible escape from the ecological collapse of their own making.

Notes

1 According to the research firm WealthX, in 2012 there were 2,000 people with net worth of $1 billion or more (185 more than in 2011), and 187,000 people with net worth of $30 million or more, who are still counted in the ultra-high-net-worth category.
2 Sotheby's International Realty, *Reside: Luxury Homes and Lifestyles Around the World*, Issue 2, Vol. 4, 2010, pp. 34–35.
3 Barbara S. Peterson, "A Jet of One's Own," *Condé Nast Traveler*, March 2013, p. 61.
4 Various private jet and jet-card companies as described in the magazine *Worth: The Evolution of Financial Intelligence*, Vol. 19, No. 6, December/January 2011, which was distributed by mail to high-income households in the Philadelphia suburbs.
5 Michelle Higgins, "New York to Dubai for $19,000", *New York Times*, 12 February 2012, Travel Section, p. 9. In addition to private suites, Emirates Airlines also offered "shower spas" with heated floors on its A380 planes.
6 Michelle Higgins, "Your Own No-Fly Zone? If Price is No Object", *New York Times*, 7 November 2010, Travel Section, p. 10.
7 Lauren Lipton, "The Informer: All That Money Can Buy", *Condé Nast Traveler*, March 2013, p. 48, p. 50.
8 Justin Catanoso, Industry Spotlight: "Flying High in North Carolina", *U.S. Airways Magazine*, July 2012, pp. 58–71. The Piedmont Triad consists of Greensboro, Winston-Salem and High Point, with a combined population of about 1.6 million.

9 Dan Pressley, Director, Horchow Travel Services, Horchow Travel 2013 brochure, p. 1. Islands visited in one of the "private jet expeditions," 11 April to 3 May 2013, include Hawaii, Samoa, Papua New Guinea, Brunei, Sri Lanka, Madagascar, The Maldives, Bali and Fiji.
10 Lipton, op. cit., p. 56.

References

Cresswell, T. (2006) *On the Move: Mobility in the modern Western world*, London: Routledge.

Hannam, K., Sheller, M., and Urry, J. (2006) Mobilities, immobilities, and moorings. *Mobilities*, 1(1): 1–22.

Jessop, B. (2006) 'Spatial fixes, temporal fixes and spatio-temporal fixes', in N. Castree and D. Gregory (eds.) *David Harvey: A Critical Reader*, New York: Blackwell.

Kaufmann, V., Bergman, M., and Joye, D. (2004) 'Motility: Mobility as capital', *International Journal of Urban and Regional Research*, 28(4): 745–756.

Nowicka, M. (2006). *Transnational Professionals and their Cosmopolitan Universes*, Frankfurt and New York: Camous Verlag.

Paglen, T. (2006) *Torture Taxi: On the Trail of the CIA's Rendition Flights*, New York: Melville House.

Paglen, T. (2009) *Blank Spots on the Map: The Dark Geography of the Pentagon's Secret World*, New York: Dutton.

Sheller, M (2007) 'Always turned on: Atlantic City as America's accursed share', in A. Cronin and K. Hetherington (eds.) *Consuming the Entrepreneurial City*, London and New York: Routledge.

Sheller, M. (2009) 'Infrastructures of the imagined island: software, mobilities and the architecture of Caribbean paradise', *Environment and Planning A*, 41: 1386–1403.

Urry, J. (2007) *Mobilities*, Cambridge: Polity.

Chapter 14

Postscript
Elite mobilities and critique

Andrew Sayer

To some extent this is an outsider's postscript: although I am writing a book called *Why We Can't Afford the Rich*, I haven't personally studied elite mobilities. While I agree that we need to know more about the rich and their lifestyles, mobilities and spending, I also want to argue for a more critical approach and one that includes a focus on how the rich *get* their money in the first place.

As Mike Savage and Karel Williams have argued, recent sociology has paid little attention to the rich, and elite studies have been seen as unfashionable, though the sociology of elite mobilities may have ambitions to become cool (Savage and Williams 2008). Studies of class may have made a comeback through inspiration from Bourdieu, with many excellent ethnographies of the working class and middle class, but the rich have largely been ignored. Yet the biggest change in class structure in most developed countries in the last four decades – the return of the rich – has largely been ignored. Strangely, even though so much has been written about neoliberalism, its class dimension has only recently been noticed. The rise of the Occupy movement in 2011, which highlighted the growing gulf between the top 1 per cent and the remaining 99 per cent, caught sociology looking the other way, predominantly downwards, and taking little interest in the economic determinants of these changes (*mea culpa* too). Sociologists have inadvertently been complicit in the common popular belief that the upper class is no more than a tiny residual group of landed aristocrats. And too often the rich have been able to hide by calling themselves 'middle class', and without being challenged by sociology for this.

So research on elite mobilities, and more generally on the rich and super-rich, is long overdue and welcome. As the contributors show, the mobility of the rich is tied up at every turn with the mobility of 'their' money. The scope to store and hide wealth is as important as the ability to move it. The global economic geography of tax havens and the webs of relations and flows which constitute them is a much under-acknowledged aspect of globalisation and the return of the rich and the emergence of a global plutocracy. In different ways, the contributors show how the lives of the rich are increasingly run via networks separate from those used by the rest of society; indeed, as others have noted, they self-exclude, and thereby cease to identify with the institutions of society that are basic to others. As Khan puts it, 'society has recessed in the minds of the elite' (Khan this volume). And yet they are generally seen in an extraordinarily favourable light, or else remain unknown to the majority: as the *Sunday Times* Rich List and the Forbes List show, most of the individuals who make up the rich and super-rich are unknown in popular culture. Several contributors demonstrate how the symbolic domination of the rich works partly through their consumption and by encouraging emulation in those below them. Of course, their symbolic domination also operates through control of media and legitimation through discourses of celebrity, but I would argue that more basically, it is sustained by an apparently innocuous discourse which legitimises the sources of income of the rich.

I would urge researchers studying the rich and their mobilities to be more critical, and to go beyond what Barry Barnes called 'the ever-so-slightly critical theory of today' (2000: 127). For example, as Featherstone notes, following Foucault, 'the enterprising self' is a central feature of neoliberalism, but the important point is that it is largely an illusory conception, and unless we show how it is so, then the critique has not really begun.

To be critical we have to be evaluative; to dismiss normative discourse as 'merely subjective' or as necessarily incompatible with objectivity is a persistent modernist delusion. Without evaluation critique is blunted and reduced to mere insinuation, which, unless the reader happens already to agree with the insinuations, is likely to prompt the question 'so what?' Why *shouldn't* someone earn – or rather get – £x million? Why shouldn't they be entitled to it? Indeed, why should they – or anyone – pay tax? Is tax not theft? It may seem outrageous that the rich can stash their cash in tax havens and escape the taxes that the little people pay, but what exactly is outrageous about this? Purely the fact of their tax avoidance or the fact of their wealth in the first place? Is their wealth legitimate? There are answers to such questions but most social scientists studiously avoid considering them, believing that they lie outside their brief.

Social science has suffered greatly from the separation of normative from positive thought over the last two centuries. Where classical political economy wrote freely and critically about opulence, vanity, greed and exploitation, modern sociology – reflecting the contemporary aversion to being 'judgemental' – takes refuge in more neutral terms such as cultural capital, taste and 'lifestyle'. For example, Adam Smith, widely misrepresented as a one-eyed apologist for capitalism, regarded the vanity that drives luxury consumption and the desire to emulate it with contempt – reasoned contempt; it was based on 'self-deceit' and it corrupted morality by distorting people's judgements of one another, so the rich are evaluated more indulgently than the poor, even for similar behaviour. He also condemned income from rent as, in effect, free-riding on the labour of others. This is at one and the same time a description and an evaluation; to fail to grasp what is problematic about rent is to fail to understand what it is; it is not a payment for the costs of producing a new good or service but for an asset which already exists. As I've argued elsewhere we need to remedy the estrangement of evaluation from description (Sayer 2011).

At the most basic level, a critical social science of elites and their mobilities needs to address the very discourse in which the rich and their activities are described, particularly economic discourse itself, for it is central to symbolic domination. It's hardly surprising that economic discourse should be highly politicised, for it concerns relations of material dependence between people. It not only names these forms of dependence – sometimes in ways that hide the dependence – but implicitly presents them as legitimate or illegitimate. As Marieke de Goede has shown, throughout the history of capitalism there have been struggles over how particular economic institutions, roles and practices should be described (de Goede 2005). Repeatedly there have been attempts to avoid objections to certain questionable activities by bringing them under more acceptable descriptions, so that, for example, activities formerly called gambling are now termed 'investment'. Any critical social science worthy of its name should approach such terms with great scepticism. Here are four examples that relate to the rich.

'Earnings'

When someone says 'I've earned £x this year', they could just mean that they have been paid £x. But, especially if they say it with emphasis – 'I've *earned* that £x' – they're likely to be implying that they have *deserved* what they have been paid; they may feel they've put in a lot of effort and done a good job. Some languages have separate words for these things, but English and many others do not. Slippage between the two meanings is very useful in leading people to assume that people get paid what they deserve. So it's not unusual for those on quite low incomes to say of the rich: 'Oh well, they've earned it so they're entitled to it.' It allows the rich to imagine that they are both deserving and special, and invites the assumption that those on low incomes are inferior. It perpetuates 'the belief in a just world', and more specifically a belief in a just economy in which what people get is what they deserve and vice versa (Lerner 1980). It also allows 'earners' of all kinds to imagine that taxation takes away what they deserve. Rather than report what the rich 'earn', we should report what they *get*, and then consider in what sense, if any, they have earned (deserved) it.

Here a crucial distinction in the history of political economy, socialist thought and taxation is indispensable: the distinction between earned and unearned income. While the former is conditional upon contributing directly or indirectly to the production and distribution of use-values, including immaterial ones such as education and health services, the latter is derived from control of assets that others need, particularly land, money and means of production, and which can thereby yield rent, interest and profit. Neoliberalism is a political economic regime in which unearned income has expanded massively, but is never identified as such in its discourse. The silence is deafening.

'Investment'

Investment is surely a good thing: the word has a halo; aren't 'investors' benefactors – if not social benefactors then at least enterprising, self-reliant individuals? But the word elides two quite different things which are not necessarily related:

i   *Object-focused definitions.* These focus on what is invested *in* (e.g. infrastructure, equipment, training) and its usefulness and benefit in the future. A school, a windfarm or a railway provides long-term benefits. They enable the production of new *use-values* – goods, services and skills and hence a better teaching environment, a cleaner source of energy, a better means of travel, a more numerate population. These are examples of what we might call real or objective investment.

ii   *'Investor'-focused definitions.* These focus on the *financial gains* to the 'investor' from any kind of lending, saving, purchase of financial assets or speculation – regardless of whether they contribute to any objective investment, or provide anything socially useful. In other words, instead of focusing on the benefits of the investment in terms of use-values, the focus is on exchange-value – how much money it yields to the investor. The financial sector uses the term investment mainly in this sense, because it is largely indifferent to where its money comes from: £1 million derived from an objective investment is no different from £1 million obtained as an interest on a loan, or stock market speculation; money is money and masks all such crucial distinctions. As long as there's a good chance of it bringing a financial return, then gambling, including gambling with other people's money, is called 'investment'. A tollbooth set up on a bridge, for extracting money out of users, could, in contemporary economic parlance, be called an 'investment' for the owners, even though the bridge already exists and hence nothing productive results, indeed even though the income is purely parasitic.

Using the same word for different things allows people to pass off wealth extraction as wealth creation. This indifference to whether individuals or institutions are funding genuine investment or merely vehicles for providing remuneration for the 'investor' is a major irrationality of capitalism, and the way we use the word 'investment' helps to conceal it.

There is no necessary link between the practices identified by these two usages of the term. While an 'investor' might get a return on a genuine investment, they might not; even if it yields them nothing personally, it may still have produced material benefits somewhere – perhaps a hospital at the other end of the country that they'll never need. They might even lose money on it, but it could still be an investment in the first sense if it brings benefits to someone. From the point of view of the second definition, such cases would be seen as *bad* investments.

Equally, those usages which focus merely on financial gains can refer to actions which produce no objective investment in anything whatsoever; indeed they may, like asset stripping, have negative effects by sacrificing long-term objective investment for short-term gains from closing production down and selling stuff off. Speculators almost always call themselves 'investors'. Many of the 'investments' made by the rich and interpreted by uncritical observers as legitimising their wealth, indeed as 'wealth creation', are primarily forms of rent-seeking or *wealth extraction.*

'The working rich'

"At the same time while the rich have recovered a good deal of ground since the 1960s, it is notable that the working rich have replaced the rentiers at the top of the income distribution table" (Featherstone this volume). But the working rich can be working at extracting rent and interest or at churning financial assets so they can skim commission and fees. Such people are '*active* rentiers', as opposed to the old passive rentiers who merely waited for unearned income deriving from their existing assets to roll in. It is naive to imagine that the extraordinary wealth of the rich is simply a reflection of some kind of productive or efficiency-enhancing economic contribution. It is primarily a product of control of assets that others need, and which can therefore be used to extract unearned income from them. 'The working rich' is another legitimising euphemism that academics need to unmask. One of the great illusions of neoliberalism – and one that has been central to the current crisis – is that extracting interest payments and rent from others are forms of wealth creation.

'High Net Worth Individuals'

This is a term used by agencies which cater to the rich such as the Forbes or the Fidelity Millionaire Outlook or Wealth Management funds; it is clearly sycophantic and misleading insofar as it (mis-)attributes the wealth of the rich to their own individual characteristics and contributions, as if power from control of assets and the basic architecture of the economy had nothing to do with it. It is blatantly ideological and should only ever be used by self-respecting critical academics in scare quotes. More generally, it is not enough to report, in postmodernist relativist vein, that the rich '(re)present' themselves in various ways. We need to know if they are *mis*-representations. Similarly, the idea that some of the rich are 'self-made' is one that any would-be critical social scientist should be able to see through (see Alperovitz and Daly 2008).

In these and a host of other ways, our economic language implies individualised explanations of the effects of economic institutions and instruments, provides gratuitous moral justifications of what are largely products of power ('earnings'), and passes off parasitic activities as productive. We need to challenge it.

Prior to the question of how the rich spend their wealth is how they get it in the first place. To answer this we need to consider the social relations through which they are able to amass their fortunes. Bourdieu would no doubt have warned that it is vital, at every opportunity, to counter the illusion that the rich are just individuals who have competed more successfully than others on a level playing field in a game in which each competitor is independent of the others, and in which there are no inherited inequalities among competitors. As Shamus Khan says, 'Elites think of themselves not as a class with particularly lineages, institutions, and associations, but instead as a collection of talented individuals who have a unique capacity to navigate our world; for the elite this capacity explains their position, and not the social trappings of class' (Khan this volume). Economic fortunes are made through social relations, often among unequals, and so these relations need to be identified. For example, the extraordinary growth of debt in recent decades raises the question of who is indebted to whom. Asset inflation is a key mechanism of enrichment through unearned income, and it primarily benefits those who own the most assets – the rich – *at the expense* of those who are asset-poor. Economics is relational.

Money itself is a social relation. It is only of value insofar as it can function as a claim on the labour and products of others, and it can do so only if those working in the real economy produce use-values for sale. The rich have vastly bigger claims on others than they do on themselves. Are we to believe that they have made a correspondingly larger contribution than others? Not even the neoliberal guru Hayek believed that, acknowledging that luck is a major influence on what people get in markets: 'the value which a person's capacities or services have for us and for which he is recompensed has little relation to anything we can moral merit or deserts' (Hayek 1960: 94; see also Hayek 1976: 74). It would be foolish to imagine that the return of the rich is the product of the rise of a new breed of 'entrepreneurs' and 'wealth creators' who are somehow so much more able than their more modestly paid predecessors of the post-war boom, and who therefore deserve to be paid more.

Rather than calling upon the super-rich to be less selfish and more responsible it would make more sense to stop them extracting wealth in the first place. In 2006 the 25 highest-paid hedge fund managers in the United States made $14 billion, three times the combined salaries of New York City's 80,000 schoolteachers. Yet economists struggle to demonstrate any benefit to society from the activities of the hedge funds (Anderson and Cresswell 2007; Eskow 2012). As John Urry notes (this volume), even a financial services insider like Adair Turner, Chairman of the UK Financial Services Authority has deemed many financial products 'socially useless'. Similarly, Andrew Haldane, Executive Director of Financial Stability for the Bank of England, commented: 'The banking industry [like the car industry] is also a pollutant. Systemic risk is a noxious by-product' (Haldane 2010). While Martin Wolf, financial editor of the *Financial Times* summarised the situation thus:

> Financial systems are important servants of the economy, but poor masters. A large part of the activity of the financial sector seems to be a machine to transfer income and wealth from outsiders to insiders, while increasing the fragility of the economy as a whole.... Banks are rent-extractors – and uncompetitive ones at that.
>
> (Wolf 2010)

Joseph Stiglitz, former Chief Economist at the World Bank, argues that the return of the rich is largely the result of a massive growth in rent-seeking, particularly in the financial sector. He argues that this not only transfers income from one group to another, but has a negative effect on the economy, because it diverts resources from productive uses which create wealth, to mere wealth extraction (Stiglitz 2012: 32; see also Kay 2012). Instead of being reinvested in production, the money is merely siphoned off to the unproductive rentier.

We need to identify the structural and symbolic changes which have allowed this amassing of wealth. Paramount amongst these were: (1) the deregulation of finance, allowing extraordinary expansion of debt and hence interest payments to the rich; (2) the shareholder value movement, extracting unearned income in dividends and benefiting from inflation in financial asset values; and (3) globalisation in allowing the expansion of sources of rent, interest and capital gains. Further, the stagnation of aggregate demand since the 1970s – itself a result of slow growth of wages and salaries – reduced opportunities for productive investment and diverted surplus capital into trading in financial assets that fuelled more asset inflation and generated new streams of rent and interest, and fees from the churning of portfolios. In David Harvey's terms, capital switched increasingly from the 'primary circuit of capital', where it was invested in the production of goods and services, to the 'secondary circuit', where it was invested in property and other financial assets, as a means of extracting wealth via rent, interest, dividends or speculation (Harvey 2007). Yet labour productivity has continued to increase since the 1970s almost as fast as in the post-war boom, but whereas then working people shared in the benefits of that growth, most of the benefits since that time have gone to the rich (Dew-Becker and Gordon 2005; ILO 2008; IMF 2007; Kristal 2010; OECD 2011; Peters 2010; Resolution Foundation 2012; UNCTAD 2012).

Recent decades have seen not only a shift in the balance between labour and capital, but a shift within the capitalist class away from productive capital to financial and rentier interests. The return of the rentier is a feature – part cause and part consequence – of the crisis of overaccumulation that has been developing in recent decades, and the growth of the secondary circuit of capital. Neoliberal prioritisation of keeping inflation low meant increased real rates of interest for rentiers. In this context the shareholder value movement gathered momentum, demanding double figure rates of return on so-called 'investments' and continual rises in share prices. The growth of financial securities greatly expanded the creation of debt, which, extraordinarily, was seen as a source of wealth creation rather than as a deadweight cost on the economy (Hudson 2012). Epstein and Jayadev show that rentier income has made a spectacular comeback since the 1970s in many OECD countries, especially in countries with limited unionisation, and hence where there was limited resistance to appropriation of economic rents by financial interests (Epstein and Jayadev 2005). Increased amounts of fictitious capital, involving claims on the value of future production – that is, on labour and what it produces – outstripped credible forecasts of production growth. Yet this diversion of investment into ways of extracting wealth from existing assets was (mis) represented as 'wealth creation' by the financial sector. This of course is only a sketch of some of the elements behind the return of the rich, but such accounts of changes in the social relations involved in the economy are needed to counter the individualistic explanations that the rich and the media propagate.

Today, the assets which they use to extract unearned income in the form of rent, interest profit and speculation include a greater proportion that are exchangeable and mobile than hitherto, not just rents from buildings but from intellectual property and securitised income streams, not just interest on loans but derivatives used to speculate on price movements and geographical differences. The days of the passive rentier, geographically symbolised in the country estate, the ownership of mines, mills, plantations overseas and land in city centres have given way to the era of the active rentier, continually seeking out the most lucrative sources of unearned income around the world, rent-seeking and continually changing the mix of assets they control to maximise returns. Whereas the old passive rentier was associated mainly with the ownership of property in particular places – a rooting to place which was symbolised in the stately home – the new active rentier is dependent on the mobility of capital and the fetish of liquidity, and their own personal mobility is very much geared to orchestrating and surfing this.

Documenting the lifestyles and behaviour of the rich without questioning the sources and legitimacy of their wealth makes me queasy; it is dangerously close to an academically restrained version of celebrity lifestyle voyeurism. The purpose of conspicuous consumption of yachts, islands, mansions and the like – typically closely coupled with tax avoidance methods designed by 'wealth management' firms – is to make a statement of the power and worth of the owner, inviting observers to infer that their disproportionate consumption is somehow reflective of their exceptional qualities. Unless we continually puncture that myth we will perpetuate it. Similarly, the way in which hyper-mobile CEOs and owners continually 'touch down' briefly in a succession of countries to make or confirm 'investment' decisions might be marvelled at as a display of executive power, but it is also an exercise in gross irresponsibility, disregarding, as it invariably does, the interests of the millions who are affected by the decisions. The new global plutocracy is a threat to democratic forces and to the well-being of billions of people. Now austerity is being imposed on low- and middle-income groups to pay for the recklessness of a financial elite who have dodged tax, privatised gains and socialised losses, engaged in insider dealing and laundered drug money with impunity, and stalled economies across the developed world, wrecking the prospects of millions of young people. We need a more critical approach.

It is especially necessary when empirical research on public attitudes to inequality suggest that as societies become more unequal they become more accepting of inequality, not less, and more intolerant of those at the bottom. In the United States, Kelly and Enns (2010) found that as inequality rose, the high- and low-income respondents on average became less supportive of spending on welfare, even though the latter were more aware of increases in inequality than most people.

In the UK, Bamfield and Horton found that even though there was some anger directed at bankers, most people judged those at the bottom more harshly than those at the top. They also noted

> a widespread belief about the ready availability of opportunity, resulting in highly individualised explanations of poverty and disadvantage [and] a belief... that benefit recipients will not go on to make a reciprocal contribution back to society through activities such as employment or caring
>
> (Bamfield and Horton 2009)

The flip side of this is of course the belief that the rich somehow deserve their wealth. Not the least of the dangers of the hypermobility and luxury consumption of the rich is the emulation it tends to induce in those below, yet it is not just the excessive consumption, and the feeding of vanity it produces, but the decline of the sense of the public good that tends to go with it. This makes it all the more important to adopt an approach which probes the sources of the wealth of the rich critically.

In reading Córdoba Azcárate *et al.*'s and Thurlow and Jaworski's contributions, I was reminded of Raymond Williams's remarkable critique, in *The Country and the City*, of the class who own stately homes, in which he brilliantly traces the interweaving of economic and symbolic domination (Williams 1968/2011). Those places which embody so much labour yet from which 'the facts of labour' are expelled, and the celebration of the owner and their 'lifestyle' are based on the unacknowledged labour of both those who service their consumption and those who provide them with their wealth in the first place. The Mexican haciendas that have now been turned into luxury hotels continue this tradition. Just as the owners of such places and their ancestors often claim to have 'built' them, when in fact they paid others to do so, owners and CEOs of contemporary firms are similarly wont to claim responsibility for what their workers have done. Impressive though they may be, luxury homes and haciendas are monuments to exploitation and unearned income, and consumption levels far beyond the reach of those who work to sustain them. They are grotesquely out of proportion with what one household working on its own could develop and manage. In a world where poverty is still widespread they are a shameful misallocation of resources. Today the vertical class relations of 'upstairs and downstairs' may have mostly been displaced horizontally to different parts of the city or of the world, but they continue in new forms. We need not only note the small armies of workers who devote their labour to providing the rich with luxuries but the dependence of the rich on the unacknowledged labour of those whose wealth they appropriate.

It is to be hoped that the sociology of the rich will not become just another fashionable subfield, its members collectively coveting their novel theories and methods in self-congratulatory style, another vehicle for demonstrating cleverness, exemplifying the condition in which, as Bourdieu put it, critique has 'retreated into the "small world" of academe, where it enchants itself with itself without ever being in a position to really threaten anyone about anything' (Bourdieu 2003: 21). More research is needed on the rich and on plutocracy, the use of the mobility of capital controlled by the rich to discipline states, the mobility patterns involved in lobbying to protect the interests of the rich, the role of tax havens in hiding profit, and to enhance their power in a host of other ways, but it needs to be critical.

References

Alperovitz, G. and Daly, L. (2008) *Unjust Deserts*, New York: The New Press.
Anderson, J. and Cresswell, J (2007) 'Top hedge fund managers earn over $240 million', *New York Times*, 24 April, www.nytimes.com/2007/04/24/business/24hedge.html (accessed 3 May 2013).
Bamfield, E. and Horton, T. (2009) *Understanding Attitudes to Tackling Economic Inequality*, Joseph Rowntree Foundation, www.jrf.org.uk/sites/files/jrf/attitudes-tackling-economic-inequality-full.pdf (accessed 3 May 2013).
Barnes, B. (2000) *Understanding Agency; Social Theory and Responsible Action*, London: Sage.
Bourdieu, P. (2003) *Firing Back*, New York: The New Press.
De Goede, M. (2005) *Virtue, Fortune and Faith*, Minnesota: University of Minnesota Press.
Dew-Becker, I. and Gordon, R. J. (2005) 'Where did the productivity growth go?', National Bureau of Economic Research Working Paper 11842, www.nber.org/papers/w11842 (accessed 3 May 2013).
Epstein, G. A. and Jayadev, A. (2005) 'The rise of rentier incomes in OECD countries: financialization, central bank policy and labor solidarity', in Epstein, G. A. (ed.) *Financialization and the World Economy*, Cheltenham: Edward Elgar.
Eskow, R. (2012) 'Don't lower taxes for billionaires. Double them', *Campaign for America's Future Blog*, 10 October, http://ourfuture.org/blog-entry/2012104109/dont-lower-taxes-billionaires-double-them (accessed 3 May 2013).
Haldane, A. (2010) 'The £100 billion question', Speech, Bank of England, March 2010.
Harvey, D. (2007) *Limits to Capital*, London: Verso.
Hayek, F. A. (1960) *The Constitution of Liberty*, London: Routledge.
Hayek, F. A. (1976) '"Social" or distributive justice' in *Law, Legislation and Liberty*, Vol. 2, London: Routledge.
Hudson, M. (2012) *The Bubble and Beyond*, Dresden: ISLET Verlag.
ILO (2008) *World of Work Report 2008: Income Inequalities in the Age of Financial Globalisation*. Geneva: International Labour Organization.
IMF (2007) *World Economic Outlook: Spillovers and Cycles in the Global Economy*. Washington DC: International Monetary Fund.
Kay, J. (2012) 'The monumental folly of rent-seeking', *Financial Times*, 21 November.
Kelly, N. J. and Enns, P. K. (2010) 'Inequality and the dynamics of public opinion: the self-reinforcing link between economic inequality and mass preferences', *American Journal of Political Science*, 54 (4): 855–870.
Kristal, T. (2010) 'Good times bad times: postwar labor's share of income in 16 capitalist democracies', *American Sociological Review*, 75 (5): 729–763.
Lerner, M. (1980) *The Belief in a Just World: A Fundamental Delusion*, New York: Plenum.
OECD (2011) *Divided We Stand: Why Inequality Keeps Rising*. Paris: OECD Publishing.
Peters, J. (2010) 'The rise of finance and the decline of organised labour in the advanced capitalist countries', *New Political Economy*, 16 (1): 73–99.
Resolution Foundation (2012) *Gaining from Growth: The Final Report of the Commission on Living Standards*, London: Resolution Foundation.

Savage, M. and Williams, K. (2008) 'Elites: remembered in capitalism and forgotten in social science', *The Sociological Review*, 56 (1): 1–24.
Sayer, A. (2011) *Why Things Matter To People: Social Science, Values and Ethical Life*, Cambridge: Cambridge University Press.
Stiglitz, J. (2012) *The Price of Inequality*, London: Allen Lane.
UNCTAD (2012) *Trade and Development Report 2012*, New York: UNCTAD.
Williams, R. (1968/2011) *The Country and the City*, London: Spokesman Books.
Wolf, M. (2010) 'The challenge of halting the financial doomsday machine', *Financial Times*, 20 April, www.ft.com/cms/s/0/f2e4dbb0-4caa-11df-9977-00144feab49a.html#axzz28nNe7PiO (accessed 3 May 2013).

Index

Page numbers in *italics* denote tables, those in **bold** denote figures.

1 per cent (ers) 2
3D printing 62–8, 244
39 Steps, The 5

Abalá 154, 160
Abramovich, Roman 40, 111
additive manufacturing *see* 3D printing
Adey, Peter 5
Adriá, Ferran 168
aeromobilities 78
Aesop's fable 198
'affluent infrastructures' 79, 244, 246
Africa *45*, 83, **84**, 202–3
air-mindedness 5
Airbus 319 Corporate Jet 81
Airbus A340 81
'alpha' territories 8
Alpina (BMW) *49*
Alps 109
Amalie Garden 217
Antigua 232
Apprentice, The 121n5
aristocracy 2, 104, 147
arrivistes 123n24
art 24, 86, 111–17, 138–9, 141
Asia-Pacific 42, *45*, 86, 104–5, 108, 113
Aston Martin *49*
Audi *49*
austerity 9, 102, 259
Australia 26, 27, 84, 103, 104
Austria 93
'authentic' landscape 206
automobilities 6, 49

Bahamas 121n9, 127n40
Bain & Company 104

'banal globalization' 33
Bank of England 233
Bank of New York 235
bankers 27–9, 36, 102, 119, 197, 201, 234, 259
Barbados 110, 126n40
Baudelaire, Charles 106
Bauman, Zygmunt 22, 32, 34, 227
beach 14, 178, 188, 197, 206, 228, 231, 246
Beaverstock, Jonathan 7, 13, 47, 153, 161, 206, 210, 242
Beck, Ulrich 220
Becker, Gary 100
Beckert, Sven 138
Beckham, David 41
Beckham, Victoria 41
Belize 93
Benidorm 197, 206
Bentley *49*
Beowulf 141
Berggruen, Nicolas 23
Bermuda 93
Bilderberg Group 12
Bildungprozess 112
billionaires 103, 104, 111, 203
bin Talal, Al-Waleed 121n7
biz jet 81
Bloomberg Billionaires Index 121n7, 122n11
Bloomberg, Michael 121n7
Blue Ocean Yacht Management 48
BMW *49*, 124n28
boarding school 28
bodies 24, 106, 147
Boeing 747, 81, 82

Boltanski, Luc 31
Bombardier 55, 56, 82
Bond, James 14
Bordeaux 113
BornRich.com 122n11
Børsen 210
Bosoms, Luis 159
botanical garden 166
Bourdieu, Pierre 35, 53, 136, 138, 141, 144, 199, 256, 260
bourgeois utopias 170
Branson, Richard 67, 101, 121n5
Brazil 9, 42, 68, 83, 84, 105
Bretton Woods 22, 233
BRICs 95, 100
Bridgewater Associates 102
Britain *see* Great Britain
Britain's Got Talent 121n5
British Empire 230, 233
British Virgin Islands 93, 110, 231, 246
Buffet, Warren 40, 47, 114, 117, 121n7, 123n20
Bugatti 48, *49*
business aviation: commercial 80–1; contribution to carbon emissions of 95; convenience of 88–9; distribution by regions of **83**; flexibility of 89; and flight tracking websites 94; growth of aircraft fleet **83**; history of 80; market for 95; and number of aircraft 82, *83*; owner-operated 81; practices in 80; productivity of 90; speed of 32, 89; status of 91–2; *see also* biz jet

Cadillac 124
Calderón, Felipe 161
Calivigny Island 246
Canada 84, 93, 103, 104
Canary Islands 232
Cannes film festival 113
Capgemini 42, 122n14
capital: circuits of 258; cultural 53, 57, 111; human 100; laundering of 235; move from productive to financial 258
capitalism: casino 195, 235; consumer 35; disorganized 4, 9; late 22; new spirit of 31; turbo 22, 237
Caribbean 95, 110, 246
Carlton, Erik 2
'car-mindedness' 5
Cathay Pacific 189–90, 245
Cato 1, 11

Caudwell, John 114, 123n20
Cayman Islands 93, 228, 231
Centre for Research on Socio-Cultural Change (CRESC) 2
Cessna 4, 82, 245–6
Chakrabortty, Aditya 13
Channel Islands (UK) 93, 232
châteaux 149
Chiapello, Eve 31
China 9, 42, 43, 68, 100, 103, 104, 105, 108, 124n26, n27, n28, 232
China Daily 113
China Merchants Bank 104
Christian Aid 232
Christie's International Real State 109
Cicero 1
climate change 3, 4, 68, 125n33
'clinical interviewing' 26
Clinton, Bill 161
Clinton, Hilary 15
coca-colonization 168
colonial encounter 3
Coloplast 216
Columbia University 137
comfort 53, 91
commons 3
Commonwealth of Dominica 93
Communist Manifesto, The 226
Condé Nast Traveller 151, 246
'confessional' modes of research 13
conservative morality 142
conspiracy theories 13
consumer culture 106
consumption: austere 105; bohemian 106; conspicuous 108, 194–206; discourses of 150; excessive 195; exclusive enjoyment of 107; normalcy of 195; 'omnivorous' 10, 136, 147; and scale-down luxuries 106; *see also* lifestyle
conviviality 196
Copenhagen 214, 216–17, 221
Cordemex 157
cosmopolitanism 8–9, 25, 33, 109, 118, 127, 144, 146, 195, 199, 205, 226, 244
Côte d'Azur 109
Cowell, Simon 41, 101, 121n5
critical discourse analysis 176, 191
Crump, Scott 63, 74
cultural egalitarians 145
'cultural omnivores' 137
Cwerner, Saulo 80
Cyprus 121, 230

Index

Dalio, Raymond 102
de Goede, Marieke 253
debt 258
Delaware 232
Dénia 197
Denmark 209–23
deterritorialized spaces 246
Diamond, Bob 121n8
digital technologies 114
Distinction 35, 199
Driving Global Wealth 100
Dubai 16, 122n9, 187, 195

ease 1, 3, 7, 10, 15, 30, 136, 140, 147, 150, 178, 206, 229, 242–3, 248
EasyJet 197
Eclipse (yacht) 40, 47
Eclipse 94
ecological collapse 248–9
ecological footprint 4
economic crisis of 1929 157
Economist, The 67, 236
Edensor, Tim 167
education 100, 114, 116, 136–7, 215, 211, 247, 254
Egypt 105
elite culture 136, 147; acquisition of 142; emotional investment in 111; presumptuous displays of 143; and talent 140
elites: American 142; composition of 137; cosmopolitan 144; cultural 136, 147; definition of 2; formations of 11, 64, 74, 241; inaccessibility of 14; invisibility of 66; mobile 16; moral legitimacy of 4; myth of self-made 62
elitism 177–8
Elliott, Anthony 195
Ellison, Larry 121n6
Elster, Jon 198–9
Embraer 82
emotional assets 113
'empty time' 30
Engels, Friedrich 226
English Premier League 111
Enron 236
enterprising self 254
Epic 94
ethnography 141–7, 153
EU Emissions Trading Scheme 95
Europe 26, 103
excess 16, 199, 206

Fascitelli, Michael D. 102
Faulconbridge, James 7, 14, 206, 242
Featherstone, Mike 194–5
Ferrari 49
Fidelity Millionaire Outlook 100
finance 12, 13, 25, 32, 35, 96, 101, 105, 228, 230, 233, 235, 237, 257
financial crisis 22, 23, 101, 107–8; *see also* economic crisis of 1929
Fine Art Fund 113
'flexibility' 29
flexions 2
flow-architectures 2, 16, 92
Fomento Cultural Banamex 159, 160
Forbes 113, 121n6, 122n11, 123n26, 151
Forbes Insights 117
Forbes List of America's Highest Paid Executives 102
Forbes List of World Billionaires 42, 43, 101, 212n7
Form Labs 63
Formentera 197
Fortune 500 85
Foucault, Michel 100, 106, 107, 143, 252, 120n3
France 93, 136–7, 424
frequent flyers 36, 245
Fused Deposition Modelling (FDM) 64

Gandia 197
Gates, Bill 40, 47, 67, 101, 117, 212n6
General Electric 68
Geneva 109, 113
Germany 43, 84
Gibraltar 93, 230
Giddens, Anthony 14
Gilded Age 138
Gini coefficient 211, 215–16
global media 194, 196
global production networks 68
Global South 68, 118, 150
global warming 4; *see also* climate change
globals: elsewhere 31, 204; and emotional geographies 34; escapism of 22; floating 31–2; symbolic power 37, 195; *see also* hyper-mobilities; 'kinetic' elites
Goldfinger 14
'good life' 35, 106, 196, 204
Google Ngram 68

Google Patent 69
Graham, Steve 196
Grand Tour 12
Grandes Ecoles 142
Great Britain 45, 102–3, 121n5, 218, 230, 232
Grenada 246
Grundtvig, N.F.S. 223
Grupo Financiero Banamex 151
Guernsey 121n9
Gulfstream 82
Gulfstream G650 90, 245
Gullestad, Marianne 212

habitus 142
haciendas 149, 156, 166, 171, 243; list of 151; project 151–3; *see also* Temozón Sur
Hammergren, John 201
Harding, David 118
'harried leisure class' 113
Harvard University 119
Harvey, David 8, 161, 257–8
Haseler, Stephen 41, 43
Hayek, Friedrich 256
hedge funds 102, 122n10
henequén see haciendas
Hernández, Roberto 151, 159
'highbrow snobs' 137, 144
High Net Worth Individuals 2, 16, 41, 47, 59, 86, 117–18, 120n2, 122n15, 228, 255; as global phenomenon 103–4; worldwide population of 43–4
Hong Kong 104, 110, 121n9, 232
Horchow Travel Services 247
HSBC 235
Hull, Chuck 63–74
Hume, David 150
hyper-mobilities 23

Ibiza 201
'Iconification' 7
immobility 8
India 9, 42, 68, 93, 100, 103, 122n15, 124n28
'individual self-cultivation' 140, 144
industrial revolution 62–74
inequality; elite perception of 141; income and 210; indicators of 23; justification of 147, 200, 212–13; legitimization of 186; and mobility 6, 9, 140; perpetuation of 136;
production of 141, 145; public attitudes towards 214, 259
infrastructure 92
innovation 107
Intergovernmental Panel on Climate Change (IPCC) 4
intermediaries 101
International Business Aviation Council 80
investment 9, 22, 25, 28, 42, 53, 100–3, 108–13, 119, 140, 158, 216, 234, 237, 245, 253–5, 258
invisible labour 179–82, 241
Isle of Man 93, 121n9

Jaguar *49*
Japan 26, 103, 105
Jávea 197
Jaworski, Adam 36
Jaws 141
Jersey 121n9
Jessop, Bob 13
JetStar 81–2
Jimmy Choo 123n24
Jobs, Steve 67, 101
John, Elton 41
Jysk 216

Kaika, Maria 7
Kaufmann, Vincent 8
Kentucky 14
Keynes, John Maynard 237
Kickstarter 63
'kinetic' elites 8
'kings and queens' history 11
Kitchen Table Society 212
Knight Frank 24, 110, 115
Kondratieff cycle 123n16
Kyttanen, Janne 65

Labuan 122n9
Lagerfeld, Karl 123n24
Lamborghini *49*
Land Rover *49*
landscape aesthetics 196
Lasch, Christopher 118
Lassen, Claus 218
Latin America 42
Latour, Bruno 66
Lauren, Ralph 102
Lear, William 82
LearJet 55, 82, 245
Lego 216

Lexus 124n28
Liechtenstein 93, 232
lifestyle: frugal 114; intensive 248; of luxury 110; mobility as a 115; 'snobs' versus 'omnivores' 136–47; super-high-carbon 57; super-rich 99, 127; and work ethic 114
Lifestyles of the Rich and Famous 105
liquid modernity 25, 227
Liverpool FC 112
Loire Valley 113
London 23, 102, 109, 114, 119, 228; Chelsea FC 111; City of 230, 233; Knightsbridge 110; libertarian nature of the City 233
Los Angeles 109
Lotus *49*
Louis Vuitton 35, 123n24, n25
low-carbon cities 8
Luttwak, Edward 24
Luxembourg 93, 232
luxury: apartments 110; aspirational ideal of 178; authentic 150; bespoke 48; cars 124n28; crafting 160, 170; discursive performance of 178; down-market 149; eccentric 200; excess of 150, 179–80; extravagant 199; garden 165–7; holidays 198; mass 108, 123n24; obscene 200; sensing 167, 170; super 108; symbolic power of 178; taste for 150; 'trickle down' 108
Luxury Property 109

Madeira 232
Madrid 119
Maersk 216
Maersk Mc-Kinney Møller, Arnold 216
Makerbot 66
Malta 121n9
Mandarin Oriental hotel 110
Marakesh 176
Marbella 176, 201
Marvin, Simon 196
Marx, Karl 3, 179, 226
Maserati 48, *49*
masses 58
Mauritius 121n9
May 1968 142
Mayan culture 167, 170
McLaren 48, *49*
Mediterranean 195, 207
'meetingness' 11
Mercedes-Benz *49*

Mérida 60
meritocracy 140
methods 14, 196, 244; *see also* 'confessional' modes of research; ethnography; mobile methods
Metro, The 121n5
Metropolitan Museum of Art 139
Metropolitan Opera 139
Mexico 84, 93, 105
Miami 14, 109
Michelin 168
Microsoft 40, 67, 121n6
middle class 103, 108, 194, 206
Middle East 95
Mills, C. Wright 11, 123n16
MIT Media Lab 63
Mittal, Lakshmi 45
'mobile free-association interviewing' 25
Mobile Lives 24, 149, 195, 204, 220
mobile methods 15, 25, 242
'mobile shadowing' 25
mobilities: as capital 242; conspicuous consumption of 50; embeddedness of 40, 59; digitized 24; high carbon 52; idea of 66; paradigm 10, 25, 66; performance of 50; power and 4; social distinguisher of 242; socio-technical perspective on 50; staging of 3; stratified 3; systemic 7, 10; typology of super-rich *46*; visibility of 147; *see also* aeromobilities; automobilities; motility
mobility-as-usual 4–7
modernity 25
Monaco 23, 109
Moody's Analytics 109
Moraira 197
Moscow 110, 113
Moss, Kate 201
motility 8
movement 17n1
Museum of Modern Art 113
Mustique 110, 176

Nader, Laura 3
narcoeconomy 248
National Business Aviation Association 85
neo-liberalism 22, 100, 107, 118, 119, 228
Netherlands 210, 232
Netherlands Antilles 232

Index

NetJets 78, 245
network capital 15
'network power' 24
networked individualism 23
networking 22
Nevada 232
New York 109, 113, 114, 119, 138, 139, 227, 233
New York Times, The 246
Nigeria 105
nobility 2
Noble *49*
noblesse oblige 118
Norway 93, 217
nouveau riche 5, 107, 108, 114

Objet 65
Occupy Movement 119, 211, 236
OECD 236
offshore 12, 99, 102, 104, 110, 118, 227, 228, 230, 234, 241, 244, 246, 249; *see also* 'secret worlds'; tax havens; treasure islands
Offshore Watch 236
oil 22, 52, 63, 67, 68, 82, 87, 96, 125n29, 248
Oracle 121n6
Orient Express, The 183
Oxfam 236

Pace, Charles 122n10
Pakulski, Jan 2
Palace of Versailles 165
Panama 122n9
paparazzi 40
'paradis fiscal' 228
Paradores 149
Pareto, Vilfredo 14
Paris 23, 109, 114
Patrón Laviada, Alejandro 158
Patrón Laviada, Patricio 158
Paulson, John 121n7
Perrot, Roy 10
philanthrocapitalism 117, 120
'philanthroentrepreneurs' 118
Philosophy of Money 116
Picasso (painting) 112
Piedmont Triad of North Carolina 246
Piper 82
plutocracy 259
Politikken 218
Ponzi schemes 232

Porsche *49*
post-modern culture 33
Power Elite, The 11
practices 4, 6, 7, 11, 16, 22, 27, 30, 35, 37, 45, 50, 153, 158, 167, 177, 196, 213, 227, 242, 253
Prada 35
'precarity' 120n4
prestige 78
principals, the 2
private business aviation 78, 96
privileged, the 2
PropGOLuxury.com 109
Protestant Ethic and the Spirit of Capitalism, The 114
psychodynamic analysis 26
public good 260
Puerto Banús 201
Putnam, Robert 199

Range Rover 49
real estate intermediaries 110
reference group 2
reinventions of self 30
Renaissance 113
rentier income 258
Revolt of the Elites 118
rich 79, 101, 104–5, 114–17, 197, 200–2, 204; ignored by sociology 251; indifference towards 202; legitimacy of 119, 252; lists 122n11; misrepresentation of 256; playgrounds 195; property 107, 109, 110; public anger 102; reference group 200, 203; representations of 256; resilience of 108; return of 251; self-exclusion 252; self-made 100; sense of responsibility 120; separation between work and leisure of 116; specialist magazines 124n28; and symbolic domination 252; working 255
Richard III 11
Richi$tan 41
Risk Society 220
robber barons 138
Rockefeller, John D. 113
Rolls Royce 48, *49*
Russia 103, 104

salaries 102
San Marino 232
São Paulo 5, 109

Sardinia 115
Savage, Mike 13, 123n16, 214, 251
Sayer, Andrew 13, 199, 213
Schultz, Theodore 100
Schumpeter, Joseph 107
Scott, John 2, 25
second homes 6, 110
secrecy 12–13, 94
'secret worlds' 227
security 110
Selfridges 123n24
semiosis 177
senses 153, 167, 170, 243
Shard 110, 126n36
South Africa 187
South America 83, 86
September 11, 2001 82, 227
Seychelles 93
Shakespeare, William 138
Shakira 161
Shanghai 113
Shaxson, Nicholas 229, 234
Simmel, Georg 108, 116
Singapore 26, 110, 121n9
Slim Helu, Carlos 40, 114, 123n20
Smith, Adam 150, 252
Social Network Analysis 62, 74
socio-technical transitions 9, 65
Soros, George 47, 121n7
South Africa 84, 105, 178, 184, 187
splintering urbanism 196
St Moritz 115
St Paul's 136, 147
Starwood Hotels and Resorts 150, 159
'stateless super-rich' 115
Stevenson, Robert Louis 37
Stratasys 64
stratification 1, 6, 10, 11, 15, 32, 66, 69, 72, 79, 203
structural stories 3
'study-up' 3
sub-prime mortgages 23, 101, 106
subaltern 10, 13
Suez debacle 233
Sugar, Alan 101, 121n5
Sunday Times, The 63
Sunday Times Rich List, The 41, 43, 252
Sundberg, Kristoffer 218
super-class, global 2
super-inclusion 10, 12
super-prime properties 115
super-rich *see* rich
sustainability 8, 52, 94, 95, 169, 170

'symbolic death' 34
Sweden 216–17
Switzerland 14, 93, 218, 229

Tarde, Gabriel 123n23
taste 137, 160, 170, 243
Tate, Henry 113
tax havens: definition of 230; 'façade' of 228, 230; mobile lives and 227; 'tax dodging' 228
Tax Justice Network 236
taxation: media 236; politics 236
'technology of the self' 143
Temozón Sur 153, 157, 160, 166, 170
Theory of the Leisure Class, The 5
Thurlow, Crispin 36
TIMCO Aviation Services 246
tourism 28–9, 149–71, 176–92, 194, 206; *see also* haciendas
travel: aspirations for 199; consumer 196; democratization of 196; excessive 204; exemplary modes of 178; as luxury 204; mass 206
treasure islands 4, 230–2
Trotsky, Leon 5
Trump, Donald 121n5
Turkey 93
Turks and Caicos Islands 230
Turner, Adair 238
Twin Towers 227

UK Financial Services Authority 238
UK Uncut 236
Ukraine 93
United Kingdom 26, 43, 84, 100, 102, 103, 232; *see also* Great Britain
United States of America 43, 68, 84, 100, 102, 103, 104, 124n28, 143, 232
Urry, John 2, 13, 23, 24, 195

Valencia 197
Vanderbilt, William 138
Vanuatu 122n9
Veblen, Thorstein 5, 194
Venezuela 83
'venture philanthropy' 118
Verdi 139
Versace 123n24
Victorian novels 147
Virgin Islands 121n9
Vornado Realty 102

Walby, Sylvia 13

Wall Street Crash of 1987 *see* financial crisis
Wall Street Journal 236
wealth 41, 113, 211; accumulation of 256–7; creation and extraction of 254; indicators 23–4; inherited 101; legitimacy of 259; possession of 107; segmentation 43
Wealth Report 109, 110, 112
Weber, Max 114, 145
welfare state 209, 223
Williams, Karel 13, 251
wine 86, 110–13, 143, 168
Winfrey, Oprah 101

World Social Forum 236
World Wealth Report 86, 104, 122n15
World, The (cruise ship) 231

X Factor 121n5

yachts 9, 21, 47, 55, 109, 195, 197, 202, 216, 242, 244, 246, 259
Yaqui 155
Yucatán 149, 171, **152**, 157, 158

Zuckerberg, Mark 62, 114, 121n5, 123n20, 147